# EDUCATION IN
# RENAISSANCE ENGLAND

# STUDIES IN SOCIAL HISTORY

### edited by

# HAROLD PERKIN

*Lecturer in Social History, University of Manchester*

◇◇◇◇◇◇◇◇◇◇◇◇◇◇◇◇◇◇◇◇◇◇◇◇◇◇◇◇◇◇◇◇◇◇◇◇◇◇◇◇◇◇◇◇◇◇◇◇◇◇◇◇

| | |
|---|---|
| THE OUTLAWS OF MEDIEVAL LEGEND | Maurice Keen |
| RELIGIOUS TOLERATION IN ENGLAND, 1787–1833 | Ursula Henriques |
| LEARNING AND LIVING, 1790–1960: A Study in the History of the English Adult Education Movement | J. F. C. Harrison |
| HEAVENS BELOW: Utopian Experiments in England, 1560–1960 | W. H. G. Armytage |
| FROM CHARITY TO SOCIAL WORK in England and the United States | Kathleen Woodroofe |
| ENGLISH LANDED SOCIETY in the Eighteenth Century | G. E. Mingay |
| ENGLISH LANDED SOCIETY in the Nineteenth Century | F. M. L. Thompson |
| A SOCIAL HISTORY OF THE FRENCH REVOLUTION | Norman Hampson |
| CHURCHES AND THE WORKING CLASSES IN VICTORIAN ENGLAND | K. S. Inglis |
| A SOCIAL HISTORY OF ENGLISH MUSIC | E. D. Mackerness |
| THE PROFESSION OF ENGLISH LETTERS | J. W. Saunders |
| EDUCATION IN RENAISSANCE ENGLAND | Kenneth Charlton |

A Sixteenth-Century Printing Shop: from J. Stradanus, *Nova Reperta* (1600).

# EDUCATION IN RENAISSANCE ENGLAND

by

Kenneth Charlton

*Senior Lecturer in Education*
*University of Keele*

LONDON: Routledge and Kegan Paul
TORONTO: University of Toronto Press

First published 1965
in Great Britain by
Routledge and Kegan Paul Limited
and in Canada by
University of Toronto Press

Printed in Great Britain by
W. & J. Mackay & Co. Ltd., Chatham

# Contents

PREFACE                                             *page* ix

ABBREVIATIONS                                            xv

## Part One: Origins

I. THE MEDIEVAL BACKGROUND                               3

II. THE RENAISSANCE DEBATE IN ITALY                     21

III. THE RENAISSANCE DEBATE IN ENGLAND                  41

## Part Two: Formal Education

IV. THE GRAMMAR SCHOOLS                                 89

V. THE UNIVERSITIES                                    131

VI. THE INNS OF COURT                                  169

## Part Three: Informal Education

VII. THE FAMILY AND TRAVEL                             199

VIII. MODERN LANGUAGES AND LITERATURE                 227

IX. MERCHANTS, NAVIGATORS AND LANDOWNERS              253

CONCLUSION                                            297

INDEX                                                 301

# Plates

A Sixteenth-Century Printing Shop: from J. Stradanus, *Nova Reperta* (1600)           *frontispiece*

I. The Medieval Tower of Knowledge: from G.
Reisch, *Margarita Philosophica* (1508)   *facing page* 80

II. (i) Medals in honour of Guarino da Verona (by
Matteo de' Pisti) and Vittorino da Feltre (by
Pisanello): from A. Chastel, *Age of Humanism*
Thames and Hudson (1963)                 81

(ii) Bishop Fox's College of Corpus Christi (the
sixteenth century buildings lie in the left background): from N. Williams, *Oxonia Depicta*
(1733)                                    81

III. Sir Thomas Elyot by Hans Holbein the Younger
(Original in Windsor Castle)              96

IV. (i) Sir Thomas More by Hans Holbein the
Younger. (Frick Collection, New York)     97

(ii) Erasmus by Hans Holbein the Younger.
(Kunst museum, Basel)                     97

V. (i) Aid to learning grammar: from John Holte,
*Lac Puerorum* (1479)                     112

(ii) Pictorial alphabet: from John Harte, *Methode
to Reade English* (1570)                  112

VI. Family Instruction: from *The Whole Booke of Psalmes*
(1563)                                    113

VII. The hazards of travel: title page of Thomas Coryat,
*Coryat's Crudities* (1611)               128

VIII. John Florio: frontispiece to his *Queen Anne's New
World of Wordes* (1611)                   129

IX. (i) Renaissance song book: from Thomas Pilkington, *First Booke of Songes and Ayres* (1605)  256

(ii) Sixteenth century surveyor's instruments:
from Cyprian Lucar, *Lucar's Solace* (1590)  256

X. The Ambassadors by Hans Holbein the Younger.
(National Gallery, London)                257

vii

XI. Title-page of Robert Recorde's arithmetic book
*Grounde of Artes* (1543)                                          272

XII. Title-page of Anthony Ashley's translation of Lucas
Wagenaer's *Mariner's Mirrour* (1590)                   273

# Preface

W ITH the growth of 'scientific' history in the mid-nineteenth century there grew up too, as Professor Hexter reminds us, the method of organizing historical investigation by means of tunnels labelled diplomatic history, political history, ecclesiastical history and so on, each sealed off from contact with the others.[1] If the historian of education is to avoid such dangers he must concern himself not merely with what went on in the classrooms of the past but with the transmission and modification of culture; not simply with the institutions through which culture is transmitted, modified and acquired, but also with the ideas which those institutions sought to put into effect, with the ways in which these ideas were set in motion, and most important of all, with the context in which and for which these ideas were developed. The historian of education must consider, too, those forces in a society—indifference, ignorance, apathy and vested interest—which resist or tend to hinder the acceptance, assimilation, and accommodation of such ideas, and which produce what has been called a 'cultural time-lag'. Again, if he limits himself to the question 'How did education affect society'? he concerns himself with only a part of the truth of the matter, and indeed attributes to education a rôle which was often not hers to undertake. He must also, therefore, inquire how far education was the product of a particular society, to what degree it changed when society changed, and to what extent new ideas and formulations were stifled or ignored by existing educational agencies. Nor must he confine himself to the question 'Who *were* educated?' He must study, too, the perennial debates about who *should* be educated and for what purposes. And what of minorities? Should their special educational needs be acknowledged? If so, should their efforts be merely tolerated or actively encouraged? Such questions lead him in the end to a particular society's views about the nature of the child and his status, the

[1] J. H. Hexter, *Reappraisals in History* (1961), p. 194.

nature of man and his destiny. These are questions we must ask
of the Renaissance.

Renaissance studies are now at the stage when some gradualist
historians can claim that there was no such thing. I do not
subscribe to that view, nor, I hasten to add, to the view that the
Renaissance was a clear break with the past. What is apparent,
however, is that Renaissance views about the nature of man
and of the child, and therefore about their education, differed
radically from those of their medieval ancestors. Humanists
gave man a prime place on this earth and produced educational
ideas appropriate to that standpoint, with the result that a highly
complicated pattern of education developed, in which outmoded
ideas jostled alongside notions which challenged the very basis
of society itself. Tradition and change were the warp and woof
of such education. The intellectual revolution, together with its
social and political concomitants, came into contact with those
traditional educational ideas and practices which had for so long
served the chivalric culture of the feudal nobility and the scholastic culture of the clergy. At the same time they created an
entirely new sector of education which arose in response to the
new culture of the merchants, the lawyers and the civil servants.
Neither the chivalric nor the scholastic culture suited the needs
of the new men of affairs. Humanism did, concerned as it was
with the civic, moral and aesthetic problems of man in society.
How to define the good life, how to lead the good life in the
busy, competitive, everyday world of affairs, how to pass this
on to future generations, these were the questions the Italian
humanists turned their minds to, and in due time the questions
were posed in England.

The dangers of putting chronological limits to the discussion
are well-recognized. Generally, however, I start with the influx
of ideas from fifteenth-century Italy, and go on to trace their
reception and modification in sixteenth-century England, concluding when they take up their journeys again as the cultural
background of the founders of colonial America. During this
period new and heretical ideas competed in men's minds against
old-established notions which could no longer be accepted without doubt or query. The medieval, and originally Platonic,
injunction to 'walk in thy calling' was one such notion to be
called in question. The literature of the period is shot through

and through with its acceptance. Yet it was the literature of a society which, though retaining social rank and degree as the necessary basis of a stable society, provided for a flexibility which allowed the Cecils, for instance, to rise in four generations from the squirearchy to marriage into the royal line, and enabled innumerable yeomen, lesser gentry, and professional men of affairs, to achieve the title of gentleman. It was an age, too, in which science and scientific inquiry were challenging traditional authority. 'Scientists' strove to emancipate themselves from the stigma which labelled their work as an irreligious probing into divine secrets, and at the same time concerned themselves with the communication of the results and applications of their work to the ordinary layman. For them science was not 'the black art', but a mode of thought and inquiry directed towards the everyday world, and ultimately devoted to the betterment of man's life on earth, a view heralded in More's *Utopia* (1516) and well on the road to general acceptance by the time Bacon's *New Atlantis* was published in 1627. The eventual coming to fruition of these ideas, 'the scientific revolution' of the mid-seventeenth century and after, institutionalized in the founding of the Royal Society, has been left to others to describe, as has the work of the Puritan followers of Comenius. These two great movements had their origins in our period, as we shall see, but they require and have received separate treatment elsewhere.

After a brief survey of the medieval background, then, a start is made on those educational ideas which arose out of Italian humanism, and which Englishmen modified to suit their own situation. One such idea, of prime importance to our theme, was that wisdom belonged as much to the world of affairs as to the cloister. More particularly, it insisted that the obligations of gentility could not be met without 'learning', previously the monopoly of the cleric. In England the view was classically stated in Elyot's *The Governour* (1531), which called on the hereditary governing class to equip itself, through a non-chivalric education, for the tasks of government.

The grammar schools, the universities and the Inns of Court were already available, it seemed, to provide such an education, and the sixteenth century did, indeed, see an influx of the sons of the wealthy into these establishments. On the other hand, certain questions remain to be answered: did these young men

really go there seeking the humanistic education which Elyot
and others enjoined upon them? Did these institutions in fact
provide such an education? And if, by and large, they did not,
as I shall hope to show, where, then, did the gentlemen of
Renaissance England get the education which they put to such
good use in national and local government?

In seeking answers to these questions it will be necessary
to go beyond the traditional institutions of education to that
informal education which the printing press and the translators
were making possible at this time, not simply for the gentleman
but also for the growing number of professional men, the clerics,
lawyers, merchants, navigators, surveyors and so on. The
problem of communication and its solution by use of the vernacular and the printing press constitute, perhaps, the most important aspect of the history of education in Renaissance England. The full implications of the maxim *verba volant, scripta
manent* are part of that history, for the Renaissance period saw
a shift from manuscript books, the arrangement of whose text
reflected the fact that it was meant to be read aloud, to the
printed book whose type was so arranged as to facilitate looking
at a page face, and even skipping over headings and sub-
headings. The emergence of a title and a title page, where
previously the first sentence or part of a sentence served to
identify the book, was merely one part of that 'elimination of
sound and voice from man's understanding of the intellectual
world (which) helped create within the human spirit itself the
silence of a spatialized universe'.[1] The printed book transformed
the listening Christian into the reading Christian, and the same
kind of change can be seen at work throughout the whole field
of education, in the traditional grammar schools and universities,
in the growing number of private schools, even, and perhaps
most important of all, in the home.

The aim, then, is to observe an idea in action, to watch the
Renaissance idea of wisdom being handled, modified, and assimilated, as Englishmen sought to perfect ways of achieving it, to
determine the uses to which it should be put.[2] Any such task

[1] Cf. W. J. Ong, 'System, Space and Intellect in Renaissance Symbolism',
*Bibliothèque d'Humanisme et Renaissance*, XVIII (1956), 222–39 and *Ramus,
Method and the Decay of Dialogue* (Cambridge, Mass., 1958), p. 318.

[2] For a theoretical discussion cf. E. F. Rice, jun., *The Renaissance Idea of Wisdom*
(Cambridge, Mass. 1958).

starts, inevitably and gratefully, with the work of W. H. Woodward and Foster Watson, and my indebtedness to them will be apparent. What I have tried to do is to marry their pioneer studies with more recent work, mostly by American scholars, and especially exemplified in L. B. Wright's *Middle Class Culture in Elizabethan England* (1935) and T. W. Baldwin's *Shakespeare's Small Latine and Lesse Greek* (1944), to produce a history of education in Renaissance England which, surprisingly, will be the first.

Parts of this book have previously appeared in print as 'Liberal Education and the Inns of Court in the Sixteenth Century', *British Journal of Educational Studies*, IX (1960), 'Holbein's "Ambassadors" and Sixteenth Century Education', *Journal of the History of Ideas*, XXI (1960), and 'Tradition and Change in Sixteenth and Seventeenth Century Education', *Year Book of Education* (1958). I am grateful to the editors of these journals for permission to use material from these articles.

Many friends and colleagues have given me advice in the writing of this book over the past seven years, especially Professor W. H. G. Armytage, Mr. Paul Coles, Mr. W. A. McNeill, Mrs. Joan Simon, Professor B. S. Yamey and the editor of this series, Mr. Harold Perkin. To each of these I offer my thanks. I am particularly indebted to Professor A. V. Judges, Professor J. P. Tuck and Mr. P. J. Wallis, whose careful and critical reading of my manuscript saved me from errors of fact and judgement. The imperfections which remain are, of course, my own responsibility.

I wish to acknowledge the expert help provided by the staff of the British Museum Reading Room and Manuscript Room, and by the Librarian and his staff of the University of Keele. Miss K. I. Ambrose was responsible for translating my original drafts into typescript, and I have to thank her for her care and skill in doing so. Miss S. I. Wood completed the typing of the final revisions.

Finally, I wish to thank my wife, whose patience and encouragement during the making of this book will scarcely be rewarded by its appearance.

KENNETH CHARLTON

*Department of Education*
*University of Keele.*

# Abbreviations

IN all quotations the spelling and punctuation have been modernized. The places of publication of books referred to is London, except where shown to be otherwise. The following abbreviations are used in the footnotes:

| | |
|---|---|
| Allen | P. S. Allen, ed., *Opus Epistolarum Des. Erasmi Roterodami* |
| *Am.H.R.* | *American Historical Review* |
| *B.J.E.S.* | *British Journal of Educational Studies* |
| *B.J.R.L.* | *Bulletin of the John Rylands Library* |
| Carlisle | N. Carlisle, *A Concise Description of the Endowed Grammar Schools in England and Wales* (1818), two vols. |
| *Ec.H.R.* | *Economic History Review* |
| E.E.T.S. | Early English Text Society |
| *E.H.R.* | *English Historical Review* |
| *E.L.H.* | *English Literary History* |
| *E.S.R.* | A. F. Leach, *English Schools at the Reformation* (1896) |
| *H.L.Q.* | *Huntington Library Quarterly* |
| *J.H.I.* | *Journal of the History of Ideas* |
| *J.M.H.* | *Journal of Modern History* |
| *J.W.C.I.* | *Journal of the Warburg and Courtauld Institutes* |
| *L. and P.* | *Letters and Papers, Foreign and Domestic, Henry VIII* |
| *M.L.R.* | *Modern Language Review* |
| *M.P.* | *Modern Philology* |
| *N. and Q.* | *Notes and Queries* |
| Nichols | F. M. Nichols, ed., *The Epistles of Erasmus* (1901), three vols. |
| O.H.S. | Oxford Historical Society |
| *P.B.A.* | *Proceedings of the British Academy* |
| *P.M.L.A.* | *Publications of the Modern Language Association* |
| *S.P.* | *Studies in Philology* |
| *T.R.H.S.* | *Transactions of the Royal Historical Society* |
| *V.C.H.* | *Victoria County History* |

# Part One

ORIGINS

# I

◇◇◇◇◇◇◇◇◇◇◇◇◇◇◇◇◇◇◇◇◇◇◇◇◇◇◇◇◇◇◇◇◇◇◇◇◇◇◇◇◇◇◇◇◇◇◇

# The Medieval Background

◇◇◇◇◇◇◇◇◇◇◇◇◇◇◇◇◇◇◇◇◇◇◇◇◇◇◇◇◇◇◇◇◇◇◇◇◇◇◇◇◇◇◇◇◇◇◇

THE modern western world, so we are told, is split into 'two cultures', the result of an educational system which increasingly separates the humanities from the sciences. The fundamental lack of communication between the artist and the scientist becomes increasingly a cause for alarm. The gap widens both at school and at university. Historically the gap is a modern one. 'The arts' had their origin in the term 'liberal arts', found first in the writings of the Greeks, and until the end of the medieval period the words 'arts' and 'sciences' were used synonymously. Indeed it was not until the twelfth century that the phrase 'liberal arts' became anything like a technical term, and even then by definition it comprehended as well as the 'arts' of grammar, dialectic and rhetoric, the 'sciences' of arithmetic, geometry, astronomy and music, the *trivium* and *quadrivium* respectively of the medieval university statutes, the essential preliminary to the further study of law, medicine and 'the queen of all the sciences', theology. The etymology of the adjective reminds us of the original purpose of liberal studies, the education of a free man, that is a free citizen in the Greek city-state of the fourth century B.C., one who would have the leisure to contribute to the administration and government of the State. Their purpose, then, was practical, though the emphasis placed on the different parts varied. In Plato 'the coping stone on top of all our liberal studies' was dialectic, a five-year course in what

3

we should now call logic, but which for Plato was to be regarded as a tool of thought and inquiry inextricably linked with the study of moral and political philosophy. As he put it, 'the course leads what is best in the soul up to the vision of what is best in things that are. Dialectic finds the eye of the soul embedded in what is really a swamp of barbarism and gently draws and raises it upwards, using the arts which we have enumerated as hand-maids in the work of conversion.' Knowledge and its attainment, then, were to be regarded as:

> a kind of conversion of the soul from darkness to light. . . . Unless a man can abstract the form of the good from all else and distinguish it by analysis; unless he makes it run the gauntlet of every proof and is eager to try it by the test not of seeming but of reality and finally unless he emerges from it with all his principles not o'er thrown, then will you not say that he does not know the real good from any other good?[1]

This was the purpose of liberal education, to find the form of the good, using dialectic as a kind of 'science of the good'.

It was a philosophical and ultimately a metaphysical view of education, one that was opposed by Isocrates, whose school at the Lyceum in fourth-century Athens rivalled Plato's Academy. And in the end it was Isocrates and not Plato who educated Greece and certainly Rome later on. Isocrates' emphasis lay on the rhetorical or oratorical side of liberal studies. For Isocrates, however, eloquence had a civic and moral purpose which nowadays we exclude when we use the term. If we use the word rhetoric it is generally in a pejorative sense, and oratory is now something suspect. Isocrates, on the other hand, linked his method with his content and purpose, all three being directed to ideas and problems involved in the moral and political affairs of the community. He was concerned with concrete problems requiring discussion and debate before decision. A truly educated man was one who had the ability to provide a solution to a problem which was best or most nearly was best suited to particular circumstances. The ability to ask the right questions, to grasp the complexity of human affairs, to make decisions, these were the virtues which Isocrates sought to foster. It was not surprising, therefore, that the Romans found his ideas more

[1] *Republic*, VIII, 533–4.

congenial to their outlook on life than they did Plato's. It was the Isocratic tradition rather than the Platonic, then, that Cicero in the first century B.C. and Quintilian in the first century A.D. chose to develop. For Cicero and Quintilian, the man of affairs was one who not only could speak eloquently and persuasively, but who also had something to say that was worth saying. The orator, in Quintilian's phrase, was 'a good man skilled in speaking' who matched his powers of speech with an elegance of life permeated by the Roman concepts of *gravitas, decorum, honestum* and *frugalitas*.

If the emphasis was placed on rhetoric, the wide scope of liberal studies remained, set out for example in texts such as Varro's *Disciplinarium Libri Novem* which added architecture and medicine to what ultimately came to be the traditional seven liberal arts. But with the advent and spread of Christianity the problem of what constituted a liberal education was enormously complicated by the need to reconcile scholarship with piety, to reconcile the truth achieved by human reason with truth achieved by divine revelation. How, in an age before there was a body of Christian literature available, could the traditional authors who had hitherto provided the content of education, provide a Christian education as well? The life of St. Jerome (A.D. 331–420) epitomizes the dilemma which faced Christians and Christian teachers in trying to formulate a course of studies. As a pupil in Rome of Donatus, the grammarian, and later as a student of theology in Gaul he had constant recourse to classical and therefore pagan texts. Then occurred one of the several spiritual crises in his life, when he suddenly gave up 'profane' studies and retreated to the desert. 'What has Horace to do with the Psalter, or Virgil with the Gospel or Cicero with the Apostle?' he asked.[1] Even then, however, he found the old texts indispensable and it was during this period that he had his famous dream in which at the Divine Judgement he was accused of being a Ciceronian rather than a Christian. Once again he renounced his classical texts, but even in the latter years of his life, when teaching in the monastery he founded at Bethlehem, he was still using them.

It was not until early in the fifth century that St. Augustine

[1] W. H. Freemantle, *St. Jerome: Letters and Select Works*, Oxford, 1938, p. 35.

of Hippo, in his *De Doctrina Christiana*, effected the reconciliation between pagan and Christian which was to provide a *modus
vivendi* for most of the medieval period. St. Augustine's solution
was to accept the disciplines of classical liberal studies, and
especially the philosophical and rhetorical bases of Greek and
Roman literature, but at the same time to seek their exemplification in Christian authors, a solution which would provide a
Christian content and at the same time a justification for the
classical basis. It was St. Augustine, too, who popularized the
idea of providing textbooks consisting of readings in each of
the liberal arts. Taking as his model the seven books of Martianus Capella, who had in turn based his work on that of Varro,
Augustine fostered a method which became traditional in the
works of Cassiodorus and Isidore of Seville, of Boethius, Bede
and Rabanus Maurus. The solution was not, needless to say,
universally applauded. Gregory the Great (540–605), for
example, who sent his missionaries to England in 597, withdrew
from the world in the midst of his secular studies 'when he saw
that many of the students rushed headlong into vice . . . lest
in acquiring wordly knowledge he might also fall down the
same terrific precipice'. Later he wrote condemning Desiderius,
Bishop of Vienne, on hearing 'that you are lecturing in profane
literature . . . for the same mouth cannot sing the praises of
Jupiter and the praises of Christ. . . .'[1] Even Odo of Cluny
dreamed of his Virgil as a beautiful vase filled with vipers, and
indeed, as we shall see, such suspicion of pagan writers was still
to be found in some sixteenth-century reformers.

By about the tenth century, however, we have a generally
accepted pattern of liberal education which had Hellenistic
origins, a mixed content and a Christian purpose.[2] It was no
longer the free man, nor the lay gentleman, but the cleric for
whom such an education was deemed appropriate, and it was in
the monasteries and later in the cathedral schools that such
education was to be found. It was from the monasteries of the
western world, for example, that the great encyclopaedic texts
of Cassiodorus and the others had come. 'Set like islands in a

[1] Cited by P. F. Jones, 'The Gregorian Mission and English Education',
*Speculum*, III (1928), pp. 337–8.
[2] Cf. P. Abelson, *The Seven Liberal Arts: a Study in Medieval Culture* (New
York, 1906).

sea of ignorance and barbarism they had saved learning from extinction in western Europe',[1] after the disappearance in the fifth and sixth centuries of those secular schools and teachers in whose hands much of the education of Roman times had rested. The Benedictine rule had laid increased stress on the obligation to study, whether by reading or writing. In his reading the monk selected from the works of the Fathers, the Lives of the Saints, the ecclesiastical histories and the Biblical commentaries of recent authors. His writing would be confined to contributing to the local chronicle or annals, producing Lives of the Saints, and multiplying copies of service and hymn books. Yet study was not the monk's prime obligation, which was to the communal life of the monastery and the daily round of prayer and worship. For the average monk, too, his monastery was his world and his reading and study confined to what the monastery's library had to offer. None of this made for the constant interchange of ideas which would enable him to go beyond the mere conservation of traditional knowledge. The Cluniac reforms of the tenth and eleventh centuries, with their emphasis on colony building and central oversight did something, it is true, to break down the growing localism of monastic life. The founders of Citeau on the other hand sought to restore the simplicity of the Benedictine rule, and St. Bernard, the Order's greatest leader, was a mystic rather than a scholar. Bec which flourished under Lanfranc and Anselm was an exception to the general picture, with an excellence which was 'almost wholly accidental'.[2]

By the eleventh century, on the other hand, a new phenomenon was appearing in the form of a constantly-moving body of students who sought masters in the cathedral churches, which were to be found not in rural retreat but in the growing urban centres, and especially in the cathedral churches of northern France, in Chartres, Orleans, Rheims, Laon and Paris. Here the bishop, bound by conciliar canon to provide for the education of the chapter, by the eleventh century had delegated his duties to a deputy, the chancellor, who in turn was aided by a *scholasticus*, a 'master of the schools'. It was to the greatest of all of these

[1] C. H. Haskins, *The Renaissance of the Twelfth Century* (Cambridge, Mass., 1927), p. 33.

[2] D. Knowles, *The Monastic Order in England* (Cambridge, 1940), p. 490.

schools, to Chartres, that students from all over Europe flocked to study with men like Bernard of Chartres and his brother Thierry, with William of Conches and Gilbert of La Poirrée. For half a century it reigned supreme as the centre of liberal studies in the literature of the Ancient World. 'We are like dwarfs that sit on the shoulders of giants. Hence we can see more and further than they, not by reason of the keenness of our vision nor the outstanding stature of our bodies, but because we have been raised aloft and are being carried by these men of giant dimensions.'[1] Under Thierry particularly, in the second quarter of the twelfth century, the whole range of liberal studies was studied at Chartres, some of his pupils going into Spain and returning with the mathematical and scientific texts then being translated into Latin from the Arabic and original Greek by men such as Adelard of Bath and Gerard of Cremona. It was at Chartres, too, that we find the first iconographical representations of the liberal arts, personified for example on the western or Royal Portal of the cathedral, where the seven arts are portrayed with the philosophers and authors associated with them. Elsewhere, in miniatures and on candlesticks as well as in stone, we find grammar, the key to all the sciences, holding a box and a key. Dialectic is represented by a snake, rhetoric is put in armour (to signify persuasion!) and astronomy is usually winged.[2]

But towards the middle of the twelfth century the influence of Chartres was being challenged by the schools in and around the cathedral of Notre Dame in Paris, where a young scholar, Peter Abelard (1074–1142), after quarrelling with his teacher William of Champeaux, the master of the cathedral school, was introducing a new method of seeking after truth, based on an

[1] The remark of Bernard is reported by John of Salisbury in *Metalogicon*, III, 4 (ed. D. D. McGarry, Berkeley, 1955), p. 167. Cf. R. Klibansky, 'Standing on the Shoulders of Giants', *Isis*, XXVI (1936), pp. 147–9.

[2] D. L. Clark, 'The Iconography of the Seven Liberal Arts', *Stained Glass*, XXIII (1933); A. Katzenellenboger, 'The Representation of the Seven Liberal Arts', in M. Clagett, G. Post and R. Reynolds, eds. *Twelfth Century Europe and the Foundation of Modern Society* (Madison, 1961), pp. 39–55; R. Klibansky, 'The School of Chartres', ibid., pp. 3–14, U. T. Holmes, 'Transitions in European Education', ibid., pp. 15–36; R. L. Poole, 'The Masters of the Schools of Paris and Chartres in John of Salisbury's Time', *E.H.R.*, XXXV (1920); L. C. Mackinney, *Bishop Fulbert and Education at the School of Chartres* (University of Notre Dame, 1957).

insistence that there was no inherent conflict between knowledge and faith, that liberal studies based even on Christian
authors ought always to be subjected to a rational test. The
tool to be used was dialectic, examplified in Abelard's *Sic et
Non*, in which opinions from different authorities are cited, not
because they are authorities but because the application of
rational thought to these would enable any contradictions in
them to be resolved and a pathway to the truth of the matter
opened up. This union of pagan and Christian teaching was, of
course, opposed by the old guard, but it made progress because
it could be justified on Christian grounds. The belief in a
personal God who, out of his goodness ordered the universe,
provided its own corollary, the possibility of understanding
such order. Reason, previously a dangerously pagan quality,
thus achieved a new dignity, in that through its use an understanding of the Divine Will could be reached. 'By doubting we
are led to enquire; by enquiry we perceive the truth.' As an
intellectual therapist Abelard was of great service to the cause
of Christian theology. His method of disputation enabled him to
go beyond the merely scriptural teaching of the past to a
theological study of the concepts themselves. Abelard did not
discover dialectic, of course. Rabanus Maurus, for instance, had
reminded his readers in the ninth century that 'logic enabled
him to penetrate into the craftiness of heretics and confute their
opinions by the magical conclusions of syllogisms'.[1] But Abelard
put it to a much more rigorous and fundamental use, allowing
it to lead him where it would and ready to accept the challenge
implicit in this. In this respect he was the Wittgenstein of the
twelfth century.

He had at his disposal very few of the logical texts of Aristotle, but as the century progressed more and more of these
became available in Latin translation, and with their aid, it
seemed, the secret to all knowledge had been found. Logic
became the *scientia scientarium*. It was an era of argument,
exciting, flexible, stimulating. The monasteries could not com-
pete in such a world—though later the Friars did, and most
successfully. In Paris the new method was pressed into the
service of theology and produced Peter Lombard's *Sentences*.

---

[1] Rabanus Maurus, *De Clericorum Institutione*, cited Abelson, op. cit., p. 72.
Abelard, *Sic et Non*, in J. P. Migne, *Patrologiae Latinae*, CLXXVIII, col. 1349.

In Italy, and especially in Bologna, it transformed the study of canon law and resulted in the *Decretum* of Gratian, the actual title of which reads *Concordantia Discordantium Canonum*. But, as so often happens, many of Abelard's followers over-stepped themselves in their eagerness to make use of 'the new logic', which instead of remaining a sharp-edged tool, became an end in itself. As Stephen, Bishop of Tournai, wrote to the Pope around 1195, 'Beardless youths sit in the chairs of the old professors and they who are scarcely pupils are anxious to be called master . . . neglecting the rules of the arts and discarding the books of good authority, with their sophistications they catch flies of senseless verbiage as in webs of spiders.' They failed to see, with John of Salisbury, that 'logic is of great value as an aid to other studies, but by itself it remains bloodless and barren'.[1] The old insistence on a wide range of studies went by the board. Lacking a Bernard or a Thierry, Chartres declined, though Orleans continued as a centre of literary studies. The great teachers were to be found in Paris and it was to these that the students flocked, for the school followed the teacher not the teacher the school, and it was on this wave of logic that the new universities were ushered in. The schools which had grown up in and around the cathedral of Notre Dame gradually, almost imperceptibly, transformed themselves into the University of Paris. The decline of the cathedral schools is reflected in the injunctions of the Third Lateran Council of 1179, repeated in those of the Fourth in 1215, to maintain masters of grammar and theology as in the past.

The 'Battle of the Seven Arts', as Henri D'Andeli called it, was decisively won by dialectic, as the statutes of the 'established' universities of the thirteenth century show.[2] If logic was the method of study, its content also was increasingly provided by the works of Aristotle, in metaphysics, in moral philosophy and in natural science. Classical literature was overshadowed as a subject of study. 'Grammar' was reduced to the elementary study of Donatus and Priscian. Rhetoric was hardly studied at all. One must not, of course, exaggerate the completeness of the victory. The new grammars, Alexander Villadei's *Doctrinale*

---

[1] Stephen of Tournai, cited by L. J. Paetow, *The Arts Course at Medieval Universities* (Urbana, 1910), p. 31; John of Salisbury in *Metalogicon*, IV, 28.

[2] Cf. L. J. Paetow, ed., *'The Battle of Arts' by Henry D'Andeli* (Berkeley, 1914).

and Everard de Bethune's *Graecismus*, both cite classical authors extensively. The *Roman de la Rose* owes much to Ovid and the *Divine Comedy* in the same way to Virgil. John of Garland's *Manuale Scholarium* relies a good deal on classical rhetoricians. Above all the *florilegia* of the thirteenth century, those useful and all-embracing collections of extracts from 'the great books', were full of the old authors. So popular were they that it is probably from them that many thirteenth and fourteenth-century authors obtained their knowledge of classical literature. This may well be cited as evidence of decline, but at least continuity was maintained despite the evil days on which literary studies had fallen.[1]

The general pattern, as we have seen, had been one of development from the great period of the Benedictine monasteries through the cathedral schools of the tenth and eleventh centuries to the universities of the thirteenth. In England, however, a slightly different picture emerges in that the cathedral schools played a much slighter part, despite the great days of these institutions in the age of Alcuin.[2] The tenth and eleventh centuries in England saw a temporary revival of monastic scholarship and learning, led by Dunstan of Glastonbury and his bishops Ethelward and Oswald, and flowering in the work of their disciples, Aelfric, Wulfstan and Byrhtferth. Their contribution to vernacular literature had no peer on the Continent, and Aelfric in particular did his utmost to spread his learning and teaching outside the monastic walls. After the Conquest, on the other hand, the Anglo-Norman monks considered themselves a race apart and their studies were almost entirely literary, centring chiefly on hagiography and the writing of history. Within this restricted field of scholarship, of course, the contributions of Eadmer, William of Salisbury and Oderic

---

[1] Cf. E. K. Rand, 'The Classics in the Thirteenth Century', *Speculum*, IV (1929), pp. 249–69. E. A. Quain, 'The Medieval *Accessus ad Auctores*', *Traditio*, III (1945), pp. 215–64. E. M. Sanford, 'The Use of Classical Latin Authors in the *Libri Manuales*', *Transactions of the American Philological Association*, LV (1924), pp. 190–248. B. L. Ullman, 'Classical Authors in Certain Medieval *Florilegia*', *Classical Philology*, XXII (1928)–XXVII (1932). R. Weiss, 'Quotations from Petronius in a Medieval *Florilegium*', *Classical Review*, LVII (1943), pp. 108–9. L. W. Jones, 'The Influence of Cassiodorus on Medieval Culture', *Speculum*, XX (1945), pp. 433–42.
[2] Cf. R. W. Southern, 'The Place of England in the Twelfth-Century Renaissance', *History*, XLV (1960), pp. 201–16.

Vitalis were considerable. But there was no disputation, no contact with inquiring minds, no fresh ideas.

Yet it was to Oxford, with no cathedral church but with a college of secular canons in the royal castle's Church of St. George and with two important monasteries nearby, that students and teachers came during the twelfth century. The town lay on the main road from Southampton to Northampton, along which scholars from Paris might travel, and we know there was considerable interchange between the two centres throughout the century. Yet we have no direct evidence to suggest why it was Oxford and not one of the several other possible centres that developed into a university town. Nor can we put a date to the beginnings of the university. The university is a peculiarly medieval institution, yet neither Paris nor Bologna nor Oxford, its three great exemplars, was the result of a decisive act of foundation whether by Papal Bull or by charter of incorporation, as Naples, say, was founded by Frederick II as a rival to Bologna in 1224, or Toulouse founded by Pope Gregory IX in 1229 as part of his campaign against the Albigensian heresy, or Prague by Pope Clement VI in 1347, or Glasgow in 1451 by Pope Nicholas V. Throughout the twelfth century we have only isolated references to students being taught at Oxford. Round about 1117 Theobald of Etampes, 'master of Oxford', was lecturing to an audience of clerks numbering from sixty to a hundred. By 1187, when Gerald of Wales read his *Topography of Ireland* to students at Oxford, he describes an academically organized society divided into several faculties each with its own doctors and masters and with students coming from a wide area, a *studium generale* in fact. It was not 'officially' recognized as such, however, until the Pope's legate Nicholas, Bishop of Tusculum, issued an ordinance in 1214 regulating affairs between town and gown after two clerks had been hanged by townsmen in 1209. Both the *universitas*, that is the gild or corporation of either students, as at Bologna, or more usually of masters (teachers) as at Paris and Oxford, and the *studium*, developed out of the *scholae* of individual teachers. In the same way the originally *ad hoc* arrangements between teacher and students were only later regularized and systematized in the statutes of the university and its colleges. Oxford was not 'founded' as a result of the migration from Paris in 1167, any more than Cambridge was by the dispersion from Oxford after the 1208 clash between town and gown.[1] Student life had similar formless origins. Before the coming of the Friars (Dominicans in 1221, Franciscans in 1224) who lived a communal life with chapel, hall, dormitory and teaching within their own convents, the students of the nascent university lived either in the houses of the townsfolk as lodgers, as Chaucer's scholar did with a carpenter's family, or in *hospitia* or *aulae* (halls), private houses in the town rented for a year or more by masters who offered lodging and some instruction for a consideration. The ordinance of 1214, already referred to, attempted in some way to regulate the rents charged by the townsfolk for these halls, but it was not until the early fifteenth century that the university, for reasons of discipline, insisted that undergraduates should reside in halls. The chief source of instruction lay in 'the schools' where the public lectures of the university were given, but the students were free to choose their own lectures as they were to choose their own form of lodging. Colleges, such as were endowed in increasing numbers in the fourteenth century, were what we would now call post-graduate institutions, where a few chosen bachelors (*socii* or 'fellows') continued their studies for a master's or doctor's degree. The colleges were not teaching institutions, they housed no undergraduates and they were very small. University College, for example, consisted of only three fellows for some time after its foundation and there were never more than six in the first century of its existence. Even Merton, the oldest and richest college had only twenty fellows by 1450. The colleges of the fourteenth century were in fact invariably overshadowed by the local monasteries and friars' convents.[2]

We have spoken of the avidity with which Aristotle's logic was read in the schools of the twelfth and thirteenth centuries, and of the way in which his scientific works were brought in

---

[1] T. E. Holland, 'The University of Oxford in the Twelfth Century', O.H.S., *Collectanea*, II (1890), pp. 137–92. H. E. Salter, 'The Medieval University of Oxford', *History*, XIV (1929), pp. 57–61. H. E. Salter, *Medieval Oxford* (Oxford, 1936).

[2] Cf. H. P. Stokes, *The Medieval Hostels of the University of Cambridge* (Cambridge, 1924). A. B. Emden, *An Oxford Hall in Medieval Times* (Oxford, 1927). H. E. Salter, 'An Oxford Hall in 1424', in H. W. C. Davis, ed., *Essays in History presented to R. L. Poole* (Oxford, 1927), pp. 421–35.

translation from Spain. Yet the Church regarded these latter, and particularly their Islamic commentators, with a good deal of suspicion, as likely to lead to heresy. Indeed the first university statutes at Paris in 1215 forbade the reading of 'the physical and metaphysical works of Aristotle', a prohibition it was felt necessary to repeat in 1231 and 1263, and it was not until the age of the great Dominicans, Albertus Magnus, Alexander of Hales and St. Thomas Aquinas, in the second half of the thirteenth century that the whole of Aristotelian thought was assimilated into Christian theology. At Oxford the introduction of Aristotelian texts dates from the first decade of the century, and thereafter was made part of regular teaching as a result of the work of men like Robert Grosseteste, John Blund, Adam of Buckfield and Robert Fishacre. By the middle of the century Aristotelian learning had taken full possession of Oxford in both the Faculty of Arts and the Faculty of Theology. As for the physical sciences and mathematics, whether Aristotelian or Arabic, despite the work throughout the twelfth century of pioneers like Adelard of Bath, Walcher, Prior of Malvern, Robert of Chester, Roger of Hereford, and the studies of the Merton school of astronomers, little science was taught in 'the schools' where logic and theology held sway.[1]

Parallel with the rise of the universities, and to a large extent dependent on it, was the growth of the grammar schools of medieval England. Hitherto the education of children had been confined either to the monasteries or to the schools of song and grammar attached to the secular cathedrals. In the former, it must be remembered, the teaching was almost wholly novitiate in preparation for membership of the community, and as such was largely moral and scriptural, together with instruction in such essential technical skills as the preparation of ink and parchment and writing in the script form current at the time. The sons of distinguished neighbours of the monastery were

[1] D. A. Callus, 'Robert Grosseteste as Scholar' in ed. D. A. Callus, *Robert Grosseteste, Scholar and Bishop* (Oxford, 1955). D. A. Callus, 'The Introduction of Aristotelian Learning to Oxford', *P.B.A.*, XXIX (1943), pp. 229–81. F. M. Powicke, 'Robert Grosseteste and the Nichomachean Ethics', ibid., XVI (1930), pp. 85–104. C. H. Haskins, *Studies in the History of Medieval Science* (2nd edition, New York, 1927), Chap. vi. C. H. Haskins, 'Arabic Science in Western Europe', *Isis*, VII (1935), pp. 478–85. C. H. Haskins, 'Adelard of Bath', *E.H.R.*, XXVI (1911), pp. 491–8.

accepted into the novices' school, though this was occasional and exceptional. From the eleventh century, however, there was a gradual increase in the kind of school which, naturally springing up near monasteries and cathedrals, and often relying on their patronage, was nevertheless not part of these institutions. The so-called 'monastic' school of St. Albans, which first appears in the records about 1100, is a good example of this.[1]

Though not of a religious institution these schools were very largely subject to their oversight, in that their master, licensed by the chancellor of the cathedral chapter, was subject to the periodic visitations of the bishop's archdeacon, and was liable to be hailed before the diocesan courts to account for any alleged misdemeanour or sin of omission. Later, the jurisdiction of the chancellor over the grammar school master extended, too, over those chantry priests whose foundations included teaching duties with their prime function of singing prayers for the souls of the founder and his kin. The parish priest and, from the late fourteenth century, the chantry priest must between them have accounted for a good deal of the teaching of children in medieval England, though in neither case would the education that they provided be very systematic or efficient. On the other hand, by the beginning of the fourteenth century there were schools, too, which like that at Hull were set up by the secular authorities and whose masters were virtually borough officials, receiving their stipend from the borough and subject to the oversight of the burgesses.[2]

Whatever the type of school, however, the process of education was almost entirely oral. Books, i.e. manuscripts, were extremely rare. Those that were in the school were probably the master's imperfect transcripts of what the scribe thought he saw in his original, itself a copy. Each day the master would read out selected portions of his text, explaining difficult words, and perpetually (and literally) rehearsing his pupils in the parts of speech and the rules of accident and syntax, relying on recitation by the pupil to check next day what had been remembered of the previous day's lesson. The pupil had no permanent

[1] D. Knowles, *The Monastic Orders in England* (Cambridge, 1949), pp. 487ff. Cf. L. Thorndike, 'Elementary and Secondary Education in the Middle Ages', *Speculum*, XV (1940), pp. 400–8.

[2] Cf. J. Lawson, *A Town Grammar School Through Six Centuries* (Oxford, 1963), pp. 15ff.

record of his exercises and such methods not surprisingly required the ever-present birch to achieve any semblance of efficiency. In such schools the grammars of Donatus or Priscian reigned supreme until in the thirteenth century they were supplemented by Alexander Villadei's *Doctrinale* (1199). Cast in hexameters, the latter was an immediate success, in university as well as school. As opposed to the continuous prose of Donatus, it not only took into account the changes which had taken place in the Latin language since the days of the Empire, but it also provided a more thorough syntax and more detailed sections on prosody and the rhetorical figures. It was in fact altogether a more comprehensive work. Also in verse was Everard of Bethune's *Graecismus* which despite its title was a Latin grammar, but neither this nor John of Garland's *Compendium Grammatice* seriously rivalled the *Doctrinale*, which survived the criticisms of the humanists to become as popular in print as it had been in manuscript.[1]

Of the different kinds or levels of education mentioned so far none was considered appropriate for the ruling class of the Middle Ages. For the nobleman and the knight a quite different kind of education was developed to prepare them for their prime duty, the service of the king in war. It was in this context that the notion of chivalry developed, at one and the same time an ideal, an institution and a system of education. In its technical sense chivalry came to England with the Conqueror and his mounted knights, for though Harold's men rode to battle they then dismounted and fought on foot. After the Conquest 'it was impossible to be chivalrous without a horse', and on this depended the first and major part of the education of a knight.[2] Practical prowess was here the prime aim. With it went a moral ideal of service to one's liege lord, in which loyalty, obedience, and trustworthiness were the virtues most sought after.

It was not until the period of the Crusades that a religious element was introduced. With the Holy Land in danger Pope Clement's famous call at Clermont enjoined on every person of noble birth, on attaining the age of twelve, the taking of a

---

[1] Cf. Abelson, op. cit., Chaps. ii, iii and iv; Paetow, *Arts Course* . . ., pp. 33ff.

[2] N. Denholm-Young, 'The Tournament in the Thirteenth Century', in R. W. Hunt, ed., *Studies in Medieval History Presented to F. M. Powicke* (Oxford, 1948), p. 240.

solemn oath before a bishop that he would 'defend to the utter-most the oppressed, the widow and the orphan and that women of noble birth should enjoy his especial care'. Such an oath achieved its highest exemplification in the Crusading Orders, the Hospitallers, the Teutonic knights and the Templars, and it was for the latter than St. Bernard drew up a *Rule* and composed *In Praise of the New Chivalry*. Bound by his oath to fight for the Christian Church against the Infidel the knight was now able to reconcile one of the contradictions inherent in his rôle in society. The pursuit and glorification of war was now given religious sanction. The principles of monasticism were adapted to the pursuit of arms. The same became true for the Monastic Knights who defended Christianity against the invading Moors in Spain in the same century. Religious idealism, together with a pattern of social behaviour towards women, now surrounded and transformed what had originated as a system of military service based on land-holding.[1]

The achieving of such an ideal required a long and arduous training, quite outside the normal scope of educational provision. It started with a groundwork of moral training at the mother's knee until the boy was seven, at which age he would be sent away from home to the household of another member of the nobility, there to serve his 'apprenticeship', first as page, then as squire. Stephen of Blois, for example, received his training at the Court of his uncle, Henry I; Henry II at the household of Robert, Duke of Gloucester; and Henry VI under Richard Beauchamp, Earl of Warwick. Nor was such instruction confined to the households of laymen. Fitzstephen, the biographer of St. Thomas á Becket, tells how 'the nobles of England and of neighbouring kingdoms used to send their sons to serve the Chancellor, whom he trained with honourable bringing up and learning; and when they had received the knight's belt sent them back with honour to their fathers and kindred'. As a page, for the next seven years of his life the boy would undertake and be taught, still under the tutelage of the womenfolk of the household, the menial tasks of household service, and particularly of service on his lord at table. At this stage, too, he would begin

[1] Cf. F. J. C. Hearnshaw, 'Chivalry and its Place in History', in E. Prestage, ed., *Chivalry* (1928), pp. 1–35. C. Dawson, *Religion and the Rise of Western Culture* (1950), pp. 181ff. E. F. Jacob, 'The Beginnings of Medieval Chivalry', in Prestage, op. cit., pp. 37–55.

to gain acquaintance with the rules and prohibitions of courtly love, both by precept and through the numerous *chansons de geste* circulating, either by word of mouth or by manuscript copy, through the courts and noble households of Europe. In addition, towards the end of this period of his training, the page would begin to pay rather more serious attention than hitherto to his physical education through running and leaping, wrestling and riding. At the age of fourteen he acquired the status of squire, when his technical training as a knight began in earnest.. Until he was twenty-one, ready to be dubbed a knight, he would be trained in the use of various weapons, in the management of horses and especially the heavy war-horse, and in the maintenance of armour. He would also perfect the less martial arts of hunting and hawking. Personal service on his lord still continued to be at the core of this stage of his training, it being emphasized that such service in no way involved a loss of dignity. In addition he would cultivate the domestic arts of music and poetry which were to play a significant part in developing in him an appreciation of the ideal of courtly love. The poetry and music of the troubadour were something much more to the knight than mere pastime and leisured relaxation after the rigours of his technical training. Through them the squire was initiated into a pattern of behaviour towards women which at best contributed to a revolution in domestic relations and the notion of good manners. Courtly love was 'a gigantic system of bigamy in which every lady was expected to have both paramour and husband, and every complete cavalier besides the wife, to whom for business reasons (i.e. the inheritance of dower and estates) he was bound, a goddess whose commands he unhesitatingly obeyed, whose cause he upheld against all-comers'.[1] The treatises on the art of courtly love, of which Andreas Capellanus's is perhaps the most famous (*c.* 1185), had their origin in Ovid, but in the chivalric tradition the ancient game of equals engaged in mutual deceit for sexual pleasure was transformed into a feudal relationship in which the lady of his choice became the knight's feudal suzerain, to whom he owed unquestioning allegiance and from whom he could expect no requite.[2]

[1] Hearnshaw, loc. cit., p. 18.
[2] Cf. J. J. Parry, ed. and trans., *Andreas Capellanus' Art of Courtly Love* (New York, 1941).

At twenty-one the squire would be ready for knighthood and would go through a highly elaborate ceremony of investiture which combined the military and the religious aspects of the chivalric ideal. As Ramon Lull put it in his *Libre del Ordre de Cavayleria* (*c.* 1280), 'the office of priesthood and of chivalry have great concordance'.[1] Invested with his arms, the symbols of his knighthood, he would before dubbing go through various rites of purification wich included bathing, the donning of white robes, fasting and keeping vigil, taking mass and listening to a sermon, and finally the blessing of his sword. With the receipt of the Church's accolade, as it were, he was now ready for the secular accolade, the ceremonial blow on the shoulders, the final act of the investiture.

Such was the training of the knight as described in the chivalric literature of the period, the *chansons de geste*, the romances, and the courtesy books.[2] It was of course, and particularly when compared with the rest of medieval education, essentially unbookish, but it must not be imagined, therefore, that the medieval knight was illiterate. He had what he imagined to be a 'healthy' contempt for clerkly education, but the reading of chivalric literature would be the aim if not always the achievement of chivalric education, and though it was a useful dramatic device for Ramon Lull's squire to find the Hermit Knight reading 'a little book' which turns out to be 'a rule and order of chivalry', such a situation was obviously considered normal enough to allow it to be used as an introductory gambit. We must not, however, unduly exaggerate the idealist nature of such an education. In England, particularly, the average knight was too busy serving the king, his liege lord, in an administrative capacity at the Shire Court or Quarter Sessions, as sheriff, escheator, constable of a royal castle or comissioner of array. Besides being bound up with the common weal, he was also particularly concerned with matters agrarian, and would therefore find one of the many contemporary manuscript manuals on estate management or estate accounting, or a copy of one of the early law books, just as useful as a copy of

---

[1] A. T. P. Byles, ed., E.E.T.S., Orig. Series, Vol. 168 (1926), p. 76. (Caxton's translation.)

[2] A. T. P. Byles, 'Medieval Courtesy Books and Prose Romances of Chivalry', in Prestage, op. cit., pp. 183–206.

*Sir Amadis* or *Sir Eglamon*, to say nothing of the great literary pieces such as *Gawain and the Green Knight* or the *Roman de la Rose*.

By the mid-fourteenth century true chivalry was in decline, if indeed it had ever existed outside its literary form. The art of war was changing and the cash nexus was invading the relationship between a lord and his man. The tournament, in the days of William the Marshal a real training for war in which as many as fifty or sixty knights a side joined in a general melée in the open countryside, was now becoming a more ordered affair altogether, and by the fifteenth century was nothing more than the safe and rather sedate tilting at the lists.[1] Indeed society as a whole was changing, and not only chivalric education but the whole concept of what education was for was changing too. In these changes we find the seeds of our theme.

N. Denholm-Young, 'The Tournament . . .', loc. cit., pp. 240–2.

# II

◇◇◇◇◇◇◇◇◇◇◇◇◇◇◇◇◇◇◇◇◇◇◇◇◇◇◇◇◇◇◇◇◇◇◇◇◇◇◇◇◇◇◇◇◇

# The Renaissance Debate in Italy

◇◇◇◇◇◇◇◇◇◇◇◇◇◇◇◇◇◇◇◇◇◇◇◇◇◇◇◇◇◇◇◇◇◇◇◇◇◇◇◇◇◇◇◇◇

SUCH was the education of the High Middle Ages. But with the growth of towns and trade, from the mid-thirteenth century onwards, we find an increasing crescendo of criticism of the traditional dichotomy between learning and the active political and social life.[1] The debate between the stoic sage and the man of affairs is an old one, and its ramifications complex, involving a consideration of the notions of wisdom, of excellence, of nobility, of happiness, of citizenship, and in the end a consideration of the questions: What is the ultimate aim of human life? What is man's destiny?

The High Middle Ages had little or no doubt about the answer. The ultimate aim of life here on earth was to prepare life in another world. Human society, as described for example by Innocent III in his *De Contemptu Mundi*, was a penal institution, the result of sin and redeemable only by grace. Worldly life was a minor episode in a cosmic picture of sin, penitence and salvation. The rediscovery and reappraisal of Aristotle, however, was to revivify the notion of a society, neither penal nor conventual but natural, rational and perfectible, ruled not by God's grace but by man's reason, which would guide him towards perfection. This was not, of course, a flight from Christianity to paganism. Rather it was a rejection of the traditional path to salvation.

[1] R. Weiss, *The Dawn of Humanism in Italy* (1947).

21

Though such ideas had been put forward in the thirteenth century, as for example by Egidius Romanus, it was not until the rise to fruition of urban life in Italy in the mid- and late-fourteenth century that they were canvassed with any degree of success.[1] Yet not without debate. On the one hand were those humanists who saw in the *vita contemplativa*, the *vita solitaria*, the only way of achieving on earth an approach to true knowledge and wisdom. Such a view was opposed, and particularly in the decades after 1400, by Florentine humanists such as Bruni, Palmieri and Alberti, who deplored the flight of the stoic sage from the responsibilities of the *vita activa et civilis*, the *vita operativa*. A bridge between these views is to be found in the life and work of Coluccio Salutati, Chancellor of Florence, admirer of Petrarch and teacher of Bruni, whose ambivalence reflects the continuance of older ideas within a new political social, economic and intellectual milieu. Like so many of his contemporaries he was, to use Leibniz's phrase, 'gros de l'avenir et chargé du passé'. In the discussion which follows we would do well to remember Huizinga's warning:–

> The transition from the spirit of the declining Middle Ages to humanism was far less simple than we are inclined to imagine it. Accustomed to oppose humanism to the Middle Ages we would gladly believe that it was necessary to give up the one in order to embrace the other. . . . Classicism did not come as a sudden revelation, it grew up among the luxuriant vegetation of medieval thought. On the other hand the characteristic modes of thought of the Middle Ages did not die out till long after the Renaissance.[2]

In considering the humanists' views, as they related to education, we shall be concerned particularly with those which had to do with the nature of wisdom, with the nature of man, and with how best he might realize the powers claimed for him. These were, of course, far from being innovations as subjects for discussion. Each had been debated both by the Ancients and by the medieval churchmen, and the debate about the active and

---

[1] Cf. K. E. Shaw, 'Egidius Romanus—a Politician's Views on Educational Theory', *Researches & Studies*, No. 19 (1959), pp. 44–55; F. Gilbert, 'The Humanist Concept of the Prince and "The Prince" of Machiavelli', *J.M.H.*, XI (1939), pp. 449–83; L. K. Born, 'The Perfect Prince: a Study in Thirteenth and Fourteenth Century Ideals', *Speculum*, III (1928), pp. 502ff.

[2] J. Huizinga, *The Waning of the Middle Ages* (1924), p. 297.

contemplative life had served as an arena in which viewpoints had striven for dominance.

Though Plato had sent his philosopher-kings back into the comparative darkness of the cave to serve their fellow-men, he had insisted that true knowledge was to be achieved only by contemplation in the brightness of the upper light. Only in this way would 'our state be administered in a spirit unlike that of other states'.[1] Aristotle had made the distinction between a practical wisdom and a theoretical wisdom on which his *Ethics* and *Politics* are, taken together, a running commentary, and the possible conflict inherent in this distinction was well-recognized by the Church. Whilst the duties and obligations to one's fellow-men were essential to the Christian life, a true union with God could be achieved only in contemplation. Though both St. Basil and St. Jerome were at pains to point out the dangers of the secluded life, and like other Christian writers insisted on comparing the virtues of the one kind of life with the virtues of the other, they nevertheless made it plain that the intellectual life of contemplation was superior in the end. The stories of Leah and Rachel and of Martha and Mary were favourite exemplifications of this theme. The superiority of the solitary life was a necessary corollary to the superiority of the state of contemplation. Both were essential to learning and wisdom.

When seeking innovations in this field of thought amongst the humanists we must be careful to distinguish between those of the fourteenth century and their successors of the fifteenth. Despite his enthusiasm for the work of the ancients, Petrarch, 'the father of humanism', could nevertheless find himself bound to the *Confessions* of St. Augustine, to whom he pours out his own in the *Secretum*. In this and more particularly in the *De Vita Solitaria* we find him championing the life of the recluse as the only way by which true knowledge might be attained.[2] True, it was not the ascetic life of solitude and poverty which had been the earlier ideal of the aloof sage, spurning wealth and material possessions, emphasizing the worthlessness of the body, and insisting on the need to inhibit the passions and

[1] *Republic*, VII, 519.
[2] Cf. J. Zeitlin, trans., *Petrarch's 'Life of Solitude'* (Chicago, 1924), and W. H. Draper, trans., *Petrarch's Secret, or the Soul's Conflict with Passion* (1911).

emotions. Petrarch's was a physical and mental withdrawal which had little to do with the life led by the hermits and ascetics to whom he refers in the Second Book of *De Vita Solitaria*. The life of retreat which he enjoyed and recommended at Vaucluse was rather one of aesthetic fastidiousness, of peaceful retreat from the cares of the busy world, away from the noise, ignorance and insensibility of the common herd. In such an atmosphere the 'whole year passes happily and peacefully as though it were a single day, without annoying company and without irksomeness, without anxieties'. Though spurning the crowd, he was by no means averse to the company of congenial companions. 'No solitude is so profound, no house so small, no room so narrow but it may open to a friend.' Nor would he deny himself the company of books, those 'cheerful associates, learned, humble and eloquent, free from annoyance and expense, without complaint or grumbling, without envy or treachery'.[1]

Petrarch's followers adhered even more firmly to the ideal of the solitary sage, in whom for them Antiquity and Christianity seemed reconciled. His pupil and friend, Lombardo della Seta, wrote his *De Bono Solitudinis* to reaffirm that frugality and indifference to material wants were the basis of the true life. Boccaccio's diatribes against family life are well known, and in his biography of Dante he reflects on Dante's unhappy fate as the philosopher who forfeited his intellectual peace by marrying and allowing himself to be drawn into public affairs. Sharing these views were the vagrant teachers and secretaries, who, without worldly ties and, in the mid-fourteenth century, still unsure of their social status as humanists, moved from court to court, making a virtue of their poverty and of their indifference to an unappreciative world.

Towards the end of the century and at its turn, however, changes were taking place in Florence which were to challenge and alter these ideas, producing a belief in the dignity of man, which was to become an integral part of humanistic thought.[2]

[1] E. H. Wilkins, *Petrarch at Vaucluse* (Chicago, 1958); Zeitlin, op. cit., pp. 181, 291–2.
[2] What follows is based very largely on the work of Hans Baron. Cf. *The Crisis of the Early Italian Renaissance* (two vols., Princeton, 1955) and *Humanistic and Political Literature in Florence and Venice at the Beginning of the Quattrocento* (Cambridge, Mass., 1955) and their bibliographies.

During the High Middle Ages the economic prosperity of Florence had been based on the financial transactions of the great families of the *Arte di Calimala*, those who dealt in foreign cloth. By the first half of the fourteenth century, however almost all these families had, in turn, suffered severe setbacks, and were gradually being replaced by the more widely-based industrial economy of the *Arte della Lana*, the woollen manufacturers. Large-scale banking continued, of course, as in the case of the Medici family, but generally the financial and social centre of Florence was now to be found in the woollen industry. It was a social shift which Dante deplored in the *Divine Comedy*, but it was a shift nevertheless which resulted in a new view of life, based on the notions of increased productivity and economic progress, where ceaseless labour for the honour of the community became a virtue in itself. As the obvious concern of a community suffering from the grave losses of trade arising from the downfall of the *Calimala*, industrial labour and the commerce associated with it gained a dignity previously unknown. The provision of work for as many as possible and the training of the population in the appropriate skills would not only cure poverty, discourage idleness and restore prosperity, but would also add to the honour of the city-state.

Here is a view of life and of education which transcended the more static medieval view. At the practical level it led to the setting up of those municipal schools which Villani noted as outstripping the traditional grammar schools. Whilst in 1338 there were four large schools of the latter kind catering for between 550 and 600 pupils, up to 1,200 pupils in the municipal schools were receiving, in the vernacular, the elements of reading and writing and accounts. Such a trend was sharpened by political events. By the 1380's the Visconti of Milan had stifled the independent life of the city-republics of northern Italy. Now, in the name of unity and nationalism, they strove to extend their Lombardy kingdom southwards, towards Pisa in the west and the Umbrian cities in the east. During the years of the Milanese wars the Florentines, with the Venetians, discovered themselves as the preservers of the civic virtues, and especially of the civic freedom which had characterized the early medieval Italian city-state. With Cicero as their model they insisted that 'when the liberty of the citizen is at stake nobody can remain a private person'.[1] Out of two generations of struggle emerged a view of life and human nature which was based on the participation of the citizen in public affairs.

But it was a view based not simply on the expediency of survival, nor again on a merely economic calculus of worldly success. Something more was needed to persuade men that there was a valid alternative to the long-accepted arguments that the spiritual was superior to the material, that the two were mutually exclusive, and that religious contemplation and intellectual speculation did in fact offer a nobler way of life. The new view based itself ultimately on the Aristotelian concept that man was *by nature* a social animal. Nature had equipped man for action. Growth to full stature required social activity and responsibility. A passionless existence in seclusion could never be the appropriate environment in which the well-rounded human personality could develop.

By denying himself access to his fellow-creatures the stoic sage denied himself the very factor essential to his own self-fulfilment. The truly virtuous man, then, became the man educated for participation in the mature, social life. Based on a confidence in human nature, the new ethic was oriented at one and the same time to study and to practical affairs. Virtue, education and civic action became indissolubly linked, having their base in the economic, political and cultural life of the community.

The leading rôle in expressing and furthering these ideas was taken by Leonardo Bruni (1370–1444). But it is in the life and works of Coluccio Salutati (1331–1406), Bruni's predecessor as Chancellor of the Florentine republic, that the ambivalence characteristic of a period of transition can be seen. Here we see a conflict between the holder of public office, striving to defend Florence's traditional civic liberty against Milan, and the scholarly humanist aware of his allegiance to Petrarch and Trecento stoic humanism. In his earliest work, *De Saeculo et Religione* (1381), Salutati extols the monastic life as the highest moral ideal. Yet by the 1390's his letters are full of praise for the active life. In one he recommends married life to his fellow men-of-letters. In another, whilst not denying that monastic seclusion might have served certain holy men, he concludes that

[1] *Tusculan Disputations*, IV, xxiii, 51.

many others have found worthiness in the *negociosa et associabilis vita*. In 1392 he had rediscovered Cicero's *Epistolae ad Familiares*. But whereas Petrarch had recoiled from what he had found in the *Epistolae ad Atticum*, Salutati found only increasing support for the active life. By 1401 he could write to the monk Giovanni de San Miniato 'while you serve only yourself . . . I try to serve all my many co-citizens'. By this time, too, he had played his part in the pamphlet campaign against Milan, adding his *Invettiva* to Cino Rinuccini's *Responsiva*, the reply to Antonio Loschi's *Invective Against the Florentines*. By the time the pamphlet had been completed and published in 1403, Florence, without allies, was on the point of triumph against her adversary. 'We alone, indeed, are the barricade and obstacle which prevent that despotic regime, which has forced so many cities and towns . . . into wretched subjugation, from completing its work throughout the whole of Italy.'

Yet despite all this, his *De Tyranno*, the work of his old age, is a reversion on the political side to the medieval concept of the superiority of the Universal Empire and the likeness of monarchy to the divine order, and on the historical side to a restatement of Dante's praise of Caesar and his denial of the rôle played by Cicero and Brutus. Equally, in his controversy with Poggio in 1405, Salutati championed the philosophy of Christian stoicism which he said had found its most perfect expression in Petrarch's work.

Salutati, then, in his last years threw over this earlier enthusiasm for *vita activa* and looked back rather than ahead. The same pattern of thought is to be found in the work of one of his most brilliant disciples, Pier Paolo Vergerio (1349–1444). Though Padua was his adopted city, Vergerio had met Salutati in Florence in 1386/7, and from the early 1390's was carrying on a voluminous correspondence with his master. His letters indeed show an even clearer and more resolute adherence to the virtues of the active life, and in 1394 he composed a reply to Petrarch's letter addressed to Cicero in Hades. Whereas Petrarch had reviled Cicero for forsaking the life of the philosopher, Vergerio applauds him for his insistence on the continued vitality of republican liberty, and the need to aim not at a stoic peace of mind but at the kind of wisdom 'which is at home in the cities and towns away from solitude'. Cicero becomes the hero, the scholar who 'troubles himself with work for the state, and shoulders the labours one must share in the interest of the *salus omnium'*. Vergerio translated these views into the field of pedagogics in his influential *De Ingenuis Moribus* (*c.* 1404), yet on his return to Padua after 1405, and during the rest of his long life, we hear no more of them.

It was left to the younger generation of humanists, who shared with Salutati the early struggle for Florentine liberties, to throw off their master's doubts and to follow through the implications of their views. Twice in his career Leonardo Bruni became involved in the fight against the Visconti, first at the turn of the century with Salutati against Giangaleazzo and later, in the 1420's, against Filippo Maria. Both occasions gave birth to writing which was significant, not only as occasional literature, but also as a contribution to the working out of what was to become a fully-developed philosophy of life based on civic humanism. His *Laudatio Florentinae Urbis*, written in 1403 or 1404, was no mere propaganda piece written in time of crisis to rouse a flagging populace. Its significance lies in its radical rewriting of the history of the city and particularly of its origins.

Traditionally one of the glories of Florence lay in its foundation by Caesar after the destruction of Fiesole.[1] The story is repeated by Villani and by Dante. Now, however, the setting up of the Empire is looked on as the end of individual liberty, and a pre-Imperial origin for Florence is claimed. Bruni stresses the significance of the early city-states of Etrutia, and the golden age is that of the Republic when 'inviolate, unshaken and thriving still was the freedom of which Rome was deprived. . . . The result . . . has been the situation which we have seen developing most perfectly in this city in the past as well as the present, namely the fact that the Florentine people rejoice in every kind of liberty and stoutly show themselves the enemies of tyrants.' Only with the decline of the Empire and the rise of the free communes had the cultural life of the Republic revived and developed. Now, once again, the commune was threatened by an ambitious tyrant. A similar interpretation is to be found in Gregorio Dati's history of Florence during the years 1380 to 1406, the first account to be written of the Visconti wars, and

---

[1] On which see N. Rubenstein, 'The Beginnings of Political Thought in Florence: a Study in Medieval Historiography', *J.W.C.I.*, V (1942), pp. 201ff.

published a year or two after their end. Significantly written in the vernacular, it was entitled *A History of the Long and Most Important Italian Wars which took place in our day between the Tyrant of Lombardy and the Magnificent Commune of Florence*. The theme was further developed in Bruni's large-scale *Historiae Florentini Populi* (begun in 1415), and was brought to a dramatic climax in his *Laudatio Johannis Strozzae Equitis Florentini*, a funeral oration modelled on that of Pericles. The death of Strozzi in battle, in 1427, moved Bruni to set down once again his political-historical analysis of Florentine *virtus*.[1]

In all of these writings, in the polemical pamphlets of Rinuccini and Salutati, and in the historiography of Bruni and Dati (which was to reach maturity in the historical writings of Machiavelli, Guicciardini and Gianotti in the sixteenth century), is to be found the basis of that type of humanism which saw as its model the scholar and publicist, Cicero.[2] With Cicero, Bruni well recognized that 'the life of retirement is easier and safer and at the same time less burdensome or troublesome to others (nevertheless) the career of those who apply themselves to statecraft and conducting great enterprises is more profitable to mankind and contributes more to their own greatness and renown'. None more than Cicero had realized the importance of letters and philosophy, yet 'to be drawn by study away from the active life is contrary to moral duty. For the whole glory of virtue is in activity.'[3]

Nor was the study and writing of history to be regarded merely as a scholarly exercise. Just as Cicero had stressed that history 'bears witness to the passing of the ages and sheds light upon reality, gives life to recollection and guidance to human existence', so Bruni recognized history as an aid to virtue, 'for the careful study of the past enlarges our foresight in contemporary affairs and affords to citizens and to monarchs lessons of incitement and warning in the ordering of public policy. From history also we draw our store of examples of moral precepts.'[4]

[1] Bruni, *Laudatio*, cited by Baron, *Crisis*, I, 50.
[2] Cf. B. R. Reynolds, 'Latin Historiography: a Survey 1400–1600', *Studies in the Renaissance*, II (1955), pp. 7–66 and E. Voeglin, 'Machiavelli's Prince: Background and Formation', *Review of Politics*, XII (1951), pp. 142–68.
[3] *De Officiis*, I, xxi and vi.
[4] *De Oratore*, II, ix; *De Studiis et Litteris* (English version in W. H. Woodward, *Vittorino da Feltre and Other Humanist Educators* (Cambridge, 1921), p. 128).

In a similar way the whole range of man's education would be a preparation for some part of public life. For the Middle Ages action and scholarship were incompatible, save for the very few. For Bruni, letters were an essential adjunct to life in the community. Education would be based on a study 'of the most approved poets, historians and orators of the past', amongst whom 'none have a more urgent claim than the subjects and authors which treat of religion and our duties in the world'.[1] Bruni's own contribution in providing texts for such a study included, besides his original works, his translations of Aristotle's *Ethics* and *Politics*, as well as the translations of Plato's dialogues which paved the way for the work of Ficino later in the century.[2]

In providing Cosimo Medici with an annotated translation of the pseudo—Aristotelian *Economics*, Bruni was contributing to a further aspect of *Quattrocento* humanism which showed his radically different position from that of Petrarch and Boccaccio. In stressing the active life Bruni and his followers were concerned not only with the life associated with the holding of public office, nor indeed only with the commercial life of Florence. Of wider and more general importance was their concern to stress the virtue of the active family life so much despised by their predecessors. A wife and family were no longer considered burdensome and likely to prove an impediment to the true philosophic life. Thus in his biographies of Dante and Petrarch it was the former whom Bruni applauded, as the divine poet who had also married, had children, held public office and even fought in the citizen-army at the battle of Campaldino.

In a similar way the justification of commerce and the accumulation of wealth as activities worthy of the virtuous citizen had for long been a matter or concern, both to the merchant and to the Church. Whilst poverty had been an indispensable part of monastic life, the Church had always recognized the need for money, not only for the sustaining of existence and the well-being of the family, but also for private alms-giving and the paying of taxes for the common good. Commercial life, too, was recognized as having virtues such as truthfulness, trust and

---

[1] Ibid., p. 133.
[2] For Bruni's translations cf. R. R. Bolgar, *The Classical Heritage and Its Beneficiaries* (Cambridge, 1954), p. 434.

justice. But with the increasing power of the commercial community, the traditional attitude of the canonists to usury and the just price had gradually been eroded, and significantly it was St. Antonino (1380–1459), Archbishop of Florence, who devoted four volumes of his *Summa Moralis* to a rationalization of this process.[1]

> If the object of the trader is principally cupidity, which is at the root of all evils, then certainly trade itself is evil. But that trade (as natural and necessary for the needs of human life), is, according to Aristotle, in itself praiseworthy which serves some good purpose, i.e. supplying the needs of life. If, therefore, the trader seeks a moderate profit for the purpose of providing for himself and family according to the becoming fortunes of their state of life, or to enable him to aid the poor more generously, or even goes into commerce for the sake of the common good (lest for example the state should be without what its life requires) and consequently seeks a profit not as an ultimate end but merely as a wage of labour, he cannot in that case be condemned.[2]

Antonino goes on to make the distinction between *valor naturalis* and *valor usualis* (value in relation to society), and justifies the taking of a percentage on bills of exchange because of their great convenience for travellers and pilgrims.

Family life and trade, then, were now respectable. Worldly success, worldly wisdom and worldly virtue now replaced the life of renunciation and mortification. Nowhere is this seen more clearly than in the picture of the Florentine merchant class which Leon Battista Alberti (1404–72) drew in his *Della Famiglia* (1434).[3] Here are to be found the fruits of Bruni's championing of the personal and social ideals of civic humanism. The four

[1] Cf. T. P. McLaughlin, 'The Teachings of the Canonists on Usury', *Medieval Studies*, II (1940), pp. 1–22, R. de Roover, 'The Concept of the Just Price: Theory and Economic Policy', *Journal of Economic History*, XVIII (1958), pp. 418–34, and J. W. Baldwin, 'The Medieval Merchant Before the Bar of the Canon Law', *Papers of the Michigan Academy*, LXIV (1959), pp. 287–99.

[2] Cited by B. Jarrett, *St. Antonino and Medieval Economics* (St. Louis, 1914), p 25. Cf. J. T. Noonan, *The Scholastic Analysis of Usury* (Harvard, 1957) and B. J. Nelson, 'The Usurer and the Merchant Prince: Italian Business Men and the Ecclesiastical Law of Restitution, 1100–1550', *The Tasks of Economic History*, Annual Supplement of *The Journal of Economic History*, VII (1947), pp. 104–22.

[3] For Alberti cf. P. H. Michel, *La Pensée de L. B. Alberti: Un Idéal Humain au XV<sup>e</sup> Siecle* (Paris, 1930); W. H. Woodward, *Studies in Education During the Age of the Renaissance* (Cambridge, 1924), Chap. iii; and C. Grayson, 'The Humanism of Alberti', *Italian Studies*, XII (1957), pp. 37–56.

books of the treatise cover the education of the young, not in a pedagogical institution but within the family and the wider community of which it is part. Thus, in what is essentially an educational treatise, we find, too, discussions of the duties of a married life, of the virtues of friendship, trust and diligence, of the obligations of the old to the young and of the young to the old. The work becomes, indeed, a detailed justification of the Florentine merchant's ethic.

Throughout, Alberti insists on the duty of the parent to provide for the education of his children, an obligation of prior importance to those of his business life. For the family reflects the pattern of the State, and in it are to be found the future members of the commune and the future heads of families. The rôle of the tutor is of vital importance. When the time comes for him to share in the education of the child he should take his place as a member of the family community, and under him every side of the child's personality will receive attention. As for the medium of instruction, both the vernacular and Latin have their part to play.[1] In the same way conversation, with his own age-group, with his tutors and with his elders, is as of much importance to the pupil as his study of books. Arithmetic, geography, meteorology are to share time with the classics in preparation for the commercial life. Music and the fine arts, too, will make their contribution to the production of an informed, well-rounded personality, who in thought and conduct might contribute to the social welfare of his family and his city. Busy-ness above all is to be encouraged. If idleness is the enemy of virtue then work takes on an ethical value alongside its aesthetic and social worth. For Alberti the poverty of Diogenes was mere affectation, the result of arrogance and vain pride. 'Riches in men's lives are like the sport of javelin-throwing; it is not the holding of the javelin in the hand but the throwing of it with skill which results in victory. In the same way it is not the possession but the use of riches which leads us to happiness.' The idea of involvement is here plain to see, and Alberti's whole life is a commentary on this. Indeed, so important does he consider the need to acquaint children with the world around them that he prefers them to be brought up in the town rather

<hr />

[1] For Alberti's contribution to the *Volgare* debate see R. Hall, *The Italian Questione della Lingua* (Chapel Hill, 1942).

than in the country, for in the former they would quickly become acquainted with vice as well as virtue. 'He who does not know the sound of the bagpipes is unable to judge whether the instrument is good or bad.'[1] The same ideals are applied in his works on the fine arts, *Della Pittura* (1435-6) and *De Re Aedificatoria* (c. 1450). The artist too, if he is to deserve the social status claimed for him by Alberti, must contribute through his art to the social life of the community: 'I will call an architect one who . . . may serve successfully and with dignity the needs of man.'[2] Just as the artist must avoid segregating himself from society so, too, his work must be appropriate not only for the private collection but also for the public place.[3] His plan for the building of an entire town reveals an architecture firmly based on his social and ethical ideals.

Almost coincident with the *Della Famiglia* was the appearance of Matteo Palmieri's *Della Vita Civile*, a dialogue whose aim was to discover 'in what consist the virtues to be desired in the perfect citizen'.[4] Here again, the ideal is to be found in a combination of the scholar and the man of affairs. Palmieri himself was born of a well-to-do merchant family, which had long concerned itself with politics. Having a thorough grounding in Latin as a boy, he first held public office at the age of twenty-six, married the following year and represented Cosimo de Medici on diplomatic missions to the courts of Naples and Rome. As in Alberti's treatise the four books of the *Della Vita Civile* deal with intellectual and physical education up to manhood, as well as discussing the moral bases of civic life. Prudence, courage, temperance and justice are singled out as the virtues to be aimed at, virtues not to be attained by means of a life of

---

[1] *Della Famiglia*, cited by Michel, op. cit., pp. 322, 316–17.

[2] Cited by A. Blunt, *Artistic Theory in Italy, 1450–1600* (Oxford, 1940), p. 10; cf. R. Wittkower, 'Renaissance Artistic Individualism', *J.H.I.*, XXII (1961), pp. 291–302.

[3] J. R. Spencer, *L. B. Alberti: On Painting* (1956), pp. 27–28; for similar ideas in an earlier period cf. H. Wieruszowski, 'Art and the Commune in the Time of Dante', *Speculum*, XIX (1944), pp. 14–33.

[4] Cf. Woodward, *Studies . . .*, Chap. iv. The importance of an education for civic responsibility is also emphasized in Maffeo Vegio, *De Educatione Liberorum* (1444); cf. the two-volume edition of the text by M. W. Fanning and A. S. Sullivan (Washington, D.C., 1933 and 1936), and V. J. Horkan, *The Educational Theories and Principles of Maffeo Vegio* (Washington, D.C., 1953).

lonely ease removed from all public activity. Only by discharging his duties in the spheres of family, business and politics can man fully realize himself. For both Alberti and Palmieri, but particularly for the latter, Cicero's *De Officiis* and Quintilian's *Institutio Oratoria* were the models to be applied to the present needs of Florentine citizens.

The ideals elaborated in Bruni, Alberti and Palmieri were translated into pedagogics in the work of Pier Paolo Vergerio, Vittorino da Feltre and Guarino Veronese. Bruni himself produced a minor educational treatise in his *De Studiis et Litteris*, addressed to Baptista di Montefeltro, younger daughter of Antonio, Count of Urbino, but the earliest and certainly the most influential of such writings was Vergerio's *De Ingenius Moribus* (*c.* 1404).[1] It was left to Vittorino and Guarino to put these ideas into practice.

In the literature of the first half of the fifteenth century, whether in the humanists' own writings or in the descriptions by pupils of their masters work, we can see worked out the pedagogical implications of the various aspects of civic humanism with which we have been concerned. The aim is plain, and common to them all: the production of a man well-versed in letters, aware of his duties to his fellow-men and equipped to carry these out. Knowledge rather than speculation is at the root of an education for the virtuous life, and hence an emphasis on ethics replaces the medieval preoccupation with metaphysics and natural philosophy. The practical wisdom of a Cicero is preferred to the theoretical wisdom of the self-contained scholar.

Antiquity, then, provided the aim of education. It provided, too, its content and three texts in particular were immediately important in this context. The first was Guarino's translation (1411) of Plutarch's treatise *On the Education of Children*. The other two were the *Institutio Oratoria* of Quintilian, rediscovered by Poggio at St. Gall in 1416, and the *De Oratore* of Cicero, a complete text of which had been discovered in the Cathedral of Lodi in 1422.[2] They provided the humanists with a statement of

---

[1] For Bruni c.f. W. H. Woodward, *Vittorino da Feltre and Other Humanist Educators* (Cambridge, 1897), pp. 123–33; for Vergerio, ibid., pp. 96–118.

[2] Cf. C. W. Super, *Plutarch on Education* (Syracuse, 1910) and K. M. Westaway, *The Educational Theory of Plutarch* (1922); Cicero, *De Oratore* (ed. and trans. E. W. Sutton and H. Rackham, Loeb Classical Library, two vols., 1942); Quintilian, *Institutio Oratoria* (ed. and trans. H. E. Butler, Loeb Classical Library,

the aims and programme of their educational labours, which are best summed up by Vergerio in his discussion of 'the liberal studies':

among these I accord first place to History, on the grounds both of its attractiveness and of its utility, qualities that appeal equally to the scholar and to the statesman. Next in importance ranks moral philosophy, which indeed is in a peculiar sense 'a liberal art', in that its purpose is to teach men the secret of true freedom. History then gives us the concrete examples of the precepts inculcated by philosophy. The one shows men what to do, the other what men have said and done in the past, and what practical lessons one may draw therefrom for the present day. I would indicate as the third main branch of study, Eloquence. By philosophy we learn the essential truth of things, which by eloquence we so exhibit in orderly adornment as to bring conviction to differing minds. And History provides the light of experience, a cumulative wisdom fit to supplement the force of reason and persuasion of eloquence. For we allow that soundness of judgement, wisdom of speech, integrity of conduct are the marks of a truly liberal temper.[1]

If the aims and content of the new education were an exemplification of civic humanism, so too was its method. The rôle of the teacher and his attitude to his pupils both reflect the new status claimed for mankind. For teacher and pupil alike was claimed a dignity hitherto denied them. No longer must teachers be of the kind described by Petrarch, 'who like disorder, noise, squalor; who rejoice in the screams of the victim as the rod falls gaily, who are not happy unless they can terrify, flog and torture. How, then, can teaching—be it of grammar or of any of the liberal arts—be a fit occupation for honourable age?'[2] A humanist himself, the teacher must carefully observe his pupils' capabilities and rationally arrange a classroom procedure appropriate to these, recognizing with Vergerio that 'children of modest powers demand even more attention, that their natural

[1] *De Ingenius Moribus*, in Woodward, *Vittorino . . .*, pp. 106–7.
[2] *Epistolae Familiares*, XII, iii, cited by Woodward, *Vittorino . . .*, p. 64.

four vols., 1920–22). Until Poggio's discovery nine out of ten medieval writers who quoted Quintilian did so from *Florilegia;* cf. P. Boskoff, 'Quintilian in the Later Middle Ages', *Speculum*, XXVII (1952), pp. 71–78. Poggio tells of his discovery in a letter to Guarino (16 December 1416), translated by M. E. Cosenza, *Petrarch's Letters to Classical Authors* (Chicago, 1910), pp, 91–95.

defects be supplied by art'.[1] Vittorino's *Casa Giocosa* was the model, where corporal punishment was only rarely resorted to, and there the teacher aimed at leading the pupil to self-discipline, by recognizing and acknowledging that the pupil was capable of it.

Here is to be found that Renaissance estimate of mankind which is at once a claim and an endorsement. It had shown itself in the specific field of the new historiography, in which tentatively appeared the notion, heretical in Petrarch's day, that the moderns were the equals of the ancients. It was reflected, too, in the humanists' insistence in their educational schemes on the importance of a study of history. That consciousness of personal distinction which characterized the men of the Renaissance (apparent, too, in their concern for bodily health and their recognition that the body was something more than a machine serving the mind) was based on an awareness of the greatness of their past, of the need to cherish and maintain the glory of their *patria* and to ensure that they were personally deserving of that *laus posteritatis* which they believed would be theirs. The good humanist's reward was fame as well as life hereafter. It was Petrarch's thirst after *fama* and his awareness that this conflicted with medieval ideals of stoicism which had promoted the outpourings of the *Secretum*. By the fifteenth century such doubts had been put aside and a dignity claimed for mankind such as had been denied by the medieval Church. Bruni, as we have seen, claimed it for the citizen. Alberti did the same for the artist, as did Vittorino for the teacher and his pupil.

In the second half of the century the claim was raised to the status of a general theory in the work of the neo-Platonists of the Florentine Academy, who worked out a philosophical gospel of the dignity of man which acted as an ideological super-structure to the earlier attempts of Bruni, Alberti and Vittorino. The theme *de dignitate et excellentia hominis* was complex and was dealt with now at one level, now at another. One was concerned with man's earthly status relative to his fellow-men, and served as a starting point for the other more speculative discussion about his place relative to the entire universe.[2]

[1] Ibid., p. 102.
[2] Cf. P. O. Kristeller, *The Philosophy of Marsilio Ficino* (New York, 1943), esp. pp. 407ff, and the review article by E. Cassirer in *J.H.I.*, VI (1945), pp.

Typical of the first was the *De Dignitate et Excellentia Hominis* of Gianotto Manetti (1396–1459) in which he passes in review the achievement of his age. Previously unknown lands, he says, have become accessible as a result of new navigational methods. Giotto's paintings compared favourably with the most famous works of ancient art. Brunelleschi's dome in Florence rivalled the Pyramids. Indeed, as Alberti had said, the dome revealed skills which 'may not have been understood or at all known by the ancients'. Bernard of Chartres's notion of modern man standing on the shoulders of the giants of Antiquity, which had remained the accepted metaphor since the early twelfth century, was now being replaced by a more critical and challenging attitude, which claimed at least parity for modern man.[1] A second strand in the discussion concerned the origin of this excellence, a query most clearly seen in the treatises *De Nobilitate* of Buonaccorso (?1391–1429), of Poggio Bracciolini (1380–1459) and of Bartholomeo Facio (1400–57). Bruni had led the way in his *Laudatio* (1403–4) in which he claimed:

equal liberty exists for all . . .; the hope of winning public honours and ascending is the same for all, provided they possess industry and natural gifts and lead a serious-minded and respected way of life; for our commonwealth requires *virtus* and *probitas* of its citizens. Whoever has these qualifications is thought to be of sufficiently noble birth to participate in the government of the republic.

Buonaccorso's treatise (for long significantly attributed to Bruni) puts the discussion in a social setting by depicting a patrician and a plebeian of ancient Rome each claiming the hand of a nobleman's daughter. The superiority of the plebeian is based on the fact that he had risen by his own effort, 'for such is the mind of mortals; resting on itself, free, and made for nobility and ignobility. In this most excellent task of humanity nobody

[1] E.g. in Alberti's dedication of his *Della Pittura* to Brunelleschi. For a wider discussion of the relationship between antiquity and the humanist cf. W. von Leyden, 'Antiquity and Authority: a Paradox in the Renaissance Theory of History', *J.H.I.*, XIX (1958), pp. 473–92.

483–501; P. O. Kristeller, 'Ficino and Pomponazzi on the Place of Man in the Universe', ibid., V (1944), pp. 220–6; E. Cassirer 'Giovanni Pico della Mirandola: a Study in the History of Renaissance Ideas', ibid., III (1942), pp. 123–44 and 319–46; P. O. Kristeller, 'Ficino and Renaissance Platonism', *The Personalist*, XXXVI (1955), pp. 238–49; and Herschel Baker, *The Dignity of Man* (Cambridge, Mass., 1947).

can accuse Nature that she had not been generous. . . . Whoever has not attained distinction should blame himself; unjustly
he complains about bad fortune.'[1]

That the adjective noble now usually denotes ethical respectability as well as high birth may well be due in the first instance
to these debates of the fifteenth century. They doubtless reflected
in some degree the humanist's felt need to justify his own position in society and to this extent the treatises are partly autobiographical, as, for example, the dialogue between Lorenzo
de Medici and Niccolo Niccoli in Poggio's *De Nobilitate* (1440).
But these early treatises also prepared the way for those of
Ficino and Pico and other members of the Florentine Academy,
especially in those aspects of their work which attempted to place
man in his cosmological setting. In his *Theologia Platonica*
(1469–74) Ficino emphasizes, like Manetti, man's skill in the
arts and places him at the centre of the universe. But the profound unrest which he sees as characteristic of man and as the
energy of his experience, can lead to the direct perception of
God in the case of very few men, and then for a brief moment
only. Pico's *Oration on the Dignity of Man* (1486) goes farther
than this and adds to mans universality a freedom to determine
his own nature.[2] This ability, innate in all men, provides him
with a challenge which can make or break him. Responding to
the challenge he can build up his own universe, the universe of
human culture. In this is to be found man's dignity and greatness. Instead of postulating an immortality of the soul, as
Ficino had done to allow everyone a perception of God, Pico
gives man his liberty for use here on earth. Man's distinction
lies in the fact that his life is determined not by nature but by
his own free choice.

> Neither a fixed abode nor a form that is thine alone nor any
> function peculiar to thyself have we given thee, Adam, to the end
> that according to thy longing and according to thy judgement thou
> mayest have and possess what abode, what form, and what functions
> thou thyself shalt desire. The nature of all other beings is limited
> and constrained within the bounds of laws prescribed by us. Thou,

[1] Baron, *Crisis* . . ., I, 365–6, II, 623, n. 22; for a fifteenth-century English
translation of Buonaccorso see *infra*, pp. 49 and 77.

[2] For a discussion of the relative position of Manetti and Pico cf. A. Auer,
'G. Manetti und Pico della Mirandola, *De Hominis Dignitate*', in *Vitae et Veritati,
Festgabe für Karl Adam* (Düsseldorf, 1956), pp. 83–102.

constrained by no limits, in accordance with thine own free will, in whose hand we have placed thee, shalt ordain for thyself the limits of thy nature. We have set thee at the world's centre that thou mayest from thence more easily observe whatever is in the world. We have made thee neither of heaven nor of earth, neither mortal nor immortal, so that with freedom of choice and with honour, as though the maker and moulder of thyself, thou mayest fashion thyself in whatever shape thou shalt prefer. Thou shalt have the power to degenerate into the lower forms of life, which are brutish. Thou shalt have the power, out of thy soul's judgment, to be reborn into the highest forms, which are divine. . . . Let a certain holy ambition invade our souls, so that not content with the mediocre, we shall pant after the highest and (since we may if we wish) toil with all our strength to obtain it.[1]

It is true, of course, that for the neo-Platonists the highest flights of intuition were to be achieved only in a life of contemplation. Similarly, their efforts to reconcile humanism and religion led them to a mysticism which rejected the more practical morality of their predecessors and relied on a more intimate, inner religious experience. In the same way their view of love, which equated it with the contemplation of divine beauty, was far removed from that of Alberti, who thought of it in terms of the emotional basis of family life. But if they differed in their ideas as to the method by which the good life might be achieved, they nevertheless embraced and took farther the current views about the dignity and worth of the human personality. They discussed and made claims for man's dignity, and in so doing raised problems concerning the origins of and man's capacity for excellence which had profound educational implications. For the optimism of their belief that the universe was essentially moral and essentially rational led to the conclusion that man's well-being lay in the development, through education, of his innate moral and rational faculties. 'I study much that I may be an educated man, but more that I may be good and free. The one makes one feel right, and the other makes one live rightly.'[2]

[1] English translation by E. L. Forbes in E. Cassirer, ed., *The Renaissance Philosophy of Man* (Chicago, 1948), pp. 224–5, 227.

[2] Vergerio, *Epistolae*, CVI, cited by J. H. Whitfield, *Petrarch and the Renaissance* (Oxford, 1943), p. 107. Cf. E. F. Rice, jun., *The Renaissance Idea of Wisdom* (Cambridge, Mass., 1958), and M. L. Colish, 'The Mime of God: Vives on the Nature of Man', *J.H.I.*, XXIII (1962), pp. 3–20.

The dangers of periodizing history and of ignoring the carry-over of medieval ideas alongside and within humanistic thought have already been mentioned. Yet with these in mind, it would still be true to say that fifteenth-century Italy saw the flowering of a humanism in which wisdom and civic virtue were united. It saw the Petrarcan compound of classical stoicism and medieval asceticism replaced by the concept of an educated citizen who consummates his *humanitas* in a life of social duty. Bruni's scholar was neither solitary nor passionless, but drew sustenance from the emotions of family life, civic business and patriotic feeling. The shift of emphasis from the learning of the professional disciplines to the joint study of literary form and the good life had taken place consciously, if at first haltingly, and had produced a concept of wisdom independent of a supernatural grace and therefore susceptible of education.

In studying classical literature the humanists worked out a method of historical and philological criticism which greatly contributed to the development of those disciplines. But their enthusiasm for the scholarly study of their texts, their philological and editorial labours, and their own original works in Latin reflected an attitude of mind which went far beyond the mere form and style of their texts. The humanists' love of classical literature went far deeper than their admiration of its stylistic felicities. It rested ultimately on the fact that in it they could find a pattern of life, which also was worthy of imitation. The Italian humanists thus produced a mental climate which in its turn influenced the political, social and educational ideals of Tudor England, to which we must now turn.

# III

<>--<>--<>--<>--<>--<>--<>--<>--<>--<>--<>--<>--<>--<>--<>--<>--<>

# The Renaissance Debate in England

<>--<>--<>--<>--<>--<>--<>--<>--<>--<>--<>--<>--<>--<>--<>--<>--<>

## I

THE golden age of English humanism has rightly been placed
in the era of Seebohm's *Oxford Reformers*[1] when scholars such as
Linacre, Grocyn, Colet, and above all Erasmus and More were
actively working to spread classical studies and more especially
to foster the study of Greek. With the exception of More, each
had studied in Italy and together they worked towards that
lettered piety which characterized the northern renaissance. Yet
it would be wrong to assume that English humanism sprang
new-born in the 1490's, conceived during sojourns in Italy and
nourished in the royally-patronized universities of the early
sixteenth century. In the first place Englishmen's contacts with
Italy and its culture were much older than this, and secondly the
strength of the humanist movement of the late fifteenth and
early sixteenth centuries had its origins in a long, virtually
continuous and certainly fruitful connexion between the two
countries. These early contacts were an indispensable preamble
to later developments.

English students had long made the journey to Italy, especially to study Canon and Civil Law. They were to be found at
Bologna as early as the second half of the twelfth century and
thereafter Englishmen appear regularly both as lecturers and

---

[1] F. Seebohm, *The Oxford Reformers* (3rd edition, 1913).

students in the registers of most Italian universities.[1] Italian influences in the field of Canon Law were strong enough for example to find their way into the legal writings of John of Salisbury and Gerald of Wales, and especially into those of Glanvil and Bracton. The great Italian writers of the *Trecento* also had their influences on Englishmen. Chaucer visited Italy twice in the 1370's and there is ample evidence in his writings to suggest that he was well acquainted with the works of Dante, Petrarch and Boccaccio. The growing attention to style to be noticed in the work of the letter writers of the Papal Curia is reflected, too, in the *Liber Epistolaris* of Richard of Bury, a collection of about 1,500 letters chosen not merely as examples of different kinds of letter, which was the usual criterion for the formularies of the period, but also for the virtues of their style. In this collection he leaned heavily on the Italian collections of Pierre de la Vigne and Thomas of Capua, and like Chaucer he met Petrarch when he visited Avignon in 1333.[2]

By the fifteenth century contact with Italy was becoming frequent and regular, with movement in both directions, the Papal Curia dispatching its representatives and Englishmen making the journey either as church officials or as students. By this time, too, as we have seen, Italian humanism was emancipating itself from its medieval surroundings. The typically medieval encyclopaedic view of knowledge, and its idea of history as a series of unconnected moralizing anecdotes had been replaced by a new historiography, a new effort to get inside the classical outlook, and in the philological field to move away from a literal rendering to one which caught the spirit of the text.[3]

At first English attempts to understand such a movement were sporadic and often unsuccessful, but the attempt was made. Italians of the merchant class, such as the representatives of the Bardi and Peruzzi, had been frequent visitors to England during the fourteenth century and had often undertaken tasks of a fiscal

[1] G. B. Parks, *The English Traveller to Italy* (Rome, 1954) I, 521ff.

[2] Cf. M. Praz, 'Chaucer and the Great Italian Writers of the Trecento', *The Monthly Review*, VI (1927), pp. 18–39 and 131–57, and R. A. Pratt, 'Chaucer and the Visconti Libraries', *E.L.H.*, VI (1939), pp. 191–9.

[3] Parks, op. cit., and E. F. Jacobs, 'To and From the Court of Rome in the Early Fifteenth Century', *Studies in French Language and Literature presented to Professor Mildred K. Pope* (Manchester, 1939), pp. 161–81.

nature for the Papal Curia.[1] In the fifteenth century, however, a regular flow of men trained in the humanistic atmosphere of the Curia began to make its influence felt in England. Poggio's visit to England in 1417–20 is a case in point.[2] His search for manuscripts was singularly unsuccessful and after his visit to Oxford he claimed that English scholars delighted more in scholastic disputation than in the new learning. On the other hand his very presence was of importance to men like Nicholas Bildestone, Chancellor to Henry Beaufort, Bishop of Winchester and Richard Petworth, Beaufort's secretary. Humphrey of Gloucester possessed some of his works, which were also later to find their way into the libraries of William Grey, Richard Bole, John Free and Henry Cranebrook, whilst at the end of the century a printed edition of his *Facetiae* was produced at Oxford.[3]

Of more immediate influence were the various papal collectors who visited England in this period, men such as Simon de Taramo, Vincent Clement and Zano Castiglione, who like Poggio and Bruni and other humanists had been trained in the Papal Chancery. Of greater importance, however, was Piero del Monte who was in England from 1435 to 1440. A pupil of Guarino, it was he who provided John Whethamstede with a copy of Bruni's Latin version of Plutarch's *Lives*, and a considerable correspondence between the two men ensued. He attracted the attention of Humphrey, Duke of Gloucester, whom he kept informed about the latest literary trends in Italy, and was also closely in touch with other English scholars such as Andrew Holes, Thomas Bekynton and Adam de Moleyns.

It was in the life and work of men such as these that the rather insubstantial origins of English humanism are to be found. Whethamstede, though in close contact with del Monte and other humanists, was interested in humanist writings more as sources of information than as models either of style and form or of a way of life to be emulated. For him they were treasure trove for his florilegial compilations and other aids to elegant allusion—his *Granarium*, *Pabularium* and *Palearium*. Though

[1] Cf. G. A. Holmes, 'Florentine Merchants in England, 1346–1436', *Ec.H.R.*, 2nd Series, XIII (1960), pp. 193–208.

[2] Cf. R. Weiss, *Humanism in England During the Fifteenth Century* (2nd edition, Oxford, 1957), pp. 18ff.

[3] S. Gibson, *Early Oxford Bindings* (Oxford, 1903), pp. 21 and 26.

these contained extracts from Xenophon, Plutarch, Quintilian, Salutati, Bruni and others, they contributed little to humanism as an idea. Yet Whethamstede was striving towards a Ciceronian style and his compilations at least made available, in however limited a sense, humanistic writings which would whet the appetites of Holes and his contemporaries, and send them off to Italy in search of the originals.[1]

But before we follow these men to Italy mention should be made of the contribution of Humphrey, Duke of Gloucester.[2] Son of Henry IV, brother to Henry V and John, Duke of Bedford, Humphrey, more than any one Englishman in the first half of the fifteenth century, furthered the cause of humanism in England. His reputation as a bibliophile was well deserved, and by importing books from Italy, chiefly through the agency of Zano Castiglione, Pier Candido Decembrio and the Florentine bookseller Vespasiano da Bisticci, he was able to build up a library which served as the foundation of humanist studies for the rest of the century. In 1439 he donated to Oxford 129 volumes and in 1444 a further 134 volumes.[3] Not all were works of the new school, of course, but the difference between the second and first collections indicated his development as humanist. The majority of the first donation were medieval texts, but included nevertheless works by Petrarch, two of Bruni's versions of Aristotle and seventeen pagan Latin authors. In the second gift, besides over twenty volumes of Latin authors, there were twenty-five humanist works, including seven of Petrarch and eight humanist versions of Plutarch and Plato. The high incidence of non-humanist works in his library should not detract from his status as humanist. Even the library of Pico had a majority of such books, and Humphrey's was a library which any Italian prince would have been glad to own.[4]

Book-collecting was only part of Humphrey's scholarship, however. He made a further important contribution to human-

[1] Cf. E. F. Jacob, *Essays in the Conciliar Epoch* (2nd edition, Manchester, 1952), pp. 183–6.

[2] Cf. K. H. Vickers, *Humphrey, Duke of Gloucester* (1907) and Weiss, op. cit., Chaps. iii and iv.

[3] The books are listed in H. Anstey, ed., *Munimenta Academica*, Rolls Series (1868), II. 758–72, and arranged alphabetically by H.H.E.C(raster), *B.Q.R.*, I (1915), pp. 131–5.

[4] Cf. Pearl Kibré, *The Library of Pico della Mirandola* (New York, 1936).

ist studies by commissioning new translations from Italian scholars. In 1433, for example, he wrote to Bruni inviting him to England and asking him to prepare a version of Artistotle's *Politics*. The invitation was declined but the *Politics* arrived in 1438, and copies of each work were quickly made for English scholars. Bruni's *Ethics* rapidly replaced the existing medieval versions, and was finally printed in Oxford at the end of the century. As a result of Humphrey's efforts Bruni was probably the best-known Italian humanist in England. A second Italian whose work he patronized was Pier Candido Decembrio, whom he commissioned to produce a version of Plato's *Republic*, and who sent him many texts from Italy, including Cicero's *Epistolae Familiares* and Quintilian's *Institutiones Oratoriae*, as well as Bruni's *Isagogicon* and Latin version of *Phaedrus*. In his household, too, Gloucester patronized Italians, by employing them as secretaries. Instead of Bruni in 1433 came Tito Livio Frulovisi, a native of Ferrara, but brought up in Venice, where he was a pupil of both Chrysoloras and Guarino. His *Vita Henrici Quinti* (*c.* 1437–8), the first 'official life' of an English king, reflected the work of Bruni and Dati and anticipated Polydore Vergil in its combination of national feeling with foreign culture, and was undoubtedly a pattern for sixteenth-century historians.[1] Frulovisi was succeeded by Antonio Beccari who served Gloucester from 1438 to 1445. A pupil of Vittorino he copied many texts for his patron in a fine humanistic hand, as well as maintaining his contacts with his fellow Italians.

As importer of books, commissioner of new translations, employer of Italian secretaries, and the patron of English students, Humphrey's contribution to the early period of English humanism was without equal, and in his day the flow of students to Italy gathered momentum.[2] They probably followed the route taken by Whethamstede, though without sharing his 'flesh quaking at the prospect of drinking the cup of that journey

[1] Details of his life and writings are given in C. W. Previté-Orton, ed., *Opera Hactenus Inedita T. Livii de Frulovisiis de Ferrara* (Cambridge, 1932), pp. ixff. An Italian translation of the *Vita* was made by Decembrio; cf. J. H. Wylie, 'Decembrio's Version of Vita Henrici Quinti by Tito Livio', *E.H.R.*, XXIV (1909), pp. 84–89.

[2] On English students in Italy see R. J. Mitchell in *T.R.H.S.*, 4th Series, XIX (1936), pp. 101–16, *E.H.R.*, LI (1936), pp. 270–8, and *Italian Studies*, VIII (1952), pp. 62–81, together with V. J. Flynn, 'Englishmen in Rome during the Renaissance', *M.P.*, XXXVI (1938), pp. 121–38.

overseas'. In 1423 Whethamstede went across to Calais, though others had used the Flemish ports. His route than took him through Picardy and Brabant, up the Rhine to Cologne, and on through Mainz, Speyer, Ulm and the Brenner Pass to Trent and the Lombardy plain and its universities.[1]

Much of the coming and going went on within the framework and under the aegis of the Church. During the fifteenth century there was a constant and increasing flow of churchman to and from Italy for one reason or another. On official church business clerics would be sent to the Papal Curia to conduct negotiations for the presentation of livings and benefices, often to seek them for themselves. Legal disputes had to be nursed and the complicated administration of papal taxation attended to. Moreover, there were always clerics in Rome on the king's business with the Papal See. At the same time, it was becoming increasingly recognized that a sound education and a professional training in both Canon and Civil Law were essential for the conduct of such business. More and more young clerics, therefore, sought dispensations to absent themselves from their cures for the purpose of study in Italy, especially for the legal studies which would fit them for lucrative posts as archdeacon or diocesan vicar-general or bishop's chancellor. Thus engaged, they would be charged with the legal business of granting probate of wills, dealing with civil and criminal cases against clerics, settling disputed contracts and marriages, and above all taking part in the heresy trials against Wycliffites. Bologna was still the centre for such studies and over half of those listed by Parks were students there, though Padua was rapidly rising during the latter half of the century and claimed about one quarter of those listed.[2] Both laws were of course studied at Oxford and Cambridge, with the prime purpose of staffing the ranks of ecclesiastical and secular officialdom. Indeed, Trinity Hall, Cambridge, the college of jurists, was founded 'for the increase of divine worship and of canon and civil learning and also for the advantage, rule and direction of the Commonwealth.[3]

[1] E. F. Jacob, 'Englishmen and the General Councils of the Fifteenth Century', in *Essays in the Conciliar Epoch*, p. 44. For details of routes and methods of travel see Parks, op. cit., Chap. xi, and M. J. Barber, 'The Englishman Abroad in the Fifteenth Century', *Medievalia et Humanistica*, XI (1957), pp. 69–71.

[2] Parks, op. cit., pp. 624–8.

[3] *V.C.H. Cambridgeshire*, III (1959), p. 362.

The early decades of the fifteenth century have been described as the Conciliar Epoch, and the great councils of the age must indeed have been important agents in the dissemination of new learning. Typical of the Englishmen attending them was Andrew Holes, who was king's proctor at Rome from 1432 to 1444, and who attended the Council of Ferrara-Florence, one of the greatest meetings of humanists of the period.[1] There Holes would meet or hear Traversari, Poggio, Chrysoloras, Guarino, Bruni, Niccolo Niccoli and Bessarion. In the same way the English ambassadors to the Council of Constance in 1415 would have met Aeneas Sylvius, Poggio and others, and it was at the Council of Basel, 1431, that Adam de Moleyns and John Whethamstede made contact with Zano Castiglione. But these were the great set pieces. Generally it was the routine traffic of church officials and students which enabled Englishmen to be introduced to humanist ideas and scholars, and Holes—the 'Messer Andreas Ols' of Vespasiano's *Memoirs*—was a typical product of the system. Pupil of Winchester, student and fellow of New College, Oxford, his many preferments are good examples of the way in which church revenues were used to subsidize education in the fifteenth century. Whilst he was at the Papal Curia from 1432 to 1444 he was constantly acquiring prebendaries, archdeaconries, and rectories, together with the necessary dispensations to permit his absentee pluralism. A great collector of books and manuscripts, host to members of the Medici circle, including Manetti, Palmieri and Carlo Aretino, he was also instrumental, along with Vincent Clement and Richard Caunton, in securing the Papal Bulls necessary for the founding of Eton College by Thomas Bekynton and Henry VI.

But men such as Holes were forerunners only, attracted by humanism without making a positive contribution of their own. A second stage in the story of humanist relations between England and Italy was reached when English students and English patrons were able to vie with the Italians in their scholarship, their bibliophily and even in their writings. This group may be regarded as providing the bridge between the nascent humanism of Bekynton, Holes and others and the full

[1] J. W. Bennett, 'Andrew Holes, a Neglected Harbinger of the English Renaissance', *Speculum*, XIX (1944), pp. 314–34.

flowering of the movement in the work of the Oxford Reformers. It included, for example, William Grey, Bishop of Ely, who not only studied at Padua and took a degree in theology there (1445), but collected a large humanist library which he later presented to Balliol College, Oxford.[1] He served as royal envoy at the Papal Curia for ten years and made himself responsible for the financing of the studies of John Free, Nicholas Perotti, and probably John Gunthorpe. He even travelled from Padua to Ferrara to attend the lectures of Guarino. Robert Flemmyng, on the other hand, was a scholar in his own right.[2] He spent three periods in Italy, as a student at Padua in 1446–52, and as king's proctor in Rome in 1458–61 and 1473–7, and like Grey heard Guarino at Ferrara. He was the first Englishman to make a serious study of Greek (whilst at Rome he was a close friend of the Papal librarian, Platina) and the library which he donated to Lincoln College, Oxford (founded by his kinsman Richard Fleming, Bishop of Lincoln) contained many Greek manuscripts which he had collected in Italy. It included, too, the now-lost Graeco-Latin dictionary, which Leland says Flemmyng compiled, as well as copies of classical and humanist authors.[3] The importance of the donation lies not simply in its humanist nature but more in that many of the books had been newly-discovered in fifteenth-century Italy and were appearing in England for the first time. Englishmen, then, as patrons, bibliophiles and scholars were beginning to emulate their illustrious predecessor Humphrey, Duke of Gloucester. But in this second period two stand out above all others. These were John Tiptoft and John Free, the first Englishmen to make an original contribution as humanists.[4]

John Tiptoft, Earl of Worcester, even more than Gloucester

[1] Cf. J. B. Mullinger, *The University of Cambridge from the earliest times to the Platonist Movement* (Cambridge, 1873), I, 397, who summarizes the full list in H. O. Coxe, *Catalogum Codicum* (1852), Pt I. Grey was one of the Englishmen whom Vespasiano included in his collection of biographies.

[2] Cf. Weiss, op. cit., *passim*.

[3] A. Hall, ed., *J. Leland, Commentarii de Scriptoribus Britannicis* (Oxford, 1709), p. 461. Weiss throws doubt on this in 'The Private Collector and the Revival of Greek Learning', in F. Wormald and C. E. Wright, eds., *The English Library Before 1700: Studies in its History* (1958), p. 128. Certainly Flemmyng owned such a dictionary.

[4] The standard biographies are R. J. Mitchell, *John Tiptoft, 1427–70* (1938) and *John Free, from Bristol to Rome in the Fifteenth Century* (1955).

was the Englishman who came closest to the Italian prince of the
Renaissance. A student at Padua, and at Ferrara under Guarino,
Tiptoft rivalled Gloucester as a book collector and patron and
outshone him as scholar. His latinity was so impressive that an
oration before Pope Pius II (Aeneas Sylvius) moved that
humanist scholar to tears.[1] Like Gloucester he offered his library
to Oxford, together with a sum of 500 marks. Though nothing
more of his projected gift was heard during his lifetime and
though only ten of his books survive, his library contained, like
Flemmyng's, many books and texts hitherto unknown in
England. Tacitus's *De Oratoribus* and Suetonius's *De Grammaticis*, for example, were brought over to England only seven
years after they had been introduced to Italy by Enoch of Ascoli
in 1455. In the same way Tiptoft's copy of Lucretius's *De
Rerum Natura* was probably the first copy of the works of that
poet to reach these shores after Poggio's discovery in Germany
in 1417. Two of Tiptoft's own translations have survived. The
earlier, a version of Cicero's *De Amicitia*, written before his
stay in Padua and probably begun whilst at Oxford, is not much
better than a scholar's exercise, closely following the original.
The other, the *Declamacion of Noblesse* (*c.* 1460), a translation
of Buonaccorso's *Controversia de Nobilitate* (1428), is highly
significant on two quite different counts. In the first place it is a
truly humanist version, elegantly written and reflecting the
spirit of the original. But more important, perhaps, Tiptoft
chose for his subject a treatise debating the nature and origin of
true nobility, a subject which, as we have seen, greatly enjoyed
the attention of the Italians of Bruni's day, and which, as we shall
see, was to play an important part in the movement of ideas in
Tudor England.[2] With his copies of the Latin classics, versions
of Greek authors and works of the leading contemporary humanists, Tiptoft made available a corpus of texts which, together
with those of Gloucester and Grey, were to prove essential for
the furtherance of humanist studies at the end of the fifteenth
and beginning of the sixteenth century.

[1] The occasion was Tiptoft's transmission of the King's obedience and con-
gratulations on Pius' accession, 1461. The source is the letter-preface of Free's
version of Synesius' *De Laudibus Calvitii* (*In Praise of Baldness*) printed by Weiss
in *B.Q.R.*, VII (1935), pp. 101–3, cf. Mitchell, *Tiptoft*, pp. 74–76, and *Free*,
pp. 145–7.
[2] Cf. *infra*, pp. 75ff.

Tiptoft's young contemporary, John Free, was perhaps the first Englishman to rank as a pure scholar of the humanities and to be recognized as such by the Italians. He spent four years with Guarino at Ferrara under the patronage of Grey, but in 1458 moved to Padua where he met Tiptoft, to whom he dedicated his Latin version of Synesius's *De Laudibus Calvitii* and whom he probably served as secretary and adviser in book-buying matters. Like Holes, and many others before him, he benefited greatly by the holding of benefices *in absentia*, for during his stay in Italy he drew the stipends of clerkships in the dioceses of Bath and Wells, Ely and Lincoln. Free's outstanding scholarship tended to overshadow the work of contemporaries like John Gunthorpe, whose studies in any case tended to be side-tracked by the ecclesiastical and political duties from which Free was discharged. John Lee, Peter Courtenay, John Chilworth, John Doggett all studied and worked in Italy during this period, preserving the continuity of English humanistic studies and bringing back the fruits of their labours to England. Unfortunately their official duties prevented them, too, from undertaking teaching in the humanities which alone would have enabled the potential that had been built up to be adequately realized.[1]

Nevertheless the books brought back by these men provided a starting point. Mention has already been made of the donations of Gloucester and Tiptoft. They were rivalled both in size and in the number of humanist works they contained by the library of William Grey, who donated his books to Balliol College, Oxford. As was to be expected the library of the Bishop of Ely contained a large number of theological works, many of them orthodox medieval treatises. His gift of 1478 however made Balliol's library supreme among the college libraries, a position held until then by Lincoln College, which had been enriched by the donation of Flemmyng in 1465. The catalogues of Lincoln College library made in 1474 of the *electione*, those books kept in circulation among the fellows of the College, show that Flemmyng's gifts included such humanist works as Valla's *Elegantiae Lingua Latinae*, Bruni's *Isagogicon* and his version of Aristotle's *Ethics*, as well as Cicero's *Orationes*, *De Amicitia* and *Epistolae ad Atticae*. In addition we find Boccaccio's *De Casibus*

---

[1] Cf. Weiss, op. cit., p. 179, and R. R. Bolgar, *The Classical Heritage and its Beneficiaries* (Cambridge, 1954), p. 311.

*Virorum Illustrium*, Guarino's version of Plutarch's *Lives*, together with a large group of classical writers including Quintilian, Pliny, Valerius Maximus, Suetonius, Virgil and Aulus Gellius.[1] Again there was the library built up by John Shirwood, Bishop of Durham, who had gone to Rome in 1486, in the company of William Sellyng and his pupil Thomas Linacre. Many of Shirwood's collection and almost all of the humanist works therein were significantly newly-printed books, including Cicero's *De Finibus, Orationes, De Oratore* and *Epistolae*, Aeneas Sylvius's dialogue *De Sonorio*, Alberti's *De Re Aedificatoriae*, Landino's *Disputationes Camaldulenses*, Plutarch's *Lives*, George of Trebizond's *Rhetorica*, together with works by Aulus Gellius, Suetonius, and Martial.[2] It was this collection which became the nucleus of the library with which Bishop Fox, Shirwood's successor at Durham, endowed his College of Corpus Christi at Oxford in 1516–17.

## II

The great age of English humanism, then, had a long tradition of humanist study behind it. What differentiated this period from those which preceded it was the nature of the teaching which was undertaken, and especially the teaching of Greek. Grocyn, Linacre and Latimer[3] traditionally dispute over the honour of being the first to do so. At any rate when Erasmus arrived in England in 1499, he found all three giving public lectures, and he wrote to Robert Fisher:

> I have found here a climate agreeable as it is helpful; and so much culture and learning, not of the commonplace and trivial sort but full, accurate knowledge of ancient Latin and Greek, so that I now have little longing to see Italy for the curiosity of seeing it. When

[1] R. Weiss. 'The Earliest Catalogues of the Library of Lincoln College, Oxford,' *B.Q.R.*, VIII (1935–8), pp. 343–59. For Italian humanist libraries cf. Pearl Kibré, 'Intellectual Interests Reflected in the Libraries of the Fourteenth and Fifteenth Centuries', *J.H.I.*, VII (1946), pp. 257–97, and D. M. Rabathan, 'Libraries of the Italian Renaissance', in J. W. Thompson, ed., *The Medieval Library* (2nd edition, Chicago, 1957). For the spread and influence during the Renaissance of Aulus Gellius's *Noctes Atticae*, cf. H. Baron, 'Aulus Gellius in the Renaissance', *S.P.*, XLVIII (1951), pp. 107–25.

[2] P. S. Allen, 'Bishop Shirwood of Durham and his Library', *E.H.R.*, XXV (1910), pp. 445–56.

[3] I.e. William Latimer, tutor of Cardinal Pole, friend of More, Fisher, Erasmus and Pace, and student with Grocyn and Linacre at Padua under Tomeo Leonico; cf. F. A. Gasquet, *Cardinal Pole and his Early Friends* (1927), Chap. vii.

I hear my Colet I think I am listening to Plato himself; who will not admire an whole world of learning in Grocyn? What mind could be more penetrating than Linacre's or more lofty or more subtle? When did nature ever create a disposition more friendly than More's or more sunny or more genial? . . . It is remarkable how thick springs up everywhere in this country the crop of classical studies.[1]

The 'crop' is less remarkable when one remembers its background and antecedents. Greek studies in England had, of course, achieved a certain renaissance in the thirteenth century with the work of Robert Grosseteste and Roger Bacon. Grosseteste had a number of south Italian Greeks in his household, among them one Nicholas the Greek, who became a canon of Lincoln and remained in England after Grosseteste's death.[2] Bacon was very much aware of the utility of a knowledge of Greek, if only for the all-important task of producing good Latin translations of the theological, philosophical and scientific texts to replace the inadequate translations then current. Greek studies, however, declined in the fourteenth century, despite the injunctions of the Council of Vienne (1312) that Greek lectures should be given at the Papal Curia and in the universities of Paris, Bologna, Oxford and Salamanca. On the other hand, as we have seen, by the middle of the fifteenth century the rapid development of Greek studies, fostered by Bruni and Ficino, was beginning to make itself felt amongst the Englishmen who visited Italy during the period.[3]

The popularity of Bruni's work had been growing steadily since Whethamstede quoted him in his *Granarium*. Duke Humphrey had acquired for his library copies of Bruni's translations of the *Ethics* and the *Politics*, of Plato's *Phaedrus*, Xenophon's *De Tyranno*, several of Plutarch's *Lives* as well as Bruni's own work the *Isagogicon*. Grey, Gunthorpe, Bole,

[1] Allen, No. 118, I, 273–4; Nichols, No. 110, I, 226.
[2] Cf. D. A. Callus, 'Grosseteste the Scholar', in D. A. Callus, ed., *Robert Grosseteste, Scholar and Bishop: Commemorative Essays* (Oxford, 1955), pp. 1–69.
[3] Cf. D. J. Geanokoplos, *Greek Scholars in Venice* (Cambridge, Mass., 1962); R. Weiss, 'The Greek Culture of South Italy in the Later Middle Ages', *P.B.A.*, XXXVII (1951), pp. 23–50, and 'England and the Decree of Vienne on the teaching of Greek, Arabic, Hebrew and Syriac', *Bibliothèque d'Humanisme et Renaissance*, XIV (1952), pp. 1–9; A. G. Little, 'Roger Bacon', *P.B.A.*, XIV (1928), pp. 265–95; and S. A. Hirsch, 'Roger Bacon and Philology', in A. G. Little, ed., *Roger Bacon Essays* (Oxford, 1914), pp. 109ff.

Flemmyng, Shirwood, and William of Worcester all added his works to their libraries. When John Doget came to write his commentary on the *Phaedo*, it was Bruni's version he used, not the traditional twelfth-century version of Aristippus.[1] The culmination of all this interest was the printing of Bruni's *Ethics* in 1479 by Theodorick Rood, the Oxford printer, the second authenticated book from an Oxford press.[2] In addition we begin once again to find Greeks living and working in England. In 1445–6, with the advice of his Council, the king disbursed cash payments to four Greeks. Of the activities in England of three of them, Manual Chrysoloras, Demetrius Palaeologos and John Argyropulos, nothing further is known, though the latter was famed for fifteen years thereafter for his lectures on Aristotle's *Ethics* in Florence, where John Tiptoft heard him. The fourth Emmanuel of Constantinople, however, is of more significance. He remained in England under the patronage of George Neville, Archbishop of York and Lord Chancellor, and later of William Waynflete for whom it is likely he taught Greek at the newly-founded Magdalen College. Eleven of the Greek texts he copied for his patrons are extant and include a Homer, a Plato, an Aristotle and a Demosthenes. Gray suggests that it was in the hope of patronage that these Greeks made the journey to England, and Emmanuel's subsequent career certainly indicates there was good reason for their doing so. Nor was he the only Greek who was able to earn a living in England at this time, for overlapping with Emmanuel from 1484 and still working in England in 1500 was another scribe, Johannes Serbopoulos of Constantinople, of whose texts ten survive. There was obviously a demand for such services in late fifteenth-century England, and it was no coincidence that the Council which advised the king, through the Regent Duke of York, to pay the four Greeks included Waynflete, Grey, Holes and Tiptoft.[3]

[1] Weiss, *Humanism*, pp. 164–7.

[2] For other Renaissance texts among early English printed books see E. G. Duff, *Fifteenth Century English Books* (Oxford, 1917), F. Madan, *Oxford Books*, I (Oxford, 1895), S. Gibson, *Early Oxford Bindings* (Oxford, 1903), and E. F. Jacob, 'The Boke of St. Albans', *B.J.R.L.*, XXXVIII (1944), pp. 99–118.

[3] H. L. Gray, 'Greek Visitors in England 1455–6', in C. H. Taylor, ed., *Anniversary Essays in Medieval History by Students of C. H. Haskins* (Cambridge, Mass., 1929), pp. 81–116. M. R. James, 'Greek MSS. in England Before the Renaissance', *The Library*, VII (1927), pp. 352–3, and Weiss in Wormald and Wright, op. cit., pp. 128–30.

As well as the Greeks there were also Italians working in England during the last decades of the century. One of them, Stephano Surigone, who rivalled Emmanuel of Constantinople as the earliest teacher of the humanities in this country, was probably teaching William Sellying at Oxford in the 1460's. Certainly William Grocyn had tuition in the rudiments of Greek, probably from Emmanuel or Johannes before he went to Italy, and later on after his return he was in residence at Exeter Hall with Cornelio Vitelli who had been brought to Oxford by Thomas Chandler, Warden of New College (1454–75).[1]

Visitors such as these provided at first hand what Grey, Tiptoft, Flemmyng and their contemporaries had provided by report after their Greek studies in Italy. More important, perhaps, they started the tradition of teaching which took root in the early sixteenth century and enabled English classical studies to come of age. And of course they sparked off a fresh wave of visits to Italy. Linacre went over in 1485 on the occasion of Sellyng's third visit. In Florence he studied Greek under Demetrius Chalcondyles and Politian, and spent more than ten years in Italy, continuing his Greek studies in Padua with Tomeo Leonico, the Artistotelian scholar.[2] He met Aldus in Venice and shared in preparing the famous edition of Aristotle with the master printer, who later included Linacre's translation of Proclus's *De Sphaera* in his *Scriptores Astronomici Veteres* (1499). It was while in Padua that his translation of Galen got under way, and he took an M.D. there in 1492.[3] On his return to England he gave More his first grounding in Greek, but spent most of his time practising medicine, becoming the king's physician in 1509 and founding the Royal College of Physicians

[1] M. Burrows, 'Memoir of William Grocyn', O.H.S., *Collectanea*, II, XVI (1890), pp. 339–40 and R. Weiss, 'Cornelio Vitelli in France and England', *J.W.C.I.*, II (1938–9), pp. 219–26.

[2] Sellyng himself had studied Greek at Bologna and had brought home many Greek manuscripts to the library of Christ Church, Canterbury. Cf. Weiss in Wormald and Wright, op. cit., p. 130. Nicholas Leonicus Thomaeus (1456–1531) read Plato and Aristotle in the Greek to his students in Padua for twenty years, after teaching Greek in Venice. He was tutor to many English scholars in Italy and dedicated works to Pace, Tunstall and Pole. Gasquet, op. cit., *passim* and Allen, No. 1479, V, 520 and note to line 180.

[3] P. S. Allen, 'Linacre & Latimer in Italy', *E.H.R.*, XVIII (1903), pp. 514–17; R. J. Mitchell, 'Thomas Linacre in Italy', ibid., L (1935), pp. 696–8; and A. Tilley 'Greek Studies in Early Sixteenth Century England', ibid., LIII (1938), pp. 221–39 and 438–56.

in 1518. Grocyn, 'the patron and praeceptor of us all' as Erasmus called him, followed Linacre to Italy in 1488, after seven years as Divinity Reader at Waynflete's Magdalen College. Like Linacre he appears to have had some Greek before going to Italy—'did not Grocyn himself learn the rudiments of the Greek language in England? Afterwards when he visited Italy he attended the lectures of the chief scholars of the day.' On his return he began his Greek lectures at Oxford, though we are no longer able to accept George Lily's *eulogia* that he was 'the first to introduce the rudiments of the Greek and Latin tongues into Britain'. His library was a large one and though about half of it consisted of standard works in theology and philosophy, the Renaissance texts included some of those which found their way into Bishop Fox's Corpus Christi College library.[1]

Colet's place in the story has been well-established by virtue of his school at St. Paul's. Yet in one sense he was the least adventurous of all his contemporaries. Though he prescribed in his statutes the reading of 'good authors such as have the very Roman eloquence joined with wisdom, especially Christian authors that wrote their wisdom with clear and chaste Latin . . . for my intent is by this school specially to increase the knowledge and worshipping of God and our Lord Christ Jesu, and the good Christian life and manners in the children', his attitude to pagan authors was still medieval in its proscription.[2] Richard Pace, successor to Colet as Dean of St. Paul's had been in Italy from 1498 to 1509. Studying with Linacre's tutor Tomeo at Padua, he was in Venice in 1504, where he delivered an oration on the study of Greek. Protégé first of Thomas Langton, Bishop of Winchester, and later of Christopher Bainbridge, Pace spent twenty of his twenty-seven active adult years in Italy, either as a student or as an agent for Wolsey in Rome, and he published the results of his contacts with Italian humanists in *De fructu qui ex doctrina percipitur* (The Profits of Learning) in which he set

---

[1] Allen, No. 241, I, 484–5, No. 363, II, 486, and Nichols, No. 230, II, 33, No. 523, II, 511. Weiss, op. cit., pp. 173–4. A list of Grocyn's books made by Linacre is printed in Burrows, loc. cit.

[2] J. Lupton, *A Life of John Colet, D.D.* (2nd edition, 1909), Appendix A, 'Statutes of St. Paul's School', p. 279. Cf. by contrast the defence of pagan literature in liberal studies in Salutati's letter to Guiliano Zonarini, Chancellor of Bologna, translated in E. Emerton, *Humanism and Tyranny* (Cambridge, Mass., 1928), pp. 290ff, and in Vives's *De Tradendis Disciplinis* (1531), translated in F. Watson, ed., *Vives on Education* (Cambridge, 1913), pp. 44ff, and 124ff.

forth in true humanist style the ways in which learning might be put to the service of the commonwealth.[1]

Yet no *school* of humanist studies arose in Oxford until the foundation of Corpus Christi College by Richard Fox, Bishop of Durham, in 1516/17. A conscious and concerted attempt at innovation in university education, its statutes provided for the first permanent Reader or Professor in Greek.[2] The Professor of Humanity was to extirpate all 'Barbarisms' from the 'beehive', as Fox called his College, by the study of Cicero, Sallust, Valerius Maximus and Quintilian. In addition, and uniquely, he was to lecture three times a week in vacation to all members below the degrees of Master of Arts on the *Elegantiae* of Valla, the *Noctes Atticae* of Aulus Gellius and the *Miscellanea* of Politian. Significantly too, Fox was at pains to stress that the third Reader of Theology, 'the science we have always so highly esteemed that this our beehive has been constructed solely or mainly for its sake', was to read the texts of the Holy Fathers and not those of their commentators, who are 'both in time and learning far below them'. Mindful of past experience and of the fruitfulness of such a procedure Fox has also provided that one fellow or scholar at a time might have leave of absence for three years to settle in Italy for the purpose of study.

The first President of the College was John Claymond, humanist, student and annotator of the classics and formerly President of Magdalen College. From Magdalen College, too, came Robert Morwent, the first Vice-President. As to the Readerships, the picture is complicated by the endowment by Wolsey in 1518 of six lectureships. Wolsey's lecturers, in fact, resided and taught at Corpus, and in the early days of the College's history Fox's scheme of Readerships was absorbed by Wolsey's. The first of Wolsey's lecturers was John Clement, who was joined shortly after by a Dr. Bliss, lecturer in Canon Law, and John Brinkwell, lecturer in Theology. Clement resigned in 1519 to concentrate on his medical studies. His place

[1] For Pace cf. Jervis Wegg, *Richard Pace* (1932). Langton and his nephew Bainbridge, successively Provosts of Queen's College, Oxford, were both well aware of the value of humanist studies, though their knowledge seems to have had little effect in the college; R. H. Hodgkin, *Six Centuries of an Oxford College* (Oxford, 1949), pp. 51–52.

[2] G. R. M. Ward, ed., *The Foundation Statutes of . . . Corpus Christi College* (1843).

was taken by Thomas Lupset, another of Wolsey's protégés, and in 1523 Lupset himself was replaced by Ludovicus Vives, the Spanish humanist. It was not in fact until 1526, when Edward Wotton returned from Italy, that one of Fox's nominees took up his duties.[1]

In addition Fox endowed the College with a library which included most of Shirwood's books from Durham, and some of Grocyn's. Naturally, this included standard medieval texts such as Vincent of Beauvais's *Speculum* in seven volumes, and Boethius's *De Consolacione* and *De Disciplina Scholarum*, as well as Duns Scotus and Bonaventura. A majority of the books, however, were Renaissance texts, most of them, and especially those from the press of Aldus Manutius, having been brought specifically for the library. The dozen or so Cicero texts derived from the Shirwood library, but there was also a full complement of Greek, including Aristotle, Plato, Xenophon, Thucydides, Herodotus, Demosthenes, Isocrates, and a two-volume Homer. The Romans were represented by Quintilian, Ovid, Juvenal and Terence, and in addition to the modern humanist works prescribed in the statutes were found Landino's *De Vita Activa et Contemplativa* and his commentary on Horace, Ficino's *Letters*, Poggio's *De Nobilitate* and *De Avaritia*, Petrarch's *Secretum*, Platina's *Vitae Pontificum*, as well as the Alberti and the Vitruvius from Shirwood's library.[2]

Here was classical scholarship thriving in England at an institutional level. Yet this was but one aspect of humanism, and one that in the end proved less important, for Tudor England at least, than another which takes us back to Colet. Colet had never been a Greek scholar (though he came to regret it), and his attitude to non-Christian literature showed a disappointing conservatism. Yet Erasmus placed him in the forefront of English humanistic studies, a position which the establishment of the school could not alone have justified. What, then, was the basis of Erasmus's estimate? The answer lies in the series of public

---

[1] P. S. Allen, 'The Early Corpus Readerships', *The Pelican Record*, VII (1905), pp. 155–9, and 'Ludovicus Vives at Corpus', ibid., VI (1902), pp. 156–60. The fullest account of Vives in England is in H. de Vocht, *Monumenta Humanistica Lovaniensia: texts and studies of Louvain humanists in the first half of the sixteenth century* (Louvain, 1934), pp. 1–60.

[2] J. R. Liddell, 'The Library of Corpus Christi College, Oxford, in the Sixteenth Century', *The Library*, 4th Series, XVIII (1937–8), pp. 385–416.

lectures which Colet began to deliver at Oxford in the Michaelmas term of 1496.[1] The fact that he took the Pauline Epistles as
his subject and not a text from one of the schoolmen, as was the
usual practice of Divinity Readers, was an innovation in itself.
But his treatment of the text and his method of approach were
equally new to his Oxford listeners. In true humanist fashion
he went straight to the heart of the matter, seeking to understand
the spirit of St. Paul's words in the light of their historical context, in a way which would reveal their practical relevance for the
Christian life.

> Counsels, precepts and exhortations replace the *ergos* and *sequiturs*
> of Abailard, for the right orientation of the will and the performance
> of right actions were of more importance to Colet than the know-
> ledge of theological distinctions and speculative conclusions. To
> approach the study of scripture with any other purpose generated,
> in Colet's opinion, only an endless variety of words and opinions
> which were well-nigh useless to the individual searching for
> example and guidance in living a Christian life.[2]

Though Colet's method was new to Oxford it was by no means
original. It was the method, for example, which Bruni, Dati and
others had used in their historical works, and which Lorenzo
Valla used in his critical studies of the Apostles' Creed, of the
Donation of Constantine (1439) and of the Bible itself. It was
the method, too, which Erasmus was to use in his work on
Jerome's *Letters* and in the production of his edition of the New
Testament.[3] 'All St. Paul's sayings must be cautiously examined,
before any opinions touching his meaning could be given,' said
Colet, examined not in the dialectical and unproductive way of
the glossators, but in the grammatical-rhetorical way of the
humanists. In other words Colet put his texts to the test of
lingustic and historical scholarship in order to extract their
Christian message. Yet he did something more than apply a

---

[1] Printed and translated by J. H. Lupton, *Colet's Exposition of St. Paul's
Epistle to the Romans* (1873), and *Colet's Exposition of St. Paul's Epistle to the
Corinthians* (1874).

[2] P. A. Duhamel, 'The Oxford Lectures of John Colet: an essay in defining
the Renaissance', *J.H.I.*, XIV (1953), pp. 493–510. Cf. R. McKeon, 'Renaissance
and Method in Philosophy', *Studies in the History of Ideas*, III (1935), 95: 'What
was sought was light rather than doctrine, love rather than knowledge, letter
rather than principle'.

[3] Cf. E. Schwarz, *Principles and Problems of Biblical Translation: Some Reformation Controversies and Their Background* (Cambridge, 1955), Chap. v.

method, something which was to prove of greater importance. In his determination to seek the 'direct practical meaning' of St. Paul he helped persuade the clergy of the importance of communicating this to their parishioners.[1] More was to make the same point in his *Letter to the University of Oxford* in 1518, as did Erasmus writing to Albert of Mainz in the following year: 'the proper task of a theologian is to instruct. I now notice that there are many who do nothing but constrain, destroy or extinguish.'[2]

The importance of such instruction was emphasized in the mystical and reforming movements of the fifteenth century when the works of Richard Rolle and Thomas à Kempis's *Imitation of Christ* achieved great popularity in England. Certainly Kempis and the Brethren of the Common Life had a profound influence on Erasmus. If, at the outset, it had tended to be the humanist ear which had listened to new ideas, by the turn of the century, in northern Europe, it was the humanist heart which reacted and transformed the message. Scholarship in the service of the flock was Colet's theme, one which reached its zenith in the sermons of Hugh Latimer, where a sensitivity to the problems of ordinary Christian life pointed to the ultimate victory of the sermon of insight over the sermon of erudition. Like Colet, Latimer stressed Christian life rather than Christian theology, the practical rather than the intellectual aspects of religion. His works echo again and again the assertion of Thomas à Kempis: 'I had rather feel compunction of the heart for my sins than only to know the definition of compunction.'[3] Latimer's concern for the mass of Christians, and especially for the poor and ignorant, led him to lay constant emphasis on the educative function of the clergy, and therefore, on the need for an educated priesthood, trained in the scholarly Erasmian tradition to take a vernacular Bible to

---

[1] Lupton, *Romans*, p. 14. The wide dispersal and popularity of Valla's works must have contributed largely to the spread and acceptance of the method. Cf. Erasmus's Preface to his printing of Valla's *Novum Testamentum Adnotationes* in 1505, Allen, No. 182, I, 407–12, Nichols, No. 182, I, 380–5, and E. H. Harbison, *The Christian Scholar in the Age of the Reformation* (New York, 1956), Chap. ii.

[2] Allen, No. 1033, IV, 102.

[3] Cf. A. Hyma, *The Christian Renaissance: a History of the Devotio Moderna* (New York, 1924) and *The Youth of Erasmus* (Ann Arbor, 1930). E. J. Klein, ed., *Richard Whitford's Translation of the 'Imitation of Christ'* (New York, 1941), p. 4. Whitford's English translation was published in 1530 and went through numerous editions.

its parishioners. From the historical and textual criticism of scholars 'learned in the three languages' would result not only an educated clergy, but equally the vernacular Bibles, the Paraphrases and Homilies through which that clergy could educate its flock. Even before the appearance of the English Bible in the 1530's Erasmus was writing in the Preface to his *Novum Testamentum*:

> The mysteries of kings it may be safer to conceal, but Christ wished his mysteries to be published as openly as possible. I wish that even the weakest woman should read the gospel and the epistles of Paul. . . . I long that the husbandman should sing portions of them to himself as he follows the plough, that the weaver should hum them to the tune of his shuttle, that the traveller should beguile with their stories the tedium of his journey.[1]

Though Colet lectured at Oxford, the traditional home of humanism in England, by the 1520's the initiative lay with Cambridge. It was in Cambridge, under the aegis of John Fisher, President of St. John's, that Erasmus had worked in 1511 and 1513 on his New Testament, though his lectures there had been poorly attended. In the 1520's, however, were to be found a new set of 'reformers', the 'Gospellers', who met at the White Hart Tavern to read Lutheran texts. Led by William Bilney, Thomas Stafford and Robert Barnes, their proselytizing activities resulted in Latimer, Coverdale, Parker and others joining their ranks. In 1519 appeared the second edition of Erasmus's *Novum Testamentum*, in which the Vulgate, printed parallel to the Greek text, showed radical revision. The profound effect it had on Bilney is recounted in his letter to Tunstall when about to stand trial on a charge of heresy. George Stafford, Reader in Divinity at Pembroke, having read the new version, began to expound the Gospels instead of Peter Lombard's *Sentences*.[2] Out of their work arose a concern over the concept of *adiaphora* which Starkey emphasized in his *Exhortation to the People Instructing them to Unity and Obedience* (1535), which

---

[1] Cited by Seebohm, op. cit. (3rd edition, 1913), p. 327.

[2] Cf. E. G. Rupp, *Studies in the Making of the English Protestant Tradition* (Cambridge, 1947), Chap. ii, and Allen G. Chester, *Hugh Latimer, Apostle to the English* (Philadelphia, 1954), pp. 10ff. Latimer described his conversion in his *First Sermon on the Lord's Prayer*, in G. E. Corrie, ed., *Sermons of Hugh Latimer* (Parker Society, 1844), I, 334–5.

Latimer made central to his own position and which became one of the principles of the Anglican *via media* as expounded by Hooker and Whitgift. The need to distinguish between the essentials of the Christian faith and those 'things indifferent' which might be left to individual conscience was one which had already occupied fifteenth-century humanists like Nicolas of Cusa, Ficino and Pico. Erasmus, writing to Paul Volz, suggested that a commission of learned and devout men might meet to draw up a brief formula of faith, 'a kind of resumé of the "whole philosophy of Christ", a resumé in which simplicity would not detract from erudition nor brevity from precision'. The aim would be to reduce the faith to a small number of articles about which agreement might be general, and to leave the rest to free discussion and belief.[1]

Yet the very concept emphasized the need for a clergy educated enough to make the distinction. Starkey made the point clear when he called for the reform of the grammar schools and universities in his *Dialogue between Reginald Pole and Thomas Lupset*.[2] The Royal Injunctions of 1547, many of them merely repetitions of the Cromwellian articles of 1538, were, however, of importance in their attention to education. Each church was to be equipped with the Great Bible, the *Paraphrases*[3] of Erasmus and the Homilies. The latter were to be read to the congregation each Sunday, and parishioners were to be encouraged to read the Bible for themselves. In addition every priest below the degree of Bachelor was to provide himself with a New Testament, in both Latin and Greek, and a copy of the *Paraphrases*, and 'diligently to study the same'. Chantry priests were enjoined to pay particular attention to their duties of 'teaching youth to read and write, and bring them up in good manners and virtuous exercises'. Further, 'to the intent that learned men may spring the more', every priest with a living worth £100 was to provide at either the university or the grammar school, an exhibition for one or more scholars,

---

[1] J. Lecler, *Toleration and the Reformation* (trans. T. L. Westow, 1960), I, 107 and 125ff. Allen, No. III, 365.

[2] K. M. Burton, ed., *Dialogue between Reginald Pole and Thomas Lupset* (1948), pp. 125 and 188–9.

[3] I.e. of the Gospels and Epistles—'something between translation and commentary, informal, informative, yet close to the text'; Harbison, op. cit., p. 87.

who 'after they have profited in good learning may be partners of their patron's cure and charge'.[1]

That there was good need for such injunctions is evidenced by the sermons of men like Latimer and Lever in the years which followed. The situation in the parishes was, as Latimer saw, closely linked with the state of divinity studies in the universities; on the one hand were the neglectful priests, on the other the unlearned:–

> Ye that be prelates look well to your office; for right prelating is busy labouring and not lording. Therefore preach and teach and let your plough be doing . . . the plough is your office and charge. . . . For how many unlearned prelates have we now this day! . . . For ever since the prelates were made lords and nobles the plough standeth. . . . They hawk, they hunt, they card, they dice . . . and by their lording and loitering, preaching and ploughing is clean gone.

Yet, 'lordling' priests apart, there were still not enough trained young clerics emerging from the universities:–

> It would pity a man's heart to hear that I hear of the state of Cambridge. . . . There be few do study divinity but so many as of necessity must furnish the Colleges; for their livings be so small and victuals so dear that they tarry not there, but go other where to seek livings; and so they go about. Now there be a few gentlemen and they study a little divinity. Alas! what is that? It will come to pass that we shall have nothing but a little English divinity that will bring this realm into a very barbarousness and utter decay of learning. It is not that, I wis, that will keep out the supremacy of the Bishop of Rome. . . . There be none now but great men's sons in colleges and their fathers look not to have them preachers so that every way this office of preaching is pinched out.

Latimer was, of course, equally concerned that parishioners should benefit from sermons, and exhorted them in typical style by recalling the anecdote of the sleepless London gentle-woman: 'one of her neighbours met her in the street and said, "Mistress, whither go ye?" "Marry", said she, "I am going to St. Thomas of Acre's to the sermon: I could not sleep at all this last night and I am going now hither; I never failed of a

[1] W. H. Frere, *Visitation Articles and Injunctions of the Period of the Reformation*, Alcuin Club Collections, XV (1910), II (1536–8), pp. 114–30.

good nap there", and so I had rather ye should go a-napping to the sermons, than not go at all.'[1]

Yet from Erasmus's Greek Testament with its revised Latin translation, through Colet's lectures and Latimer's sermons, down to the vernacular Bible and devotional literature, humanism at one level or another manifested itself in both the religious and academic spheres, and could not but have its effect on the lives and minds of all sorts and degrees of people. Scholars back from Italy, Fisher at Cambridge, Fox at Oxford, Latimer in the pulpit, each made their contribution.

Thomas More had not studied in Italy and his studies at Oxford had been cut short by his father in favour of the Inns of Court, yet he was at the very centre of Greek studies in England in the early decades of the sixteenth century. A pupil of both Linacre and Grocyn, More acquired a remarkable facility in the language as Richard Pace testified:—

> no one ever lived who did not first ascertain the meaning of words and from them gather the meaning of the sentences which they compose—no one I say, with one single exception, and this is our own Thomas More. For he is wont to gather the forces of the words from the sentences in which they occur, especially in his study and translation of Greek. This is not contrary to grammar but above it, and an instinct of genius.[2]

With William Lily he produced a volume of Greek epigrams in translation, the *Progymnasmata*, in which they took the original epigram from the *Anthologia Graeca* and then each produced a rival Latin rendering. Like Erasmus he translated some of Lucian's dialogues and the rhetorical declamation *Tyrannicida*, to which both he and Erasmus composed replies.[3] During the

---

[1] Corrie, op. cit., I, 65–66, 178–9 and 201. For similar criticisms by Thomas Lever cf. E. Arber, ed., *Thomas Lever, Sermons* (English Reprints, 1895), pp. 120ff. For a fuller discussion cf. N. Wood, *The Reformation and English Education* (1931), Chap. v.

[2] *De Fructu* . . ., quoted in translation by T. E. Bridgett, *Life and Writings of Sir Thomas More* (1891), p. 12.

[3] *The Anthologia Graeca* was first published in Florence in 1494. The translation by More and Lily must have been among the earliest made in England. Cf. C. R. Thompson, *The Translation of Lucian by Erasmus and St. Thomas More* (New York, 1940), pp. 9 and 12ff. For a review of Erasmus's study of Greek cf. Allen, I, Appendix VI, 592–3 and A. Hyma, 'Erasmus and the Oxford Reformers', *Nederlands Archief voor Kerkgeschiedenis* N.S. XXV (1932), pp. 69–72 and 97–136 and ibid., N.S., XXXVIII (1951), pp. 65–85.

controversies which followed the publication of Erasmus's *Praise of Folly* (1514), More joined with his friend in refuting the criticism of Martin Dorp. The Dutch scholar had suggested that Erasmus might be better employed writing a *Praise of Wisdom* instead of the projected edition of a Greek New Testament, which he considered to be superfluous when the Vulgate quite adequately preserved the essential truth of the Scriptures. More followed Erasmus's reply of May 1515 with one of his own in October, in which he reiterated Erasmus's defence of Greek studies. A similar defence is to be found in More's letter to Oxford University in 1518, where he refers to a sermon preached in the University in which humanist education in general and the study of Greek in particular were considered 'trivial, if not a positive hindrance to the spiritual life'. Indeed the preacher went on to aver that simple country folk and the unlettered fly quicker to heaven, quicker presumably than those who wasted their time with the trivialities of *litterae bonae*. The sermon was yet another episode in the war between the 'Greeks' and 'Trojans'. More's rejoinder was sharp and full of authority. He wrote:–

> To whom is it *not* obvious that to the Greeks we owe all our precision in the liberal arts generally and in theology particularly? . . . Few will question that humanist education is the chief, almost the sole reason why men come to Oxford . . . some should also pursue law in which case the wisdom that comes from the study of humane things is requisite; and in any case it is something not useless to theologians; without such study they might possibly preach a sermon acceptable to an academic group but they would certainly fail to reach the common man . . . from whom could they acquire skill better than from the (classical) poets, orators and historians? . . . they build a path to Theology through Philosophy and the Liberal Arts which this man condemns as secular.[1]

Such was the chief burden of the case for the defence, and Erasmus and More spent most of their lives writing on this theme. *Ad fontes*—'back to the sources'—was no mere pendatic

[1] Allen, No. 337, II, 91–114; cf. Schwarz, op. cit., pp. 162ff for other similar criticisms of Erasmus. E. F. Rogers, ed., *The Correspondence of Thomas More* (Princeton, 1947), pp. 27ff, and 111ff. Cf. T. S. K. Scott-Craig, 'Thomas More's Letter to the University of Oxford', *Renaissance News*, I (1948), pp. 17–24, which includes a new translation.

cry of the ivory-towered scholar. The roots of Christianity lay
in the Greek language. Without the study of Greek, theologians
deprived themselves of access to an important corpus of biblical
and patristic literature. As Erasmus put it:–

> My whole purpose in life has always been two-fold: to stimulate
> others to cultivate *bonae litterae*, to bring the study of *bonae litterae*
> into harmony with theology . . . and to initiate a process which
> would impart to *bonae litterae* a truly Christian note. . . . Secondly
> that the study of theology on its present conventional lines might
> itself be improved and enlightened by theologians acquiring a
> better knowledge of classical Latin and Greek and an improved
> critical taste in literature as a whole.[1]

This was the general purpose. Embodied in it were two main
tasks which faced the humanist scholar. First he had to emancipate himself from the dead weight of scholastic irrelevancy
which had hidden from sight the basic questions of the Christian
life. 'Where in the Scriptures do you find a statement of
Aristotle or Averroes? (asked More). Where any mention of
first and second intentions? Where any mention of complica-
tions and restrictions? Where any mention of formalities or
quiddities or even ecceities with which everything is now
crammed full?'[2]

Second, and more important perhaps, the humanist had to
show that the natural ethics found in classical pagan literature
were complementary rather than opposed to Christian ethics:–

> I had rather lose Scotus and twenty more such as he than one
> Cicero or Plutarch. Not that I am wholly against them, neither, but
> because by the reading of one I find myself become better whereas
> I rise from the other I know not how coldly affected to virtue but
> most violently inclined to cavil and contention.[3]

The end-product of a humanist education should be not a better
disputant, nor simply a better philologist, but a better man, and

---

[1] Allen, No. 1581, VI, 8, translated in H. A. Mason, *Humanism and Poetry
in the Early Tudor Period* (1959), p. 88.

[2] *Ratio Seu Methodus*, cited by E. L. Surz, 'The Oxford Reformers and Scholas-
ticism', *S.P.*, XLVII (1950), pp. 547–56. Cf., too, W. K. Ferguson, 'Renaissance
Tendencies in the Religious Thought of Erasmus', *J.H.I.*, XV (1954), pp. 506ff.
The same complaint is found in *Utopia*, Everyman edition, p. 71.

[3] N. Bailey, ed., *The Colloquies of Erasmus* (1878), I, 182, cited by Surz, op.
cit., p. 556.

throughout their writings Erasmus and More stressed that it was the practical ethics of the ancients that was of value. The Utopians were skilled in both Latin and Greek and Hythloday's 'pretty fardel of books' contained the best of both literatures. Yet these in themselves were not enough. 'The chief and principal question is in what things, be it one or more, the felicity of man consisteth.' This was the question which concerned Utopia's philosophers, in contrast to the schoolmen's obsessional disputations over instants, relations, quiddities and the like. The pedantic haggling over details had obscured the real purpose of classical studies which was to produce better men and better Christians, who thereby could play a fruitful rôle in the life of the community.[1]

It was at this point that More realized the dilemma which faced him. If humanist study was to be regarded as a preparation for the world of affairs, the humanist could not shirk the decision of entering that world. If, as he believed, society could be reformed through education, he could scarcely turn his back on the sick world which he described in *Utopia*. The false pleasures and above all the sin of pride, which the Utopians picked out for special condemnation, were there all around him. More's was no academic dilemma for he had often in his early days thought of retreating to the monastic life. When in his youth he resolved, as Stapleton records,

> to put before his eyes the example of some prominent layman on which he might model his life he called to mind all who at that period either at home or abroad enjoyed the reputation of learning and piety (and) finally fixed on John Pico, Earl of Mirandula who was renowned in the highest degree throughout the whole of Europe, for his encyclopaedic knowledge and no less esteemed for his sanctity of life.[2]

It was therefore no merely philological interest which moved More to translate the *Life* of Pico, which the latter's nephew had written in 1496. Significantly, too, More chose to translate three of Pico's letters. In one, to his nephew, Pico warns the boy of the trials and tribulations of life at Court.

---

[1] *Utopia*, Everyman edition, pp. 15, 72, 81–82.
[2] T. Stapleton, *The Life and Illustrious Martyrdom of Sir Thomas More* (trans. P. E. Hallett, 1928), p. 10.

Of the court and service of this world there is nothing that I need to write unto thee, the wretchedness whereof the experience itself hath taught thee and daily teacheth. In obtaining the favour of the princes, in purchasing the friendship of the company, in ambitious labour for offices and honours, what an heap of heaviness there is! How great anguish, how much business and trouble, I may rather learn of thee than teach thee. . . .

In another, a reply to one in which Andrew Corneus, a friend, had urged Pico to give up his study of philosophy in order to serve a prince, Pico writes :—

Philosophers . . . love liberty; they cannot bear the proud manners of estates;[1] they cannot serve. They dwell with themselves and be content with the tranquillity of their own mind. . . . I therefore abiding fairly in this opinion, set more by my little house, my study, the pleasure of my books, the rest and peace of mind than by all your kings' palaces, all your common business, all your glory all the advantages ye hanker after and all the favour of the court.[2]

The problem of a choice between the active and contemplative life was obviously being turned over in More's mind at the time he made his translations (*c.* 1504–5), but with the accession of Henry VIII in 1509 there seemed at last good reason for serving his prince. Leaving on one side the effusions of the occasion in his Coronation 'epigram'—'a poetical expression of good wishes by Thomas More of London'—More obviously felt that here was an opportunity to serve a prince who shared his ideas about the value and purpose of classical studies. 'He now gives the good men honours and public offices, which used to be sold to evil men. By a happy reversal of circumstances learned men now have the prerogative which ignoramuses carried off in the past. . . . What can lie beyond the powers of a prince whose natural gifts have been enhanced by a liberal education?'[3] Nor was More alone in his optimism. In a letter

---

[1] I.e. princes.

[2] W. E. Campbell, ed., *The English Works of Sir Thomas More* (1931) I, 364–5 and 370; cf. S. E. Lehmberg, 'Sir Thomas More's Life of Pico della Mirandola', *Studies on the Renaissance*, III (1956), pp. 61–74, and 'English Humanists, the Reformation and the Problem of Counsel', *Archiv für Reformationgeschichte*, LII (1961), pp. 74–91.

[3] L. Bradner and C. A. Lynch, *The Latin Epigrams of Thomas More: edited with translations and notes* (Chicago, 1953), pp. 19 and 141.

to Erasmus telling him of the accession of the king and urging him to return to England, William Blount, Lord Mountjoy, reported 'the other day he wished he was more learned. I said that it is not what we expect of your Grace, but that you will foster and encourage learned men. Yea, surely, said he, for indeed without them we should scarcely exist at all.'[1] And events proved that there was every justification for their raised hopes, when Erasmus could write in 1518,

> The king, the most sensible monarch of our age is delighted with your books and the Queen is well instructed—not merely in comparison with her own sex—and is no less to be respected for her piety than her erudition. With such sovereigns those persons have the greatest influence who excel in learning and prudence. Thomas Linacre is their physician, a man whom it is needless for me to characterise, when by his published books he has made himself sufficiently known. Cuthbert Tunstall is Master of the Rolls. . . . Thomas More is one of the Council. . . . Pace, with a character near akin, is the king's secretary. . . . William, Lord Mountjoy, is the head of the Queen's household and John Colet is the preacher. I have only named the chief people . . . a palace filled with such men may be called a Temple of the Muses rather than a court. What Athens, what Porch, what Lyceum would you prefer to a court like that?[2]

Flattery of royalty could possibly have been a factor in More's poem, though he was certainly not given to the practice. The Letters of Mountjoy and Erasmus related to situations in which exaggerated praise was neither necessary nor appropriate, and were obviously sincere and enthusiastic reports. The humanists' high hopes for the new reign were indeed well-grounded. And yet More hesitated. He set out his dilemma in the first book of *Utopia*, where he debates the conflict between the scholar's duty to learning and truth and his duty to his prince and fellow-citizens. The prince's need for good counsel was undoubted, 'for from the prince, as from a perpetual well-spring cometh among the people the flood of all that is good or evil'. At the

---

[1] Allen, No. 215, I, 450, Nichols, No. 210, I, 457–8. The same optimistic note is sounded in Castiglione's *The Courtier*. Though not published until 1528 the work was written in 1516.

[2] Allen, No. 855, III, 356–7, Nichols, No. 805, III, 421–2; cf. Allen, No. 832, III, 303; Nichols, No. 790, III, 361; and Allen, No. 919, IV, 22; Nichols, No. 585, III, 399.

same time the humanist must serve with a pragmatic attention to the real world and its everyday problems, and not according to 'school philosophy . . . which thinketh all things meet for every place'. On the other hand Italian experience had shown that more often than not humanists had been called into the service of a prince only to buttress a predetermined policy. Instead of leading along the paths of virtue and enlightenment, the humanist might find himself expediting a policy which ran quite contrary to his humanist ideals. Erasmus apparently found no difficulty. He served through his writings, constantly preaching the cause of lettered piety, of Christian humanism, whilst at the same time safeguarding his independence. Whether through his philological and grammatical works, or through his didactic treatises for princes, his manuals for Christian knights, his handbooks for the guidance of youth, or most important through his Greek New Testament, to say nothing of his continuous stream of letters, he kept up a barrage of fire and counter-fire. Yet Erasmus avoided rather than solved the dilemma of which More was so painfully aware. His didactic works, brilliantly setting forth the ideal to be arrived at, rarely provided a practical guide as to how such an aim might be achieved within the context of an actual social-political organization. Erasmus's naïve belief that to write was enough prevented his hearing the ridicule which might laugh a humanist's ideals out of court.[1]

Yet despite his doubts More plunged into the life of the Court. He had been active in the legal affairs of the City of London both on behalf of the Mercer's Company and as Under-Sheriff, in which office he represented the City in litigation before the royal Courts. It was during and immediately after his Netherlands mission (1515) that *Utopia* was written. In 1517 he was in Calais on diplomatic business for the king. By the time he wrote his letter to the University of Oxford (1518) he was obviously a member of the Court. Reluctant as he was to take on the 'heap of heaviness', as a humanist he had no alternative. Pico's advice must be put aside and the model found in the *vita activa* of Salutati, Bruni and Alberti. Nor indeed did More follow their model in political life only. Alberti's

---

[1] *Utopia*, Everyman edition, pp. 19, 34, 41–42. Cf. Paul Coles, 'The Interpretation of More's *Utopia*', *Hibbert Journal*, LVI (1958), pp. 365–70, and J. H. Hexter, *More's Utopia, the Biography of an Idea* (Princeton, 1952), pp. 113ff.

insistence on the educational rôle of the father and the family was nowhere more apparent than in More's own household— *scholam ac gymnasium Christiana religionis*, as Erasmus called it.[1] If More had doubts about putting humanistic studies to the service of the State, Wolsey had none. His own household was a veritable school of affairs, 'a nursery for the Court', in which a good many of the king's servants, Pace, Gardiner and Cromwell among them, acquired the first rudiments of political and administrative expertise. Wolsey's projected school at Ipswich and Cardinal College at Oxford, as well as his patronage of young scholars, each had as its aim the ultimate production of educated royal servants. The king, too, of course, became increasingly aware of the value of such men, especially when the question of his divorce was pending, and on the advice of Cranmer he sought the opinions of the universities of Europe on the question of his marriage's validity. Cranmer himself was sent to Germany, Croke and Stokesley to Italy, Reginald Pole to Paris, whilst at the same time the humanistic scholar Sir Thomas Elyot was sent as ambassador to the Court of Charles V to secure Charles's neutrality in the coming conflict. Having entered the royal service More's fears progressively appeared to him to be justified and his letter to Erasmus makes clear his relief on relinquishing the chancellorship in May 1532.[2] With the reins of government in the hands of Cromwell, the patronage of young scholars was undertaken on the explicit understanding that they would be directed to the furtherance of the king's policies. Cromwell's protégés were more often than not to be found in the household which Reginald Pole set up in Padua, an establishment which stood comparison with those of Grey and Tiptoft. Twenty years had elapsed since Linacre and his generation had studied the humanities in Italy, but Leonico was still teaching there and his tutorship of Pole and his colleagues and their scholarly association with humanists like Bembo and Longolius maintained the link. Pupil of Linacre and Latimer, Pole himself was one of those who benefited from the patronage of the king. His first visit to Italy in 1519 was brief, but he returned in 1521 with an annual stipend of £100 from the king.

---

[1] Allen, No. 2750, X, 139. Cf. Stapleton's description in Stapleton, op. cit., Chap. x.

[2] Stapleton, op. cit., pp. 78–79.

Padua was by this time recovering from the results of the war of the League of Cambrai, Erasmus had called it the 'Athens of Europe', and in 1533 Thomas Winter, Cromwell's natural son and at that time a member of Pole's household, wrote to his father, 'There are professors of sciences here such as I have never hitherto heard, philosophers into whom the mind of Aristotle seems to have migrated, and civil lawyers and physicians than whom there are none more learned.'[1]

It was the chance of studying Civil Law that attracted Thomas Starkey when he joined Pole there in 1532 or 1533. In 1534 he wrote to Cromwell :–

> Because my purpose then was to live a politic life I set myself now these last years past to the knowledge of the civil law, that I might thereby make a more stable and sure judgement of the politic order and customs used among us here in our country. After this manner in diverse kinds of study I have occupied myself, ever having in mind this end and purpose at the last here in this commonalty where I am brought forth and born, to employ them to some end; and though in them I have not most profited, yet diligence and will hath not lacked thereto, but whatsoever it is that I have the goodness of God attained into I shall most gladly apply it to the service of our prince, and thereby reckon myself to attain a great part of my felicity.[2]

In the following year Starkey returned to England to become chaplain to the king, and later to prepare his *Dialogue between Reginald Pole and Thomas Lupset*. The biographical letter of dedication to the king repeats the ideas and aims which he had communicated to Cromwell and in the *Dialogue* itself he sets out the abuses which he sees around him. His analysis of the state of affairs in England and his suggestions of ways and means of remedying it show that this was no theoretical treatise, but a practical attempt to explain how a humanist education, for the nobility, for the clergy, for the lawyers, as well as for the prince, could play its part in putting the commonwealth to rights.

Running through the *Dialogue* are two themes. One is the

---

[1] *L. and P.*, VI, 314, Winter to Cromwell, 7 April 1533.
[2] S. J. Herrtage, *England in the Reign of Henry VIII: Starkey's Life and Letters*, Pt. I, E.E.T.S., Extra Series, XXXII (1878), p. x; cf. J. A. Gee, *The Life and Works of Thomas Lupset* (New Haven, 1928), p. 147.

nobility's neglect of learning, the other the unwillingness of some scholars to put their learning at the disposal of the State. Pole himself is criticized on these latter grounds:–

> Of this, Master Pole, many men do you accuse, saying that since you have been of your country so well nourished and brought up, so well set forward to gather prudence and wisdom, you ought now to study to maintain and advance the weal of this same your country, to the which you are bounden no less than the child to the father, when he is, by sickness or age, impotent and not of power to help himself. You see your country, as me seemeth, to require your help, and as it were cry and call unto you busily for the same, and you—as drowned in the pleasure of letters and private studies —give no ear thereto, but forgetting her utterly suffer her still to want your help and succour upon your behalf, not without great injury.[1]

Pole defends himself against the charge but after a lengthy discussion agrees with Lupset 'that every man ought to apply himself to the setting forward of the common weal, every man ought to study to help his country'. Nor must the scholar and nobleman be accused of mere ambition in their willingness to serve the prince,

> when men desire to bear office and to rule to the intent they may establish and set in their country, this common weal which you have before described . . . it is the highest virtue that is in any noble stomach and is a certain argument of true nobility; for sluggish minds live in corners and content themselves with private life, whereas very noble hearts ever desire to govern and rule to the common weal of the whole multitude.[2]

To achieve this for the clergy, who have an important part to play in the common weal, the grammar schools and universities must be reformed, and here the recently published *De Liberis Recte Instituendis* of Cardinal Sadoleto (Venice, 1533) is recommended.[3] For the nobility a new kind of institution is suggested,

---

[1] K. M. Burton, ed., *Dialogue* . . . (1948), p. 22. Cf. Edmund Harwell's similar criticism in *L. and P.*, V, No. 301, p. 75.

[2] Op. cit., pp. 36 and 191.

[3] Ibid., pp. 181–2 and 188–9. Cf. E. T. Campagnac and K. Forbes, eds., *Sadaleto on Education* (1916), and R. M. Douglas, *Jacopo Sadoleto, 1477–1547: humanist and reformer* (Cambridge, Mass., 1959).

certain places appointed for the bringing up together of the nobility, to which I would the nobles should be compelled to set forward their children and heirs, that in a number together they might the better profit. To this use turn both Westminster and St. Albans and many others. . . . For like as monks and religious men living together exercise a certain monastical discipline and life, so they nobles being brought up together should learn there the discipline of the common weal. . . . Here they should learn how and after what manner they might be able and meet to do and put in exercise that thing which pertaineth to their office and authority, and so, plainly and fully, to be instruct in the administration of justice both public and private.[1]

Contemporary with Starkey in Padua was Richard Moryson, one of a group of scholars of poor birth which included John Friar, Henry Cole and George Lily, all of whom studied under Tomeo Leonico whilst enjoying the patronage of Pole. Moryson himself was a product of Wolsey's Cardinal College. After graduating B.A. in 1528 he moved to Cambridge where he met Latimer, Gonell and Cranmer. He joined Pole's household in 1532 and though he enjoyed the benefits of Pole's great generosity his letters to Cromwell and Starkey constantly plead poverty and the need for further help. 'Are you two ashamed or afraid to maintain the life of studies of one? Has your love of letters and learned men grown so cold? Pole has returned Aristotle to me, but I am in great want of the Greek Commentaries. . . .' In a similarly pleading letter to Cromwell he offers to come home if Cromwell thought he could serve the State, but would prefer to continue and complete his studies.[2] This in fact is what he did, continuing his Greek studies with George Lily and becoming fluent in Italian and German. He returned to England in 1535 in the service of Cromwell, ultimately becoming his secretary. In the following year the Pilgrimage of Grace brought into the open criticism of Henry's policies which it became Moryson's task to defend. The burden of complaint was complex and seldom unanimous, but an important element in the mixture and one which made the Pilgrimage an aristocratic rather than a democratic movement, was the reaction against the king's policy of promoting men of

[1] Op. cit., pp. 169–70.
[2] *L. and P.*, IX, 103, Moryson to Starkey, 16 August 1535, and X, 372, Moryson to Cromwell 29 February 1536.

low birth to positions of trust and authority. Wolsey and Cromwell were the obvious examples, but of course Moryson himself, and many like him, were also the target of criticism. The result was the preparation by Moryson of two pamphlets, *A Lamentation Against Rebellion* (1536) and *A Remedy Against Sedition* (1536), later to be followed by *An Invective Against the Great and Detestable Vice, Treason* (1539).[1] Together they form not only a defence of immediate policies, and therefore perhaps are too readily classed as occasional literature, but also a reasoned attempt to explain and justify the basis of these policies. The latter involved a redefinition of the concept of nobility and its educational implications, one which reflected the loosening of social ties which characterized even this early Tudor period. Moryson's pamphlets voice once again the humanistic doctrine that virtue not birth was the indispensable criterion of nobility. 'True nobility is never but where virtue is . . . this only to be the way of promotion and here nobility to consist. What shall we need to endeavour ourselves unto, when whatsoever we do we must be tried by our birth and not by our qualities?' Moryson's own personal struggle against poverty made it all the more important to him to insist that riches and high birth were not enough. Indeed in a letter to Cromwell in 1536 he confessed that he would not now wish to have been born of rich parents, for it was almost thought disgraceful in England to be noble and learned.[2]

### III

We are not here primarily concerned with the political theories of Starkey and Moryson, though each implied the duty of non-resistance to a divinely appointed and liberally educated prince, who was nevertheless himself subject to the law. Their social theories are, however, of greater relevance to our present purpose. Arising out of a political situation of great complexity, they reflected a climate of opinion whose background was wider than the particular problems of enclosures, debased coinage, and dissolved monasteries which prompted their work. In

[1] Cf. W. G. Zeeveld, 'Richard Moryson, Official Apologist for Henry VIII', *P.M.L.A.*, LV, Pt. 1 (1940), pp. 406–25.

[2] W. G. Zeeveld, *Foundations of Tudor Policy* (Cambridge, Mass., 1948), pp. 209 and 95.

essence they exemplify an anglicization of Italian ideas about the nature of nobility and gentility and their connexion with virtue and education. This meant on the one hand a rejection of that chivalric education which had been considered appropriate for the ruling class in the past, and on the other a secularization of the concept of wisdom, with its corollary, the justification of the *vita activa* as the educated man's vocation.

We have seen that Englishmen had become acquainted with these ideas during their studies in Italy. But in order to take root and thrive such ideas needed an appropriately fertile soil in England, a soil which was in fact being prepared during the latter half of the fifteenth century. During that period a decline took place in the economic fortunes of the great landowners. Faced not only with a shortage of labour and of tenants, but also with a fall in land values and in the profits of cultivation, they 'tried to stabilize their incomes by sub-letting estates to men small enough to live on them and substantial enough to afford them. . . . Some of them bought demesne farms or whole manors outright, others appeared merely as tenants ('farmers'), but all of them represented a new and rising class.[1] With their living costs rising and their incomes falling the old aristocracy had to face, too, a growing social criticism of their way of life and of their failure to fulfil their traditional obligations. Some, apprehensive of the narrowing of the gap between themselves and the middling men to which we have referred, attempted to reverse the trend by a 'revival' of chivalry and all its trappings. They attempted to accentuate the differences between themselves and their 'inferiors' by conspicuous consumption on dress and household effects, on hunting, hawking and the tournament with their elaborate ritual and costly equipment, on personal bands of retainers, all of which reflected an age in which, as Huizinga has shown, beauty was ousted by pomp and magnificence, in art as in chivalry.[2]

Texts such as *The Book of Hawking, Hunting and Blazing of Arms*, commonly called the *Boke of St. Albans* (1486), provided instruction in these matters.[3] Malory's *Morte D'Arthur*, printed

[1] M. M. Postan, 'Some Social Consequences of the Hundred Years War', *Ec.H.R.*, XII (1942), pp. 11-12.

[2] Huizinga, *Waning of the Middle Ages*, Chap. xiv.

[3] Cf. E. F. Jacob, 'The Boke of St. Albans', *B.J.R.L.*, XXVIII (1944), pp. 99-118.

by Caxton in 1485 and Wynkyn de Worde in 1498, pointed out how useful such knowledge was, 'wherefore, as we seemeth, all gentlemen that bear old arms ought of right to honour Sir Tristram for the goodly terms that gentlemen have and use . . . that thereby, in a manner, all men of worship may dissever a gentleman from a yeoman, and from a yeoman a villain. For he that gentle is will draw into him gentle tatches, and to follow the customs of noble gentlemen.'[1] But times were changing. Caxton's epilogue to the *Boke of the Ordre of Chyvalry* (1484) regretted the increasing neglect of 'feates of arms', horsemanship and weapon-skill, whilst the author of the *Boke of Noblesse, addressed to Edward IV on his Invasion of France, 1475*, deplored how

> of late days, the greater pity is, many a one that (hath) been descended of noble blood and borne to arms, as knight's sons, esquires and of other noble gentle blood, set themselves to practice strange faculties . . . as to learn the practice of the law or custom of the land or of civil matters, and so waste greatly their time in such needless business as to occupy courts holding, to keep a proud countenance at sessions and shire holdings, also there to embrace and rule among your poor and simple commons of bestial countenance that lust to live in rest.[2]

Yet even those who had detected the strength and changing direction of the wind faced the growing competition of the 'ungentle' who were already regularly appearing in Parliament, and who under the first two Tudors were chosen, as a matter of policy, to be the king's servants, officials and even ministers. Just as humanists staffed the Papal Curia and the princely Courts of fifteenth-century Italy, so too that most princely of princes, Henry VIII, chose men well-versed in the ideas and ideals, the methods and the skills of humanism, whether as chancellor, ambassador or clerk.

The literature justifying and buttressing such a trend was voluminous. In opposition to the reassertion of chivalric ideals it offered a re-definition of nobility and gentility based on merit

---

[1] Caxton's edition of *Morte D'Arthur*, modernized by A. W. Pollard (three vols., New York, 1936), II, 9. A facsimile edition of the Wynkyn de Worde printing (1498) was published from the unique copy in the John Rylands Library (Oxford, 1933).

[2] J. G. Nichols, ed., *The Boke of Noblesse* (Roxburghe Club, 1860), pp. 26–28.

and service, whose Italian origins we have already discussed. Chaucer had already hinted at it in the *Wife of Bath's Tale*, when he defined a gentleman:—

> Who ever loves to work for virtuous ends
> Public and private, and who most intends
> To do what deeds of gentleness he can
> Take him to be the greatest gentleman.
> Christ wills we take our gentleness from him
> Not from a wealth of ancestry long dim.

A more striking example, though by no means untypical, was John Tiptoft's *Declamacion of Noblesse*,[1] a translation, as we have seen, of Buonaccorso's *Controversia de Nobilitate* (1428). The work was printed by Caxton in 1481 and later became the source of the earliest English secular drama, Henry Medwall's *Fulgens and Lucres* (*c.* 1497).[2] The plot concerns the rivalry between the nobleman Publius Cornelius Scipio and the commoner Gaius Flammenius for the hand in marriage of Lucres, daughter of the wealthy citizen Fulgens. Cornelius boasts of the nobility of his birth and the wealth of his parents, whilst his youth has been devoted to the cultivation of the accomplishments appropriate to his station—'hunting, hawking, singing and disport'. Gaius on the other hand refers to his studies in philosophy and the classical language and literature, and rests his case on the fact that his rival refers only to the deeds of his ancestors and his inherited riches, whereas true nobility lies in a man's own virtue:—

> noblessness resteth neither in riches nor in blood but in a free and noble courage which is neither servant to vice nor to uncleanness, but is exercised in cunning (i.e. knowledge) and virtue. And he that is endued with such courage deserveth best to be called noble, worshipful and excellent.[3]

In the *Declamacion*, as in the *Controversia*, the question is put to the Roman Senate, from whom, however, no decision is

---

[1] Printed in Mitchell, *Tiptoft . . .*, Appendix I, pp. 215–41.

[2] Edited by F. S. Boas and A. W. Reed (Tudor and Stuart Library, Oxford, 1926); a photographic facsimile has been printed in the Henry E. Huntington Facsimile Reprints Series (New York, 1920), with introduction by Seymour de Ricci.

[3] Mitchell, op. cit., pp. 221, 234.

forthcoming. In the play, on the other hand, Lucres herself
makes the choice, in favour of Gaius Flammenius,

> For in this case I do him commend,
> As the more noble man since he this wise,
> By means of his virtue to honour doth arise[1]

Exactly the same sort of attitude and argument had been put
forward in Palmieri's *Della Vita Civile*: 'He who seeks fame in
the ability of past generations deprives himself of honour and
merit. A pitiable creature is he who lives on the reputation of
his ancestors. A man who deserves honour should offer himself,
not his genealogy.'[2]

It was an argument which would find ready acceptance among
a socially-ambitious group of merchants, lesser landowners and
officials, who derived great satisfaction from *Gentleness and
Nobility* (1529?), 'a dialogue between the merchant, the knight
and the ploughman disputing who is a very gentleman and who
is a nobleman and how men should come to authority'. Each of
the disputants makes his claim in turn and for different reasons,
but the judgement lies with the philosopher who concludes:—

> The thing that maketh a gentleman to be
> Is but virtue and gentle conditions
> Which as well in poor men often time we see,
> As in men of great birth or high degree
> And also vicious and churlish conditions
> May be in men born to great possessions.[3]

They found their views confirmed in Sir Thomas Elyot's
*Image of Governance* (1541), where the Emperor Severus chides
his minister Frontinus for recommending a young nobleman to
his service on the grounds of his ancient stock and great substance.

> I had thought ye had ever esteemed the stock by the fruit, and not
> the fruit by the stock. No man commendeth the boughs or branches
> because the stem of the tree is long or straight . . . if the stock

---

[1] Boas and Reed, op. cit., p. 81.

[2] Cited H. Baron, 'The Historical Background of the Florentine Renaissance',
*History*, N.S., XXII (1938), p. 318.

[3] A. C. Partridge and F. P. Wilson, eds., *Gentleness and Nobility* (Malone
Society Reprints, 1950), lines 1123ff. Cf. K. W. Cameron, *Authorship and Sources
of Gentleness and Nobility* (1941).

be never so fair if the boughs be rotten or seer the owner will shred them and throw them into the fire . . . a good child reneweth and augmenteth the praise of his parents, the ill child raseth out of men's hearts the father's honour and benefit. . . . Therefore speak no more of him but search for some other in whom sincerity and temperance be joined with wisdom. Such a one if he be of an ancient house shall bring to our palace an honourable remembrance of his noble progenitors, and as well to noble as to unnoble shall be an excellent pattern or precedent. If he be of late come to worship his own advancement shall engender in noble men honest envy either to exceed him in virtue or at least to be judged equal to him. To poor men it shall be an allectife and root of good hope that they be in the rank where the reward is dealt.[1]

Nobility of birth, then, had to be supplemented by 'vertue and connyng' before it could make an individual worthy to govern. As Ascham was later to put it,

nobility without virtue and wisdom is blood indeed, but blood truly without bones and sinews; and so of itself without the other very weak to bear the burden of weighty affairs. But nobility governed by learning and wisdom is indeed most like a fair ship having wind and tide at will. . . . Therefore, ye great and noble men's children if you will have rightfully that praise and enjoying surely that place which your fathers have and elders had and left unto you, you must keep it as they got it, and that is by the only way of virtue, wisdom and worthiness.[2]

But even virtuous wisdom was not in itself enough. Essential to the new concept was the application of these qualities to the service of the common weal. As Barclay observed :—

> Certainly in learning we spend the time in vain,
> Except the deed follow, all perfectly to blind
> Which we at beginning conceived in our mind
> Since doing is the fruit and learning but the seed.[3]

Erasmus, as so often, summed it all up in a few sentences :—

useful occupations should be respected and sluggish indolence not graced with the title of nobility. I should not strip the well-born

---

[1] Op. cit., pp. 76–77. Parallel passages are to be found in Elyot's *The Governour* (1531) (ed. H. H. S. Croft, two vols., 1883), II, 29ff, and Moryson's translation of Vives's *Introduction to Wisdom* (1540), Sig. B ii *verso*.

[2] *The Scholemaster* (1570) (ed. J. E. B. Mayor, 1863), pp. 39–40.

[3] Alexander Barclay, *The Mirror of Good Manners* (1523).

of their honour if they follow in the footsteps of their forefathers and excel in those qualities which first created nobility. But if we see so many today who are soft from indolence, effeminate through sensual pleasure, with no knowledge of any useful vocation but only charming table fellows, ardent gamesters (I would not mention any of their obscene practices), why I ask you should this class of persons be placed on a higher level than the shoemaker or the farmer? In former times leisure from the baser activities was granted the best families not so they might indulge in wanton nonsense but so that they might learn the principles of government.[1]

Erasmus's criticism was only one in a constant stream of complaint against the idleness and ignorance of the aristocracy. Edmund Dudley, writing in 1509, was of the opinion, that 'the nobleman and gentlemen of England be the worst brought up for the most part of any realm in Christendom', an estimate confirmed by the Italian Secretary of the Venetian Ambassador Francesco Capello.[2] Nor was the complaint confined to England. Thomas Niger preaching to the Fifth Lateran Council, complained that 'A fine intellect and high station rarely are joined together. How many of the crowd of nobles busy themselves with culture? How many of them are learned or patrons of learning? . . . the school for the liberally educated is a prison and the instruction a punishment. They scorn studies and they hate the studious.'[3]

Pace's horn-blowing gentleman was unashamed: 'I swear by God's body I'd rather that my son should hang than study letters. For it becomes the sons of gentlemen to blow the horn nicely, to hunt skilfully, and elegantly to carry and train a hawk. But the study of letters should be left to the sons of rustics.'[4] But he was fighting a losing battle. Idleness was the great emblem of aristocratic pride in More's *Utopia* and the hunt, with

[1] L. K. Born, ed., *The Education of a Christian Prince* (New York, 1936), p. 226.

[2] D. M. Brodie, ed., *The Tree of Commonwealth* (Cambridge, 1948), p. 48; C. A. Sneyd, ed., *A Relation of the Island of England* (Camden Society, XXXVII, 1847), p. 22.

[3] Cited by E. L. Surz, *The Praise of Pleasure* (Cambridge, Mass., 1957), p. 81. For French examples cf. J. H. Hexter, 'The Education of the Aristocracy in the Renaissance', *J.M.H.*, XXII (1950), pp. 1–20.

[4] Cf. F. J. Furnivall, *Education in Early England* (E.E.T.S., 1867), pp. xii–xiv.

I. The Medieval Tower of Knowledge: from G. Reisch,
*Margarita Philosophica* (1508).

II. (i) Medals in honour of Guarino da Verona (by) Matteo de'Pisti) and Vittorino da Feltre (by Pisanello): from A. Chastel, *Age of Humanism* Thames and Hudson (1963).

II. (ii) Bishop Fox's College of Corpus Christi (the sixteenth-century buildings lie in the left background): from M. Williams, *Oxonia Depicta* (1733).

its elaborate ceremonial and ritual, came in for sharp criticism in Erasmus's *Praise of Folly*. Both merely echo an attitude which we find in Alberti's *Della Famiglia* (1434), and which as we have seen had become an essential part of Italian humanism: 'A gentleman without letters whatever his race will be taken for a rustic, and for myself I would wish to see young noblemen more often with a book in their hands than a sparrow hawk.'[1]

The old chivalric education had not aimed at producing a lettered aristocracy, and it had taken the renewed interest in the works of Cicero and Quintilian to reveal the unreality of the distinction that had grown up between the man of words and the man of action. The challenging of traditional concepts about the nature of nobility now produced, in the early sixteenth century, a new genre of didactic literature. Its origins lay in the medieval *De Regimine Principe* class of literature.[2] But whereas the medieval texts concentrated on an education expressed in terms of an ideal prince and emphasized the institutional basis of his power, those of the Renaissance widened their scope to include the education of those serving the prince, stressing the personal qualities of those who rule and showing a greater concern for the practical problems of government. In the Tudor shift from military to civil service the knight became the gentleman, and the term nobility tended to be replaced by gentility and civility. Yet the change in terminology should not be allowed to obscure the essential continuity of the discussion: 'a reconciliation of the old type with the new—the knightly with the civic and the scholarly—produced an ideal of personality, of the complete man of modern society, which stands for the final and harmonious picture of personality as the Renaissance had fashioned it.'[3] It is not surprising, then, that the schemes of education outlined in the literature found a place for training in horsemanship and 'feats of arms' alongside studies in philosophy, history, and law, though the reasons for the inclusion of such training had now changed. No longer was its purpose strictly vocational. Instead it was included as one of several parts each contributing in its own distinctive way to the

[1] Michel, op. cit., p. 200.
[2] Summarized in L. K. Born, op. cit., Chaps. iv and v.
[3] W. H. Woodward, *Studies* . . ., p. 245.

production of a 'well-rounded' man, later to be called 'the compleat gentleman'.

The new education as outlined in the literature of the day had, in fact, three parts to its curriculum. First were the 'exercises' already mentioned, the carry-over of the knightly ideal, horsemanship, skill in the use of arms, wrestling, dancing and so on. Second came the predominantly Italian emphasis on 'manners', and third, the newest aspect, were the 'studies', in moral and political philosophy, history, law, modern languages, mathematics, astronomy. The first strand in the recommended pattern had little practical expression in England, though Fortescue had described it as a part of the educational system at the fifteenth-century Inns of Court and Sir Humphrey Gilbert was to include it in the curriculum of his 'Queene Elizabethe's Achademy'. It achieved greater success, however, on the Continent in the Courtly Academies of the late sixteenth and seventeenth centuries. The other two strands, though distinguished for purposes of analysis, were, of course, closely interwoven and both might find a place in any one text of the period. On the other hand, each may be said to have its own epitome. The classic discussion of behaviour appropriate to the upper class was to be found in Baldassare Castiglione's *Il Cortegiano* (1528), describing life and manners of the Court of the Montefeltre, Dukes of Urbino, whilst Sir Thomas Elyot's *The Governour* (1531) served as the model exposition of studies for those who were to serve the prince. Each came to be the standard work in its respective field. Those that followed, and there were many such, merely continued the pattern set by Castiglione and Elyot, though more often than not with less skill. Together these two works provide the pattern of the scholar-gentleman, yet each had its own emphasis. For Castiglione chivalry was still the core of the matter, though of a social rather than a martial kind. His courtier was accomplished rather than learned, able to hold his own in the gallant company of the Court. Skilled as a lover in both the sensual and the Platonic senses, having a flair for the fine arts especially in poetry and music, he aimed to conceal his skill and accomplishments with an air of nonchalance. Castiglione described it as *sprezzatura*. Hoby translated it, misleadingly if not inaccurately, as 'recklessnesse'. A word coming closer to the sense of Castiglione would perhaps be 'effortlessness', a quality sought after by Renaissance painters no less than courtiers.[1] Refined delicacy, *urbanitas*, *galanterie*, these are the words which are most appropriate to Castiglione's courtier.

Elyot's concern was with a more sober character altogether, and he considered the sphere in which the subject moved as important as the subject himself. 'I have enterprised to describe in our vulgar tongue the form of a just public weal, which matter I have gathered as well of the sayings of most noble authors (Greeks and Latins) as by my own experience, I being continually trained, in some daily affairs of the public weal . . . almost from my childhood.' He goes on to explain that he writes 'to the intent that men which will be studious about the weal public may find the thing thereto expedient compendiously written. And for as much as the present book treateth of the education of them that hereafter may be deemed worthy to be governors of the public weal . . . I have therefore named it *The Governour*.'[2] Elyot's Governor was interested primarily in politics and ethics. Duty, responsibility, obligation, these were the key concepts. Seemly behaviour and the social graces, though they had a part in his life, were on a different level of importance. On the other hand, if a man like Sir William Cecil came nearest to the ideal which Elyot sought, Sidney, Spenser and Raleigh owe more to Castiglione. We would do well, however, to avoid emphasizing too much the differences between the two patterns of life and education: each had its part to play.[3]

As each text provided a model for behaviour so, too, each was followed by works in the same vein. *Il Cortegiano* was known in England in the original shortly after its publication in 1528, and was translated into English by Sir Thomas Hoby in 1561.[4] The Italian texts which followed Castiglione's were in their turn added to the growing number of translations of foreign works appearing in England. Della Casa's *Galateo* (1550) was

---

[1] Cf. R. J. Clements, 'Michaelangelo on Effort and Rapidity', *J.W.C.I.*, XVII (1954), pp. 301–10.

[2] *The Governour* (ed. H. H. S. Croft, two vols., 1883), I, cxci–cxcii.

[3] On what they had in common cf. Albert Menut, 'Castiglione and the Nichomachean Ethics', *P.M.L.A.*, LVIII (1942), pp. 309–21.

[4] Cf. Pearl Hogrefe, 'Elyot and "The Boke called Cortegiano in Ytalion" ', *M.P.*, XXVII (1929–30), pp. 301–9. Further editions of Hoby's translation appeared in 1577, 1588 and 1603, whilst a Latin translation by Bartholomew Clerke, first published in 1571, was reprinted in 1577, 1578, 1593, 1603 and 1612.

englished by Robert Peterson in 1576. William Pettie's translation in 1581 of the first three books of Guazzo's *La Civile Conversazione* (1574) was completed with a translation of the fourth by Bartholomew Young in 1586.[1] In 1595 appeared William Jones's *Nennio, or a Treatise of Nobilitie*, a translation from the Italian of Giovanni Battista Nenna, and this was followed three years later by John Keper's translation of Annibale Romei's *Discorsi* (1586) under the title of *The Courtier's Academy* (1598). Any refinements in the behaviour current in the Elizabethan Court owed their origin as much to literature of this sort as they did to the direct example of Italian visitors or of those Englishmen who had witnessed for themselves the court and city life in Italy.

In the same way the ideals expressed in Elyot's work were further spread by other texts which used his as a model. We find a common pattern in works such as the anonymous *Institucion of a Gentleman* (1555), Laurence Humphrey's *The Nobles: or of Nobilitie* (1563), Ascham's *Scholemaster* (1570), Lyly's *Euphues* (1580), and the long line of *Advices to a Son* which were generalized in works like James Cleland's *Institution of a Young Noble Man* (1607) and Henry Peacham's *The Compleat Gentleman* (1622). All agreed that the basis of true nobility lay in virtue and wisdom, acquired through the new education and applied to the service of 'the publicke weal'. An educated governing class had become essential to the welfare of the State, and each writer in one degree of detail or another put forward the sorts of studies appropriate to such a situation. Humphrey's may stand as example for them all. After stressing the need for instruction in grammar, rhetoric, logic and 'civility of manners' he goes on:—

> But since in a nobleman tendeth to a common weal wear he with daily and nightly study Aristotle's and other writings of civil knowledge, know he the country's ordinances, laws and manners (together) with the foreign states. . . . Read he also all writers of nobility, Erasmus *The Institution of a Christian Prince*, Sturmius's learned *Nobility* . . . and almost all Plutarch's works, in them as mirrors to see himself. . . . The neighbour study to this is

[1] For the widespread influence of Guazzo on English life and letters cf. J. Lievsay, *Stefano Guazzo and the English Renaissance, 1575–1675* (North Carolina, 1959).

historical knowledge, many ways available . . . be he also skilful in the *Chronicles* of his country . . . and both all antiquity and the law and statues of our own realm wherein so skilful ought he to be as he dare professeth. . . . The Mathematicals have their manifold profit; arithmetic can he not waste. Geometry much helpeth to placing, planning and conceiving of buildings. Great delight and profit bringeth Geography . . . and astrology (i.e. Astronomy).[1]

We have seen how the stream of ideas flowed into England from Italy, how what has been called civic humanism, classically expressed in the writings of Bruni and Alberti, was assimilated in those of Elyot; how the refinements of court life, characteristic of late fifteenth-century Italy, became known in England largely by way of translations; above all how it came to be recognized, though not without opposition, that an educated governing class, made ready by its education to serve the prince and the common weal, was a prime need in the modern State as it was developing during the sixteenth century.

The question must now be asked, how and where did this new class get its new education? The answer would seem obvious: in the existing institutions of learning, the grammar schools, the universities, the Inns of Court. When the admissions Registers and histories of these institutions are examined this indeed is what we find. More and more the sons of the gentry are sent to these places, so much so indeed that Latimer, Ascham and others complain that no longer is there a place for the poor scholar.[2] It was a trend which has been seen as being of incalculable benefit to the nation, one which was responsible in Elizabethan times for a House of Commons whose quality surpassed all its predecessors.[3] But a second question still remains. Did these sons of the gentry and nobility in fact receive at these institutions the special kind of education which was now considered necessary for the future man of affairs? The new ideas undoubtedly arrived in England. Did they have any appreciable effect on the existing institutions of education? To this problem we must now turn.

[1] *The Nobles*, Sigs. Y v–vi.
[2] Cf. Corrie, op. cit., p. 179, and Ascham's letter to Cranmer, 1547, in Strype, *Memorials of Thomas Cranmer* (Oxford, 1840), I, 242–3.
[3] A. L. Rowse, *The England of Elizabeth* (1950), p. 503; J. E. Neale, *The Elizabethan House of Commons* (1949), Chap. xv.

## Part Two

FORMAL EDUCATION

# IV

<hr>

# The Grammar Schools

<hr>

W E have seen the importance attached to grammar schools by the humanists. The Tudor sovereigns, too, expressed their zeal for these institutions, though for very different reasons. Yet the traditional picture of schooling in Renaissance England is curiously two-faced. On the one hand the Reformation enacted by Henry VIII and his son Edward VI has been described as being responsible for the crippling of school education in England by the dissolution of educational institutions based on monastic and other religious houses as well as on chantries and gilds. Yet on the other, the large number of grammar schools bearing the names of these sovereigns is cited to show that they were personally active in providing essential patronage for the spread of grammar school education.

The first view was formulated by A. F. Leach in his *English Schools at the Reformation* (1896) and *Schools of Medieval England* (1915), and has been widely accepted by historians of the period.[1] It was based on the assumption that education in the pre-Reformation period was provided by the secular cathedrals and collegiate churches together with the private

[1] What follows is based largely on the studies of Joan Simon, 'A. F. Leach on the Reformation', *B.J.E.S.*, III (1954/5), pp. 128–43 and IV (1955/6), pp. 32–48, and 'The Reformation and English Education', *Past and Present*, No. 11 (1957), pp. 48–65; cf. W. N. Chaplin, 'A. F. Leach: a reappraisal, *B.J.E.S.*, XI (1962–3), pp. 99–124, and J. Simon, 'A. F. Leach: a reply', ibid., XII (1963–4), pp. 41–50.

endowments of chantry, social gild, and priest's service. The monastic contribution he discounted, so that almost all the damage was done as a result of the chantry legislation of Edward VI, when schools were 'swept away . . . or if not swept away, plundered or damaged'.[1]

Leach was able to arrive at this conclusion in the first place by exaggerating the amount of schooling provided in the secular cathedrals and collegiate churches, which by the end of the fifteenth century were but a shadow of their former selves as educational and cultural centres. As to the chantry legislation, Leach was particularly guilty of special pleading. He ignored to a very large degree the *intent* of the chantry legislation to amend the 'great part of superstition and errors in Christian religion' by converting chantry endowments 'to good and Godly uses, as in the erecting of grammar schools, to the education of youth in virtue and godliness, the augmenting of the universities and the better provision of the poor and needy'.[2] To that purpose the Commissioners sent out to effect the dissolution were especially enjoined to note any endowments devoted to the poor and to education, and particularly to report on any chantry priests engaged in teaching, whether enjoined by their endowment to do so or not. True, the intent of a piece of legislation is not necessarily its execution and this was true of the dissolution legislation, yet (as Mrs. Simon has shown) where teaching was taking place this was duly noted and provision made for the school to be 'continued', with a fixed stipend for the teacher paid by the Crown, and with no religious duties attached. Indeed the Commissioners went further and recommended the setting up of schools where none had existed before, as at Newent in Gloucester, or advised the transference of endowments, from Week St. Mary, for example, where 'the said school is in decay by reason it standeth in a desolate place', to Launceston which was in need of a well-endowed school. At Liverpool, again, though they found the school not being kept according to the foundation, they nevertheless granted a stipend.[3] More important than these, however, were the many cases

[1] *English Schools at the Reformation*, I, 6.

[2] 1 Edward VI c. 14 in A. F. Leach, *Educational Charters and Documents* (Cambridge, 1911), pp. 472–3.

[3] *E.S.R.*, II, 83, 33–35 and 40–41, 115–16, 120 and 125.

where local inhabitants bought back or were granted the land or rents of the former endowment for the upkeep of a school, often with the same master, a supplemented endowment and a reorganized curriculum set out in statutes. At Ipswich the burgesses had been running a school since 1477. The foundation which Wolsey was in process of setting up, however, was dissolved and was ultimately taken over by the Corporation in 1566 after the master had been 'continued'. At Stafford the dissolution of both the Collegiate Church of St. Mary and the chantry of Thomas Countre resulted in the continuance of the chantry schoolmaster, Humphrey Peckenham, and the setting up in 1550 of 'the Free Grammar School of King Edward VI' at the instance of the newly-incorporated borough, with further endowment to provide for two masters. In the same way, the 'Free Grammar School of King Edward VI' at Shrewsbury (1552) was financed from the tithes of the dissolved colleges of St. Mary and St. Chad at the instance of the 'Bailiffs, Burgesses and inhabitants of the town'.[1] The King Edward VI grammar school at East Retford originated with a chantry of Thomas Gunthorpe, parson of Bosworth, 'in agreement with the bailiffs and burgesses of Retford' (1518). At the dissolution, with the help of Robert Holgate, Archbishop of York, the borough petitioned to receive a grant of the lands of the former chantry towards a re-endowment of the school, which was completely reorganized with detailed statutes drawn up by Holgate himself. In some cases, even, the chantry lands were bought back by the locality without any further official refoundation, as at Ilminster, Leeds, Towcester and Little Waltham.[2]

The same pattern appears in connexion with the disolution of those abbeys which were patrons of the local grammar school. At the dissolution of the abbey of St. Albans, for instance, the local inhabitants, led by the former abbot, petitioned for and obtained a private Act of Parliament to reconstitute the school which would be governed by the newly-enfranchised borough (1553). After the dissolution of the abbey at Reading the

[1] I. E. Gray and W. E. Potter, *Ipswich School 1400–1950* (Ipswich, 1950), pp. 31–33; C. G. Gilmore, *History of the King Edward VI School Stafford* (Oxford, 1953); pp. 13–14; J. B. Oldham, *History of Shrewsbury School 1552–1952* (Oxford, 1952), p. 4.

[2] Carlisle, II, 280; *V.C.H. Somerset*, II, 451; *V.C.H. Yorks.*, I, 457; *V.C.H. Northants.*, II, 227–9; *V.C.H. Essex*, II, 553.

patronage of the school came to the Crown, which granted letters patent to Leonard Cox, the master, in person, the rights being transferred to the town in 1562. The historian of Westminster School has described the dissolution as 'a blessing in disguise', which inaugurated a new era in the life of the school, first under Alexander Nowell and then under Nicholas Udall.[1]

Also inquired into under the terms of the Chantry Acts were those pre-Reformation schools which had been endowed by a social gild, as at Stratford, Ludlow, Louth, Chipping Norton or Saffron Walden. In these cases we find the schools reconstituted either under the aegis of the newly-enfranchised borough, or under the reconstituted gild itself acting as a corporation in its own right. In the same way schools such as Walthamstow, Cromer, Stockport, and Horsham, whose original endowment by City Companies were associated with a chantry or priest's service, were now freed of their former association and continued under the supervision of the Company.[2]

In all these various ways, then, means were found, where a demand existed, to maintain continuity and improve existing provision. In addition, however, Leach failed to take into account the growth of purely lay-sponsored education which, as we have seen, had begun to gather momentum in the fifteenth century and which continued with added strength throughout the sixteenth century. Of the newer schools in the early part of the sixteenth century, Stephen Jennyngs' foundation at Wolverhampton (c. 1512) was placed under the control of the Merchant Taylors Company. The school at Bridgnorth (Salop) was already, in 1503, in the hands of the local Court of Burgesses. In 1512 John Colet's school at St. Paul's, a rival to that run by the Dean and Chapter, was placed under the control of the Mercer's Company, for (as the founder said) he found 'less corruption in a body of married lay men like the Mercers than in any other order or degree of mankind'.[3] Such activity, untouched by the chantry legislation, was continued after the Reformation. Schools were founded by merchants like Sir Andrew Judd, skinner, at Tonbridge (1553), Lawrence Sheriff,

---

[1] *V.C.H. Herts.*, II, 56–57; *V.C.H. Berks.*, II, 245ff; L. E. Tanner, *Westminster School: a History* (1934), p. 4.

[2] *E.S.R.*, II, 185–6, 234–5, 239–40, 243–4; *V.C.H. Essex*, II, 522.

[3] G. P. Mander, *History of Wolverhampton Grammar School* (Wolverhampton, 1913); Carlisle, II, 340; Allen, No. 1211, IV, 518.

grocer, at Rugby (1567), and Peter Blundell, wool merchant, at Tiverton (1599), and by lawyers like Sir Roger Chomeley at Highgate (1562), Richard Lord Rich at Felsted (1564), Roger Marwood at Sandwich (1563) and Sir Anthony Browne at Brentwood (1557). Others owed their foundation to clerics such as Matthew Parker at Rochdale (1565), James Pilkington at Rivington (1566), and Alexander Nowell at Middleton (1572), whilst the Rev. Thomas Alleyn provided for the triple foundation of Uttoxeter, Stone and Stevenage in 1558.

Many of these schools sought and received a charter from the sovereign, and it was this practice which has given rise to the legend of the Tudor patrons of education. We have seen how many King Edward VI grammar schools arose out of local initiative. In the same way the title of 'the Free Grammar School of Queen Elizabeth at Ashbourne' (Derbyshire) hides the fact that its Charter was obtained, in 1585, 'at the instance of Sir Thomas Cockaine of Ashbourne, knight, William Bradbourne of the Lee, Thomas Carter of the Middle Temple, with Thomas Hurt and William Jackson of Ashbourne and other persons inhabiting the same town'. Similarly the Queen Elizabeth's Grammar School at Rivington owed its foundation to the energies of James Pilkington, the first Protestant bishop of Durham, who provided the school with its own detailed statutes.[1]

Leach's picture, then, may be faulted on these two counts, namely that many schools which came within the purview of the commissioners were in fact 'continued' and improved, and that even then there was a parallel stream of lay foundations untouched by the chantry legislation. In addition he grossly overstrained the evidence for the existence of particular grammar schools in the Middle Ages. More important than this, however, he ignored the fact that the reformers themselves were passionately interested in education and well-recognized the value of schools in the propagating of their ideas. Sir Walter Mildmay, the Surveyor-General of the whole chantry operation, was intimately involved in the schools of his own county of Essex, as well as being the founder of Emmanuel College, Cambridge,

---

[1] N. J. Frangopulo, *The History of Queen Elizabeth's Grammar School, Ashbourne, 1585–1935* (Ashbourne, 1939), p. 23; M. Kay, *The History of Rivington and Blackrod Grammar School* (Manchester, 1931), Appendices I and II.

devised expressly for the training of clergy and destined to become the centre of Puritan ideas in Elizabethan Cambridge. Far from 'crippling' schools, the Reformation put many of them on a more solid foundation by placing them in the hands of a middle class which provided the chief demand and had an interest in their survival.

It also produced a lay teaching profession, in the sense that the teacher was no longer responsible for the religious observances of the chantry priest. Yet if the organization was secular, the aim was undoubtedly and increasingly more precisely religious. The accepted connexion in the minds of both Romans and Reformers between religion and education was made explicit in a variety of ways: by the statutory enactments of the Tudor sovereigns, the diocesan injunctions to parish vicars and curates, the episcopal licensing of teachers, and the detailed injunctions and prescriptions with which individual grammar schools were surrounded by their statutes and ordinances.[1] Founders went farther than the mere inclusion of phrases such as 'good manners and godly behaviour' or 'virtue and learning' in their statutes. They prescribed regular attendance at church and the saying of daily prayers, and included explicit instructions to the master that the children were to be taught the Lord's Prayer, the Ten Commandments, the Catechism and the like. Archbishop Holgate, indeed, went so far as to compose his own prayers for the children of East Retford and to include them in the statutes of the school.[2] The gentlemen petitioning the Queen to sanction the founding of the grammar school at Ashbourne cited as the first of their reasons that 'the said town of Ashbourne is situate in the Peak of the county of Derby, a very rude county utterly void of preachers to teach either young or old their duties either to God or Her Majesty and therefore in great need of schools for the good bringing up of youth'; and went on to show that:

> for want of schools the youth of that county follow the old tradition of men and rather cleave to papistry, than to truth of the gospel. . . . For want of schools they know not God nor Her Majesty's laws, but are given over to wickedness and vices such as swearing, drunkenness, whoredom, idleness and such like to the great dis-

[1] For Catholic education cf. A. C. F. Beales, *Education Under Penalty* (1963).
[2] Carlisle, II, 282. Bishop Pilkington did the same for Rivington Grammar School, J. Whitaker, *Statutes and Charter of Rivington School* (1837), pp. 165–6.

pleasure of God, contempt of Her Highness and to the great damage and hurt of the Commonwealth.[1]

It is not surprising that the Queen lent her name to the foundation of men who could juxtapose God's and Her Majesty's laws, who recognized the grammar school as a nursery of 'preachers to teach' and who, on top of all, were willing to provide the money for such a foundation. The case became even more attractive when the masters at these schools could be bound not only by subscription to the Act of Uniformity and the licensing and oversight by the ordinary of the diocese, but also by an oath such as the master of Kirkby Stephen School was bound by in 1566:–

> I do swear by the content of this book that I shall freely without exacting any money diligently instruct and teach the children of this parish and all others that resort unto me, in grammar and other humane doctrine according to the statutes thereof made, and I shall not read to them any corrupt doctrine, or reprobate books or work set forth at any time contrary to the determination of the universal catholic church, whereby they may be infected on their youth in any kind of heresy or corrupt doctrine or else be induced to insolent way of living, and further shall observe all the statutes and ordinances of this school. . . .

The statues themselves go on to enjoin that he shall especially instruct his young scholars 'in good manners, well and comely, and from all maner of theft, lying, swearing and filthy talking he shall restrain; and also to his scholars he shall interpret and read those authors which may induce them and lead them to virtue, goodliness and honest behaviour and the knowledge of humanity, but not to wantoness or sauciness'.[2]

This kind of prescription was regularly included in school statutes, irrespective of denomination. Sir Andrew Judd's statutes for Tonbridge School (1553) in the reign of Mary insisted that the master be 'whole in body, well reported, Master of Arts in degree (if it may be) . . . and by examination found meet both for his learning and his dexterities in teaching as also for his honest conversation (i.e. good moral character) and for right undertaking of God's true religion now set forth by public authority whereunto he shall stir and move his scholars', a prescription which was almost exactly matched by the 1559

[1] Frangopulo, op. cit., p. 26.    [2] Carlisle, II, 715 and 717.

Injunctions of Elizabeth 'that no man shall take upon him to teach, but such as shall be allowed by the ordinary (of the diocese) and found meet as well for his learning and dexterity in teaching as for sober and honest conversation, and also for right understanding of God's true religion . . . (and) that all teachers of children shall stir and move them to do reverence to God's true religion now truly set forth by the proper authority'.[1] The particular case of Richard Lord Rich provides a good example of Tudor capacity for compromise in education and religion. The first Chancellor of the Court of Augmentations in 1536, it was as Lord Chancellor that he affixed the Great Seal to the foundation deed of the grammar school at Bury St. Edmunds in 1550. In the reign of Mary, whom he served in a variety of capacities, he set up a chantry for the poor at Felsted to replace the dissolved Holy Trinity Gild, and under Elizabeth (1564) converted it into the foundation for a lay grammar school with additional endowments, to provide the basis of the present Felsted School.[2]

The picture of English schools at the Reformation and after cannot yet be filled in with systematic accuracy. Detailed research, county by county, will be necessary before this will be possible. Yet the outlines of that picture would seem to show educational provision in many cases surviving the chantry legislation and on an improved basis, but in any case being constantly reinforced and renewed by lay foundations which reflected the general trend of secularization in philanthropy as a whole. Professor Jordan's work has already made it clear, for example, that previous estimates of the number of schools which were founded or refounded in the latter half of the sixteenth and early part of the seventeenth centuries have been far too low.[3] As to the schools themselves, they were no longer primarily nurseries for the priesthood, though of course their pupils included sons of clerics and others who were destined

---

[1] D. C. Somervell, *A History of Tonbridge School* (1957), p. 16; W. H. Frere, ed., *Visitation Articles and Injunctions of the Period of the Reformation* (1910), III, 21.

[2] M. Craze, *A History of Felsted School, 1564–1949* (Ipswich, 1955), pp. 20–23, 27–28.

[3] W. K. Jordan, *Philanthropy in England 1480–1660* (1959), pp. 279–92, cf. P. J. Wallis, 'A Register of Old Yorkshire Grammar Schools'. *Researches and Studies*, No. 13 (1956), pp. 64–104.

Th:Eliott Knight

III. Sir Thomas Elyot by Hans Holbein the Younger (Original in
Windsor Castle, Crown copyright Reserved).

IV. (i) Sir Thomas More by
Hans Holbein the Younger.
(Frick Collection,
New York.)

IV. (ii) Erasmus by Hans
Holbein the Younger.
(Kunstmuseum, Basel.)

for holy orders. The out-moding of chivalric education meant that the sons of the nobility were now, for the most part, taught by private tutors in their own homes, yet increasingly the sons of the squirearchy, of lawyers, and of merchants were, together with the traditional group of 'poor and needy scholars', filling the grammar schools, sometimes, it was complained, to the detriment of the latter.

Not all grammar schools were of equal status in this respect, of course. Bess of Hardwick and her second husband, Sir William Cavendish, sent their sons to Eton, whilst Sir Philip Sidney and Fulke Greville were pupils together at Shrewsbury, 'the largest school in England' as Camden described it in 1586. Camden himself was a pupil at the greatest of London schools, St. Paul's; so was Thomas Lupset, protégé of Thomas Cromwell, and so, too, that other Tudor antiquary, John Leland. With Sidney and Greville at Shrewsbury were the sons of the old Shropshire families of Jasper More, Roger Charlton, Thomas Corbett, Andrew Sandford and so on. And alongside the sons of the gentry at Repton we find Charles Hope, son of a yeoman, John Bancroft, son of a husbandman, Gilbert Barton, son of a carpenter, and others of like degree. Thomas Wolsey, butcher's son, was a pupil at Ipswich School before, in more prosperous times, he planned its refoundation. Samuel Harsnett, son of a baker and later Archbishop of York, had his early schooling at Colchester Grammar School. Not far away Chelmsford Grammar School included amongst its pupils Philemon Holland, 'translator general of the age', and John Dee, scientist, astrologer and alchemist. Unfortunately school registers and admissions books for the period are few, and those of the smaller rural grammar schools have not survived, if indeed they were ever kept with any degree of continuity. School histories, too, tend to concern themselves only with their most famous pupils. Fortunately, however, the admissions books of St. John's College and of Gonville and Caius, which alone record the status of their students' parents, provide ample evidence of the sons of yeomen, husbandmen and tradesfolk going up to Cambridge from their local grammar schools alongside the sons of the gentry and mercantile aristocracy.[1]

[1] H. G. Maxwell-Lyte, *A History of Eton College* (1889), pp. 152–3; Oldham, op. cit., pp. 6–7; R. B. Gardiner, *Admissions Registers of St. Paul's School* (1884),

The usual age of entry into the grammar school was six or seven, though of course this varied. More often than not, too, qualifications of literacy were imposed as a condition of entry. Eton's statutes required 'a competent knowledge of reading and the grammar of Donatus and of plain song'. When he founded St. Paul's school in 1509 Colet insisted that the master 'must first see they know the Catechism and also that he [*sic*] can read and write competently, else let him not be admitted in no wise', a requirement that was included almost *verbatim* in the statutes of Merchant Taylors' School (1561). The refoundation statutes of Canterbury Grammar School (1541) were even more precise in their ordering that 'No one shall be admitted into the school who cannot read readily, or does not know by heart in the vernacular the Lord's Prayer, the Angelic Salutation, the Apostle's Creed and the Ten Commandments. Those who are wholly ignorant of grammar shall learn the accidents of nouns and verbs as it were out of class. When they have learned these they shall be taken into the first class.' Similarly, Sir Nicholas Bacon's statutes for St. Albans Grammar School (1570) went so far as to insist that 'none shall be admitted into this school but such as have learned the accidence without book and can write indifferently'.[1]

This latter requirement, however, was exceptional, and generally the 'petties', as these younger pupils were called, would be those 'coming to learn the figures and characters of letters until such time as they can read perfectly, and sound and pronounce their words distinctly'.[2] Traditionally such education as was required before starting on the grammar course proper would generally be provided outside the grammar school either by the parish priest or, when directed to do so as part of the endowment, by the chantry priest. In 1520, however, Robert Sherborne, Bishop of Chichester, advised the master of his

[1] Maxwell-Lyte, op. cit., pp. 581–2; Lupton, *Life of Colet*, p. 227; H. B. Wilson, *A History of Merchant Taylors School* (1812), I, 16; Leach, *Educational Charters*, p. 465; Carlisle, I, 517.

[2] Guisborough (Yorks.) Statutes, 1561, cited by T. W. Baldwin, *Shakespeare's Small Latine and Less Greeke* (Urbana, 1944), I, 430.

pp. 18–19; Gray and Potter, op. cit., p. 14; *V.C.H. Essex*, II, 504–5 and 52; M. Messiter, *Repton School Register, 1557–1910* (1910); J. E. B. Mayor, *Admissions to the College of St. John* (1882); J. A. Venn and S. C. Venn, *Admissions to Gonville and Caius* (1887).

foundation at Rolleston in Staffordshire to encourage his brighter pupils 'so that they may act as pupil teachers, to teach small boys who may be brought to him the alphabet and first rudiments', a practice which Bishop Oldham's trustees followed in their statutes for Manchester Grammar School (1525), and one which was virtually inevitable in the small rural grammar school.[1] The new statutes of Bury St. Edmunds School could still insist, in 1550: 'let them seek elsewhere the ability to read and write. Let ours give nothing but the rules of grammar and the learning of the Latin and Greek tongue'; but Bishop Pilkington was being more realistic when he acknowledged, in his statutes for Rivington (1566), that 'though it is to be wished that none be admitted to the schools but that can read, yet in great need the usher shall teach such to read and learn the Short Catechism in English as have not learned it . . . (and) if the number of petties that learn to read be more than the usher can well teach, some of the eldest scholars by course may be appointed by the master and governors to help him'.[2]

The writing school within Christ's Hospital, with its writing master and two teachers of the petties, was exceptional, as was Ruthin's prize of 'a silver pen to him that excels other in writing well'.[3] The second half of the century did, however, see a general improvement in provision for this level of schooling, particularly in the appointment of ushers specifically charged with the teaching of petties, though as might be expected such instruction came low in the order of priorities. At the King's School, Peterborough, for example, 'All such as cannot write' were to 'learn to write two hours that (Saturday) afternoon and in like manner every day one hour if it may be spared, as betwixt eleven and twelve or twelve and one'. At Kirkby Stephen writing lessons were confined to 'holidays and half-holidays', at Houghton-le-Spring 'on playing days and after supper', and at Heighington on 'festival days and other convenient times', when the master was to set them copies without extra salary or pay. William Dugard, the master of Colchester

[1] A. F. Leach, *The Schools of Medieval England* (1915), p. 289; A. A. Mumford, *Manchester Grammar School* (Manchester, 1919), p. 479.

[2] *V.C.H. Suffolk*, II, 314; Whitaker, op. cit., pp. 206–7.

[3] E. H. Pearce, *Annals of Christ's Hospital School* (2nd edition, 1908), pp. 146ff; L. S. Knight, *Welsh Independent Grammar Schools to 1600* (Newtown, 1926), p. 120.

Grammar School managed to get the best of both worlds. 'If any desire to write, my course is to take 20s. in hand and for that 20s. to teach (at by-times not hindering their progress in other learning) so many several hands as they will learn so long as they come to school'.[1]

The size of the school was, of course, a factor of importance here. The smaller schools, inadequately endowed, inevitably found themselves ill-equipped to meet the needs of their pupils, and it was these schools and their pupils which Mulcaster had in mind when he criticized the teaching of petties in his *Positions* (1581), and when he produced his *Elementarie* in the following year. By the end of the century, however, most grammar schools of any size would have an usher 'able at least to teach the introduction of grammar and inferior Latin books to the first two forms, as also to teach English books and fair writing, cyphering and casting accounts, the better to train up the young beginners in the ABC, Primer, Catechism and such other English books whereby they may attain to the perfect reading of the English tongue'.[2] It would be more generally accepted, too, that 'the letter is the first and simplest impression in the trade of teaching and nothing before it. The knitting and jointing whereof groweth on very infinitely as it appeareth most plainly by daily spelling and continual reading, till partly by use and partly by argument the child gets the habit and cunning to read well, which being once gotten what a cluster of commodities doth it bring withal'. The necessary division of labour was even recognized in episcopal licences which began to distinguish between those teachers licensed *ad instruendum puerorum in literis grammaticalibus* and those *in facultate legendi et scribendi*.[3]

More attention, then, was being paid to the teaching of the Three R's, though, of the three, arithmetic—'cyphering and casting of accounts'—was not yet generally considered essential in this context. Nor were the drawing and music which Mulcaster included in his *Elementarie*. The reason is not far to seek, for this pre-grammar school education, like its counterpart in

---

[1] *V.C.H. Northants*, II, 209; Carlisle II, 718; *V.C.H. Durham*, I, 395 and 399; *V.C.H. Essex*, II, 505.

[2] Aldenham Statutes, 1600, *V.C.H. Herefordshire*, II, 84.

[3] R. H. Quick ed., *Positions by Richard Mulcaster* (1818), pp. 233ff and 256; W. E. Tate, 'Episcopal Licensing of Schoolmasters in England', *Church Quarterly Review*, CLVII (1956), pp. 426–32.

the quite separate 'elementary schools' of the eighteenth and nineteenth centuries, was basically religious in aim. The immediate and perhaps most important purpose of learning the arts of reading and writing was to enable the child to master the elements of his religious life, the Lord's Prayer, the Ten Commandments, the Creed and the Seven Sacraments. The first of these would be included with the alphabet and syllables on that most ancient of educational apparatus, the Horn Book. Later this developed into the small printed booklet, whose title *An ABC with Catechism* covered a wide variety of compilations and which often included a selection of graces before and after meals and various admonitions to virtuous living. This became, in its various forms, the child's primer, and served both as an elementary reading book and as a first book of religious instruction, providing at the same time a convenient gathering together of prayers for adults with no great claim to education.[1] The primer proper shed the ABC section and became the printed counterpart of the medieval Book of Hours, of which *A Goodly Prymer in Englishe* (1535), *The Manual of Prayers or the Primer in Engliysh and Laten* (1539) and *The Prymer in Englyshe and Latyn set forth by the King's Majestie* (1545) are typical examples. These rather more substantial volumes of religious education and exercise included a calendar, an almanack for finding the dates of Easter and other movable feasts, the Little Office of Our Lady, the seven Penitential Psalms, the Litany of the Saints, etc., to which basic structure would be added other liturgical and popular devotions. With the Reformation these were largely replaced by the Book of Common Prayer, whilst catechetical instruction came to be finally standardized in Alexander Nowell's *Catechism*, first published in Latin in 1570, translated into English in the same year by Thomas Norton, into Greek in 1573 by William Whitaker, and suitably abridged into the *Smaller* and *Middle Catechism* soon after. The various forms of Nowell's work soon replaced the catechisms of the earlier Reformation, including that of Calvin which had been translated into English in 1566. They were expressly enjoined upon all schoolmasters

---

[1] One has been printed in facsimile, E. S. Shuckburgh, ed. *The ABC Both in Latyn and in Englysshe* (1889); cf. C. C. Butterworth, 'Early Primers for the Use of Children', *Papers of the Bibliographical Society of America*, XLIII (1949), pp. 374–82.

in the Canons of 1571 and repeated in those of 1603, and were prescribed in many school statutes of the period.[1]

The Tudor sovereigns and their advisers were thus well aware of the importance of early religious training and made provision accordingly. Educationists, too, were recognizing the importance of a sound grounding in the elements of the English language, not merely as a part of religious education, nor indeed simply as an essential precursor to the grammar school course, but also as part of the wider movement which sought to elevate the English language as a medium of literary expression, with the attendant problems of standardizing spelling and pronunciation. Mulcaster's *Elementarie* (1582) which starts as a treatise on the teaching of reading and writing, becomes a detailed defence of the English language and an analysis of its basic characteristics and possibilities.

> Some be of the opinion that we should not write of any philosophic argument . . . in our English tongue because the unlearned understand it not, the learned esteem it not, as a thing of difficulty to the one and no delight to the other. For both the penning in English generally and my own penning in this order, I have this to say. No one tongue is more fine than other naturally, but by industry of the speaker, which upon occasion offered by the government wherein he liveth endeavoureth himself to garnish it with eloquence and to enrich it with learning. The use of such a tongue, so eloquent for speech and so learned for matter, while it keeps itself within the natural soil, it both serves the own turn with great admiration and kindles in the foreign which came to knowledge it a great desire to resemble the like.

He calls, too, for 'a perfit English dictionarie' in which would be gathered 'all the words which we use in our English tongue whether material or incorporate, out of all professions, as well learned as not, and besides the right writing, which is incident to the alphabet, would open into as therein both their natural force and proper use', and as an earnest of which he himself

---

[1] Cf. C. C. Butterworth, *The English Primers 1529–45* (Philadelphia, 1953); H. C. White, *Tudor Books of Private Devotion* (Madison, 1951), and E. Birchenough, 'The Prymer in English', *The Library*, 4th Series, XVII (1937–8), pp. 177–94; G. E. Currie, ed., *A. Cathechism written in Latin . . . with the same translated into English by Thomas Norton* (Parker Society, Cambridge, 1853); A. M. Stowe, *English Grammar Schools in the Reign of Queen Elizabeth* (New York, 1908), pp. 110ff.

provides a list of nearly ten thousand words 'as may easily direct our general writing'.[1]

Mulcaster was by no means original in his concern for the teaching of reading and his recognition of the wider problems it involved. Earlier systematic discussions are provided in John Hart's *Orthographie, Conteyning the Due Order and Reason How to Write or Printe the Image of Manne's Voice Most Like to the Life or Nature* (1569) which he followed with *A Methode or Comfortable Beginning for All Unlearned Whereby They May Bee Taught to Reade English in a Very Short Time with Pleasure* (1570), the latter including a pictorial alphabet, and 'in a great letter the Christian belief, the ten commandments of God, and the Lord's Prayer, where the syllables are sundered for the ease of all learners old and young'.[2] At a lower level were works such as Thomas Newbery's *Booke in Englysh Metre After the Great Marchaunt Man Called Dives Pragmaticus, very pretty for children to rede whereby they may the better and more readyer rede and wryte wares and implements in this world contayned* (1563) in which men of various trades and occupations come to the shop of Dives Pragmaticus to buy his wares, the names and spelling of which he provides in metrical form, with a good ration of mild humour:–

> I have ladels, scummers, aundryons and spits,
> Dripping pannes, pothookes, ould cats and kits
> And pretty fine dogs without fleas or nits.
> What lack you my friend? Come hither to me.[3]

William Bullokar's *Amendment of Orthographie for English Speech* (1580), on the other hand, was an attempt at a standardized pronunciation and notation of these sounds in the Roman, Italian, Chancery and Secretary hands, which he followed up with phonetically-rendered translations of the Psalter, Aesop's *Fables* and Cato's *Distichs* (1585).

---

[1] E. T. Campagnac, ed., *The First Part of the Elementarie* (Oxford, 1925), pp. 267 and 187. For Ascham's contribution to the discussion cf. L. V. Ryan, *Roger Ascham* (1963), pp. 279ff.

[2] Both the *Orthographie* and the *Methode* are reprinted in B. Danielsson, *John Hart's Works on English Orthography and Pronunciation* (Stockholm, 1955); cf. E. J. Dobson, *English Pronunciation, 1500–1700* (Oxford, 1957).

[3] John Rylands Facsimiles, No. 2 (Manchester, 1910), Sig. A iiii *verso*.

The first attempt to discuss the whole range of petty instruction was Francis Clement's *Petie Schole with an English Ortho-graphy, wherein by rules lately prescribed as taught a method to enable both a childe to read perfectly within one moneth and also the imperfect to write English aright. Hereto newly added 1. verie necessorie precepts and patterns of writing the secretary and Romane hands. 2. to number by letters and figures. 3. to cast accompts* (1587). Like the first part of William Kempe's *Education of Children in Learning* (1588) and the whole of Edmund Coote's *The English Schoolmaster* (1596), Clement's work was a thoroughly practical manual for those who taught reading, writing, spelling and arithmetic and even goes so far as to give instructions for the making of ink and the correct way to choose a quill and cut it. Significantly, Mulcaster, Kempe and Coote were all masters of grammar schools, Mulcaster at Merchant Taylors', Kempe at Plymouth and Coote at Bury St. Edmunds, and the care with which the method of teaching the petties is detailed is a further reminder of the growing recognition of the importance of the elementary stages of education in the vernacular, half a century and more before the followers of Comenius were at work in this country. Coote's book was so popular that it reached a twenty-fifth edition in 1635 and a fifty-fourth in 1737. It made use of a full range of pedagogical techniques, from the use of dialogue and recapitulation to graded reading exercises (complete with moral content) at the end of each chapter. One such exercise was 'this speech made only of the words taught before':–

> Boy, go thy way up to the top of the hill and get
> me home the bay nag, fill him well and see he be fat,
> and I will rid me of him, for he will be but dull, as
> his dam, yet if a man bid well for him I will tell
> him of it, if not I do but rob him and so God will
> vex me and may let me go to hell . . .
>
> I met a man by the way this day who when he saw me
> hit me a blow that it did swell, for that I did not stir
> my cap when I did meet him.[1]

[1] E. Coote, *The English Schoolmaster* (1596), pp. 5 and 7; cf. B. Daniellson, 'A Note on Edmund Coote; Prolegomena for a critical edition of Coote's "English Schoolmaster" ', *Studia Neophilologica*, XXXII (1960), pp. 228–40, and J. W. Adamson, *The Illiterate Anglo-Saxon* (Cambridge, 1946), pp. 56–57.

More advanced reading exercises are provided in the form of a short Catechism, a prayer, various graces before meals, and extracts from the Bible and the Psalms, the treatise concluding with a short section on arithmetic and an alphabetically arranged vocabulary with instructions on how to find words in it.

This kind of education continued almost inevitably in the grammar school proper, statutes and reluctant 'grammarians' notwithstanding. John Brinsley, master of the grammar school of Ashby-de-la-Zouch (Leics.), writing in 1612, made it clear that:—

> it is an extreme vexation that we must be toiled among such little pettys and in teaching of such matters, whereof we shall get no profit, nor take any delight in our labours . . . it were much to be wished that none ought to be admitted to the grammar school until they were able to read the New Testament perfectly and that they were in their Accidences or meet to enter, . . . (indeed) there might be some other school in the town for those little ones to enter them. It would help some poor man or woman who knew not how to live otherwise and who might do well if they were rightly directed . . . yet nothwithstanding where it cannot be redressed it must be born with patience and wisdom as a heavy burden.[1]

But the aim always was to get on with the real business of the day, the study of Latin grammar—'the portal of all knowledge whatsoever', as Aeneas Sylvius had called it. In his *Regulae Grammaticales* (c. 1418), Guarino had described it as 'the art of speaking correctly and writing properly and of reading with understanding the work of (Latin) prose writers and poets', and this was the prize sought by Ascham in his *Scholemaster* (1570), Mulcaster in his *Positions* (1581), Kempe in his *Education of Children in Learning* (1588), Brinsley in his *Ludus Literarius* (1612) and *Consolacion for our Grammar Schools* (1622), and Charles Hoole in his retrospective *New Discovery of the Old Art of Teaching School* (1660). It was the goal which, in theory at least, every 'mayster of the grammar schole' presented to his pupils.

The child's study of grammar fell into two fairly well-defined parts, supervised in the larger schools by the usher and the

---

[1] E. T. Campagnac, ed., *Ludus Literarius or The Grammar Schoole*, (1917) p. 13.

master respectively. Under the usher the boy's life would be bounded by parsing and construing, the making of Latins or 'vulgars' and the building up of a vocabulary. Drill and repetition would be the dominant method. The rudiments mastered, he would then, with the master, proceed to the real end of these preliminary exercises, Latin composition, i.e. the writing and speaking of themes, letters, verses and orations in imitation of the classical authors whose texts he would read. As Kempe summarized it, 'first the scholar shall learn the precepts, secondly he shall learn to note the examples of the precepts in unfolding other men's works; thirdly to imitate the examples in some work of his own; fourthly and lastly to make somewhat alone without an example'.[1]

During the fifteenth century the grammars of Donatus, Priscian and Dolensis (Alexander Villadei) were replaced in Europe by those of Guarino, Sulpitius, and Perottus. In England from the 1480s to the 1530s a whole series of new texts were produced by successive masters of the grammar school of Magdalen College, Oxford, which though owing a good deal in the way of structure to Donatus, nevertheless made a serious attempt to overcome the difficulties of presenting the rules of accidence and elementary syntax to young scholars in grammar schools. The earliest of these, John Anwykyll's *Compendium Totius Grammatice* (1483), explicitly acknowledges its debt to Valla, Servius and Perottus in its running title. Whereas Anwykyll's work was in Latin, the *Lac Puerorum or Mylke for Children* (1479) of John Holte, usher at the school under John Stanbridge, goes a stage farther in the simplification of presentation by being written in English, even to the extent of using English names such as 'bidding mood', 'shewing mood', 'asking mood' and so on instead of the usual technical terms. To help illustrate and elucidate his points, Holte also made use of drawings in the shape of a hand showing the arrangement of cases, with a bunch of tallow candles to indicate the declensions. The book was graced with prefatory and concluding epigrammatic verses by Sir Thomas More, and obviously filled a gap, being printed by both Pynson and Wynkyn de Worde.[2] These early works were,

---

[1] *Education of Children in Learning* (1588), Sig. F.2.
[2] Cf. W. Nelson, 'Thomas More, Grammarian and Orator', *P.M.L.A.*, LVIII (1943), pp. 337–52.

however, in their turn replaced by the various grammatical texts of John Stanbridge and his pupil Robert Whitinton, the Stanbridge grammar in fact being specifically prescribed in the statutes of Manchester and Reading Grammar Schools. The improvements effected in these new texts became apparent when the tabular presentation in Stanbridge's *Accidence* ( ?1520)

| | |
|---|---|
| Amo/as/at | I love |
| Doceo/ces/cet | I teche |
| Lego/gis/git | I rede |
| Audio/is/it | I here |

is compared with the continuously running lines of Donatus and the deplorable doggerel of Alexander. For the pupils of his school at St. Paul's Colet produced a short accidence of his own, the *Aeditio*, which was used alongside William Lily's two short books on syntax, the one, *Rudimenta Grammatices* in English and the other, *De Constructione octo partium orationis*, for more advanced teaching, in Latin. It was this latter text which Erasmus himself revised at Colet's request.

In the second decade of the century, then, there were plenty of home-produced 'grammars' from the two rival 'schools' of Stanbridge-Whitinton and Colet-Lily.[1] Indeed such proliferation apparently resulted in some confusion, for various moves were made in the 1520s towards the standardizing of grammar teaching by the production of a uniform grammar. In 1529 the Convocation of Canterbury drew attention to the fact that

> whereas either through the plague raging in places where public schools are or through the death of a master, it often happens that a boy who has begun to learn grammar for a year or two under one teacher is obliged to leave him to go to another teacher who has another method of teaching, so that he is almost laughed at by all; and so it happens that those who are still raw in grammar, suffer great loss in the progress of their learning.

it was therefore decreed that 'there shall be one uniform method of teaching, throughout the whole province of Canterbury'.[2] A committee consisting of the Archbishop, four bishops, four

---

[1] Cf. E. Pafort, 'A Group of Early Tudor School Books', *Library*, 4th series, XXVI (1946), pp. 227–61; H. S. Bennett, 'A Check-List of Robert Whitinton's Grammars', ibid., 5th Series, VII (1952), pp. 1–14.

[2] Leach, *Educational Charters* . . . p. 447.

abbots and four archdeacons was directed to compile the desired text in the course of the next year, though nothing seems to have come of the project. Wolsey, too, suggested the benefits of a uniform grammar in his foundation at Ipswich in the same year. Such uniformity would obviously appeal to the king, and in the late 1530s a committee was set up to produce a 'royal grammar'. The Lily-Colet-Erasmus texts were chosen as the basis of the new version, with the result that the Royal Grammar was produced in two parts in 1540–2, one in English and one in Latin. These were the works which were later to be bound up together with a common title page headed *A Shorte Introduction of Grammar* and destined to be known as Lily's Latin Grammar.

The preface ran,

> Henry VIII . . . to all schoolmasters and teachers of grammar within this realm, . . . to the intent that hereafter they (English children) may the more readily and easily attain the rudiments of the Latin tongue, without the great hindrance which heretofore have been through the diversity of grammar within this our realm and all our dominions, as ye intend to avoid our displeasure and have our favour, to teach and learn your scholars this English introduction here ensuing and the Latin grammar annexed the same, and none other, which we have caused for your ease and your scholars speedy preferment briefly and plainly to be compiled and set forth. Fail not to apply your scholars to learning and godly education.

The Royal Grammar continued to be prescribed in the Royal Injunctions of both Edward VI (1547) and Elizabeth (1559), as well as by the Ecclesiastical Canons of 1571 and 1604, and remained the standard, though by no means the only, grammar until the introduction of the Eton Grammar in 1758. An indication of the success of 'Lily's Grammar' may be judged by the fact that William Flower, to whom was granted in 1573 the privilege of printing the work, transferred his 'right' two years later to six assigns who paid him a yearly rent of £100 for it. Again, during Elizabeth's reign, at a time when 1,250 copies of a book constituted an ordinary 'edition', 10,000 copies of the grammar were allowed to be printed annually.[1]

[1] F. Watson, *The English Grammar Schools to 1660* (Cambridge, 1908), p. 255. The text is reproduced in facsimile from the 1567 edition in V. J. Flynn, ed., *A Shorte Introduction of Grammar* (Scholars Facsimiles and Reprints, New York,

Having memorized their accidence and the elementary rules of construction, the pupils would now be made to apply the 'precepts' by constructing illustrative sentences—the 'making of Latins' or the 'making of vulgars'—and thus begin acquiring vocabulary. For these exercises they would have the aid of a wide variety of new texts, ranging from John Anwykyll's *Vulgaria Terentii* (c. 1483), a collection of sentences from Terence with subjoined English translations, to the texts of Stanbridge and Whitinton and William Horman of Eton, who produced a book of 319 pages including 3,000 sentences arranged topically, with the English sentence followed by Latin.[1] Though texts such as these shed a good deal of light on life in the Tudor schoolroom, the lively touches of humour we find in them must have been swamped by the daily grind and drudgery of examining sentences word by word, phrase by phrase, and rule by rule. The procedure was soundly denounced by Vives in his *De Tradendis Disciplinis* (1531), where he suggested what was later to be called the method of 'double-translation' as expounded by Ascham in *The Scholemaster* (1570). It was a method, too, which Sir Thomas More's daughter, Margaret, had used in her studies, which John Palsgrave recommended in the introduction to his translation of *Acolastus* and which William Cecil advised his son to use, following John Cheke's habit with his own students. This direct imitation of the 'best authors' had also been recommended by Erasmus in his *De Ratione Studii*, where he expresses his impatience 'with the average teacher of grammar who wastes precious years in hammering rules into children's heads. For it is not by learning rules (he goes on) that we acquire the power of speaking a language but by daily intercourse with those accustomed to express themselves with exactness and refinement and by the

[1] B. White, ed., *The Vulgaria of John Stanbridge and the Vulgaria of Robert Whittinton* (E.E.T.S., Orig. Series, No. 187, 1932); M. R. James, ed., *William Horman's Vulgaria* (Roxburghe Club, 1926).

1945). For discussions of the make-up of the work cf. V. J. Flynn, 'The Grammatical Writings of William Lily, ?1468–?1523', *Papers of the Bibliographical Society of America*, XXXVII (1943), pp. 85–113, C. G. Allen, 'The Sources of Lily's Latin Grammar: a review of the facts and some further suggestions', *The Library*, 5th Series, IX (1954), pp. 85–100; J. P. Tuck, 'The Latin Grammar Attributed to William Lily', *Durham Research Review* (1951), pp. 33–39.

copious reading of the best authors.'[1] Ascham and Brinsley both recommended the popular edition of Cicero's *Epistles* by John Sturm for the purpose, but teacher and pupil would also have at their disposal collections of other models such as the *Colloquies* of Erasmus, of Petrus Mosellanus and of Marthurin Corderius, Vives's *Lingua Latinae Exercitatio*, Castellion's *Dialogorum Sacrorum*, Aesop's *Fables* and the *Distichs* of Cato.

To supplement such texts, Nicholas Udall, master of Eton, produced his own *Floures for Latine Speaking* (1533), which John Higgins later augmented in his *Floures of Eloquent Phrases of the Latine Speach gathered out of all the sixe comoedies of Terence* (1575); Richard Taverner produced similar works by translating Erasmus's *Proverbs or Adagies with new additions gathered out of the Chiliades of Erasmus* (1539) and compiling *The Garden of Wisdome* (1539) from the *Apophthegmata*. All or any of these would provide models both of construction and vocabulary, which, together with the 'continual rehearsal of things learned' recommended in the Royal Grammar, would now put the pupil in a position to attempt the composing of themes, letters, verses and orations and to maintain a systematic reading of Latin authors.[2] For prose and letters Cicero was the universal model, for verse Ovid and Horace, for orations, the pseudo-Cicero *Ad Herennium* together with Aphthonius and Quintilian. In this, the rhetorical side of the pupil's training, the two main virtues to be aspired to were copiousness of vocabulary and variety of style. The reading of Latin authors and the keeping of a commonplace book, in which could be written down words and idiomatic phrases from 'authoritative' sources to be used in the various written and oral exercises, formed the background to the main business of writing and speaking Latin.

In a proliferation of texts produced to aid both teacher and pupil one above all stands out, Erasmus's *De Duplici Copia Verborum ac Rerum*, the *De Copia* of so many school statutes and book lists of the period. Written in 1512 at the request of Colet

---

[1] W. H. Woodward, ed., *Desiderius Erasmus Concerning the Aims and Methods of Education* (Cambridge, 1904), pp. 163–4; cf. Ryan, op. cit., pp. 104–6, 244–5, 266–8.

[2] Cf. F. Watson, ed., *Early Tudor Schoolboy Life: The Dialogues of Vives* (1908); W. T. Chase, ed., *The Distichs of Cato: a famous medieval text book* (Madison, 1922).

for use in his school at St. Paul's, it ran into over a hundred editions during the sixteenth century, was translated, epitomized, and pirated, and became the standard work in grammar schools all over Europe.[1] The first part of the work is an extended vocabulary arranged to provide alternative words with which to elaborate a statement already made, whilst the second, and smaller, part details the different ways in which the statements might be arranged in the form of various figures of speech. To help pupils learn the definition and classification of these figures recourse could be had to the *Epitome* of Susenbrotus or the *Tabulae* of Mosellanus, which, as Vives had recommended, could be 'hung up on the wall so that it will catch the attention of the pupil as he walks past it and force itself upon his eyes'.[2] But these were later replaced by texts produced by Englishmen, most of them translations and abridgments of continental works. Leonard Cox's *Arte or Crafte of Rhethoryke* ( ?1529), for example, was mostly a translation of Melanchthon's *Institutiones Rhetoricae* (1521) and was written, as Cox explains, for those of his pupils at Reading grammar school who might become 'advocates or proctors in law, or else apt to be sent as their prince's ambassadors or to be teachers of God's word . . . and finally to all them that have anything to propose or to speak before any company whatsoever they be'.[3] Richard Sherry, headmaster of Magdalen School, 1534–40, based his *Treatise of Schemes and Tropes* (1550) on Erasmus's *De Copia*, Mosellanus's *Tabulae* and the *Ad Herennium*. Five years later he revised the work 'especially for such as in grammar schools do read most eloquent poets and orators', and renamed it *A Treatise of the Figures of Grammer and Rhetorike*, each section of the Latin text being followed by an English translation. Richard Rainolde's *Foundacion of Rhetorike* (1563) on the other hand, was a very free version of perhaps the most famous of all school books on rhetoric both in the ancient world and in the Renaissance, the *Progymnasmata* of Aphthonius of

[1] Cf. J. K. Soward, 'Erasmus and the Apologetic Text-Book: a study of the *De Duplici Copia Verborum Ac Rerum*', *S.P.*, LV (1957), pp. 123–35, and H. D. Rix, 'The Editions of Erasmus' *De Copia*', ibid., XLIII (1947), pp. 595–618.

[2] F. Watson, ed., *Vives on Education* (Cambridge, 1913), p. 134.

[3] Op. cit., Sig. A ii *verso*. For a discussion of the date of this edition cf. F. I. Carpenter, ed., *Leonard Cox, The Arte or Crafte of Rhethoryke* (Chicago, 1899), pp. 10 and 19.

Antioch (flor. 3rd century, A.D.). Rainolde used the sixteenth-century edition of Richard Lorich, first published in 1537 and englished in 1572. But the book was widely used in England even before 1572.[1] The copy which Sir Thomas Egerton used, for example, was a Frankfurt edition of 1553, and the book was recommended in many school statutes, as well as by Ascham, Brinsley and Hoole. Brinsley's chapter 'Of making themes . . .' is, indeed, very largely based on Aphthonius. Again, Henry Peacham's *Garden of Eloquence* (1577), 'a dictionary of rhetorical and grammatical terms necessary for the understanding and attaining of perfect style', was based largely on Susenbrotus, with additions from Melanchthon and Erasmus amongst others.

All of these were traditional expositions of the Aristotelian-Ciceronian analysis of the arts of rhetoric and logic, of which Thomas Wilson's *Rule of Reason* (1551) and *Arte of Rhetorique* (1553) were the classic English interpretations. In 1543, however, Peter Ramus had produced his revolutionary *Dialecticae Institutiones*, which was followed by the *Institutiones Oratoriae* (1545) and *Rhetorica* (1548) of his friend Audomarus Talaeus. These in their turn inspired English imitators. Dudley Fenner's *Artes of Logicke and Rethorike* (1584), for instance, provided schoolmasters with a concise summary of both Ramus and Talaeus in one volume, whilst William Kempe's section on logic and rhetoric in his *Education of Children in Learning* (1588) is Ramistic in its treatment. The most famous of school texts which favoured the new method was the *Ramae Rhetoricae . . .* (1597) of Charles Butler, master of the grammar school at Basingstoke, whose book went through ten editions during the seventeenth century and was highly recommended by Brinsley. But the immediate impact of the new order was slight and Aphthonius' *Progymnasmata* with its fourteen different types of elementary exercises in theme-writing, ranging from

---

[1] F. R. Johnson, ed., Richard Rainolde's *Foundacion of Rhetorike* (Scholar's Facsimiles and Reprints, New York, 1945); cf. W. G. Crane, *Wit and Rhetoric in the Renaissance* (New York, 1945); cf. W. G. Crane, *Wit and Rhetoric in the Renaissance* (New York, 1937); K. R. Wallace, 'Rhetorical Exercises in Tudor Education', *Quarterly Journal of Speech*, XII (1936), pp. 34–39, and F. R. Johnson, 'Two Renaissance Text Books of Rhetoric: Aphthonius' *Progymnasmata* and Rainolde's *A Booke Called the Foundation of Rhetorike*', *H.L.Q.*, V (1944), pp. 427–41.

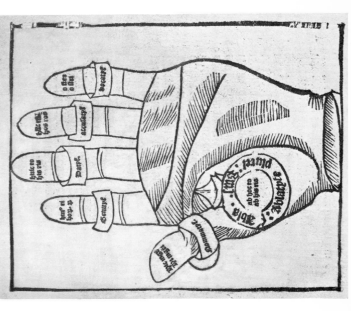

V. (i) Aid to Learning Grammar: from John Holte, *Lac Puerorum* (1479).

V. (ii) Pictorial Alphabet: from John Harte, *Methode to Reade English* (1570).

VI. Family Instruction: from *The Whole Booke of Psalmes* (1563).

the retelling of a fable or myth, through the *narratio* (a short narrative or an historical, poetical or judicial topic), the *chria* (a theme on the saying or deed of some famous person) and the *sententia* (on some wise saying or proverb) to the *thesis* or *consultatio* (a speech marshalling arguments for one side or another of some debatable abstract proposition) and the *legislatio* (for or against a proposed or existing law), remained the model. In these conciseness of style and pithiness of phraseology played no part. Amplification and ornamentation were the thing. The aim at all times would be Ciceronian fluency, with carefully constructed, well-rounded periods expressing an abundance of illustrative material. The exercise of 'varying' which was used as a means towards this end is well-illustrated by Shakespeare's Dauphin in praise of his horse :–

> *Dauphin:* I will not change my horse with any that treads but on four pastens. Ca! ha! he bounds from the earth as if his entrails were hairs, le cheval volant, the Pegasus, chez les marines de feu! When I bestride him I soar, I am a hawk. He trots in the air; the earth sings when he touches it; the basest horn of his hoof is more musical than the pipe of Hermes.
>
> *Orleans:* He's of the colour of nutmeg.
>
> *Dauphin:* And the heart of the ginger. It is a beast for Perseus; he is pure air and fire, and the dull elements of earth and water never appear in him, but only in patient stillness, while his rider mounts him; he is indeed a horse and all other jades you may call beasts.
>
> *Constable:* Indeed, my lord, it is a most absolute and excellent horse.
>
> *Dauphin:* It is the prince of palfreys: his neigh is like the bidding of a monarch and his countenance enforces homage.
>
> *Orleans:* No more cousin!
>
> *Dauphin:* Nay, the man hath no wit that cannot from the rising of the lark to the lodging of the lamb vary deserved praise on my palfrey. It is a theme as fluent as the sea; turn the sands into eloquent tongues and my horse is argument for them all.
>
> (*Henry V*, III, vii, 11–37).

Imitation of classical models was, of course, basic to this method of rhetoric teaching. As an aid to this, Brinsley recommended that the student make an analysis of the model before going on to compose his own theme, dividing the model first into its component parts, 'as exordium, narratio, confirmatio, confutatio and conclusio', and marking these in the left hand margin before going on to note the various rhetorical devices used in the text in the other: 'and in the latter side of the page towards the right hand to set the several tropes or figures, but in two or three letters. As for metonymia, efficientia no more but met, effic, or the like, marking some time under the word in which they are.'

What was true of theme-writing applied also to letter writing, and here again the teacher and pupil would have the help of manuals especially designed for the purpose. More often than not the statutes of the school laid down in detail the sort of work expected, as at Rivington where

> the elder sort must be exercised in devising and writing sundry epistles to sundry persons, of sundry matters, as of chiding, exhorting, comforting, counselling, praying, lamenting, some to friends, some to foes, some to strangers; of weighty matters or merry, as shooting, hunting, etc., of adversity, of prosperity, of war and peace, divine and profane, of all sciences and occupations, some long and some short.[1]

The most popular text was Erasmus's *De Conscribendis Epistolis* (1421). A shorter and perhaps easier book was that of Christopher Hegendorf (1537), though this was rivalled later in the century by the texts of Macropaedius which went through many editions in the seventeenth century.

A final aid which the pupil would have at his disposal in his exercises in composition would be the dictionaries of the period.[2] The dictionaries on which the medieval boy had relied, such as those of John of Garland, were being replaced by the end of the fifteenth century by modern works such as the *Promptorium Parvulorum* (*c.* 1440) ('a Storeroom for Young Scholars'), an alphabetically arranged English-Latin dictionary grouped under *nomina* and *verba*, and the *Ortus Vocabularium* (1500) ('The Garden of Words'), a Latin-English compilation which ran to at least twelve editions between 1500 and 1533. The younger pupils would make use of John Stanbridge's *Vocabula*, a Latin-English word list which ran into seventeen editions (1496–1631) and which itself owed a good deal to Perotti's *Cornu-*

---

[1] Whitaker, op. cit., pp. 216–17.
[2] Cf. D. T. Starnes, *Renaissance Dictionaries* (Austin, 1954).

*copiae*. The words were arranged under topics in the tradition of the medieval vocabularies and *nominales*, a practice which was continued in the rather more elaborate works of the mid-century especially compiled for schools, such as John Withals's *Shorte Dictionarie for Yonge Beginners* (1556) which was perhaps the most widely-used text of its kind.[1] Richard Huloet's *Abcedarium Anglico-Latinum* (1552) was alphabetically arranged and was enlarged by John Higgins in 1572 to include French words on the model of John Veron's *Dictionariolum Puerorum Tribus Linguis, Latina, Anglica et Gallica Conscriptum* (1552). Huloet's *Dictionarie* (1572), on the other hand, consisted of English phrases and sentences expressed in a variety of ways in Latin, much the same kind of pattern as was used by John Baret in his *Alvearie* (1573), a triple dictionary, English-Latin-French, which included some Greek terms, and which Abraham Fleming revised and enlarged in 1580.[2] In his 'Address to the Reader' Baret explains how he came to compile the work, and incidentally throws some light on classroom methods of the period:—

> About eighteen years ago, having pupils at Cambridge studious of the Latin tongue, I used them to write epistles and then together and daily to translate some piece of English into Latin, for the more speedy and easy attaining of the same. And after we had a little begun, perceiving what great trouble it was to come running to me for every word they missed (knowing then of no other dictionary to help as but Sir Thomas Elyot's *Librarie* which was come out a little before), I appointed them certain leaves of the same book every day to write the English before the Latin, and likewise to gather a number of fine phrases out of Cicero, Terence, Caesar, Livy etc., and to set them under several titles, for the more readily finding them again at their need. Thus within a year or two they had gathered together a great volume which (for the apt similitude between the good scholars and diligent bees in gathering their wax and honey into the hive) I called the book their Alvearie, both for a memorial by whom it was made and also by this name to encourage others to the like diligence for that they should not see their worthy praise for the same unworthily drowned in oblivion.

All of these dictionaries were arranged in ways that would

[1] Cf. D. T. Starnes, 'An Elizabethan "Dictionarie for Yonge Beginners" ', *Studies in English*, XXIX (1950), pp. 51–76.

[2] Cf. J. H. Sledd, 'Baret's "Alvearie", an Elizabethan Reference Book', *S.P.*, XLIII (1946), pp. 147–63.

specifically facilitate the preparation of Latin themes, etc., in the upper forms of grammar schools. Peter Levins, on the other hand, went a step farther when he produced his *Manipulus Vocabulorum, a dictionarie of English and Latine words* (1570). He compiled it, he said, not simply 'for scholars that want variety of words, but also for such as use to write in English metre' and towards that end, therefore, he set the English before the Latin.[1]

The 'Librarie' of Sir Thomas Elyot, which Baret mentions as having come out 'a little before', was the *Bibliotheca Eliotae: Eliot's Librarie* (1538, revised 1542), the first of the great Latin-English reference dictionaries of the English Renaissance. It was enlarged in 1548, and again in 1552 and 1559, by Thomas Cooper, Master of Magdelen School 1549–67, whose dictionary became the standard work, until it in its turn was replaced by Thomas Thomas's *Dictionarium Linguae Latinae et Anglicanae* (1587, and numerous other editions). These would be to the sixteenth-century pupil what 'Lewis and Short' and 'Smith' are to today's students. Costing in the region of fifteen shillings or more it is not surprising that evidence of their being in school libraries is confined to well-endowed schools like St. Albans, Felsted or Colchester.[2] Baret had obviously made use of Elyot's work in his school in Cambridge, and doubtless Cooper's would be in use at the Magdalen College School, but the importance of these dictionaries at this stage lies not so much in their possible use by pupils, but in the provision they made for the grammar school masters of a thoroughly humanistic attitude to lexicography as the handmaiden of both pure classical Latin and a standardized English.

The study of Latin language and literature, then, remained the chief concern of the grammar schools as hitherto. What of the two other languages, Greek and Hebrew, which the reformers of the period had pronounced to be indispensable? Erasmus recommended the concurrent study of Greek and Latin not only on the grounds that 'within these two literatures are

---

[1] Cf. H. B. Wheatley, ed., *Manipulus Vocabulorum* (Camden Society, XCV, 1867).

[2] For the prices of schoolbooks cf. Baldwin, op. cit., I, 178, 374ff, 394, 422, 490ff; H. S. Bennett, 'Notes on English Retail Book Prices, 1480–1560', *Library*, 5th Series, V (1950), pp. 172–8, and F. R. Johnson, 'Notes on English Retail Book Prices, 1550–1640', ibid., 5th Series, V (1950), pp. 83–112.

contained all the knowledge which we recognise as of vital importance to mankind', but also because 'the natural affinity of the two tongues renders it more profitable to study them side by side than apart'. Elyot, in *The Governour*, also wished the child to learn Greek and Latin authors at the same time or else to begin with Greek, for 'if a child do begin therein at seven years of age he may continuously learn Greek authors three years and in the meantime use the Latin as a familiar language'.[1] Vives, too, in his *De Tradendis Disciplinis* recommended that both should be taught.

Yet it is unlikely that anything more than lip service was paid to Greek and Hebrew in the general run of grammar schools. The statutes of East Retford (1552) graphically express the common attitude when they add, almost as an after-thought, 'and the said master shall teach the scholars of this (fourth) form the Greek grammar, and also the Hebrew grammar if he be expert in the same, and some Greek authors, so far as his learning and convenient time will serve thereunto'. Colet had prescribed that the 'Master of St. Paul's be learned in Greek if such may be got'; and Lily, the first High Master, must have been one of the very few Englishmen of his day to be so qualified.[2] As we might expect, the position improved somewhat later in the century, and whereas Greek was not included in the 1530 curriculum of Eton, the 1560 revision of the statutes prescribed the elements of grammar for the two highest forms. St. Bees, Norwich, Rivington, Bangor and Shrewsbury all included Greek in their statutes, and when those for Harrow were revised in 1591 Greek grammar was to be started in the Fourth Form, prior to reading Demosthenes, Isocrates, Hesiod, Heliodorus, and Dionysius of Halicarnassus in the Fifth.[3] In the first half of the century the grammar of Theodore of Gaza was most frequently recommended, though Thomas Ashton, of Shrewsbury School, preferred that of Clenardus. The prime reading was the Greek New Testament, as recommended at St. Saviour's (1562), Norwich (1566) and Blackburn (1597),

[1] *De Ratione Studii* (1511), translated in W. H. Woodward, *Erasmus*, p. 163. *Governour*, Book I, Chap. x.

[2] Carlisle, II, 283; M. L. Clarke, *Classical Education in Britain, 1500–1900* (Cambridge, 1959), p. 12.

[3] Baldwin, op. cit., I, 312.

with the authors mentioned in the Harrow statutes providing supplementary or advanced reading. 'Let them and the form above them (i.e. Third and Fourth Forms) read a dozen daily verses out of the Greek Testament before the saying of the parts', was Charles Hoole's recommendation. Brinsley, too, starts his boys with the Greek grammar and Testament which would be followed by 'some of the purest authors . . . as namely Isocrates, Xenophon, Plato and Demosthenes'. Yet only at Westminster, perhaps, first under Nowell and Grant and later under Camden, would pupils achieve the standard reached by Sir Thomas Bodley as a result of his father's tuition while in exile in Geneva, where he was able to attend lectures at the University in Greek, Hebrew and Divinity. It was while he was headmaster at Westminster that Edward Grant produced the first Greek grammar in English. This was later adapted by William Camden, whose book became for Greek studies what Lily's was for Latin, until it was superseded in the eighteenth century by Busby's Greek grammar as Lily's was by the Eton Grammar. Certainly there were very few schools which could emulate Westminster's Greek plays performed by the pupils.[1]

As for Hebrew there is little evidence to show that it was taught in any but a small number of schools. Sir James Whitelocke, a pupil of Mulcaster at Merchant Taylors', reported that he was there 'well-instructed in the Hebrew, Greek and Latin tongues', though it was unlikely that he was equally well-instructed in all three. When he was Dean of Westminster, Lancelot Andrewes, another pupil of Mulcaster, used to send for the boys of the upper forms to teach them Greek and Hebrew, and Charles Hoole refers to a later generation of Westminster boys as being able to 'make orations and verses in Hebrew'. Brinsley recommended Hebrew for the upper forms and hoped that a study of Hebrew Old Testament and Greek New Testament would enable the boys 'to speak the words of God indeed with facility, authority, and power'. Hoole has his Sixth Form reading Hebrew on three mornings a week, using Johannes Buxtorf's *Epitome*, the Psalter, the Old Testament and

---

[1] C. Hoole, *A New Discovery of the Old Arte of Teaching School*, ed. E. T. Campagnac (Liverpool, 1913), p. 169; Brinsley, op. cit., pp. 239 and 222ff; *The Life of Sir Thomas Bodley . . . written by himselfe* (Oxford, 1647), p. 2; Watson, *English Grammar School . . .*, pp. 496ff.

our common Church Catechism in Hebrew which was printed for the Company of Stationers in four languages A.D. 1638. . . . It is not very difficult to attain to (he claimed) because it goeth word for word with our English and is not so copious in words as the Greek and Latin. And whereas many defer the Hebrew to be learned at the University, I may say it is rarely attained there by any that have not gotten (at least) the rudiments of it beforehand and at a grammar school.[1]

Generally, however, Hebrew was neglected, only rarely appearing in the statutes of schools and even then expressing a pious hope on the part of the founder, as at East Retford 'if (the teacher) be expert in the same' or at Blackburn 'if any be willing or fit thereunto'.[2]

The speaking and writing of Latin, then, predominated. Something must be said, however, about the traditional picture of the English grammar school as a place where the boys were forbidden to speak any language other than Latin, a prohibition which included their own language.

> Boys were not taught Latin, they were taught *in* Latin, they were not allowed to utter a single vernacular word whilst at school. . . . No teaching of any kind in the vernacular existed anywhere before 1550 or thereabouts. . . . If Shakespeare crept unwillingly to school he did so because there he would be confronted by a Master who spoke nothing but Latin and who would birch him if he spoke an English word to another boy.[3]

The plausibility of such a picture is enhanced by reference to those school statutes of the period which explicitly forbade the use of the vernacular. Oundle statutes (1556), for instance, insisted that the boys speak Latin to each other 'as well in the school as coming and going to and from the same'. At Rivington (1566) it was prescribed that 'In the school they that can must

---

[1] J. Bruce, ed., *Liber Famelicus of Sir James Whitelocke* (Camden Society, LXX, 1858), pp. 12–13; Hoole, op. cit., pp. 191, 194, 201; Brinsley, op. cit., p. 226.

[2] Carlisle, II, 284; G. A. Stocks, ed., *Records of Blackburn Grammar School*, I (Chetham Society, N.S., LXVI, 1909), pp. 74–75.

[3] E. P. Goldschmidt, *The Printed Book of the Renaissance* (Cambridge, 1950), pp. 8–9. Cf. W. Nelson, 'The Vernacular Tongue in English Education', *Renaissance News*, IV (1951), pp. 39–40, and 'The Teaching of English in Tudor Grammar Schools; *S.P.*, LXIX (1952), pp. 119–43; J. P. Tuck, 'The Beginnings of English Studies in the Sixteenth Century', *Durham Research Review*, No. 7 (1956), pp. 65–73.

speak nothing but Latin and the younger sort must learn every day to amend.' The Hawkshead statutes (1586) went even further, declaring that the pupils were to 'continually use the Latin tongue or the Greek tongue within the school as they are able'.[1]

On the other hand two points should be made. In the first place, the difficulties of implementing these provisions must have been enormous, as Brinsley was quick to show.[2] But more important than this, even a summary glance at what went on in Tudor grammar schools will show that in the teaching of Latin grammar the use of English was not only a necessary expedient but also something recognized by masters to be of positive educational value, though English as a separate subject never appeared on a school time-table. At the end of the fifteenth century it would have been impossible to talk about *the* English language. Caxton's early printing ventures soon revealed the difficulties arising from the lack of standardized spelling and pronunciation, and Andrew Boorde could declare, 'The speech of England is a base speech to other noble speeches as Italian, Castilian and French'.[3] Both Elyot in his *Castell of Health* (1541) and Ascham in his *Toxophilus* (1545) felt bound to apologize for and defend their use of English as a literary medium. Yet the general trend was towards a recognition of the possibilities of the vernacular. For Mulcaster, nearly forty years later, there was no doubt and certainly no need for apology: 'I do not think that any language be it whatsoever is better able to utter all arguments, either with more pith or greater plainness than our English tongue is. . . . I love Rome but London better; I favour Italy but England more, I honour the Latin but I worship the English'.[4] The motives underlying the many eulogies of this kind were mixed, of course. Renaissance humanism and the *questione della lingua* debates in fifteenth-century Italy had paved the way. The movement which produced the vernacular translations of the Bible as a necessary part of the Reformation further contributed to the discussion about the status of the vernacular languages. Most important of all, however, was the

[1] Carlisle, II, 217; Kay, op. cit., p. 173; Carlisle, I, 656.

[2] *Ludus Literarius*, pp. 212, 214, 219.

[3] F. J. Furnivall, ed., *Andrew Boorde's 'First Booke of the Introduction of Knowledge' 1547* (E.E.T.S., Extra Series, X, 1870), p. 122.

[4] *Elementarie*, pp. 274 and 269.

growing feeling of national pride which prompted Mulcaster, for instance, to see the use of the vernacular as yet another way of indicating England's emancipation from Papal subservience.

We have already seen how at petty level more attention was being paid to the pupil's native tongue. In the grammar school itself the use of dictionaries, the compiling of commonplace books and constant exercising in translation and composition must have made the Tudor schoolboy well aware of the grammatical complexities of his own language. Already in the early fifteenth century English was being used in grammatical texts, as in the anonymous short Latin grammar written for the College of St. Mary Magdalene, at Battlefield near Shrewsbury, and the *Parve Latinitates* (1434) of John Drury, schoolmaster of Beccles, in Suffolk.[1] Some of the earliest of the printed grammars, as we have seen, also made use of English in their texts. But, in addition, as the sixteenth century progresses more and more evidence points to instruction in the grammar of English and an insistence that the writing of good English must accompany the writing of good Latin. The first step in translating a piece into Latin was the grammatical analysis of the English. As Lily put it in his *Rudimenta*, 'When I have an English to be turned into Latin I shall rehearse twice or thrice and look out the verb, the nominative case cometh before the verb and answereth to the question who or what?' Nicholas Udall, in his *Floures for Latine Spekynge* (1533), emphasized the need for skill in both English and Latin. In the Dedicatory Letter to his translation of Seneca, *The Myrrour or Glasse of Maners* (1547), Robert Whitinton explains that he has 'adjoined the text of Latin with the translation in English to the intent that . . . schoolmasters, teachers and readers following the old tradition of expert and learned men may instruct their scholars in good and honest manners in both tongues English and Latin'. Again, in his English version (1553) of Cicero's *De Officiis*, a textbook which remained popular for the remainder of the century, Nicholas Grimald stresses the importance 'as well in the English as in

---

[1] Cf. S. B. Meech, 'An Early Treatise in English Concerning Latin Grammar', *Essays and Studies in English and Comparative Literature* (University of Michigan Publications in Language and Literature, XIII, 1935), 81–125; M. R. James, *The Western MSS in the Library of Trinity College, Cambridge* (Cambridge, 1900–5), III, 301–8; and S. B. Meech, 'John Drury and his English Writings', *Speculum*, IX (1934), pp. 70–83.

the Latin to weigh well properties of words, fashions of phrases and the ornaments of both'.[1]

It was in order to provide a grounding in such work that William Bullokar produced his *Shorte Introduction on Guiding to Print, Write and Reade Inglish Speech* . . . (1580). As he had insisted in *Amendment for Orthographie* . . . (1580) English 'must be the foundation to such as desire further learning' and his *Shorte Introduction* . . . would enable its readers the better to understand their Latin grammar. Bullokar followed this up with a *Bref Grammar of English* (1586), but the first comprehensive English grammar for use in schools was the *Logonomia Anglica* (1619) of Alexander Gill, the elder, successor to Mulcaster as High Master of St. Paul's and teacher of John Milton.[2] The book was divided into four sections, *Literae, Etymologia* (i.e. Accidence), *Syntaxis* (with a rhetorical section on schemes and tropes) and *Prosodia*, thus providing a grammar and rhetoric for the English language. A second part of the *Logonomia* which was to have been devoted to Logic would have thus completed a kind of Trivium for English, but it seems not to have been produced. The *Literae* section is an orthography, teaching a phonetic system of writing English and in the rest of the book the illustrative quotations from English writers as well as the English in his paradigms are given in the author's own phonetic spelling. Spenser was obviously his favourite, with quotations from the *Faerie Queene* outnumbering all others, which include, however, George Wither, Samuel Daniel, Philip Sidney, John Davies, Ben Jonson and Edward Dyer. The practice of including examples of English literature in school texts was by Gill's time increasingly popular, and collections such as Francis Meres's *Palladis Tamia: Wit's Treasure* (1595), William Vaughan's *The Golden Grove, moralized in three books* (1600) and R. Allott's *England's Parnassus or the Choysest Flowers of our Modern Poets* (1600), provided convenient material for the schoolmaster's use. In this period, too, were produced the first English dictionaries for schools; not dictionaries in the true sense but collections of

---

[1] Grimald, *To the Reader*, Sig. CC vii, and Nelson, S. P., LXIX (1952), pp. 119–43.

[2] Cf. D. L. Clarke, 'Milton's Schoolmasters: Alexander Gill and his Son Alexander', *H.L.Q.*, IX (1946), pp. 129–33; A .Barker, 'Milton's Schoolmasters', *M.L.R.*, XXXII (1937), pp. 526–36.

'hard words', such as Robert Cawdrey's *Table Alphabeticall* (1604) and John Bullokar's *English Expositor, teaching the interpretation of the hardest words in our language* (1616), which was still being produced, in a twelfth edition, in 1719.

One must not, of course, overemphasize the place of English studies in the grammar schools of the sixteenth and early seventeenth centuries, but the prohibition of English speaking in Tudor school statutes must be put in context, and interpreted as referring to those hours of school life devoted to the speaking of Latin and not as an absolute prohibition. Arthur Golding's plea, in his prefatory poem to Baret's *Alvearie* (1580) for a standard English grammar on the lines of the Royal Grammar was not heeded, but it is significant that Brinsley included in his *Consolacion for Our Grammar Schools* (1622) a separate section on 'English' following those on Latin, Greek and Hebrew, and in it he recommended Gill's *Logonomia*. The great period of English scholarship in the origins and structure of the English language was yet to come with the work of Wallis and Wilkes and their contemporaries in the Restoration period, but the groundwork was already being laid in the fields of grammar, pronunciation and lexicography.[1]

What most contributed to the quality and kind of education which went on in the grammar schools of Renaissance England, however, was the quality of the masters who taught in them. The evidence provided by the statutes and time-tables of the period must be matched with the way in which the prescription was carried out. Certainly the practising schoolmaster did not go short of advice, for he was faced with a wealth—some would say welter—of precept and exhortation, much of which was not only based on practical experience but went so far as to anticipate some of the better-known writings of Comenius and his followers in the mid-seventeenth century.

Contact with the Continental Renaissance was direct. Erasmus' texts, as we have seen, were widely recommended and used, but for the educational ideas of the Renaissance, Englishmen went above all to Juan Luis Vives (1492–1540), the Spanish humanist who had worked with Erasmus at the Trilingual College of Louvain and who visited England regularly

[1] Cf. D. T. Starnes and G. E. Noyes, *The English Dictionary from Cawdrey to Johnson, 1604–1755* (Chapel Hill, 1946).

during the period 1523–8, spending part of his time teaching in Fox's 'bee-hive' at Corpus Christi, and the rest at the Court of Henry VIII. More and Erasmus eulogized the young scholar. Elyot, Ascham, Mulcaster, Brinsley, and others recommended his works—and absorbed his ideas into their own writings. His lively dialogues about everyday life, the *Linguae Latinae Exercitatio* (1585), were prescribed at Eton, Westminster, Shrewsbury, Rivington, Hertford and many other schools. His *Introductio ad Sapientiam* (1524) was used at Eton, Westminster, Shrewsbury and Norwich, and his *De Tradendis Disciplinis* (1531), with its insistence on the need to observe the child and to adapt both aim and method to his needs, its call for a humane relationship between master and pupil, its advocacy of the vernacular in the earlier stages of education and its thoroughly humanistic approach to the study of the classics, provided much of the theoretical basis for sixteenth-century innovations in English education.

Such was the positive side of the picture. Unfortunately, as in so much of educational history, the negative side loomed large and practice in the majority of schools, particularly in the smaller grammar schools, showed a gloomier face. Much of the humanists' plea for the continuance of the cheerful atmosphere of Vittorino's *Casa Giocosa* was submerged by a brutality towards boys which not only, and not surprisingly, reflected the violence of personal life which remained part of the Tudor scene, but also found a new sanction in the Calvinistic insistence of the essential depravity of man. Zwingli's was a still small voice against the chorus of both the sadistic and the sincere who insisted, as John Wesley did two centuries later, on the maxim 'beat them betimes'.[1] Other factors must, of course, be taken into account. With the master and the usher sharing between them the whole work of the upper and lower schools, 'classes' were large and discipline inevitably fierce. In addition their pay was miserably small. At the beginning of the century the master's salary would be in the region of £10 per annum and the usher's £5. By the middle of the century this had generally risen to £15 and £10 respectively, and at the end of the century a master would be lucky to get £20, with the usher receiving

---

[1] E. B. Castle, *Moral Education in Christian Times* (1958), Chap. v, summarizes sixteenth and seventeenth-century views on the punishment of children.

£10, increases which could hardly be said to be sufficient to keep pace with the inflation of the period, during which prices had increased about six-fold. A house or room was often provided, free of rent, the master and usher could supplement their incomes by admission and quaterage fees, and occasional sums came their way in the form of cockpenny, victor penny, potation penny and other kinds of levy. But these could rarely be counted a substantial increment, and increasingly founders were following the practice laid down in the statutes of the Manchester Grammar School (1524), which expressly forbade the taking of such fees. Moreover, the payment of schoolmasters was often jeopardized by trustees who were corrupt or who inefficiently let the endowed lands of the school on long leases at unfavourably low rents. Even Richard Mulcaster had a long and hard fight with his governors of the Merchant Taylors Company to achieve regular payment and occasional increases in salary. Compared with other professional men, whose office frequently enabled them to enjoy the benefits of the recognized, indeed built-in, practice of bribes and perquisites of all kinds, the schoolmaster had to rely on a salary that was lamentably small and his quality was therefore correspondingly low.[1]

Schoolmasters of high quality were, of course, to be found. Richard Mulcaster, Alexander Gill and Richard Brinsley had a national reputation. There were less well-known masters, too. Richard Michill, for example, master at Heptonstall in the West Riding, was a scholar of Magdelen College, Oxford, a good Latinist and '*in trivialibus artibus bene multumque versatus*', and Peter Carter of St. John's College, Cambridge, who was master of the grammar school at Whalley in Lancashire for twenty years, before moving on to the schools in Bolton, Wigan and Preston, produced his own *Annotationes in Dialectica Johan Setoni*, which was printed with Seton's texts in 1562/3 and subsequently appeared in eleven further editions before 1631.[2] Men such as these, presumably, recognized the responsibility of their task, and deserved the eulogy of Erasmus when he claimed that 'To be a schoolmaster is next to being a king. Do

[1] For bribery and patronage cf. J. E. Neale, 'The Elizabethan Political Scene', in *Essays in Elizabethan History* (1958), pp. 59–84. For schoolmasters' salaries cf. Stowe, op. cit., pp. 180–3.

[2] A. Raine, *History of St. Peter's School, York* (1926), pp. 74–78; A. J. Hawkes, 'Peter Carter, 1530–1590', *N. and Q.*, CXCVI (1951), pp. 356–7.

you count it a mean employment to imbue the minds of your fellow citizens in their earliest years with the best literature and with the love of Christ, and to return them to their country honest and virtuous men? . . . Even among the heathen it was always a noble thing to deserve well of the State and no one serves it better than the moulder of raw boys.' Mulcaster was doubtless setting an ideal standard when he insisted that the master

> besides his manners and behaviour which require testimony and assurance, besides his skill in exercising and training the body, must be able to teach the three learned tongues, the Latin, the Greek and the Hebrew, if the place required so much, if not so much as is required . . . he must be able to understand his writer, to master false prints, unskilful dictionaries, simple conjectures of some smattering writers concerning the matter of his training and be so appointed ere he begin to teach, as he may execute readily and not make his own imperfection to be a torture to his scholar . . . he must have the knowledge of all the best grammars, to give notes by the way still . . . hardness to take pains, constancy to continue, and not shrink from his trade.

It is unlikely, too, that Samuel Harsnett, Archbishop of York and founder of Chigwell Grammar School in Essex, found the paragon whom he prescribed in his statutes for the school in 1629:—

> Item, I constitute and appoint that the Latin schoolmaster be a graduate of one of the Universities, not under seven and twenty years of age, a man skilful in the Greek and Latin tongues, a good poet, of sound religion, neither Papist nor Puritan, of a grave behaviour, of a sober and honest conversation, no tippler nor haunter of alehouses, no puffer of tobacco and above all that he be apt to teach and serve in his government. And all elections otherwise made, I declare them to be void *ipso facto*, and that as soon as the schoolmaster do enter into Holy Orders, either Deacon or priest, his place to be come void, *ipso facto*, as if he were dead.[1]

Such men doubtless existed and were willing to take on the hazardous duties of schoolmastering, but they must have been few. Abraham Fraunce, we may presume, was indulging his feeling more than a little when he fulminated against

[1] Allen, No. 364, II, 154; *Positions*, p. 235; Carlisle, I, 417–18.

the swarming rabble of our cloystrell curates which when their fathers have either compounded with their landlord for some pelting vicarage or paid ready money for a better parsonage, convey themselves to Cambridge or Oxford, where having once known the price of an admission, salting and matriculation, with the entertaining of Freshmen in Rhetoric schools, they return whence they came with their mother's wit and father's learning carefully kept together that when they have wearied men with reading scarce true English on the Sunday, all the week after they may plague poor boys with false Latin in a belfry.[1]

On the other hand the Act Books of the dioceses up and down the country are likely to provide a rather more objective picture, and in them we find reference to schoolmasters like John Ireland of Halifax, who was found to be completely ignorant of Latin, had never learned the first rudiments of grammar and could not read English.[2] In between the Richard Michills and the John Irelands lay a mass of pedantic Holofernes who turned education into a grind of mechanical repetition, or, as William Lily called it, 'continual rehearsing'. What Rabelais referred to as 'verbosination' and the 'gymnastics of nothingness', Milton was still, a century later, calling 'gerund grinding'. The ideal which Guarino had set forth and which the masters of Magdalen College School had accepted very soon degenerated into mere rote work, a pattern of education which four hundred years of grammar-schooling later Edward Thring could describe as the 'schoolboy's briar patch', in which 'for various reasons, the power of Latin and Greek as mental training is not understood. . . . As exercises of memory they are bad. The schoolboy especially does not understand what he is about. It is a perfect wilderness to him.'[3]

Thomas Nash, in *Summer's Last Will and Testament*, echoes what must have passed through the mind of many a boy: 'Here, before all this company, I profess myself an open enemy to ink and paper. I'll make it good upon the Accidence body, that in speech is the devil's pater noster. Nouns and Pronouns, I pronounce you traitors to a boy's buttocks; Syntaxis and Prosodia you are tormentors of wit, and good for nothing but to get a

---

[1] *Lawyer's Logicke* (1588), Sig. A4 verso.
[2] Raine, op. cit., p. 75.
[3] E. Thring, *Theory and Practice of Teaching* (2nd edition, 1885), p. 104.

schoolmaster twopence a week.' Elyot, who may perhaps be regarded as a more sober witness, is equally critical, however: 'Lord God! (he lamented) How many good and clean wits of children be nowaday perished by ignorant schoolmasters.' In the upper school, too, where themes and verses 'were wrung from poor striplings like blood from a nose', the schoolmaster tended to be unaware of the danger inherent in all humanism, the danger of failing to distinguish in fact between means and ends, despite Sir Thomas More's reminder, in his prefatory epigram to Holt's *Lac Puerorum*, that the work was to be regarded as *janua nostra*, 'our gateway'.[1] The search for variety and inventiveness which Erasmus had advocated in his *De Copia* had led to what Bacon called 'that delicate and polished kind of learning . . . the cobwebs of learning, admirable for their fineness of thread and work but of no substance or profit'. Rhetoric, which Cicero, Quintilian and the humanists had meant to be an essential tool in the hands of the educated man of affairs had now, paradoxically, become the trade mark of the cloistered pedant, mere Ciceronianism. It was a trend which led Nizolius to produce a lexicon based exclusively on the writings of Cicero, which persuaded Bembo to swear never to use any Latin expression not found in Cicero, which could allow Thomas Browne to translate *Festina lente* (the motto of the press of Aldus Manutius) as 'celerity contempered with cunctation', and which led Sir Philip Sidney to wish that 'the diligent imitators of Tully and Demosthenes (most worthy to be imitated) did not so much keep Nizolian paper books of their figures and phrases as by attentive translation (as it were) devour them whole and make them wholly theirs'.[2]

At first sight it would seem that the Renaissance produced the great age of the English grammar schools which, surviving the shock of the Reformation, enjoyed royal patronage, were supported by enlightened and learned founders, and benefited from schoolmasters who had fully assimilated the educational ideas of humanism, with a wealth of humanist texts to guide both founder and teacher. All of this, moreover, was taking place

[1] R. B. McKerrow, ed., *The Works of Thomas Nashe* (Oxford, 1958), III, 279–80; Croft, I, 163; Milton, *Tractate of Education*, in *Works* (Columbia Edition, New York, 1931) IV, 278.

[2] Bacon, *Works*, III, 284 and 286; Sidney, *Apology for Poetry*, in C. G. Smith, ed., *Elizabethan Critical Essays* (Oxford, 1904), I. 202.

VII. The Hazards of Travel: Title-page of Thomas
Coryat, *Coryat's Crudities* (1611).

Around the portrait oval:

IOANNES FLORIVS AVGVSTÆ ANNÆ ANGL:SCOT:FRANC:ET HIB:REGINÆ PRÆLECTOR LING:ITALICÆ

ÆT: 58. A:D: 1611.

CHI SI CONTENTA GODE

*En virtute suâ contentus, nobilis arte,*
*Italus ore, Anglus pectore, uterq̃ opere*
*Floret adhuc, et adhuc florebit; floreat ultra*
*FLORIVS, hâc specie floridus, optat amans.*

Gul:Hole sculp:

*Tam fœlix utinam,*

VIII. John Florio: Frontispiece to His *Queen Anne's New World of Wordes* (1611).

in an age of demographic growth and increasing urbanization, which would provide an increasing demand for grammar school education. Yet such a picture would be as incomplete as it was misleading; misleading in that it is a picture of prescription rather than practice, and incomplete in that it ignores certain features of the period which were unlikely to contribute to the well-being of the schools.

In the first place it ignores the extreme degree of uniformity imposed on the schools by successive sovereigns for religious and political ends, a uniformity in which the episcopal licence rather than ability to teach became the criterion, and which resulted in a prescribed Grammar, a prescribed Catechism, a prescribed Primer and ultimately a prescribed Bible. To a lesser degree this uniformity was enhanced by the common practice of basing the statutes of a newly-founded school on those of an already-existing foundation. The statutes of Saffron Walden, for example, were revised in the 1520s 'in accordance with the method of Eton and Winchester'. When the grammar school at Cuckfield was freshly endowed by William Spicer in 1528, it was laid down that the master teach 'in the method followed at Eton'. The statutes of Sherborne in 1565 were based on those of St. Paul's, whilst Westminster's new statutes of 1560 were based on Malim's *Consuetudinarium* from Eton. Such practices might, of course, be justified, as they are in the educational programmes of the underdeveloped countries today, as the best means of creating a standard, but this is hardly in keeping with what purports to be a golden age.

Nor can we accept as complete the picture put forward by W. K. Jordan in his *Philanthropy in England*, when he attributes the increase in the number of newly-founded grammar schools to the 'determination of donors to extend and strengthen educational opportunity', thus displaying 'an almost obsessive confidence that thereby the ignorance from which poverty sprang might be dispelled, that youth might be encouraged and that a way might be cleared for all men of talent and ambition'.[1] Professor Jordan has provided an enormous amount of information which clearly shows the increase in the total number of endowed schools. Whether, in the light of the price revolution, the *value* of their endowments increased in the degree which he

---

[1] *Philanthropy in England, 1480–1660* (1959), pp. 279ff.

claims, must be doubted. But his interpretation of the motives underlying such endowments must also be questioned, for it attributes to the wealthy of the sixteenth and early seventeenth centuries a view of society and education held in their day only by visionaries like John Knox and the Comenian Puritans, and in the nineteenth and twentieth centuries by liberal democrats. Any explanation of educational foundation in the period must take into account the fact that the money which went into the endowment of grammar schools represented an attempt on the part of men rising in the social scale to achieve a respectability in the upper ranks of society which money alone could not yet ensure, and at the same time enabled them to indulge in an acceptable form of traditional charity, for which the supporting of monasteries, the founding of chantries and the building of parish churches had in former times provided an outlet.

Renaissance England had within it the seeds of a truly explosive expansion of grammar school education, both in provision and in content and method. Instead, the sovereigns of the period, faced with religious atomism, political danger and economic dislocation saw the schools as an important instrument with which to maintain public order and achieve political and religious conformity. Instead of acting as breeding grounds for humanist ideas, a distinct possibility at the beginning of the period, the grammar schools became instruments of national policy, a means of strengthening the State against religious innovation. The grammar schools of Renaissance England had become to the nation what the voluntary elementary schools of the nineteenth century were to their various demoninational sponsors, instruments for maintaining the *status quo*. It was not until the age of Thomas Arnold that a further attempt was made at the humanist study of the classics, and even later, into the twentieth century, that the grammar schools came to be regarded as instruments of social change, as a ladder up which those 'capable of profiting' could ascend.

# V

◇◇◇◇◇◇◇◇◇◇◇◇◇◇◇◇◇◇◇◇◇◇◇◇◇◇◇◇◇◇◇◇◇◇◇◇◇◇◇◇◇◇◇◇◇

# The Universities

◇◇◇◇◇◇◇◇◇◇◇◇◇◇◇◇◇◇◇◇◇◇◇◇◇◇◇◇◇◇◇◇◇◇◇◇◇◇◇◇◇◇◇◇◇

THE grammar school has always been the traditional road to the university and in the sixteenth century the move was usually made at what for us would be the early age of fourteen or fifteen. Some younger brothers would go up to university with their elder brother at an even earlier age, but this became less frequent as the period progressed. Indeed the average age of entry tended to rise in the latter part of the sixteenth and early seventeenth centuries. Some founders of grammar schools carefully linked their foundations with particular colleges, following the examples of Wykeham and Henry VI in associating Winchester with New College, Oxford, and Eton with King's College, Cambridge. Alexander Nowell, for instance, linked his grammar school at Middleton in Lancashire (1572) with Brasenose, Oxford; the new charter of Westminster (1560) associated the school with Christ Church, Oxford and Trinity College, Cambridge. In much the same way Sir Thomas White linked his College of St. John at Oxford with the Merchant Taylors' School in London by reserving thirty-seven places in the college for pupils of the school.[1]

Traditionally freshmen lived in a hall or hostel in the town, the colleges being communities of graduate fellows, mostly clerics, but with a few Canon or Civil lawyers, studying for a Master's or Doctor's degree. Only occasionally was provision

[1] Carlisle, I, 706 and II, 62 and 100–1.

made for a very few 'poor scholars', i.e. undergraduates. The sixteenth century, however, saw what were to be fundamental changes in the university system, stemming from the disappearance of the halls and the development of the modern college tutorial system. The changes in the colleges were of two kinds. In the first place, they no longer remained the preserve of graduate fellows. Besides increasing the provision for poor scholars they also began to accept undergraduate 'commoners', as fee-paying members of the college, some of them, the *commensales* or gentlemen-commoners or fellow-commoners, being the sons of the nobility and the gentry who paid extra fees and even shared the fellows' table.[1] Secondly, having absorbed the function of the medieval halls, the colleges also became teaching institutions, with the fellows taking on the teaching duties hitherto the responsibility of the university and carried out in the main by the Regent Masters, those younger fellows of colleges who were M.A.s of under three years standing. As a result of this, too, the fellows increasingly came to regard their fellowship as a position for life, instead of until such time as they completed their post-graduate studies, though they were still statutorily obliged to resign on marrying or on taking up an ecclesiastical benefice. Whereas the medieval hall had no *raison d'être* without the university, the sixteenth century college now tended to become a very much self-contained unit, providing its own teachers and providing for its own students, often in conflict with and powerful enough to resist the parent body whenever the interests of the two did not coincide.

The change was not of course an abrupt one. The pattern had been set in the first half of the fifteenth century by the founding of colleges which expressly provided for the teaching of undergraduates who were to live in the college. William Byngham's foundation of God's House (*c.* 1439) at Cambridge, for example, had the precise aim of providing an establishment in which could be trained masters of grammar, able and willing to go out to teach in grammar schools—the first teachers' training college, in fact. When the college was newly endowed and refounded as Christ's College, by Lady Margaret Beaufort

[1] For details of fees paid by the various classes of student in the first decade of the seventeenth century cf. G. H. Wakeling, *Brasenose Quartercentenary Monographs*, XI (1909), pp. 16–17.

and Bishop John Fisher it retained its special characteristic as a place in which undergraduates lived and were taught. In the same way, and perhaps more influentially, William Waynflete's statutes for Magdalen College, Oxford (1482) provided, in addition to the usual foundation, for three Readers (i.e. lecturers) in Natural Philosophy, Moral Philosophy and Theology, who were to instruct the thirty Demies and all other comers, secular or regular, without fee. More significant for the future, places were made available for twenty *commensales*, 'the sons of noble and worthy persons, friends of the College', who were to pay for their own maintenance as well as their tuition.[1] Other colleges were founded in the fifteenth century on the old pattern, St. Catherine's (1473) for instance, but it was the new which was followed by Fisher at St. John's (1516) and Fox at Corpus Christi (1516). By the middle of the century Henry VIII's own foundation of Trinity College, Cambridge (1546) provided for fifty-four pensioners in addition to the usual foundation of scholars and fellows. Today, All Souls, Oxford, alone remains a medieval college of graduates.

Teaching by the university, of course, continued and might have received added impetus by the founding of the Regius professorships in 1540. But in the event these did little to keep up attendance in 'the schools', i.e. the lecture halls. The tide was turning towards the colleges. The small exclusive communities of graduates were being transformed into large bodies of teachers and undergraduates who now 'lived in'. In the Cambridge of Erasmus most undergraduates lived in halls, the university Grace Books for the period 1488–1511 making frequent mention of these establishments and their students— though chiefly in connexion with inter-hall feuds and riots! In the Grace Book for the period 1542–89 not a single reference is to be found.[2] Trinity Hostel was still in existence in 1540, and St. Nicholas Hall is mentioned in the Edwardian statutes, but of the twenty which John Caius listed in his *History* (1574), all of which had been in existence during his lifetime, not one

---

[1] H. Rackham, ed., *Early Statutes of Christ's College* (Cambridge, 1927), prints and translates the statutes of both God's House and Christ's College; cf. A. H. Lloyd, *Early History of Christ's College* (Cambridge, 1934), pp. 11ff; H. A. Wilson, *Magdalen College* (1899), pp. 38–41.

[2] M. Bateson, ed., *Grace Book B* (Cambridge, 1903) and J. Venn, ed., *Grace Book Δ* (Cambridge, 1910).

remained at the time of writing. At Oxford in 1550 only eight halls survived with 200 students in residence, and these had all but disappeared by the end of the century.

At the same time the Heads and Masters of colleges were becoming increasingly important and powerful. Both within their own houses and within the general government of the universities, they built up positions which were further strengthened by Whitgift's statutes for Cambridge in 1570 which, besides reducing the power of the Bishop of Ely in the matter of visitations, drastically curbed the influence of the Regent Masters. As Whitgift, himself Master of Trinity in 1567–70, put it, 'A Master of a College hath perpetual office, he is the chief governor of that society, and all the members thereof owe duty and obedience unto him, as to their head, he hath authority to punish and to see laws executed, neither do I think that either archbishop or bishop claimeth greater authority and jurisdiction over their provinces and dioceses than is due to the master of his College.'[1] Whitgift was not merely claiming this power. He, and others like him, enjoyed it, and the authority of the Master was to remain undiminished until it came under the fire of the University Commissioners in 1856.

The vehemence of Whitgift's insistence on his authority may merely have reflected the controversial times in which he lived (his words were in reply to Thomas Cartwright). But he was also reiterating what earlier university men had felt important, and this gives us a first clue to the reasons why these changes in the concept of a college's function had been taking place. For, initially, Byngham's and Wykeham's and Fisher's concern had been for a closer supervision of the life and studies of prospective clerics. The medieval halls were small, they lacked continuity, their discipline was ineffective and often not binding. A student who disliked the regimen of one hall was free to move to another of his choice. With students living, dining and studying in a college devoted to 'true learning and true religion', control would become the more effective, it was felt. It is no coincidence, of course, that such an attitude became more insistent in the Tudor period, when 'true religion' was 'royal religion' and when both universities were faced with a succession

[1] J. Ayre, ed., *The Works of John Whitgift* (Parker Society, Cambridge, 1851–3), II, 179–80.

of royal visitations which led to royally approved statutes. Moreover, lay Chancellors could and did, on the sovereign's behalf, control elections to Fellowships and Masterships, as well as award degrees, grant leaves of absence, and legalize pluralities by royal mandate and royal dispensation. In 1536 it was legislated that all those proceeding to a degree must take the oath of supremacy. In 1571 Convocation at Oxford laid it down that no student would be admitted 'unless he have under the Vice-Chancellor's hand for the time being a certificate of his subscription both to the articles of Religion and Her Majesty's Supremacy'. In 1576 a general statute, in English, insisted amongst other things on subscription to the Thirty-Nine Articles on taking a degree. There was little difference between the two universities in what Professor Butterfield has called 'an unattractive submissiveness to organized power'.[1]

We have already seen how the humanists' ideas of an educated gentleman engaging himself in affairs of State, having survived the transition from civic to princely Italy, moved on to England there to be translated into a monarchical milieu by Elyot and others. It should be noted, first of all, that nowhere does Elyot, writing in the 1520s (the book was published in 1531) suggest that his future governors should attend university in order to acquire the new kind of education; the means for instruction, as it had been for Elyot himself, was to be the private tutor. And yet from the 1540s onwards we find an increasing number of gentle-born youth making their way to the universities of Oxford and Cambridge and living as commoners or pensioners in the colleges. As Hexter has put it, 'Beginning some time in the reign of Henry VIII, the sons of the titled nobility of England swarm into those citadels of clerkly training, the English universities'.[2] And this 'invasion', as Sir John Neale has called it, gathered force as the century progressed. Of the first hundred entries in the register of Gonville and Caius, which starts in 1560, twelve have parents designated as esquire, seventeen as gentlemen, eight as merchants or citizens of London, four as

---

[1] L. L. Shadwell, ed., *Enactments in Parliament Concerning the Universities of Oxford and Cambridge* (O.H.S., 1911–12), I, 119; S. Gibson, *Statuta Antiqua Universitatis Oxoniensis* (Oxford, 1931), pp. 403ff and 421; *V.C.H. Cambridge*, III, 336.

[2] J. Hexter, 'The Education of the Aristocracy in the Renaissance', *J.M.H.*, XXII (1950), p. 4.

nobleman, knight, Doctor of Medicine, and Doctor of Divinity, and fifty-nine as of *mediocris fortunae*. This latter classification, however, must not be taken too literally, as it included some whose families qualified for the Herald's Visitation and were therefore of the class of *armigeri* (esquire), as well as others who belong to the gentry class. During the period 1584–1604, on the other hand, the registers show twenty-six esquires, twenty-three gentlemen, forty-one *mediocris fortunae*, twelve yeomen, nine clergymen, six citizens of London, one sheriff, one doctor of laws and one *tenuis fortunae*. The college was still recruiting its students from a fairly wide social range, but the proportion from the gentry who entered as commoners was obviously rising steadily. At Queen's College the total number of commoners in 1531 was fourteen. In 1565 there were twenty, in 1570 forty, in 1581 seventy, in 1612, 184. At St. John's in 1573 there was a total of 271 persons in residence, including the master, fifty-one fellows, seventy-eight scholars, eighty-nine pensioners and forty-six sizars, the old 'poor and needy scholars' who were 'working their way through college' by waiting at table and acting as personal servants to the fellows and gentlemen-commoners. Hexter has further indicated that whereas in the period 1550–75 there were five undergraduates who matriculated at Oxford as *filii plebei* to every three who described themselves as gentlemen's sons, by the beginning of the century the proportion was six gentlemen to five plebeians.[1]

All this time the total number of undergraduates in the universities was rising. At the Queen's visit to Cambridge in 1564, the total number was 1,200. In 1573 Dr. Caius reckoned it to be nearly 1,800. By 1597 the numbers were well over 2,000, and by 1620, 3,000.[2] The picture was much the same at Oxford. As we have seen, not all of the increase resulted from the influx of the sons of nobility and gentry, but the proportion of places they took up was certainly rising.

Of the late 1530s Fuller remarked, 'there was now a general decay of students no college having more scholars therein than

[1] Hodgkin, op. cit., pp. 71–72; C. H. Cooper, *Annals of Cambridge* (Cambridge, 1842–5), II, 316; Hexter, loc. cit., p. 8, from the figures of A. Clark, *Register of the University of Oxford* (Oxford, 1889), II, 414.

[2] Cooper, op. cit., II, 206–7, 315–16, 568; cf. J. Simon, 'The Social Origins of Cambridge Students, 1603–40', *Past and Present*, No. 26 (November, 1963), pp. 58–67.

hardly those of the foundations, no volunteers at all, and only persons praised in a manner by their places to reside'. In 1545, in a letter to Cranmer, Ascham was complaining too, but this time because too many sons of wealthy parents were depriving poor men's sons of places. In 1549, Latimer, lamenting the shortage of educated clergy, attributed it to the fact that 'there be none now but great men's sons in Colleges and their fathers look not to have them preachers', the traditional occupation of a university graduate.[1]

It is on the strength of this undoubted influx that Sir John Neale postulates 'a cultural revolution' which was to have an important influence on the quality of the Elizabethan House of Commons. 'It still remains true (he writes) that the effectiveness of an assembly is inevitably and profoundly reflected by the quality of education its members have received', and he goes on to show that in the 1563 Parliament, out of a total of 420 members, sixty-seven had been at either Oxford and Cambridge and 108 at the Inns of Court, thirty-six attending both. Thus, 139 members had received 'a higher education'. In 1584 out of a total membership of 460, 145 had attended the 'universities and 164 the Inns. With ninety members attending both institutions this gives a figure of 219 in receipt of higher education. Of the 460 members of the 1593 Parliament 161 were university men and 197 had been at the Inns. One hundred and six had been at both, so that a higher education is claimed for 252 members. 'Little wonder (Neale concludes) that the House of Commons showed initiative and ability when—the stage reached in 1593 —43 per cent of the members possessed a legal education and 54 per cent had been to university or Inns of Court or both'.[2]

Renaissance ideas about the education of the governing class had flowed into England and as we have seen there is ample literary evidence to show that these ideas were being urged upon the governing class. It would seem that the governors were indeed sending their sons to the institutions of higher education

[1] M. Prickett and T. Wright, eds., *History of the University of Cambridge . . . by Thomas Fuller* (1840), p. 235; Ascham to Cranmer (January 1545) in J. A. Giles, ed., *Whole Works . . .* (1865), I, 69; Latimer, *Sermons* (Parker Society, Cambridge, 1845), p. 179.

[2] J. E. Neale, *The Elizabethan House of Commons* (1949), pp. 302ff.

in order to receive a training which would equip them for their future life of service at both local and national levels. Nowhere, however, is evidence given that this was the prime motive for going to university. Nor, and more important, is it inquired whether, once entered on the College Admission Book, they spent time and energy on the studies enjoined on them, nor whether in fact such studies as Elyot had recommended were being provided in the universities of Renaissance England. It becomes necessary, therefore, to seek evidence of the good intentions of this new class of undergraduate and then to consider the courses which were being provided.

Direct evidence of the first kind, of course, is hard to find and difficult to assess, but at the very least one would expect such students, given the kind of motives attributed to them or to their parents, to complete the four-year course, especially as it was during the last two years of the course that particular emphasis was laid on clear thinking and practical 'exercises' in public speaking. In fact, the vast majority of gentlemen-commoners and pensioners stayed for only a year or at most two, and when Neale's figures are more closely examined their somewhat misleading nature becomes apparent. In the 1584 Parliament, as Neale himself indicates, only fifty-four of those who 'attended' went on to take a degree, a mere 12 per cent of the total membership of the House. In 1593 the number was sixty-two out of 161, 13 per cent of the total. If we look more closely at the 127 country gentry of the 1584 Parliament who had already held county office, eight had attended the universities of whom six took a degree. Of the further thirty-three country gentry members who gained county office after 1584, eleven attended university of whom three stayed to take degrees. Similarly, of the thirty-five Crown officials in that Parliament, only four out of the thirteen who attended university gained a degree. Of these degreed men, Sir Francis Knollys, Treasurer of the Household, is counted as a university man because he registered at Magdalen in 1564, though he was also admitted to Gray's Inn in the same year and received an M.A. by royal mandate in 1598. Christopher Hatton, Vice-Chamberlain of the Household, was a gentleman-commoner at St. Mary's Hall in 1555 but went on to the Inner Temple without taking a degree, whilst Sir Francis Walsingham, Principal Secretary of State, was admitted to King's in 1548 at the ripe age of twelve, and was registered at Gray's Inn at the age of sixteen.[1]

Professor Hexter is more careful in his choice of words: 'Greys, Brandons, Manners's, Cecils and Devereux *all appear on the College Registers* between 1525 and the end of the century six peers of the Howard family alone *matriculate* at Oxford or Cambridge.' When he investigates the educational careers of the nineteen men 'who served in the lieutenancy commission between 1607 and 1619 in Northamptonshire, most (of whom) had come of age in the reign of Elizabeth' he is careful to report that 'almost four-fifths were *exposed to some kind of higher learning*, almost three-fifths *spent time* at the universities and well over a third topped their university experience *with a dab* and *sometimes* much more than a dab of education in the laws of England'.[2] Yet he arrives at the same conclusion as Neale by the same process of inference from the Admission Register and Matriculation List.

Of course, the fact that this class of student did not go on to take a degree does not of itself prove anything if it can be shown that their studies were continuous, relatively complete and earnestly undertaken. Yet there is little evidence that whilst they were up at university the sons of gentlemen who were later to serve the State displayed any great seriousness of purpose. Indeed there is evidence to show that the university authorities were on occasion in doubt as to whether they should be treated as *bona fide* students or not. In the Decrees and Orders of 1576 provision was made to exempt 'Lords and knight's sons and heirs of esquires not being graduates' from the prohibition of dress other than the scholarly black. Generally, however, efforts were made to insist that they were conscientious in their studies, Balliol for example insisting that every commoner be assigned to a master or a fellow as tutor and perform the same academic exercises as a scholar. Such regulations, on the other hand, and there were many more like them, seem not to have made any material difference. In 1561 for instance Robert Beaumont was complaining of 'licentious youth . . . and our

[1] Hazel Matthews, 'Personnel of Parliament of 1584–5', unpublished M.A. Thesis, University of London, 1948; Evelyn Trafford, 'Personnel of Parliament of 1593–4', unpublished M.A. Thesis, University of London, 1948.

[2] Loc. cit., pp. 8–9 (my italics).

epicures and careless worldlings'. Cecil made much the same sort of complaint in the following year. In 1578 a decree was promulgated to provide for

> the restoring of the ancient modesty of students, scholars and all others that shall be accounted the same . . . but especially by suffering of sundry young men, being the children of gentlemen of wealth at their coming to the same university, contrary to the ancient and comely usage of the same . . . (which) shall become rather a storehouse or a staple of prodigal, wasteful, riotous, unlearned and insufficient persons to serve or rather to unserve the necessity of the realm both in the church and civil policy.[1]

Failure to attend lectures and exercises—and, to be fair, the neglect of the lecturers themselves—had for long been a continuous complaint, so that when the Queen visited Cambridge in 1592 the 'committee concerning Her Majesty's Entertainment' took no chances and made elaborate arrangements to ensure that for the period of the visit at least, lectures would be both given and attended, even going to the length of naming the individual lecturers and disputants—a modern duty-roster with a vengeance. At Oxford the same sort of situation prevailed, provoking in 1585 the cry that 'our commoners are daily multiplied and daily grow out of order. They are bound to no exercise in this house, they are under no correction, neither will the President suffer them to be brought, although diverse times it hath been earnestly sought for. There be none in all this town farther out of order or more disobedient to all kinds of sorts than they.'[2]

There is abundant evidence, in fact, to show that the influx of the sons of the gentry into the universities did not produce a zealous group of undergraduates, eager to equip themselves for the future. But even had they wished to do so, would they have been able to acquire an education in the *studia humanitatis*?

---

[1] Gibson, op. cit., p. 404; *V.C.H. Oxford*, III, 83; *S.P. Dom. Eliz.* XIX, No. 54, cited by H. C. Porter, *Reformation and Reaction in Tudor Cambridge* (Cambridge, 1958), pp. 111–12; J. Heywood and T. Wright, eds., *Cambridge University Transactions during the Puritan Controversy* (1854), I, 217.

[2] A. Clark, ed., *Register of the University of Oxford* (Oxford, 1889), p. 229; W. D. Macray, ed., *Register of Members of Magdalen College Oxford*, N.S. II (Oxford, 1897), p. 107. See also the deposition of William Cooke, ibid., III., 11ff.

This particular question, which both Neale and Hexter over-look, must now be looked at from the point of view of both university and collegiate studies.

Much of the teaching at university level remained as it had been during the medieval period, laid down as to method and curriculum in the statutes of the universities, which, though subject during the sixteenth century to successive scrutiny and 'revision' at the beginning of each reign, were modified very largely to suit religious policy and could not be regarded as curricular changes to any great degree. This kind of teaching was carried out, as in the past, by the Regent Masters in 'the schools' from nine o'clock to eleven in the forenoon. These 'ordinary lectures'—the *lectiones cursoriae*—consisted in the reading through of a set text, usually Aristotle, and the making of short comments on its subject matter.

Changes in the curriculum and the traditional methods of teaching at university level were, however, attempted from the end of the fifteenth century by the separate endowment of 'professorships', 'readerships' or 'lectureships'. The terms were used indifferently to describe such endowments as the Lady Margaret Divinity Lectureships (1497) at each of the universities, which were permanently endowed in 1502, each with an independent stipend of £20 per annum. The lectures were to be given on four days a week during term and the Long Vacation from such theological works as would be approved by the Chancellor and Doctors of the university. These were the *lectiones solennes*, formal lectures in the modern sense, giving an exposition of a particular point or question. Though the method was new, we do well to remind ourselves of the innate conservatism of the educational system by noting that the first of the Lady Margaret lecturers, Edmund Wylford, used the *Quodlibeta* of Duns Scotus as the basis of his lectures.[1] In the same way, Sir Robert Rede endowed three readerships in philosophy, logic and rhetoric at Cambridge with stipends of £4 per annum each, and in 1535 the Visitors to Oxford established public lecture-ships in Greek at Magdalen, in Latin at Merton and Queen's, and in Greek and Latin at New College and All Souls. Most impor-tant, in 1540, Henry VIII set up the five Regius Professorships

[1] Gibson, *Statuta*, pp. 300ff; Cooper *Annals*, I, 247. *V.C.H. Oxford*, III, 17.

in Divinity, Greek, Hebrew, Civil Law and Physic, each with an annual stipend of £40. By the institution of such lectureships as these it was obviously hoped not only to supplement but also to improve the standard of university teaching, and much was expected of the new professorships, especially when John Cheke was appointed to the Chair of Greek and Sir Thomas Smith to that of Civil Law. But the hope that university studies would be stimulated was in the event disappointed. Neither Cheke nor Smith remained at Cambridge for more than three years, and Ascham wrote eloquently of the gap left by Cheke's departure for Court in 1542.[1] In an age of inflation the fixed stipends soon bore no relation to current needs, and by the time James I had augmented the stipends of both the Lady Margaret readerships and the Regius Chairs, by granting the revenues of the rectories of Terringham and Townsham, a tradition of nonlecturing had become accepted in practice if not in theory. In 1570 Parker reported to the Queen that 'in your university of Cambridge not two in the whole are able or willing to read the Lady Margaret Lecture'. At Oxford in 1576 it was found necessary to remind the King's readers and the Lady Margaret lecturers of their duties, and to lay down fines of 6s. 8d. for noncompliance, a reminder which was repeated in 1581, but with a similar lack of success.[2] Again in 1602 a detailed statement to Archbishop Whitgift concerning 'Disorders tending to the decay of learning and other dissolute behaviour' referred to the fact that 'of those who should read four times a week some read not four times a year'.[3] The period of violent religious change in the mid-century had, of course, contributed to the decline in the universities which John Jewel characterized as 'a dismal solitude . . . without learning, without lecturers, without religion'. Throughout the second half of the century we find constant exhortation, backed on occasion by threat of fine, to attend both the ordinary and the specific lectures. But attendance was not forthcoming and when renewed efforts were made in 1599 to enforce attendance in accordance with the statutes the

---

[1] *Toxophilus* (1545), in Giles, *Whole Works* . . ., III, 67, cf. Ryan, op. cit., pp. 18ff.

[2] J. Bruce and T. T. Perowne, ed., *Correspondence of Matthew Parker* (Parker Society, Cambridge, 1853), p. 374; Gibson, *Statuta*, pp. 407 and 423.

[3] G. Peacock, *Observations on the Statutes of the University of Cambridge* (1841), p. 61, no. 1.

students claimed that the statutes allowed either attendance or a fine and that they were ready to pay the latter.[1]

In addition to the statutory lecturing of the Regent Masters and the newly endowed lectureships to which we have just referred, the university was responsible for the 'exercises' of the students which took place in the schools every Monday, Wednesday and Friday afternoon in term. In these the student was meant, through the medium of the traditional disputation and declamation, to apply the formal precepts in logic and rhetoric received in both university and collegiate lectures to the practical business of public speaking and debate. The orations which the students produced for these 'exercises' were intended as practical tests for the sophisters, those in the last two years of their undergraduate training, acting as essays would for the modern student. The disputations were also to be attended by the second-year men, who were thus introduced to the elaborate pattern of procedure between the respondent and his two opponents, supervised by a Regent Master as moderator. It was taken for granted, of course, that the student had had some introduction to this kind of work in the grammar school composition of themes on rhetorical patterns, and would continue the keeping of commonplace books, an essential and universal part of an undergraduate's work, and one which Richard Holdsworth reminded his pupils would 'furnish you with a quantity of syllables, perfect your Latin and supply you in copiousness of word and good expressions, and also raise your fancy to a poetic strain'. The Determinations which an intending Bachelor performed in 'the schools' during lent, were a final public demonstration of an undergraduate's proficiency in the art of public speaking, as well as a recognition of his fitness to proceed to higher studies. Thus, by his early and continuous study of grammar the student familiarized himself with the Latin language and its structure. Through logic he learned to think precisely and without irrelevance, and by rhetoric to convey his thought in a manner which would persuade his hearers of the rightness of his argument.[2]

The argument that printed books were now available and,

[1] Jewel to Peter Martyr, in H. Robinson, ed., *Zurich Letters* (Parker Society, Cambridge, 1842), I, 11, 40, 77; Clarke, *Register*, p. 10.

[2] For technical details of exercises and examples of *theses* or *quaestiones* set for M.A. candidates cf. Clarke, *Register*, pp. 21ff and 169ff.

therefore, made the 'ordinary' lectures of the Regent Masters obsolete, was often put forward, though no attempt was made to modify the method of this type of elementary teaching. The same point could not, however, be made about the *lectiones solennes*, and yet both student and lecturer were neglectful of this type of teaching too. Of all the teaching undertaken by the university the exercises, perhaps, would have been the most useful for the intending man of affairs, who would need to be able to organize his argument and present it in the most persuasive manner. Yet once again, we find evidence of continual neglect by both teacher and student. In an address to the university in 1547 Walter Haddon deplored the neglect of 'the common schools', a term which, he claimed, was becoming something of a misnomer, both in respect of attendance at lectures and participation in the exercises. John Caius's *History*, written in 1548, paints the same kind of picture, and the behaviour of the students seems not to have changed when Harrison wrote his *Description of England* (1577), for at that time

> most of them study little other than histories, tables, dice and trifles. . . . Besides this, being for the most part either gentlemen or rich men's sons they oft bring the university into much slander. For standing upon their reputation and liberty, they ruffle and roist it out, exceeding in apparel and hunting riotous company, (which draweth them from their books into another trade) and for excuse they are charged with breach of one good order think it sufficient to say that they be gentlemen which grieveth many not a little.[1]

But as we have seen the university was no longer the sole provider in the sixteenth century. The colleges were now beginning to provide instruction within their own walls, though as Walter Haddon said, with reference to the new royal foundation of Trinity College, they were never intended to provide alternative teaching nor to become 'a hiding place in which to remain wrapt in private meditations.'[2] The admission of commoners did not at first necessarily mean that collegiate tuition was provided for them. In the sixteenth century, however, it increasingly became the practice to provide in the statutes of the new founda-

[1] F. J. Furnivall, ed., *William Harrison's Description of England* (New Shakespeare Society, Series VI, Pt. I, 1877), pp. 77–78.
[2] Mullinger, *Cambridge*, II, 96.

tions for college lecturers and readers, and to insist that students be attached to particular tutors who would be responsible for their moral welfare as well as their academic studies. The very detailed statutes of the new royal foundation of Trinity College, Cambridge (1546), and those for Sir Thomas White's foundation of St. John's, Oxford (1560), best exemplify this, but the revisions of the statutes of older colleges also show the same trend. At Queen's College, Oxford, for instance, lectureships in Greek, logic and theology were set up, and Brasenose amended its statutes to establish lectureships in philosophy and humanity in 1555, Greek in 1578 and Hebrew in 1628.[1]

Few of these additions, however, showed many signs of a serious attempt to introduce Renaissance studies into the colleges; although we might have expected Henry VIII's foundation of Trinity to follow the lead of Fox, at Corpus Christi, in fact the works of Aristotle predominate among the prescribed texts.[2] What was new was the provision of regular lectures at collegiate level, and perhaps more important for the future the institution of the college tutor.

It has been claimed that it was through this collegiate teaching that the gentlemen of Renaissance England obtained the education which fitted them for service to the State, and that the college tutor was the key figure in this education.[3] Two claims are made for the latter. The first is that, surrounded by the 'neglect and irresponsibility of the (university) lecturers', the college tutor showed 'dedicated attention' to his pupils, and that the 'burden of undergraduate education fell on more vigorous, adaptable and stimulating methods of instruction that developed simultaneously within the colleges.' Secondly, that it was through the college tutor, the statutory curriculum of the university notwithstanding, that modern studies fit for the education of a Renaissance gentleman became the norm. Curtis quotes with approval, for example, Lady Bacon's description of the universities in 1564, which was published with her translation of John Jewel's *Apology*. Yet, like Fortescue's late fifteenth-century description of the Inns of Court, this must surely be regarded as

[1] *V.C.H. Oxford*, III, 134, 209.

[2] Mullinger, *Cambridge*, II, Appendix A prints the statutes of the college.

[3] M. H. Curtis, *Oxford and Cambridge in Transition, 1558–1642* (Oxford, 1959), Chap. iv.

a eulogistic description of what ought to have happened rather that what in fact did happen.

The burden of Curtis's case rests, however, on the evidence provided in the 'Directions for a Student in the University' of Richard Holdsworth, Fellow of St. John's, 1613–20, and Master of Emmanuel, 1637–43, in which is found a remarkably 'modern' course of suggested reading, as well as evidence of the conscientious way in which Holdsworth regarded his duties as a tutor. He emphasized rhetoric at the expense of logic, and he paid particular attention to the way in which an undergraduate tackled his studies. Moreover, though Holdsworth relied almost entirely on Aristotle in the first two years of the course, no mention ever being made of Ramus or of English texts based on Ramus, his selected readings from classical literature were all that a humanist could have wished for, including in the first year Cicero, Terence and Ovid, as well as Erasmus's *Colloquies*, Valla's *De Elegantiis* and Vigerius's *Idiotismes* for the study of rhetoric. Later, Horace, Juvenal, Lucan and Plautus together with Livy, Florus, Quintus Curtius and Suetonius were to be read, whilst Greek authors would include Aesop, Hesiod, Theocritus, Demosthenes and Homer.

Holdsworth was a tutor at St. John's College, Cambridge, one of the earliest and most famous of the humanist foundations on which, with Fox's Corpus Christi, Wolsey's Cardinal College and the royal foundations, so many humanist hopes had been centred. But the foundation of Saint John Fisher became, during Elizabeth's reign, a notorious centre for Protestant dissension and faction, with fellow divided against fellow. Curtis's picture of 'dedicated attention' accords ill with Porter's description of Cambridge at this time, and with the continual charge and counter-charge and consequent injunctions, admonitions and exhortations which fill the pages of Elizabethan university history. We may perhaps—though not certainly—dismiss Bucer's criticism 'that the greater part of the Fellows are either most bitter Papists or profligate epicureans, who as far as they are able, draw over the young men to their way of thinking and imbue them with an abhorrence of sound Christian doctrine and discipline', as nothing more than sectarian invective, but there was no doubt in Parker's mind that matters were no better when he wearily wrote to Cecil, 'If your honour will hear their challenges ye shall hear such cumbrous trifles and brabbles that ye shall be weary. . . . Scholars' controversies be now many and troublous; and their delight is to come before men of authority to show their wits; and I cannot tell you how such busy sorts draw to them some of the graver personages to be doers, *an ex sinceritate et ex bona conscientia nescio.*' The detailed statement to Whitgift in 1602, furthermore, made it quite clear that 'the dissoluteness and roguishness of some tutors was proving the undoing of many students both in learning and in manners', and even if these were in the minority, the purchase of fellowships and the 'corrupt resignations', whereby 'resigned places pass to scholars designed by the resigners at very excessive cost to their parents', would hardly contribute to a teaching body working with 'dedicated attention'.[1] The latter practice had in fact been growing since Henry VIII's reign, had been noted by the visitors of the college during the Magdalen controversies in 1585 and called forth the comment in 1595, 'I hear thou art in preferring grown too partial, thou lovest thyself sinisterly, and have quite forgotten me thy mother, it is thy sister's fault as well as thine, You both of you prefer such unto your favours, grace them with degrees and give them places.'[2]

Holdsworth was undoubtedly a remarkable tutor, though his reading list was so exhaustive and detailed that it is unlikely that any but the best of his pupils could make much of it. But in any case he was teaching too late for him to stand examplar for the period which produced Neale's Members of Parliament. Whitgift, on the other hand, may be regarded as one of the more conscientious tutors during the earlier period, and his college (Trinity) had become one of the most popular for gentleman-commoners in Cambridge. But his tutorial accounts for the early years of the 1570's show that though he bought plenty of Ciceros for his pupils, his philosophy text was the traditional *Dialectica* of John Seton, written as the author explained in order to make Aristotle intelligible. The two other texts most frequently

[1] Bucer to Calvin, 1550, in H. Robinson, ed., *Original Letters Relative to the English Reformation* (Parker Society, Cambridge, 1846–7), II, 546; Parker to Cecil, 1565, in Bruce and Perowne, op. cit., p. 249; Peacock, op. cit., p. 61, n. 1; *V.C.H. Oxford*, III, 178.
[2] W. C., gent., *A Letter from England to her Three Daughters, Cambridge, Oxford and the Inns of Court* . . . (1595), in A. B. Grosart, ed., *Occasional Issues of Unique or Very Rare Books*, XV (1881), p. 40.

mentioned in the accounts are Aristotle's *Organon* and *de Physica* and we find little evidence of humanist texts being bought for his pupils. Similarly the scheme of teaching drawn up in the 1570s by Robert Norgate, Master of Corpus Christi College, shows a daily routine of one hour of Aristotle's natural philosophy, and elementary lectures in Greek grammar and construction and rhetoric in the afternoon with Cicero as the text.[1] Again, one of the most famous tutors of the period, John Preston of Queen's, 'the greatest pupil-monger in England in man's memory', who numbered the fourth Earl of Lincoln, the two sons of Sir Henry Yelverton, the sons of Sir Henry Capel and the son and heir of Lord Saye and Sele amongst his students, was characterized by another of his pupils, Thomas Ball, as one who 'adoreth Aristotle as his tutelary Saint'. The same kind of traditional teaching is to be found in the evidence provided by the account books of Joseph Mead, Fellow of Christ's College, 1613–18. Among the books he purchased for his pupils Aristotle reigns supreme, sometimes though *de Anima* or the *Organon*, but more often through the medium of that universal uncle of early seventeenth-century students, Bartholomew Keckermann, who produced manuals in logic, natural philosophy, ethics, rhetoric, theology, Hebrew and even geography, most of them Aristotelian in origin and method. Curtis also quotes the 'Rules' of James Duport, Fellow of Trinity and Master of Magdalene after the Restoration, but even as late as this he was advising his pupils, 'in your answering reject not lightly the authority of Aristotle, if his words will permit of a favourable and a sure interpretation. . . . Follow not Ramus in logic nor Lipsius in Latin, but Aristotle in one and Tully in the other.'[2]

It would seem, then, that the inferential claims of Neale and the more direct championship of Curtis need serious qualification. Certainly Curtis's claims for 'the creative role of Oxford

---

[1] Cf. S. R. Maitland, 'Archbishop Whitgift's College Pupils', *British Magazine*, XXXII (1847), pp. 361–79, 508–28, 650–6 and XXXIII, 17–31, 185–97 and 444–63; Porter, op. cit., pp. 50–51.

[2] T. Bull, *Life of Reverend Dr. Preston* (1628), ed., E. W. Harcourt (1885), p. 9; J. Peile, 'On Four MS Books of Accounts kept by Joseph Mead, Fellow of Christ's College with his pupils between 1614–33', *Cambridge Antiquarian Society Communications*, XIII (1909), pp. 250–61; for Keckerman see W. T. Costello, *The Scholastic Curriculum at Early Seventeenth Century Cambridge* (Cambridge, Mass., 1958), *passim*; G. M. Trevelvan, 'Undergraduate Life during the Protectorate, *Cambridge Review*, 22 May 1943, pp. 238–40, prints Duport's *Rules*.

and Cambridge in English thought and society' go too far towards the eulogistic, especially when he writes:—

> They were the chief agent for maturing and broadening the intel-
> lectual classes of England. They did more than any other institution
> to develop a body of trained and cultivated men who used their
> learning and knowledge to direct the political fortunes of their
> nation to guide the taste and manners of their fellows, to preserve
> and clarify, to criticize and revise the beliefs and ideals of their
> culture. They helped to instil the moral and religious ideals that
> were common to Englishmen and to provide a common general
> education to the more highly educated and influential members of
> the intellectual classes. On the other hand they made important
> contributions to the cohesiveness of English society. They helped
> to nurture the highest moral and religious ideals to which English-
> men subscribed, facilitated associations among Englishmen of all
> classes, promoted the growth of a community of feeling and atti-
> tude, and improved the means of social mobility.[1]

It was precisely in the sixteenth century that the universities
ceased to be the true *community* of scholars which had been their
chief characteristic in the medieval period, and it is naïve to
claim that 'Yeomen's sons and earl's sons, merchant's sons and
heirs of the landed gentry were all bred together in learning'.[2]
They lived together within the walls of a college, but whether
the earl's son, dining as a gentleman-commoner at the fellows'
table, took much cognizance of the yeoman's son is highly doubtful. Again, though 'education' came to be expected of the upper
class, it never of itself 'improved the means of social mobility'.
This is a twentieth-century concept. In the Renaissance period it
was landed wealth which first and foremost enabled a man to
rise in the social scale, and it simply was not true that 'learning,
gained in institutions open to men of all sorts, was a means of
social advancement which increased the flexibility of the social
system and reduced the chances that narrow pride on one side
and frustration on the other would embitter the relations between the aristocracy and the other classes of English society'.[3]
At university, of course, that essential of Tudor and Stuart
society, connexion, could be acquired or furthered. The gentry

---

[1] Op. cit., p. 262.
[2] Ibid., p. 269.
[3] Ibid., p. 271.

sent their sons to university primarily for social rather than educational reasons, as a useful, indeed necessary form of conspicuous consumption. It was for this reason, too, that in the history of the universities in England the late sixteenth century stands out as the age when a young man's 'university days' first came to be regarded as a period for the 'sowing of wild oats', an attitude of mind which predominated until the era of grant-aided students, which started in earnest only after the Second World War. A gentleman of Renaissance England fitted himself for his future rôle of governor more often than not *after* he left university, as we shall see.

Curtis's claim for the modernity of university studies must also be modified, though in this case less drastically. Most of the evidence he adduces in this respect stems, as we have seen, from Holdsworth's *Directions*. He supplements this by reference to the books found on the shelves and recorded in the inventories of undergraduates who died whilst still at university. The statutes, he maintains, tell us nothing of what was actually studied. Yet Holdsworth's work and the undergraduate books to which Curtis refers relate to the second and third decades of the seventeenth century, too late to buttress the claims of Neale and Hexter, and in any case are not sufficiently typical to use as the basis for a general assessment of university studies.[1] Though tuition in mathematics and science, for example, was available, it was not systematically organized and relied very largely on the interests and enthusiasms of what must have been a minority of tutors. It would, of course, be surprising if it were found to be otherwise. The universities aimed at the conservation of knowledge and the provision of 'liberal studies', and in the eyes of the university authorities the new mathematics and science, with their anti-Aristotelianism and their emphasis on practical applications, would hardly be deemed appropriate for such purposes. The Edwardian statutes had, indeed, included mathematics in the first-year course, and amongst the prescribed texts was the new algebra of Giralamo Cardan, the *Ars Magna* ( 1545). But there is no evidence that anyone lectured on it, and the subject was, in any case, omitted in the Elizabethan revision of 1570. William

---

[1] For an exhaustive treatment of Cambridge in these years cf. H. F. Fletcher, *The Intellectual Development of John Milton, II: the University of Cambridge Period* (Urbana, 1961), which also prints Holdsworth's 'Directions', pp. 623–55.

Buckley, whom Cheke had sent to King's College, Cambridge, in 1548, to teach mathematics, produced a text of his own, *Arithmetica Memorativa* (1567)—in Latin hexameters, almost thirty years after Robert Recorde's *Grounde of Arts* had shown how to set out a mathematical textbook. Though Recorde was a fellow of All Souls for a time, not one of his books found its way into his college's library.[1] John Dee taught mathematics in the universities of Louvain, Paris and Rheims, but refused an invitation to do so in Oxford in 1554, and his famous preface to Henry Billingsley's translation of Euclid emphasized the practical utility of such a study, especially for those 'very good and pregnant English wits, of young gentlemen and of others, who never intend to meddle with the profound search and study of philosophy, in the universities to be learned.' By the turn of the century there were, undoubtedly, tutors and students interested enough to study the new mathematical and scientific texts, though (in the words of John Wallis) 'not as a formal study, but as a pleasing diversion, at spare hours. . . .'[2] What Curtis's lists show is that 'modern' books were available, and that some few undergraduates read them with the help and guidance of exceptional tutors like Holdsworth.

As to the statutes, whether university or collegiate, though they do not necessarily tell us what actually went on, we cannot ignore them as Curtis would have us do. Revised and repeated as they were, they certainly reflected the considered view of the most senior and responsible members of the universities as to the kind of studies necessary to achieve the aims of a university in Renaissance England, studies which they believed could and would be undertaken and carried through. Cecil, for example, in 1601 ordered the Vice-Chancellor (yet again, it seemed) to ensure that 'all duties and exercises of learning be diligently and duly performed according to the Statutes and Orders of the University',[3] and Laud, indeed, went so far as to have a digest of the new statutes of 1636 prepared, because (as

[1] W. W. Rouse Ball, *A History of the Study of Mathematics at Cambridge* (Cambridge, 1889), p. 13; R. T. Gunther, *Early Science at Oxford* (1922), I, Pt. 2, p. 21.

[2] Billingsley, *Euclid*, Sig. A iiii; Wallis, in an autobiographical letter to Thomas Smith, 29 January 1697, in T. Hearne, ed., *Peter of Langtoft's Chronicle* (1810), I, cxlvii.

[3] Cited by Costello, op. cit., p. 8.

he wrote) 'since the publishing of the new statutes there hath been some complaint made that the younger sort cannot have access often enough to the statute book which is reserved in every particular college thereby to know all hours for lectures and all other duties required of them. Hereupon it was thought fit that an abridgement of them should be made especially of those which concern manners and exercise.'[1] There were, one presumes, then as now, three types of student, those who attended to what was prescribed, those who didn't and managed to enjoy a lively social life, and those few brave souls who made the most of what extra-curricular instruction and inspiration was provided by a similarly small body of university teachers.

The method of study, based as it very largely was on the lecture, the disputation and the declamation, remained scholastic throughout most of the seventeenth century, and Aristotle, 'whose authority is paramount', remained the lynch pin of university studies, as the many surviving notebooks and commonplace books of the more diligent undergraduates remind us. If the university is to be regarded as a market of ideas it could hardly be said that either Oxford or Cambridge traded in *new* ideas. Certainly both showed every sign of reluctance to accept new ideas and to assimilate them into their courses of study. Nor did they make any great effort to modify their courses to meet the supposed needs of the new type of student who filled the expanding colleges. Scholasticism was certainly in decline during the seventeenth century but it took an unconscionable time in dying, and 'unless scholasticism is appreciated as the pattern of undergraduate (and post-graduate) thinking it is impossible to understand seventeenth-century Cambridge or what came out of it'.[2] And this remains true even when it is remembered that it was at Cambridge (to a lesser degree at Oxford) that the works of Peter Ramus and Talaeus found their chief supporters. Despite the advocacy of men like Laurence Chaderton, Gabriel Harvey, William Temple and William Gouge in the schools and colleges of Cambridge, Ramus's attempt to reorganize or 'methodize' the scholastic curriculum—for his aim was neither

[1] W. Laud, *Works*, V, 189–90. The abridgement was made by Thomas Crosfield, cf. F. S. Boas, ed., *The Diary of Thomas Crosfield* (1935), pp. xiv–xv.

[2] Costello, op. cit., p. 4. Cf. Locke's criticism of its continued influence in *Thoughts Concerning Education* (1690).

to abolish it nor to introduce 'modern' studies in its place—
failed to make any permanent impact. His work and his supporters produced notorious controversy in the last three decades
of the sixteenth century, and Ramistic texts, whether direct
translations or works based on his method, poured from the
presses. As we have seen, one of the most popular of school texts
was Charles Butler's *Rhetoric* (*Rhetoricae Libri Duo*, 1597, etc.),
which produced eight editions in half a century and was recommended by both Brinsley and Hoole. Yet we search in vain for
Ramistic texts among those bought or recommended by Whitgift, Mead, Holdsworth and Duport (who explicitly rejects
Ramus), though Dr. Thomas Worrall of Brasenose recommended Ramus to his pupil Richard Matten.[1]

Indeed, far from the simplification which Ramus and Talaeus
aimed at, the trend in logic seemed towards more and more
commentary on Aristotle, and in rhetoric towards a Ciceronianism which reached its ultimate in John Lyly's *Euphues*. The
anonymous seventeenth-century tutor who complained that 'we
are burdened with a variety of dialectics, and unless God hears
our cry Aristotle is likely to have more commentators than contexts'[2] was merely repeating what John Seton felt, about 1540,
when, as he tells us, he produced his *Dialectica* because 'modern
writers want rather to embellish the subject than to make it
understood'. With its elaborate and repetitious patterns, its
iterations and alliterations, its grouping of similes and its extravagant illustrations drawn from strange sources, in Euphuism
rhetoric ran riot. Ralph Lever was already complaining in 1573
that 'Ciceronians and sugar-tongued fellows labour more for
fineness of speech than for knowledge of good matter; they often
speak much to small purpose and shaking forth a number of
choice words and picked sentences (they) hinder good learning
with fond chat.' In 1580 Philip Sidney warned his younger
brother Robert that Ciceronianism was then 'the chief abuse of

---

[1] Clark, *The Lives of Sundry Eminent Persons of the Later Age* (1683), p. 183.
The best work on Ramus is W. T. Ong, *Ramus, Method and the Decay of Dialogue*
(Cambridge, Mass., 1958). For the English Ramists cf. W. S. Howell, *Logic
and Rhetoric in England 1500–1700* (Princeton, 1956), pp. 173–281; H. S. Wilson
and C. A. Forbes, eds., *Gabriel Harvey's Ciceronianus* (University of Nebraska
Studies in English, No. 4, 1945); and H. S. Wilson, 'Gabriel Harvey's Orations
on Rhetoric', *E.L.H.*, XII (1945), pp. 167–82.
[2] Cited by Costello, op. cit., p. 45.

Oxford'. Bacon repeated the criticism in a famous passage in *The Advancement of Learning*, and the historian of the Royal Society's early years provides us with a significant commentary on the longevity of the method:—

> Who can behold without indignation how many mists and uncertainties these specious tropes and figures have brought our knowledge. How many rewards which are due to more profitable and difficult arts have been still snatched away by the easy variety of fine speaking? . . . They[1] have therefore been most rigorous in putting in execution the only remedy that can be found for this extravagance, and that has been a constant resolution to reject all amplifications, digressions and swellings of style; to return back to the primitive pureness and shortness when men delivered so many things almost in an equal number of words. They have exacted from all their members a close-marked, natural way of speaking, positive expressions, clear senses, a native easiness, bringing all things as near in mathematical plainness as they can and professing the language of citizens, countrymen and merchants before that of wits and scholars.

Modern scientists may well demur at the ambiguity of the last sentence, but here we have the origin of the 'note' and 'communication' of the modern scientific journal.[2]

As further evidence of what was regarded as the inappropriateness of university studies for the education of the future governors, we may cite the many schemes put forward in Renaissance England with the express purpose of providing an alternative to the old chivalric education. Few of these schemes thought of the university as the appropriate place for such an education. Thomas Starkey, for instance, in his *Dialogue* (*c.* 1533–6) suggested that

> Likewise as we have in our Universities colleges and common places to nourish the children of poor men in letters (whereby as you see, cometh no small profit to the common weal), so much more we should have, as it were, certain places appointed for the bringing up together of the nobility to which I would the nobles should be compelled to set forward their children and heirs, that

[1] I.e. the Fellows of the Royal Society.

[2] *The Arte of Reason Rightly Termed Witcraft* (1573), Sig. i *verso*; W. A. Bradley, ed., *The Correspondence of Philip Sidney and Hubert Languet* (Boston, Mass., 1912), p. 223; Bacon, *Works*, III, 283–4; and T. Sprat, *A History of the Royal Society of London* (1667), pp. 112–13.

in as much together they might better the profit. To this use turn bothWestminster and St. Albans and many other.[1]

Starkey was here primarily criticizing the education of the nobility by private tutor as recommended by Elyot, but the existing institutions were regarded as appropriate only for the education of the clergy, and a quite separate establishment was deemed necessary for the education of the nobility. When Sir Nicholas Bacon drew up, with Thomas Denton and Robert Cary, a scheme for the education of statesmen for Henry VIII, he suggested it be carried out in London, and though he did not indicate a site for a later scheme for the education of the royal wards, he quite plainly did not intend the studies he prescribed to take place in the universities.[2] Again, Sir Humphrey Gilbert's elaborate scheme for 'the erection of an academy . . . for the education of Her Majesty's wards and others, the youth of nobility and gentlemen' indicated that London was to be its setting, and not Oxford and Cambridge, this having the added advantages that 'the other Universities shall then better suffice to relieve poor scholars, where now the youth of nobility and gentlemen taking up their scholarships and fellowships do disappoint the poor of their livings and advancements'.[3] And when Gresham College, the only one of such schemes to be put into practice, was founded in 1598, it, too, was sited in London.

The significance of the siting of these projected academies is further reinforced by the curriculum they advocated. Though Starkey did not give a detailed course of studies, he constantly emphasized the need for an all-round education, which ministered to the needs of the body as well as of the mind and the soul, and throughout he makes clear the practical end of such an education. Bacon's earlier scheme was for the especial provision of statesmen well-versed in the laws of the land and was based on the study of French and Latin. For his later scheme five schoolmasters were to be assigned, 'The first to read a lecture of the temporal or civil law and one other *de disciplina militari*. The second to teach the Latin and Greek tongue to whom for

---

[1] Op. cit., p. 169.

[2] The earlier scheme is printed in E. Waterhous, *Fortescutus Illustratus* . . . (1663), pp. 539–46, the later piece in J. Conway Davies, 'Elizabethan Plans and Progress for Education', *Durham Research Review*, No. 5 (1954), pp. 2–3.

[3] F. J. Furnivall, ed., *Queene Elizabeth's Achademy* (E.E.T.S., Extra Series, VIII, 1869).

assistance an usher would be joined, able to teach them to write fair. The third the French and other languages. The fourth music and qualities thereupon depending. The fifth to ride, to vault, to handle weapons, and such other things as thereto belongeth.'[1] Cecil, himself Master of the Court of Wards, had a household full of young noblemen sent to him to guide their education. There they were instructed in Latin, French and cosmography as well as 'writing and drawing, . . . riding, shooting, dancing, walking and other commendable exercises'.[2] On the other hand whilst the curriculum he prescribed for those under his own roof was thoroughly and typically humanistic he nevertheless produced a memorandum for the Parliament of 1559 'That an ordinance be made to bind the nobility to bring up their children in learning at some university in England or beyond the sea from the age of 12 to 18 at least', at a time when he well knew the universities were at their lowest ebb after the reign of Mary, and would certainly not provide the kind of education he was providing for those in his care.[3]

The most comprehensive scheme of higher education put forward at this time was that of Sir Humphrey Gilbert, whose plan for a 'Queen Elizabeth's Achademy' clearly shows the gulf which lay between what was considered necessary for the education of 'the youth of nobility and gentlemen' and what was general in the universities. Situated in London to be close to the court, it would be both grammar school and university. Masters for Latin and Greek, Hebrew, logic and rhetoric would be assisted by four ushers. Great emphasis was to be placed on spoken English. Those in charge of the higher studies were to take especial care to point out the practical aspects of the work. The Reader in Moral Philosophy, for instance, was to emphasize the political significance of his subject matter. The two mathematicians would concentrate, respectively, on arithmetic and geometry, 'which shall be only employed to Imbattelings, fortifications and matters of war with the practice of Artillery and use of all manner of instruments belonging to the same', and cosmography and astronomy, relating 'the practices there-

---

[1] J. Conway Davies, loc. cit., p. 2.

[2] Ibid., p. 4.

[3] Considerations Delivered to the Parliament, 1559, in *H.M.C.*, *Salisbury MSS.* (1883), I, 162.

of only to the art of navigation, with the knowledge of necessary stars, making use of instruments appertaining to the same'. There were to be lecturers in French, Italian, Spanish and High Dutch (i.e. German), and besides Readers in Civil Law and Divinity, a Lawyer 'who shall read the grounds of the common law . . . and . . . set down and touch exquisitely the office of a Justice of the Peace and sheriff'. The Physician was, against all university practice, to teach in the English tongue and to combine theory and practice with appropriate demonstrations, and together with the Reader in Natural Philosophy would carry out experiments, the results of which were to be delivered annually in writing for the benefit of posterity. In addition precise and detailed provision was made for the acquisition of the 'accomplishments' which were considered an essential part of a humanistic education. A Riding Master was to 'teach noblemen and gentlemen to ride, make and handle a ready horse, exercise them to run at Ring, Tilt, Tourney and course of the field . . . and also to skirmish on horseback with pistol', the handling of which would be taught by a 'perfect-trained soldier' who would also be responsible for practice in 'all kinds of skirmishings, imbattelings, and sundry kinds of marchings, appointing among them some one time some another to supply the rooms of Captains and other officers, which they may very well exercise without arms and with light staves, instead of Pikes and Halberds'. A 'Master of Defence' would take care of instruction in the other weapons of the day, 'the rapier and dagger, the sword and tergat, the grip of the dagger, the battle axe and the pike'. As for the less martial accomplishments, the young gentlemen would be taught dancing and such musical instruments as 'the lute, the Bandora and cyttern, etc.'

Most of this was as far removed from what went on in the universities as could be imagined, and, as we have suggested, other motives must be sought to explain the influx of the gentle-born into the universities of Renaissance England. Meanwhile, these institutions remained the sole training ground for the nation's clergy, though the sixteenth century did see the disappearance of the monastic habit from the schools and streets of Oxford and Cambridge.

As we have seen, in the early years of the century both Oxford and Cambridge, in their turn, had become centres where the techniques of humanism and the study of the ancient languages produced critical editions and texts of both the Bible and the works of the Christian Fathers, with the prime motive of attempting a reform of the Church from within. As a corollary to this, they constantly preached the need for an educated clergy. With the coming of the Reformation and the greater emphasis on individual responsibility in religious life, a new feature in the educational programme appeared, namely the need for an educated flock, a provision which further heightened the need for a reformed clergy. The universities, therefore, as the training ground of the clergy, became key institutions in the religious life of the country, a point well-recognized by both the sovereign and the Church hierarchy. Jewel's affirmation that 'as learning is dangerous and hurtful without religion, so religion is unable to *defend itself and to convince the gainsayers* without learning', serves to remind us not only of the way churchmen were aware of the need for both scholarship and education, but also that scholarship was considered but a means to an end, something to be put to the service of the Church.[1]

The problem was clearly seen. How far did the universities provide what was wanted? It is clear that the senior members of the English Church were, with some few remarkable exceptions, learned and conscientious in their efforts to see that both pastors and flock were better educated. But the universities, fearful in the 1540's for their continued existence and too busy during Elizabeth's reign with religious controversy, produced no great theological scholars who could compare, say, with Martin Bucer and Peter Martyr. Hooker, who immediately comes to mind, became a fellow of his college, Corpus Christi, Oxford, after taking an M.A. in 1577 and for two years read the Hebrew lectures at the university as deputy to Thomas Kingsmill, the Regius Professor. But he resigned his fellowship on marrying and after serving as Master of the Temple, took various rural livings which enabled him to produce his great defence of the Anglican settlement, *The Laws of Ecclesiastical Polity*, far removed from the petty strife of the universities. Parker, Cox, Aylmer and Sandys were all scholars in their own right, yet the era of the Christian scholar in the universities is to be found in

[1] J. Ayre, ed., *Works of John Jewel* (Parker Society, Cambridge, 1845–50), II, 980–1 (my italics).

the first decades of the century rather than the last. Controversial writing abounded but could not compare with the contributions of Colet and the other Erasmians.

The same negative tale must be told of the study of Greek and Hebrew, a scholarly knowledge of which, it was hoped, would help solve the problems of the Church. As Erasmus put it in 1501, 'Latin erudition, however ample, is crippled and imperfect without Greek: we have in Latin at best some small streams and turbid pools, while they have the clearest springs and rivers flowing with gold. I see it is the merest madness to touch with the little finger that principal part of theology which treats of the divine mysteries without being furnished with the apparatus of Greek.'[1] Yet despite Erasmus' efforts, despite Fox's foundation of what was to be England's *collegium trilingue*, despite the endowment of the Regius Professorship in Greek, no important school of Greek studies developed in the universities. Cheke left Cambridge after only three years as the first Regius Professor and 'even Cheke cannot be mentioned in the same breath as Turnèbe or Dorat or Henri Estienne or Scaliger in France or as Victorius in Italy or as Camerarius in Germany. He read the classics widely and critically and was a competent translator of Greek authors, but he could not have edited a Greek text and, to judge by the only two specimens that we have, his Greek prose and verse were decidedly poor quality.'[2] When Sir Thomas Pope projected the foundation of Trinity College, Oxford, in 1555, he was urged by Pole to give greater attention to the study of Greek. Pope replied, 'I like the purpose well but I fear the times will not bear it now. I remember when I was a young scholar at Eton the Greek tongue was growing apace, but the study of it of late is much decayed.'[3] Andrew Downes, who held the Chair at Cambridge from 1585 to 1625, had made his name as a Greek scholar with his notes to the works of Chrysostom, but his predecessor Bartholomew Doddington was Regius Professor for twenty-three years (1562–85) without making any impact on the world of learning, and though his generation produced a few

[1] Allen, No. 149, I, 352; Nichols, No. 143, I, 313.
[2] A. Tilly, 'Greek Studies in England in the Early Sixteenth Century', *E.H.R.*, LIII (1938), pp. 221–39 and 438–56; Ingram Bywater, *Four Centuries of Greek Learning in England* (Oxford, 1919).
[3] Cited by Tilly, loc. cit., p. 453; cf. R. R. Bolgar, *The Classical Heritage and its Beneficiaries* (Cambridge, 1954), pp. 327–8.

translations, mostly of books having some bearing on the theological controversies of the day, certainly there was nothing to compare with the wide range of interest of the humanists of the early part of the century. The notebooks of the students have little in them to demonstrate their interest in or acquaintance with Greek studies, which is not surprising when we consider Seth Ward's report that when he came across some old mathematical texts in Sidney Sussex College he could find no one to help him, 'the books were Greek, I mean unintelligible, to all the fellows'.[1] None of this, of course means that Greek was not taught at all at the universities. But what was taught was of an elementary kind, as both university and collegiate statutes make clear. It was not, in fact, until the eighteenth century that the universities of England produced, in the persons of Bentley and Porson, scholars with an international reputation who could and did produce the kind of critical editions of which Erasmus would have approved.

If Greek studies made no great show in the latter half of the century and after, those of Hebrew were in an even worse case in both universities. At Cambridge neither of the Regius Professors, Thomas Wakefield (1547–75) and Edward Lively (1575–1605) seems to have lectured, and William Gouge 'became an excellent Hebrician', according to his father's *Life*, only by private study with one Philip Ferdinand, of whom William Eyre of Emmanuel reported that only whilst Ferdinand remained did there exist 'a slight hope' that by his means 'a certain knowledge of the language might be kept alive in the university'.[2]

At the higher levels of scholarship, then, the universities had little to offer the Church other than polemic. It is not surprising therefore, that their rôle in the training of the nation's clergy was not particularly distinguished either, despite the founding of Emmanuel College (1583) and Sidney Sussex College (1595) expressly for that purpose. Indeed, the very fact of their foundation is a reflection of the serious shortage of educated clergy, notwithstanding the constant urgings by the reformers, both before and after the Reformation, of the absolute necessity of such men for the continued health of the Church and its members.

[1] W. Pope, *Life in Seth Ward* (1697), p. 10.
[2] Mullinger, *Cambridge*, pp. 416–18.

Henry VIII was deploring the lack of trained clergy and the poor state of the universities long before the burnings and deprivations of Mary Tudor's reign left England desperately short of parish clergy. Latimer, as we have seen, regretted that whilst so many gentlemen's sons were entering university so few of their parents 'would have them preachers', and later on Ascham pointed out that more and more these new entrants were depriving those poor men's sons who were likely to enter the Church of places which traditionally had been theirs. Paradoxically, too, certain aspects of the Reformation itself had contributed to a situation in which career prospects in the Church were no longer as attractive as they had once been. The bishops had been deprived of a large proportion of their land and its revenues, whilst the taking over of church lands by laymen meant that tithes and the right of presentation to livings now fell into hands which were more concerned with obtaining revenue than with maintaining a stipend sufficient to attract 'learned' clergy. Inflation further depressed what was essentially a fixed-income class. Although the average income of benefices had rather more than doubled during the century, Whitgift could still complain, as Archbishop of Canterbury, that more than half of the benefices were worth no more than £8–£10 per annum, that one thousand of these were as low as £2 per annum and that only four hundred were worth more than £30 per annum.[1] The loss of old fees, the abuse of impropriations, the rise in prices, and the increasing number of married clergy with family responsibilities (by 1585 as many as two-thirds of the nation's clergy were married) all contributed to a situation in which most of England's clergy were 'more interested in husbandry, than in divinity'. 'What man of reason will think that eight pounds yearly is able to maintain a learned Dunce when every scull in a kitchen and groom of a stable is better provided for?' asked one critic. Latimer went to the heart of the matter in his usual practical way: 'They have great labours and therefore ought to have good livings that they may commodiously feed their flock; for the preaching of the word of God unto the people is called meat . . . not strawberries.' Yet by the end of the century Sandys was still able to complain: 'was there ever any time, any age, any nation, country or kingdom when and where the Lord's

[1] P. M. Dawley, *John Whitgift and the Reformation* (1955), pp. 202–3.

messengers were worse entreated, more abused, despised and slandered than they are here at home ?'[1]

The picture was not entirely black, of course. Not all impropriators were like those 'corrupt patrons', who, John Jewel complained in a sermon at St. Paul's Cross in 1583, 'engross and gather with their hands many livings . . . yet leave to take charge over the people blind Sir John, not only lack-Latin, but lack-honesty and lack-conscience and lack-religion'.[2] There were some, such as Henry Hastings, third Earl of Huntingdon, who systematically sought out and preferred suitably educated men for the livings in his hands. Huntingdon's own household seems to have been a veritable seminary for the training of clergy, and it was he who persuaded the corporation of Leicester to pass an ordinance in 1562 enjoining a member of every household to attend lectures given in St. Martin's Church every Wednesday and Friday. He founded the school at Ashby and reorganized the free school at Leicester, endowing both with scholarships to the universities for 'earnest students of divinity who would set their minds to become preachers of the Gospel of Christ in the Church of England'.[3]

The clergy of London must also be excepted from the general picture of ill-educated and depressed clerics. The prospect of a larger stipend, either as vicar or curate, tended to attract the better-educated cleric, but, in addition, London had a large number of lectureships available for such men, who were willing and able to preach. Even so, by the end of the century, though 75 per cent of beneficed clergy in London were graduates, only 50 per cent. of the curates were university men.[4] When Whitgift became Archbishop in 1583, two-thirds of all clergymen were non-graduates and less than one-sixth were sufficiently educated to be licensed as preachers. By the end of the century one-half were licensed, a tribute to Whitgift's constant efforts to improve

[1] J. Strype, *Whitgift*, I, 534; Latimer, *Sermons*, I, 62; J. Ayre, ed., *Sermons of Edwin Sandys* (Parker Society, Cambridge, 1841-2), II, 350.

[2] Jewel, *Works*, II, 999-1000.

[3] M. Claire Cross, 'Noble Patronage in the Elizabethan Church', *Historical Journal*, III (1960), pp. 1-16; and *The Free Grammar School of Leicester* (Leicester, 1953).

[4] Cf. H. Gareth Owen, 'Parochial Curates in Elizabethan London', *J. Ecclesiastical History*, X (1959), pp. 66-73; and 'Lectures and Lectureships in Tudor London', *Church Quarterly Review*, CLXII (1961), pp. 63-76.

the situation. On the other hand, Injunctions at both national and diocesan level could not hope to be more than partially successful in producing a 'learned' priesthood when the Church failed to suppress the simony and pluralism which depressed its own clergy. The cause of uniformity also militated against improvement, as for example in the case of 'prophesying', which originally started, with the approval of the bishops, as weekly or fortnightly meetings for the study of the Scriptures. Most effective in the south-east and in Lancashire, and enjoying the support of Grindal, they were regarded with suspicion by Whitgift who set about suppressing them as possible seed-beds of dissent. Laud reacted in exactly the same way when a group of merchants in London, the Lay Feoffees, collected funds in the 1610's and 1620's with the express intent of buying out lay patrons in order to appoint lecturers, augment stipends and fill the livings they controlled with 'learned priests'.[1]

The real crux of the matter was the production of clergymen who could preach. The 'learned priests' were those who could preach, and though this was true of both Armenian and Puritan, it was the latter who placed the greater emphasis on preaching ability in their clergy. When he entered the pulpit the preacher considered himself, in a sense, no longer as a member of a hierarchical institution but as a direct expounder and interpreter of the word of God, and he justified this claim as much by his superior learning as by his 'call'. This is not to claim any originality for the Puritans, of course. The sermon was a proved and efficient method of exposition and exhortation, traditionally much more important than the liturgical part of the service. Manuals for the preacher about the art of preaching abounded in the medieval period and especially after the coming of the Friars in the thirteenth century.[2] The beneficed clergymen in the English Church would almost certainly have been introduced to logic and rhetoric in his grammar school course, at however

---

[1] Cf. E. M. Kirby, 'The Lay Feofees', *J.M.H.*, XIV (1942), pp. 1–35; and I. M. Calder, 'A Seventeenth Century Attempt to Purify the Anglican Church', *Am.H.R.*, LIII (1948), pp. 760–75.

[2] Cf. T. M. Charland, *Artes Praedicandi: Contribution à l'histoire de la rhétorique au moyen âge* (Paris, 1936); William A. Hinnebusch, *Early English Friars and Preachers* (Rome, 1951), Chap. xvi; G. R. Owst, *Literature and Pulpit in Medieval England* (2nd edition, Oxford, 1961), Chap. iv, and *Preaching in Medieval England* (Cambridge, 1926), Chap. vii.

lowly a level. He would also most probably have been exercised in the art of notemaking at sermons. He may or may not have gone on to university, as we have seen. But in either case he could rely on the help of the manuals coming off the presses in the second half of the sixteenth century in increasing numbers. *The Preacher, or Method of Preaching* (1574), for example, was an English translation by John Horsfall of a work by the Dane, Niels Hemmingsen (*Nicholas Hemminge*) 'out of which the true and faithful ministers of Christ may learn plainly and orderly to break and distribute the word of God unto the people and flock committed to their charge'. Here the traditional pattern of rhetorical utterances is set out, starting with the *exordium* and following through the *treatise* and the *digression* to the *conclusion*, distinguishing on the way the various kinds of sermon—the parenetical ('that which consisteth in exhortation'), the persuasible, the consolatory, and the chiding—together with hints about the use of commentaries and the training of the memory. John Ludham's *The Practis of Preaching otherwise called the Pathway to the Pulpit* (1577), a translation of the Latin text of Andreas Geradus, followed much the same pattern, whilst Thomas Blundeville's *Arte of Logicke* (1599) was written 'especially for such zealous ministers as have not been brought up in any university'. Keckermann's *Rhetorica Ecclesiasticae* (1608), on the other hand, was obviously designed for the university graduate. Richard Bernard's *The Faithful Shepheard* (1607), extensively revised in 1627 and going through many editions thereafter, was directed towards a much wider audience, being

> very profitable (as Bernard claimed) both for young students who intend the study of theology (herein being also declared what arts and tongues first be learned, what kind of authors to be read, and books necessary in the beginning, and which in the first place), as also for such ministers as yet have not attained to a distinct order[1] to study, write, meditate, and to preach methodically, both for their better discourse in delivering the word, and the people's understanding in learning and memory in retaining the same.

The majority of such manuals were, of course, of Puritan origin, exhorting the preacher to adopt that 'plain, English'

---

[1] I.e. those not yet licensed to preach.

style which characterized the best Puritan sermon literature and which owed a good deal to the new logic and rhetoric of Ramus and Talaeus. McIlmaine, who produced the first English translation of Ramus, made it clear that his work was intended not merely for university scholars, but for lawyers, teachers, writers and preachers :—

> If thou be a divine this method willest thee that in place of the definition, thou set forth shortly the sum of the text which thou has taken in hand to interpret; next to part thy text into a few heads, that the auditor may the better retain thy sayings. Thirdly to entreat of every head in his own place with the ten places of invention . . . and lastly make thy matter plain and manifest with familiar examples of authorities out of the word of God.[1]

An early example of this pattern of proceeding is the sermon preached by John Stockwood, Master of Tonbridge Grammar School, at St. Paul's Cross in 1578. Having stated his text Stockwood went on, 'I will use no fore-speech or entrance, garnished and set out with some rhetorical flourish to win at your hand . . . my plain and simple handling of this text without curious and picked out words and terms . . . knowing that the word of God, simply and plainly handled is able without the help of the persuading speech of man's wisdom to pierce even to the heart.' He then went on to divide his text into three 'general points', each of which he subdivided into 'branches' from which in due course is drawn a 'doctrine' or moral.[2] The practical nature of these manuals which introduce the less educated preacher to this pattern is well illustrated by Bernard's *Faithful Shepheard* in which he recommends that the preacher get to know his congregation, for

> from the knowledge of his auditory, what errors are amongst them, what practice of virtue, what vices generally or in particular callings, who comfortless or discouraged and need consolation . . . like a physician skilful of his patient's disease he may fully administer a right potion . . . to have this knowledge it is fit for the pastor to be resident in his charge and to converse familiarly with his people, seeing and observing them.[3]

[1] R. Makylmenaeum, *The Logike . . . of P. Ramus, Martyr* (1574), p. 13.
[2] J. Stockwood, *A Sermon Preached at Paules Cross on Bartholomew Day 24 August 1578* (1578), p. 4.
[3] Op. cit., p. 7.

We may take it that those clergymen who had attended university had also been reasonably assiduous students, and certainly by the end of the century the evidence suggests that an increasing number of 'learned' clergy were being turned out by the universities. Mention must finally be made of the two other professional subjects studied at university, medicine and law. The study of Canon Law had been prohibited by Henry VIII as being incompatible with the doctrine of Royal Supremacy, and despite the increasing need for Civil Law in the workings of Star Chamber, the Court of Requests and the Councils of the North and of Wales, very little was done at the universities to provide instruction in it. Henry VIII had included a Chair of Civil Law amongst his Regius Professorships, though it was not until the appointment of Alberico Gentili to the Chair at Oxford in 1587 that anything worthwhile was done, whilst the attempt of the Edwardian Commissioners to convert All Souls, Oxford, and Trinity Hall and Clare Hall, Cambridge, into collegiate centres for the study of Civil Law came to nothing. Faced with the jealous safeguarding of vested interests by the common lawyers of the Inns of Court, who had their own system of legal education, it is not perhaps surprising that the civilians failed to maintain themselves and their studies.

As to the university study of medicine, most physicians preferred to go abroad, after taking a B.A., preferably to Padua, and then, on their return, to become incorporated members of their universities by means of a grace which admitted them in the rank and degree of their Continental university. What medical study went on at Oxford and Cambridge was almost entirely a study of the 'approved authors', Hippocrates, Galen, and their commentators, and it was typical that John Caius's introduction of Vesalian anatomy into his college of Gonville and Caius became a study of Vesalius's text, *De Humani Corporis Fabrica* (1543), rather than a practical training in his methods. The great stir caused by Paracelsus and his insistence on the importance of chemistry in medicine, fostered in England by the translations and works of John Hexter and George Baker in the last quarter of the century, had little effect on medical education in the universities. Indeed, 'the English Hippocrates', Thomas Sydenham, is reported by John Ward as preferring to take apprentices—'Physick is not to be learned by going to universities . . . one had as good send a man to Oxford to learn shoemaking as practising physick.' Even the College of Physicians, founded in 1518 on the initiative of Padua-trained Thomas Linacre, who was its President until his death in 1524, was largely a Galenist stronghold, using Linacre's translations of Galen's texts. It did, however, undertake a good deal more practical medicine and anatomy than the universities.[1] It was during his Lumleian lectures, which he gave twice a week at the college for forty years, that William Harvey announced his observations concerning the circulation of the blood. 'I profess to learn and teach anatomy not from books but from dissections, not from the tenets of philosophers but from the fabric of nature', he later wrote, and it was Harvey's work which John Mapletoft, the Gresham professor in medicine, described when in his first lecture he treated 'of such new inventions of anatomy as I think may be most useful and best requite your time and patience'.[2]

Dr. Curtis has described the period 1558–1642 as one of 'transition'. Certainly changes were taking place in the universities of Renaissance England—increasing royal control, influx of the sons of the aristocracy and gentry, growth of collegiate teaching and collegiate influence in the government of university affairs. But none of this was cultural change, least of all the cultural revolution which Neale and Curtis claim. The seeds of a possible revolution (if the word is to be used at all) were sown in the universities in the early decades of the century, but very few of them germinated. Most lay dormant in what became inhospitable soil. Here and there evidence is seen of what might have been. But such stirrings were the result of the interest and predilections of individuals, and these examples of the *studia humanitatis* at work failed to become general practice, accepted

[1] Phyllis Allen, 'Medical Education in Seventeenth Century England', *Journal of History of Medicine and Allied Sciences*, I (1946), pp. 115–43; P. H. Kocher, 'Paracelsan Medicine in England, 1570–1600', ibid., II (1947), pp. 451–81; Charles Severn, ed., *Diary of Reverend John Ward* (1839), p. 242; W. D. Sharpe, 'Thomas Linacre, 1460–1524: An English Physician and Scholar in the Renaissance', *Bulletin of the History of Medicine*, XXXIV (1960), pp. 233–56; C. C. Gillespie, 'Physick and Philosophy: a study of the influence of the College of Physicians of London upon the Foundation of the Royal Society', *J.M.H.*, XIX (1947), pp. 210–25.

[2] *De Motu Cordis* (1628), Dedication to President and Fellows of Royal College of Physicians (Everyman edition, 1907), p. 8; J. Ward, *Lives of the Professors of Gresham College* (1740), p. 275.

and institutionalized by the university authorities. The changes we have noted were political and social, not cultural. George I's Regius Professorships of History and Modern Languages aimed in an explicit way at re-introducing civic humanism into university studies, but they foundered on what by then had become the traditional rock of non-lecturing. It was not, in fact, until the mid-nineteenth century, with the setting up of the Combined School of Law and History, and the second attempt, under the leadership of Benjamin Jowett, to resuscitate the notion of classical languages and literature as a basis for humanistic study, that the ideals and programmes of Bruni and Erasmus and Bishop Fox began to be recognized and actively taught once again. Even then science had to rely on the newly-founded British Association for the Advancement of Science for its furtherance, as it had on the Royal Society in the seventeenth century. Internal reform had to await those who reacted in a positive and constructive way to the pressures of public opinion, as formulated for example in the *Edinburgh Review*, and in the Reports of the University Commissioners. It was only then that 'In some of us liberalism soon took the practical shape of an effort to reform and emancipate the university, to strike off the fetters of medieval statutes, to set it free from the predominance of ecclesiasticism, and *recall it to its proper working and restore it to the nation.*'[1]

[1] E. Abbott and L. Campbell, eds., *Life and Letters of Benjamin Jowett* (1897), I, 176–7 (my italics).

# VI

◇◇◇◇◇◇◇◇◇◇◇◇◇◇◇◇◇◇◇◇◇◇◇◇◇◇◇◇◇◇◇◇◇◇◇◇◇◇◇◇◇

# The Inns of Court

◇◇◇◇◇◇◇◇◇◇◇◇◇◇◇◇◇◇◇◇◇◇◇◇◇◇◇◇◇◇◇◇◇◇◇◇◇◇◇◇◇

OXFORD and Cambridge, then, were the traditional seats of higher education in England. But by the beginning of the seventeenth century Sir George Buck could claim for London the honour of being 'the third university of England', and pride of place among 'all the Colleges, ancient schools of privilege and houses of learning and liberal arts within and about the most famous city of London' he assigned to the Inns of Court, the seats of legal education.[1]

In the thirteenth century the study of the law in England had meant the study of the Roman and cosmopolitan law of the canon and civil codes. But during that century we see, too, the development of the kings' law in those royal courts which the Normans had originated. In 1223 the Court of Common Pleas, which was to become the most important of the royal courts of law, was fixed at Westminster, and so it was in London that we find the common lawyers congregating. In addition, it was under Edward I that the practice began of selecting the king's judges or justices from the ranks of these common lawyers instead of from the Church or the administration. This choosing of the Bench from the Bar became normal practice in the fourteenth century, and reflected the growth of a lay legal profession, replacing in the

---

[1] *The Thirde Universitie of England* . . . (1612). He was repeating a point made by William Harrison in the Second Book of his *Description of England* (ed., F. J. Furnivall, New Shakespeare Society, Series VI, Pt. I, 1877), pp. 82–83.

king's courts the old ecclesiastical lawyers who had practiced in both secular and ecclesiastical courts. Both trends arose out of the gradual development of an ordered legal system based on royal writ and statute and carried on in the king's courts at Westminster. By the end of the fourteenth century both the English common law and the English common lawyer may be said to have come of age.

The king's courts did not, of course, sit throughout the year, and the 'terms' during which they sat, Hilary, Easter, Trinity and Michaelmas, were brief, lasting only about three weeks. It was necessary, therefore, for the lawyers to find temporary accommodation, and it was not surprising that they often chose to live 'in common', at first in small groups with family or geographical associations.[1] Later they found it both more convenient and more profitable to rent larger and more permanent *hospitia* which ultimately became the four 'greater' Inns, Gray's Inn, Lincoln's Inn, Inner Temple and Middle Temple, in and about Holborn and Chancery Lane, not far away from the courts, but remote from the noise and bustle of the city within the walls. It was in these *ad hoc* circumstances that the lawyers began to think of themselves as a profession, expert in their calling (though still retaining the title *Esquier apprentice du loy* as practising barristers), making a sufficient and sometimes a lucrative living out of their work, and by 1400 subjecting themselves to regulation by their peers. This living together and the growing sense of common interest resulted, too, in a feeling of responsibility for the training and behaviour of those younger members of the profession, the *addiscentes apprenticii*, who sat in that part of the court which came to be known as 'the crib', learning court procedure, and listening to the pleadings and arguments of their seniors. The judges themselves were aware of this, too, and it was C. J. Bereford, the first common lawyer to be raised from the Bar to the Bench, who replied to a point-making Sergeant, 'Really I am much obliged to you for your challenge, and that for the sake of the young men here and not for the sake of us who sit on the Bench.'[2]

[1] Cf. S. E. Thorne, 'The Early History of the Inns of Court, with special reference to Gray's Inn', *Graya*, No. 50 (1959), pp. 79–96; and D. S. Bland, 'Chaucer and the Inns of Court', *English Studies* XXXIII (1952), pp. 145–55.

[2] W. S. Holdsworth, *A History of English Law* (1922–38), III, 479, citing *Year Books 3 Edward II* (Selden Society, XX, 1905), p. 36.

But sitting and listening in court and making notes of the proceedings was not the most efficient way of studying the law and preparing for a profession, and gradually the practice of arguing about the day's cases over supper back at the hostel provided the germ which was to make the Inns of Court educational institutions as well as clubs for practising lawyers. The younger members (whose 'dues' also contributed to the financial stability of the club) were encouraged to formalize their arguments and to frame them in the context of court procedure, the seniors intervening on points of information and procedure and perhaps providing a summing up and a decision. It was but a short step from this to the regulation of Lincoln's Inn in 1428, which required those barristers normally resident in London and the county of Middlesex to remain in residence and pay commons during the periods between terms, the vacations, so that formal instruction could continue. In the 1430's we have records of the younger barristers covenanting to remain in residence, e.g. 'Hayworth has promised to continue every Christmas and a month every Lent and a month every harvest (i.e. before the Michaelmas Term) this three years next coming.' Then in 1442 it was enacted that every person admitted to membership should continue during the three years next after his admission, for two weeks before the opening of Hilary Term, for three weeks before Easter and for three weeks before Michaelmas, and that those already admitted who had not 'continued' should now be required to do so. What had started as unorganized, *ad hoc* lodging halls for practising lawyers during term time were, by the end of the fifteenth century, highly-organized and prosperous communities which had taken on the self-appointed task of providing professional instruction for their younger members both in term and during 'the Learning Vacations'. The parallels between the development of the Inns of Court and the growth of the colleges of Oxford and Cambridge has been pointed out by Professor Thorne,[1] but the comparison must not be stretched too far. The Inns were purely secular establishments whereas the colleges were ecclesiastical. While the Inns called their own members to the Bar, it was the university not the colleges which granted degrees. Nor had the Inns endowments with which to

[1] Loc. cit.

sustain the studies of poor and needy scholars. Indeed, as Fortescue tells us—

> In these greater Inns a student cannot well be maintained under eight and twenty pounds a year, and if he have a servant to wait on him (as for the most part they have) the expense is proportionately more, for this reason, the students are sons to persons of quality, those of an inferior rank not being able to bear the expenses of maintaining and educating their children in this way . . . so that there is scarce to be found, throughout the kingdom an eminent lawyer who is not a gentleman by birth and fortune.[1]

The picture we have of the system of legal education provided at the Inns of Court in the Renaissance period is an unusually clear one. Most accounts are based on a series of contemporary descriptions of which the earliest, and perhaps the most famous, is that of Sir John Fortescue in his *De Laudibus Legum Angliae* (*c.* 1468–71). Alternatively, recourse has been had to John Stowe's *Survey* (1598), to Sir George Buck's *The Third Universitie of England*, first published in 1612 and appended to later editions of Stowe's *Annals*, or to the later account of Sir William Dugdale in his *Origines Judicales* (1666). Each of the last three supplemented his reliance on Fortescue by quoting the account which Thomas Denton, Nicholas Bacon and Robert Cary produced for Henry VIII about 1540, when he was considering setting up 'an House of Studentes wherein the knowledge as well of the pure French and Latin tongues as of your Grace's lawes of this your realm should be attained'.[2] In addition there are the records of the governing bodies of the four Inns, which provide us with evidence of the day-to-day life in the Inns.

The pattern of a law student's education was a complicated one. He began, sometimes after coming down from university, at one of the Inns of Chancery of which there were ten in Fortescue's day. Originally housing the clerks of Chancery who prepared the original writs for the king's courts, they had during the fifteenth century been progressively taken over by law students who spent two years there acquiring the rudiments of the law before moving on to one of the four Inns of Court,

[1] S. B. Chrimes, ed., *Sir John Fortescue, De Laudibus Legum Angliae* (Cambridge, 1949), p. 117.
[2] Printed in Edward Waterhous, *Fortescutus Illustratus* . . . (1663), pp. 539–46. A similar document, Cott. MSS., Vitelius Cix, *temp.* Henry VIII, has been printed in W. Herbert, *Antiquities of the Inns of Court* (1804), pp. 211–22.

where the student would be admitted as an Inner Barrister.[1]
For seven years he kept his commons and undertook his 'exercises' at his Inn during the terms and Learning Vacations, after
which he was eligible, on producing a certificate stating he had
duly continued his exercises, for call to the Bar of the House and
the rank of Utter (or Outer) Barrister.[2] Three years later he
would be allowed 'to make public profession and practice of the
law in all courts and to give counsel unto all clients'. Even now
his legal education was not considered complete, not in fact
until he had 'continued' as Utter Barrister for from ten to twelve
years.[3] The call to the Bar was merely an inception, though
giving the recipient a new status. As R. J. Fletcher has put it,
'Utter Barristers differed from "young gentlemen under the
Bar" very much as a third-year man differs from a freshman.'
Having thus 'continued', that is having conscientiously undertaken the various 'exercises and learnings' incumbent upon him,
the young lawyer was now eligible to be called upon to provide
the series of lectures called Readings and ultimately to become
a member of the Bench of the Inn, the governing body of the
House. It was from amongst those distinguished members of the
Bench who had been called upon to 'read twice' that the Crown
appointed the Serjeants-at-Law, who thereupon left the Inns of
Court for their own *hospitia* in Fleet Street and Chancery Lane.[4]

The 'exercises' or 'learnings' which the student had to undertake were of three kinds. As a newly-admitted Inner Barrister
he had to cultivate the art of *bolting*, which consisted of conver-
sational arguments upon cases and questions put to him by a
Bencher and two Utter Barristers sitting as his judges in

---

[1] The term 'barrister' derived from the *barrae*, or forms, on which students
sat during the exercises. For a discussion of the changing meanings of the word
cf. W. C. Bolland, 'Two Problems in Legal History', *Law Quarterly Review*,
XXIV (1908), pp. 392–402. For Chancery cf. T. F. Tout, 'The Household of
Chancery and its Disintegration', in H. W. C. Davis, ed., *Essays in History
presented to Reginald Lane Poole* (Oxford, 1927), and 'Literature and Learning
in the English Civil Service in the Fourteenth Century', *Speculum*, IV (1929),
pp. 365–89.

[2] One is printed in R. J. Fletcher, ed., *The Pension Book of Gray's Inn* (1901), I,
27; cf. the order of 12 June 1572, ibid., p. 12.

[3] Sir Edward Coke, *Reports* (1602), Preface, cites twelve years, but there was
a wide variability; cf. J. D. Walker, ed., *Black Books of Lincoln Inn* (1897–1902),
which gives a list of members, 1573–4, with dates of admission and calls to Bar and
Bench.

[4] Their ceremonial leave-taking is described in *Black Books*, I, 278–81.

private.[1] Later he participated in *moots*, a form of public disputation within the House which took place every evening after supper, during Term and the Learning Vacations. At the moots an Utter Barrister propounded a case before a Reader and two other Benchers. Each of the Benchers then argued the merits and demerits of the case, with the mover having the last word. This completed, two Inner Barristers, one acting as plaintiff, the other as defendant, then declared some action 'even as Serjeants do at the Bar in the King's court to the Judges,' after which an Utter Barrister 'argued questions within the case'. In all such disputations it was the invariable rule that the junior member— 'the youngest in continuance'—argued first, whether Inner Barrister or Bencher. The latter spoke in English but all other participants were bound to plead and reason in Law French. The mootings thus provided some opportunity for learning for all ranks. Their object being to promote ready speaking, the topic or case was not announced to the disputants until called upon to discuss it. The case, in fact, was laid upon the salt cellar at supper and 'none was to look into it upon pain of expulsion'.[2]

More advanced than either bolts or moots were the *Readings* which were given, in Law French, twice a year in the mornings of the Learning Vacations. The earliest Readings, dating from the early fifteenth century, consisted of general lectures on the 'old statutes', i.e. those prior to Edward III, but by the middle of the century these had developed into elaborate and detailed expositions of statute law, where successive Readers, lecturing on four mornings a week for four weeks, covered the most important chapters of Magna Carta, the statutes of Merton, Marlborough, Westminster I, Gloucester, Westminster II and so on, the one taking up where his predecessor had left off, until the whole cycle of statutes had been covered. Whereas in 1430 the cycle lasted about four years, by the end of the century the Readings had developed such a complexity that it took ten to twelve years to complete the cycle.[3] During the sixteenth century, however, it became the practice for the Reader to choose

---

[1] To 'bolt' is to sift (flour). Cf. *Pension Book*, p. 17 n. 1.

[2] J. F. Macqueen, *A Lecture on the Early History and Academic Discipline of the Inns of Court and Chancery* (1851), p. 18.

[3] Cf. S. E. Thorne, *Readings and Moots at the Inns of Court in the Fifteenth Century* (Selden Society, LXXI, 1954, for 1952). For a list of Readings in print and MS. cf. Holdsworth op. cit., V, Appendix II, pp. 447–9.

his own statute, and by that time too the Reading lasted for only three weeks. The Reading for the Summer Vacation, usually allocated to a recently-elected Bencher, started on the first Monday after Lammas Day, and for this reason was sometimes also referred to as the August Reading. The Lent Reading, starting on the first Monday of Lent, was the more important of the two for the Reader was normally a 'Double Reader', i.e. a Bencher of some seniority and distinction called upon to read for a second time. Very often a Double Reading was a signal for elevation to the rank of Serjeant-at-Law. The invitation to read carried with it also an obligation to entertain a good deal at the Reader's expense. The Reading itself, 'the precursor of seminar methods',[1] was a series of formal lectures, which included a discussion of difficult legal terms contained in the chosen statute, the pointing out of 'such inconveniences of mischiefs as were unprovided for', and the raising of various doubtful points of law with their suggested interpretation. Each lecture of the Reading was followed by general discussion by members of the Inn, the youngest Utter Barrister having the usual privilege (and ordeal) of speaking first. He would 'rehearse' one of the points or questions propounded by the Reader in an effort to prove him in error or doubt, and after the general discussion, in which Serjeants and Judges would often take part, the Reader was given the opportunity to refute the objections and confirm his own interpretation. Generally the Reading and discussion lasted for 'two hours or thereabouts' each morning. A similar type of exercise also took place in the Inns of Chancery, when as part of their training, senior Utter Barristers of the Inns of Court acted as Readers. In addition to these formal exercises the student would, of course, spend the mornings of the Law Terms in the courts themselves listening and watching and making notes.

The connexion between these exercises and the rhetoric of the period was noted by Elyot who described the moot, for example, as

> an exercise wherein is a manner, a shadow or figure of the ancient rhetoric . . . where first a case is appointed to be mooted by certain young men containing some doubtful controversy, which is in the head of a declamation called *thema*. The case being known they which be appointed to moot examine the case . . . whereof

[1] C. H. Williams, 'Early Law Readings', *B.I.H.R.*, III (1925–6), p. 97.

may rise a question to be argued that of Tully is called *constitutio*.
. . . Also they consider what pleas on every part ought to be made
and how the case may be reasoned, which is the first part of
rhetoric named *invention*, then appoint they how many pleas may
be made for every part and in what formality they should be set,
which is the second part of rhetoric called *disposition* . . ., etc.[1]

But, as he pointed out, it was difficult to achieve true eloquence
when the language of communication was Law French, 'which
lacketh Elocution and Pronunciation, two of the principal parts
of rhetoric' and which could also produce the written report that
'Richardson An. Just. de C. Banc. al Assises at Salisbury in
Summer 1631 fuit assault per prisoner la condemne pur felony
que puis son condemnation ject un brickbat a le dit justice que
narrowly mist et pur ceo immediately fuit indictment drawn per
Noy envers le prisoner et son dexter manus ampute et fix al
Gibbet sur que luy mesme immediatement hange in presence de
Court.'[2] Denton and his colleagues, like Elyot, had recom-
nended a 'purification' of the language of the law but without
avail. In the courts themselves English had been the medium of
argument since Edward III's reign, though the pleadings remained in Law French and the writs and statutes in Law Latin.
Not until 1650 did English become the official language of the
courts.

This, then, was the system as outlined by Fortescue and
others. Hierarchical in structure and dialectical in method, it
provided a long basic training for those who wished to become
professional lawyers. Yet the descriptions were all of them descriptions of a system as it should be. Fortescue, for example,
was writing, in his exiled old age, a treatise for Prince Edward,
son of Henry VI, and as his most recent editor indicates 'he is
obviously and deliberately saying the best he can: he is definitely
writing a panegyric, not a balanced survey. Moreover he obtains
his effect largely by concentrating almost exclusively on what we
may call the theoretical as distinct from the actual aspect of the
institutions and laws with which he deals.'[3] As W. S. Holdsworth

[1] Croft, op. cit., Book I, Chap. xiv. Cf. D. S. Bland, 'Rhetoric and the Law
Student in Sixteenth-Century England', *S.P.*, LIV (1957), pp. 498–508.
[2] Cited by F. W. Maitland, *English Law and the Renaissance* (Cambridge,
1901), p. 68, n. 40; cf. G. E. Woodbine, 'The Language of the English Law',
*Speculum*, XVIII (1943), pp. 395–436.
[3] Chrimes, op. cit., p. ciii.

has pointed out, in practice all was not well with the system.[1] Citing Dugdale, the *Black Books of Lincoln's Inn* and the *Pension Book of Gray's Inn*, Professor Holdsworth dated the beginning of the decline of the system from the late sixteenth century. Yet a closer look at the records of all four Inns suggests that the seeds were already being sown at the end of the fifteenth century and that the decline was proceeding throughout the sixteenth.

The pattern of decline may be traced by reference first of all to the students, and then to those who taught them. There can be no doubt that the attitude of a large number of students at the Inns of Court to their work and their behaviour in and out of the Inns left much to be desired. Taking into account the natural *joie de vivre* of young men, the records nevertheless show that this was rarely offset by a parallel devotion to study at the appropriate times. Again, the members were generally older than their university counterparts, many having come to the Inns from university, and their behaviour was often dangerous and sometimes vicious. Fighting, theft and licentiousness often appear in the records. At one end of the scale we have insolence to the officers of the House and 'ragging' in the presence of the Benchers. At the other end a case such as that dealt with on 20 May 1506, when Miles Hibbert and five others were each fined 3s. 4d. for 'breaking the door of the White Hart in Holborn at night and beating the housewife of the same to the scandal of the society, and also for frequenting a brothel, in Holborn called John Hasylrykke's House'.[2] At each of the Inns similar situations had to be dealt with by the Benchers who regularly, and apparently ineffectually, tried to regulate the behaviour of the students.

More important, however, is the fact that from the last decade of the fifteenth century the exercise of mooting was progressively neglected. Admittedly, the only records we have for the early part of this period are those from Lincoln's Inn, but there is no reason to believe that the behaviour of its students and members differed in any radical way from that of members of the other Inns. In the Trinity Term of 1494, for example, we

---

[1] W. S. Holdsworth, 'The Disappearance of the Educational System of the Inns of Court', *University of Pennsylvania Law Review* LXIX (1921), pp. 201–22.

[2] *Black Books*, I, 139.

find John Mynors, William Ayllyff and Richard Eryington being fined 'for not keeping or preparing the moots for two days as they ought, when divers Benchers were prepared to hear the moots'. Later in the same year, on 30 November, Mynors and Ayllyff with seven others, were again fined—this time 40*d.* —for a similar offence, 'in consequence whereof the Benchers and the rest of the Society had to do without'. The failure of the moot through non-attendance of students continued to be a regular occurrence until, in the Trinity Term 1513, it was ordered that 'all the Utter Barristers being in Commons in Hilary Term, should be amerced at 20*d.* a piece for loss of one moot the same term. If any one refuse to pay on first asking, then 6/8*d.*'[1] Nor did the situation improve with the passage of time and repeated orders from the Masters of the Bench. The accounts of the Inn are full of recorded fines for failure to moot. On 4 May 1559, an order was made that the fine for a 'moote-faille', previously 20*d.*, 'shall be 13/4*d.* for the Utter Barrister assigned to moot and 5/- for every other Utter Barrister then in Commons'. The order was repeated on 6 February 1560, 23 May 1560 and 21 November 1560, apparently without avail, for on 2 February 1562 more stringent measures were ordered and the fines raised to 20*s.* and 6*s.* 8*d.* respectively.[2] Yet the failure to attend continued.

A similar picture is seen in the Middle Temple. During the 1570's the number of students so charged was between ten and twenty each time the 'parliament' met, with fines of 20*s.* apiece in each case. On 13 May 1575 it was ordered that 'no vacationer shall be admitted to Commons until he had paid his fine to the Treasurer'. Yet at the next parliament eighteen vacationers were fined. When on 25 May 1582, twenty-eight absentees were recorded, another stratagem was resorted to in that 'all gentlemen absent last Lent should not be fined but shall keep another vaction'. In 1585 and 1586 forty-one and forty-two students respectively paid fines for non-attendance.[3] The situation was not helped of course, by the allowed practice at all of the Inns of 'special admissions', whereby members were admitted 'at the

[1] Ibid., pp. 101, 102, 172; cf. C. T. Martin, ed., *Middle Temple Records: Minutes of Parliament* (1904), I, 44, 84, 121, 133, etc.

[2] *Black Books*, I, 326, 329, 330, 332, 335, etc.; cf. F. A. Inderwick, ed., *A Calendar of Inner Temple Records* (1896, etc.), I, 143, 211–12, 257.

[3] *Middle Temple Records*, I, 207, 251, 274ff, etc.

instance of' some influential member and were 'pardoned all vacations and burdens within the Inn', as for example, in the case of Master Dynham, son of Thomas Dynham, knight, who was 'admitted and pardoned all vacations and burdens within the Inn in consideration that his father is a Fellow of the society and a well-wisher of it. He paid 26s. 8d'.[1] Complaints were already being made about the practice in the late fifteenth century, though without effect, for such admissions provided a valuable source of income for the Inns, sometimes in cash, sometimes in kind.

Yet the students, the Inner Barristers and junior Utter Barristers were not alone in their default. Those senior members of the House, Benchers and senior Utter Barristers, who by virtue of their attendance at and participation in the various exercises had an important part to play in the education of the students, similarly failed to honour their obligations. In the Michaelmas Term of 1496 William Cattelard 'having lost three vacations at Bench, it is considered that he shall pay 36/8d beyond the 20/- he has already paid, unless he keep vacation at the Bench before the time of his second reading'.[2] During the Easter Term of 1502 a general consideration of the situation produced the following from the Governors and Benchers :—

Agreed by the Governors and Benchers:
Whereas very often for lack of good and diligent study on the part of the Fellows at the Utter Bar, the instruction of the moot is of no profit to the students or the hearers, and on various occasions issue has been joined between them; And doubts in the moot, put, as of old, to the great instruction (of the students) were not shown nor understood by reason of the said default, to the great detriment of the hearers and of the students of the Society: The cause of which appears to be in the Fellows at the Inner Bar, because the moot is not taken nor written by any of them at the time of its assignment, nor is it delivered to the Fellows of the Utter Bar at a fitting time so that they may have profitable study thereof, as the ancient use was: Therefore, to emend and correct this great defect it is agreed that if the moot, at the time of its assignment be not written by two of the Inner Bar at least, then all of the Inner Bar, being in commons, shall pay 12d for each default;

[1] *Black Books*, I, 193.
[2] Ibid., p. 107.

provided always that if one only shall write it, he shall be discharged from the penalty: . . . And if they of the Utter Bar refuse to receive the moot so offered to them before the end of the mass (mess?) then each of them of the Utter Bar being in commons, shall lose 20d for each default.[1]

Year by year, however, the fines continued until on 14 November 1510 it was ordered

by Robert Reed, knight, Chief Justice of the King's Bench, John Boteler, a Justice of the same, John Aleyn, Baron of the Exchequer, John More, Serjeant-at-Law, John Nuport and John Nudegate, Serjeants-at-law-elect, and the Governors and others of the Bench of Lincoln's Inn, in order to preserve and continue the learning within the Inn as hitherto, that everyone called to the Bench shall keep all vacations at Autumn and Lent from the time of his call until his first Reading under penalty of 20s. for each vacation not kept. After his first Reading, he shall keep five vacations during the next three years under penalty of 5 marks for each vacation not kept.[2]

By 1557 the penalty for newly-called Benchers who failed to keep the Learning Vacations had risen to £5, though again the records show that this, too, failed as a deterrent. It might, of course, be objected that the records refer only to the rule-breakers and ignore the majority who worked hard and conscientiously. But the records do more than show isolated examples of misdemeanour. The defalcations were widespread enough and regular enough for those in authority to feel it necessary to issue general warnings 'for the benefit of the whole house'. In addition, whereas at the beginning of the century fines for non-attendance were recorded individually, by the mid-century it was found necessary, at the Middle Temple for example, to record it as 'all who ought to have attended . . . and did not are fined 20s.' and 'Each Master who missed last Autumn vacation should forfeit 20s.'

Even the Readings were not immune. As early as the Easter Term of 1502 William Elys of Lincoln's Inn was fined 13s. 4d. 'for that he being Reader for Lent past went away in the third week of his Reading'. By the end of the reign of Henry VIII we

---

[1] Ibid., pp. 126–7; cf. *Middle Temple Records*, I, 58.
[2] *Black Books*, I, 161, cf. *Middle Temple Records*, I, 12, 34, 41, 42, etc., and the General Orders promulgated in 1552, 1559, 1561, etc.

find Benchers reluctant even to accept the invitation to read. On 2 February 1540, for example, Mr. Rushton was fined £5 for not reading. Others preferred, and were apparently allowed, to make a composition instead, for on 29 August of the same year Mr. Menell paid £6. 13s. 4d. 'not to be Reader next Lent, as he should according to his anciently'. On 2 February 1542 Mr. Lane, having been appointed Lent Reader this year for his Second Reading and wishing to be 'pardoned forever' was ordered to pay a fine of £10, which was later reduced to £6.[1] At Gray's Inn such *ad hoc* arrangements had by the mid-century apparently become regular enough to necessitate a general ruling 'that whosoever should be chosen Reader, were he for his first or second reading elected, in case he refuse he should forfeit ten pounds to the use of the house'. In the 1550's fines ranging from £3. 6s. 8d. to £10 were imposed on Benchers of the Middle Temple for failure to read.[2] On 7 May 1562 Mr. Scrope of Lincoln's Inn was 'discharged of both of his readings on payment of £40'. On 1 July 1565 his colleague Mr. Newdigate paid £20 to be discharged from his Second Reading. Once again a general ruling was promulgated in an effort to check the trend. On 14 November 1588 the Masters of Lincoln's Inn ordered that 'everyone hereafter called to the Bench and accepting it shall read his first reading in his term on being appointed; in default he shall pay £40 and shall be removed from the Bench'.[3] Despite this the accounts of the Treasurer Robert Owen presented in November of the next year show that Humphrey Bridge paid only £13. 6s. 8d. in discharge of his obligation to read for a second time, whilst Richard Wheler is allowed to compound for both Readings on payment of £30. On 28 January 1595 Mr. Henry Townshead was fined £30 for refusing to act as Lent Reader, 'and if not paid before Ascension Day, £40'. Later in the year, having paid £13. 6s. 8d. he is excused the rest of his fine.[4]

The practice of failing to complete a full set of lectures also continued unchecked throughout the century, until in 1591

[1] *Black Books*, I, 125, 225, 229; cf. *Inner Temple Records*, I, 72, 73, 77, etc.

[2] *Pension Book*, I, 496, *Middle Temple Records*, I, 100ff.

[3] *Black Books*, I, 336, 346, II, 10. Disbenching and a fine of £40 was already the penalty in the Inner Temple, *Inner Temple Records*, I, 146, 191.

[4] *Black Books*, II, 12, 39, cf. *Inner Temple Records*, I, 158, 164, 172, 177, etc.; *Middle Temple Records*, I, 104, 109, 112, 115, 118, etc.

The two Chief Justices and Chief Baron (of the Exchequer) and all the residue of the Justices of both Benches and the Barons of the Exchequer well perceiving that these late examples of short and few readings are so dangerous as they are not longer to be suffered, have thought it very necessary that the same readings and charges of the readers shall be from henceforth used as followeth:

First of all single readers in every of the said Houses of Court shall continue every of their Readings by the whole space of three weeks, or till Friday in the third week after the beginning of every such Reading at the least; and that there shall be as many Readings in every of the said three weeks as by the ancient orders of the same house have been accustomed. And if there shall be any cause, allowed by the Benchers of the said House for fewer Readings there shall be, not withstanding any such cause, three Readings in every of the said three weeks at the least, any order to be taken to the contrary notwithstanding.

And to the intent that the charges of the same Readings may not be over-great and burdenous to the same Readers it is ordered that . . . no such Readers shall allow any greater diet in the Hall . . . either in wine or in meat that was allowed usually before the first year of the Queen's Majesty's reign.[1]

Even when the Readings were honoured on many occasions they failed to fulfil their intended purpose. With Judges and Sergeants present many Readers looked upon the occasion as an opportunity to impress their seniors rather than instruct their students. Sir Francis Bacon, when introducing his Lent Double Reading at Gray's Inn in 1600 on the Statute of Uses, insisted that his

meaning is revive and recontinue the former ancient form of reading . . . being of less ostentation and more fruit than the manner lateley accustomed. For the use then was, substantially to expound the statutes by grounds and diversities . . . and not to stir conceits and subtle doubts, or to contrive a multitude of tedious and intricate cases, whereof all, saving one, are buried and the greater part of that one case which is taken is commonly nothing to the matter in hand. But my labour shall be in the ancient course to open the law upon doubts, and not to open doubts upon the law.[2]

[1] *Black Books*, II, 20–21.
[2] *Works*, VII, 396.

Sir Edward Coke, in similar vein, having dilated on the possibilities of Readings as forms of instruction goes on:—

> but now readings having lost the said former qualities have also lost the former authorities: for now the cases are long, obscure and intricate, full of new conceits, liker rather to riddles than lectures which when they are open they vanish away like smoke, and the readers are like to lapwings who seem to be nearest their nests when they are farthest from them, and all their study is to find nice evasions out of the Statute.[1]

The Judges and Benchers were certainly aware of the trend of events as regards both mooting and Reading. The Judges Orders of 1557 laid down amongst other things that moot cases 'should not contain more than two points arguable' and that none of the Bench should argue more than two points. Similar complaints and orders were deemed necessary in 1594. The Benchers of the Middle Temple, replying to an order 'That the readings be held out the whole three weeks as in ancient time and the former good orders for diet and guests to be admitted in readings be observed', remarked that the order 'agrees with our ancient orders and was now very necessary to be thoroughly reviewed and duly observed'. Similarly, to the order 'that the Readers be always moved to make their course short, not containing above two or three points at the most and those upon the Statute head or as near as may be', the Benchers replied, 'This was the ancient order of the House and they intend to renew it by authority of their Parliament.'[2] Again, in 1600, the Benchers of Lincoln's Inn 'for a more especial care and vigilant eye to be had upon the whole estate of this fellowship', ordered amongst other things that 'one other Double Reader or Ancient Bencher, one other Single Reader and one or two other of the puisnes of the said Bench . . . shall in like manner be selected for that year Directors of and for the learned exercises of all sorts as well within as without this House to be performed by any of the Fellows of the same House'.[3]

And so it continued throughout the sixteenth century. Failure

---

[1] *First Part of the Institutes* (1628), p. 280b.

[2] *Black Books,* I, 320, II, 33–34; cf. *Inner Temple Records,* I, 192; *Middle Temple Records,* I, 111–12, 339ff.

[3] *Black Books,* II, 66.

to 'keep vacations' by both teacher and taught, truncated Readings, Readings irrelevant to the needs of the student, failures to read, abuse of the social concomitants of a Reader's duties had all contributed to the decline of an educational system which had lost a good deal of its relevance for large numbers of those who attended the Inns of Court. The imposition of fines or individual offenders, general rulings from the Bench 'for the attention of the whole house', Judges Orders promulgated to apply to all Inns of Court and Chancery—these followed each other with a regularity which can point only to their ineffectualness. Judges Orders were issued successively in 1591, 1594 and 1596. They were repeated in 1606, 1614, 1627 and 1629. None succeeded in halting the decline which by the outbreak of the Civil War was complete.[1]

The reasons for the decline of the system of legal education at the Inns of Court were obviously complex but the answers to two questions might profitably be sought. In the first instance, why did the Readers and Benchers fail to honour their obligations in the education of the students? Secondly and more important, why did the students behave as they did and why did they fail to study and exercise in the manner prescribed for them?

The answer to the first is relatively simple and has two main features. Sixteenth-century England was by comparison with previous centuries a fluid society, with a tremendous amount of land changing hands. It is not surprising, therefore, that it was a litigious age and that the profession of the law, i.e. the common law, flourished. Many members of the Inns consequently felt it a burden to have to forsake the courts to take part in the exercises arranged for the students. The result was a high degree of absenteeism. Yet others found themselves in a dilemma, for the way to promotion in the legal hierarchy lay through the Inns of Court, and, as has been pointed out, an invitation to read was often the signal for promotion to the Bench of the House and even to a Serjeanty. The process of Reading, therefore, with

---

[1] Efforts were made to revise the exercises and Readings at the Restoration, but without any lasting success. For comments on legal education during this period cf. Roger North, *A Discourse on the Study of the Laws* (1824). A suggestion that the moots be revived was made by Robert Lowe to the Commission of Inquiry on the Inns of Court in 1855. Lord Atkins, *The Moot Book of Gray's Inn* (1924), describes the founding of the present Gray's Inn Moot Society and contains reports of the moots held under its auspices.

its elaborate ritual of entertaining and dining (the right people) and its opportunities for showing one's skill and erudition, was something of a temptation for one who aspired to high rank in his profession. Many of those who accepted the invitation to read used it for their own purposes, and its original aim was forgotten.

The students present more complex problems. Two facts are not in dispute—their increased numbers and their unsatisfactory behaviour. Admissions Books and various 'orders of the house' attempting to restrict numbers provide us with evidence for the first,[1] the records of the Inns for the second. Indeed the irregular behaviour of the students was early recognized outside of the Inns. In 1524, for example, in the Court of the Star Chamber 'the ancients of the Inns of Court with the Readers and Principals of all the Inns of Chancery being present, it was advised them that they should not from henceforth suffer the gentleman students among them to be out of their houses after six of the clock in the night without very great and necessary cause, nor wear them any manner of weapons'.[2] Later in the century (1554), Henry Machyn, citizen and merchant taylor of London wrote in his diary, 'The XIIth day of June was a great affray between the Lord Warden's servants of Kent and the Inns . . ., Gray's Inn and Lincoln's Inn, and some slain and hurt.'[3] In his *Memorials of the Holles Family*, Gervase Holles refers to Sir John Holles's sojourn at Gray's Inn from 1583, which Professor Neale cites as an example of 'this changing fashion, of incalculable benefit to our civilisation'. Gervase goes on, however, 'there he continued some years which he spent not fruitlessly (as most of our Inns of Court gallants do) but took good impressions'.[4] Sir John was obviously not a typical 'Inns of Court

---

[1] Cf. *Inner Temple Records*, I, 223, 276–8, 468ff; *Middle Temple Records*, I, 110, 200.

[2] John Bruce, 'An Outline History of the Court of Star Chamber', *Archaeologia*, XXV (1834), p. 380; cf. the Star Chamber case *temp.* Henry VIII, cited in *Pension Book*, pp. xxv–xxvi.

[3] J. G. Nichols, ed., *Diary of Henry Machyn, Citizen and Merchant Taylor of London, 1550–63* (Camden Society, XLII, 1848), p. 65.

[4] Neale, *The Elizabethan House of Commons*, p. 305, and A. C. Wood, ed., *Gervase Holles' Memorials of the Holles Family, 1493–1456* (Camden Society, 3rd Series, LV, 1937), p. 89; cf. similar testimony of Sir James Whitelock concerning his brother, Edmund, in J. Bruce, ed., *Liber Famelicus of Sir James Whitelock* (Camden Society, LXX, 1858), pp. 7–8.

man', who by the end of the century had become notorious enough to figure in the literature of the day:–

> Who's younder
> Deep mouth'd hound that bellows rimes like thunder
> He makes an earthquake through St. Paul's Churchyard.
> Well fare his Lent his 'larum shall be heard.
> Oh! he's a puisne of the Inns of Court
> Come from the university to make sport
> With his friend's money here. . . .[1]

The explanation of this situation lies in the fact that as attendance at Inns of Court increased throughout the sixteenth century the purpose of attendance changed too. Though writers like Elyot and his successors had insisted on some legal training so that a gentleman might better serve the State, this was an ideal to which the Inns of Court made little practical contribution. It would seem that a large proportion of the increased membership of the Inns was made up of those who had been sent in order to obtain the social cachet so avidly sought by the rising gentry of the Elizabethan period. The picture of the Inns of Court described above hardly fits in with the ideal of 'finishing a gentleman's education with some study of the law'.[2]

Amongst those who wished to follow the profession of the law there were, of course, those who made the most of what opportunities were available, those bright stars whose abilities and aspirations enabled them to rise above the defects of the system. Edmund Plowden for example who was a Middle Temple student in the mid-century, refers to the benefits derived from his studies in the Preface of his *Commentaries*, published in 1571. Sir Simonds D'Ewes looked back in the same way to his studies at the Middle Temple.[3] There were many

---

[1] Everard Guilpin, *Skialethia* (1598), Satire 5, printed in G. B. Harrison, ed., Shakespeare Association Facsimile, No. 2 (1931). One need hardly mention those 'Swingebucklers . . . little John Doit, and black George Barnes and Francis Pickbone and Will Squele' who were Justice Shallow's contemporaries at the Inns of Court; cf. John Earle's description of the 'Inns of Court Man' in *Microcosmographie* (1628).

[2] Neale, op. cit., p. 304; cf. *Pension Book*, p. xxxii: 'The reigns of Elizabeth and her successors were the palmy days of the old system of education'; and A. L. Rowse, *The England of Elizabeth* (1950), p. 366: 'The Elizabethan era was the golden age of their history'.

[3] J. O. Halliwell, ed., *The Autobiography and Correspondence of Sir Simonds D'Ewes* (1845), I, 305–6.

others. Yet this will not justify the assumption that all who entered did so to acquire 'a legal education'. The records point to the assumption that the majority did not.

Yet even those who became professional lawyers contributed to the decline by their perfunctory attendance at the exercises. How then did they acquire their expertise? The answer here lies in the fact that a change in the *method* of acquiring a legal education was taking place during the sixteenth century. As Professor Thorne has put it, 'Students . . . had begun to read for the bar rather than listen.'[1] Though the budding lawyer could become lawyer only through the institution of the Inns of Court, the foundations of his professional knowledge were more and more coming to be based on his own study (for there were no tutors at the Inns) of the printed texts, and though Coke warned his readers that both reading and practice were necessary parts of the legal education, he was as much commenting on the neglect of the past as recommending for the future.[2]

In the early days of the Inns, and indeed before they became recognizable institutions, the student of the common law had few texts for his guidance. Copies of the statutes existed, as did those collections of court cases which came to be known as the Year Books. In addition there were the great treatises of the law by Glanvill, Bracton, Fleta and Britton. Different in kind from these were the concise manuals of legal maxims, information and forms of action such as the *Brevia Placita*, which listed the various pleas in the king's courts, cited the writs, declarations and defences appropriate to particular actions, as well as showing the methods of pleading in a plea of land or a plea of trespass. But all of these were in manuscript, and the treatises particularly would be far too expensive for the student, who had to rely on his own notes taken during court proceedings.

Very soon after the coming of printing to England, however, printers readily saw the possibility of a lucrative market in law books. The earliest printed law books were those collections of statute law, produced in the early 1480s by Lettou and Machlinia, which came to be known as the *Old Abridgment*. In 1528

---

[1] *Readings and Moots*, p. xvii.
[2] *First Part of the Institutes*, p. 70; cf. the texts recommended by Coke in his Preface to *Reports*, Pt. III (1602), Sigs. Ciii–iv.

John Rastell produced his *Magnum Abbreviamentum* in which each statute included in the collection was abbreviated in its original language. Later both he and Robert Redman printed editions in English which came to be the standard reference texts. The earliest collections of cases, gathered by their regnal year and therefore called the *Year Books*, were also printed in the 1480s. These, too, were produced in abridged form with cases arranged alphabetically, the first to be printed being that attributed to Nicholas Statham (*c.* 1490) and known thenceforth as *Statham's Abridgment*. This was later superseded by Sir Anthony Fitzherbert's *La Graunde Abridgement* in three volumes (1514–16), which was itself enlarged and rearranged by Sir Robert Brooke in 1573. Fitzherbert and Brooke remained the standard collections of case law in abridged form and ran through many editions, until the posthumous publication of Henry Rolle's *Abridgment* which 'marked a new departure in the literature of abridgments' by including with its digest of cases, summaries of both parliamentary proceedings and statutes.[1] The last regnal year for which cases were printed as Year Books was 27 Henry VIII (1535–6), though the Year Books continued to be printed throughout the sixteenth century, very largely by Richard Tottell, whose cheap productions obviously served a widespread market.

In addition to the Year Books themselves and their various abridgments the student and lawyer could in the second half of the century refer to the *Reports*, private collections of cases with commentaries, which were more scientifically arranged than the Year Books and were reports of judicial decisions rather than records of procedure and pleadings as the Year Books were. The most famous *Reports* were those of Sir Edmund Plowden (1571) and Sir James Dyer (1585). Both collections enjoyed great vogue until they were overshadowed by the great collection of Sir Edward Coke, covering cases from 1572 to 1616, and published in thirteen parts (of which two were posthumous) from 1600 to 1659. Coke's *Reports* became so authoritative as to have almost the force of law in the courts of the seventeenth century, consisting as they did of a systematic statement of the principles of common law as exemplified in the cases which came before him.

[1] Holdsworth, op. cit., V, 376.

Like the manuscript *Year Books* the manuscript collections of precedents and writs were also printed in large numbers, the earliest being the (*Old*) *Natura Brevium* (1496) which went through at least seventeen editions in French and eleven in English before 1600. Another version was produced by Sir Anthony Fitzherbert in 1534, the *New Natura Brevium*, of which there were at least eight sixteenth-century editions. In the same way Pynson's *Book of Entries* (1510) passed through many editions and enlargements, culminating in Coke's great 700-page edition in 1614. 'What availeth the serjeant or apprentice the general knowledge of the laws (he wrote) if he know not withal the form and order of legal proceedings in particular cases and how to plead and handle the same soundly and most for his clients' advantage? . . . if in the pleading whereof there be found error though the right be good the cause faileth.'[1] Despite this the student did need to have some 'general knowledge of the laws', and for this he could rely on what might be called the philosophical treatises. Though Coke recommended as 'right profitable' the printed editions of Glanvill and the other medieval writers most students would probably have agreed with William Fulbecke's comment that 'their books are *monumenta adorandae rubiginis* which be of more reverence than authority'.[2] Their place, in any case, was taken in the second half of the sixteenth century and after by the *Reports* of Plowden, Dyer and Coke and by the latter's four volumes of *Institutes*, the first of which comprised an up-to-date commentary on what was probably the most famous and certainly most-used law book of the period, Thomas Littleton's *Tenures*. Originally published ( ?1480) in Law French and englished in 1532, at least sixty editions, either in French or English, were published before 1600. Even its inferior predecessor, the *Old Tenures* (*temp.* Edward III), ran into eleven printed editions during the same period. 'How commodious and profitable unto gentlemen students of the law be these three books, that is to wit *Natura Brevium*, the *Old Tenures* and the *Tenures* of Mayster Littleton experience proveth and the books themselves declare (wrote William Rastell in 1534), for like as a child going to school first learneth his letters of the A.B.C. so they that intend

---

[1] Coke, *Book of Entries* (1614), To the Reader.
[2] *A Direction or Preparative to the Study of the Law* . . . (1600), p. 27.

the study of the law do first study of these iii books'.[1] Littleton not only answered the usual question 'What do I do in court?' but also tried to give a scientific account of land law, answering as well the question 'What is the law?' His book was an indispensable source of reference and it is not surprising that many of the editions were of what we would call hip-pocket size. Coke even went so far as to describe it as 'the ornament of the Common Law, the most perfect and absolute work that was ever written in any humane society'.

Two other works of the treatise variety must also be mentioned here. The first is John Perkins's *Profitable Booke Treating of the Lawes of England*, originally published in Law French in 1530 and translated into English in 1555. Like Littleton, though in less masterly fashion, Perkins tried to provide the law student with a systematic view of the grounds of land law and his book was much read in the sixteenth century, as its many editions show. John Doddridge's *English Lawyer* (1631) was a later work, which aimed at 'describing a method for managing the laws of this land and expressing the best qualities requisite in the student practiser, judges and fathers of the same'. Its chief interest lies in its insistence on the need for a liberally educated lawyer and in its attempt to provide a reasoned and logical basis for the English common law. In this, Doddridge, a Justice of the King's Bench, drew on the twin criteria of reason and conscience which were the basis of that other branch of law, Equity, which had been developed through the Court of Chancery, the Court of Requests and the Conciliar Courts (Star Chamber, High Commission, of the North, and of the Marches) during the sixteenth century. He refers in this connexion to another law treatise which had a very wide influence in the period, the *Doctor and Student* of Christopher St. Germain, originally published in Latin in 1523 and enlarged and englished in 1531.[2] It appeared when the courts which relied on the Civil Law rules of evidence and procedure were at the height of their influence and popularity, when humanists like Starkey

---

[1] Preface to his collected edition of twelve law books (1534).

[2] Cf. F. L. Baumer, 'Christopher St. Germain, the Political Philosophy of a Tudor Lawyer', *Am.H.R.*, XLII (1937), pp. 631–51; P. Vinogradoff, 'Reason and Conscience in Sixteenth Century Jurisprudence', *Law Quarterly Review*, XXIV (1908), pp. 373–84; and S. E. Thorne, 'St. Germain's "Doctor and Student" ', *The Library*, 4th Series, X (1930), pp. 421–6.

were criticizing the common law as 'over confused . . ., infinite and without order or end. There is no stable ground (he continued) nor sure stay . . . the subtlety of one serjeant shall invert and destroy all judgement of many wise men before time received'. During the 1530s there seemed some slight chance of a 'reception' of Roman law in England, though this did not in fact take place. Nevertheless, the civilian approach to the law, and St. Germain's book in particular undoubtedly influenced the common lawyers, in their efforts to systematize their common law books.[1]

Many of the books we have referred to were obviously designed for those who professionally studied or practised the law, and some of the small manuals were bound up together to provide a kind of compendium. Rastell produced a collection of twelve such texts in 1534, Thomas Berthelet one of seven in 1540, and many others followed. There was one class of book, however, which was written especially for those who were not professional lawyers, but who, by virtue of their office of Justice of the Peace or simply by being landowners, required some guidance in the law and its processes. As the author of the *Institucion of a Gentleman* (1565) put it,

> To be a Justice of the Peace in the country as a stay for simple men and helper of their causes by way of arbitrement or otherwise to end their contention and stint their strife . . . is a goodly ministration and office for a gentleman . . . and though such be not fully well-learned in the laws yet it behoveth him to have some knowledge therein and chiefly in things belonging to his office.[2]

It was for this purpose that the *Boke of the Justice of the Peas* was compiled. The earliest manuscript versions date from 1422 and their popularity is attested by the large number of copies which have survived. The first printed edition appeared in 1506 and ran to thirty-two editions before the end of the century. It was followed by Sir Anthony Fitzherbert's *L'office et authoryte de Justyces de Peas* (1538) published in both Law French and in English, the former of which ran to twelve editions and the latter to eleven. This remained the standard text until Elizabeth's 'stacks of statutes' necessitated a new work, William

---

[1] Starkey, op. cit., p. 173.
[2] Op. cit., Sig. D. vii *verso*; cf. B. Putnam, *Early Treatises on the Practice of the Justices of the Peace in the Fifteenth and Sixteenth Centuries* (Oxford, 1924).

Lambard's *Eirenarcha* (1581), whilst Fitzherbert's book was completely revised in 1583. These two texts, together with Michael Dalton's *Country Justice* (1618), provided the local justice with a concise and practical *vade mecum* designed specifically 'to somewhat further the good endeavour of such gentlemen as be not trained up in the continual study of the laws'.[1] As Dalton put it,

> withal I observe the business of the Justices of the Peace to consist partly in things to be done by them out of their sessions and sometimes privately, and peradventure upon a sudden without the advice or association of any other, and partly at the sessions of the Peace. Of things of this last kind I purpose in this treatise not to meddle . . . but for the private and sudden help of such justices of the peace who peradventure have not read over the former writers . . . and not conversant with the study of the laws for their ease principally I have published this work.[2]

Dalton was referring here, of course, to the J.P.'s powers of summary justice in petty criminal cases and to the enormous amount of administrative duty that fell to his lot. It is not surprising, then, that Fitzherbert, Lambard and Dalton each covered topics ranging from drunkenness, theft, rape, riot and routs to the apportionment of the rates, the making of market regulations, non-attendance at church, employment of vagrants, relief of the poor and the repair of highways and bridges. In each and every case their books provided essential guidance for the overworked J.P.

But even if he did not take office the country gentleman, whether of ancient lineage or of the new mercantile (or legal) interest intent on establishing a landed family, as landowner needed to know some law. For not only was society changing, the law, the feudal land law, was changing too, as the king tried to retain the benefits of feudal incidents on land (as for example by the Statute of Uses) and the lawyers on behalf of their clients sought to circumvent it. Leases for lives and fixed rents for long terms were being replaced by short leases, in an effort to meet the price revolution. Title deeds became all-important as lawyers sought security of title to lands which a generation previously had belonged to monasteries or the ancient aristo-

---

[1] *Eirenarcha*, Proheme.
[2] *Country Justice*, Epistle to the Reader.

cracy. The common lawyers meanwhile waxed fat as they developed increasingly elaborate and technical instruments to transmit land free of such feudal burdens as wardship and marriage and relatively safe from the remote or dormant title. The speculative purchaser buying to improve and re-sell, the owner anxious to provide for his heirs and at the same time to make the most of his rent-roll, increasingly needed to safeguard himself by knowing something of the law. Already in the middle of the fifteenth century Agnes Paston was reminding her son Edmund, then at Clifford's Inn, 'Think only of the day of your father's counsel to learn the law, for he said many times that whosoever should dwell at Paston should have need to learn how to defend himself.'[1] In 1607 James Cleland was still making the same point when he recommended the study of the law in his *Institution of a Young Nobleman*, 'to the intent by these means he may be able to defend himself from the crafty, subtle surprising of the world and to give his friend and neighbour good counsel, to maintain a poor widow and a little orphan from wrong and oppression'[2].

In such a litigious age a book like Thomas Phayer's *Newe Boke of Presidents* (1534) became indispensable to a landowner and his steward, for in it they would find

> many notable and goodly precedents of practice of all sorts, forms and fashions, as well for the assurance of lands, both free and copyhold, as for all manner of bargains, covenants and other matters belonging to the law . . . as indentures, deeds, feoffments, dowers, jointures, bonds, releases, acquittances, warrants, exchanges, charters, patent of offices, fairs and immunities, letters of safe conduct, bills of complaints, titles, pleas and answers, letters of testimony with divers other instruments. . . .[3]

Towards the end of the century, William West produced a similar work the *Symbolaeographia which may be termed the Art, Description or Image of Instruments, Covenants, Contracts, etc.* (1590), which together with a copy of one of the many editions of Littleton's *Tenures* would at least put a landowner in a position to 'defend himself'. Most landowners, too, would have jurisdiction as lord of the manor, and here they would have the

---

[1] J. Gairdner, ed., *The Paston Letters* (1904), I, 58.
[2] Op. cit., p. 95.
[3] Op. cit., Sig. Aii.

benefit of a long tradition of texts, dating back to thirteenth century manuscript manuals, which provided a concise summary of procedure and scope of jurisdiction. Whether based on the Latin manuscript text *Modus tenendis curiam baronis* or the French *La Court de Baron*[1] the printed versions of the sixteenth century found a ready sale and ran into many editions, as was the case with John Kytchin's *Jurisictions or the Lawful authority of Courts Leet, Courts Baron, Court of Marshalseys, Court of Pypowder and Ancient Demesne together with the most necessary learning of Tenures and all their incidents* . . . (1580), written as Kytchin said in his Epistle Dedicatory, 'for the direction of such as keep courts . . .' He continued, 'I have collected all such cases out of our Books of Law so that those who either have not the said Books at large, or have them and yet want time to peruse them, may here for sweatless labour receive satisfaction in exchange.' Alternatively the lord of the manor would find a printing of the original text bound up in the *Compendia* to which we have already referred.

Many others besides the professional common lawyer were especially interested in the law, and if the lawyer himself was beginning to *read* for the Bar, the printed book was also becoming the stand-by of the layman. It was from books such as those we have mentioned that the country gentlemen who comprised the predominant class in the Elizabethan House of Commons, and who ruled in one way or another the English countryside, obtained their legal background. Though traditionally the Inns of Court had housed the sons of the nobility and the gentry who had no intention of making the law their profession, the system of education there was in no way geared to their supposed special needs, so that it would have been virtually impossible, even with the best will in the world—and this was notably absent as we have seen—for such a student to acquire 'in a year's residence after Oxford and Cambridge enough law to settle the disputes of tenants of the family estate or act as Justice of the Peace in his home county'.[2]

This is not to claim that they derived nothing from their

---

[1] Cf. F. W. Maitland and W. P. Baildon, eds., *The Court Baron* (Seldon Society, IV, 1890).

[2] C. Bowen, *The Lion and the Throne: the Life and Times of Sir Edward Coke* (1957), p. 57; cf. J. A. Williamson, *The Tudor Age* (1953), p. 8.

stay, but that their stay was unlikely to have made the significant contribution to the initiative and ability of the House of
Commons which Professor Neale claims for it. We can hardly
claim that those who did 'attend' the Inns of Court were seeking
what Elyot had hoped they would seek, and even had they so
wished it is unlikely they would have found what they sought.
They may well during their stay have caught something from
the cultural life of the Inns, whose patronage of drama and the
masque during the Mesne or Dead Vacations has yet to be
satisfactorily placed in the history of English literature and
culture. But we must take care not to attach too much significance to Ben Jonson's much-quoted dedication of *Every Man
Out of His Humour* to 'the noblest nurseries of humanity and
liberty, the Inns of Court', for an *Epistle Dedicatorie* can hardly
be expected at this time to be other than fulsome in its tenor.
Our conclusion must be, therefore, that the contiguity in the
sixteenth century of an ideal vigorously expressed and a desire
on the part of the gentry to send their sons to the Inns of Court
has resulted in the Inns being given an exaggerated place in the
history of what we call a liberal education.

# Part Three

INFORMAL EDUCATION

# VII

The Family and Travel

P ERHAPS the stablest feature of European culture and certainly its oldest educational institution is the family. Since
Aristotle it has served as the pattern of the State, and for
the Christian, God is the Father as, for the Roman Catholic, the
Pope is Papa. Both the State and Church were merely the
family writ large. The heads of both institutions had the same
obligations to their respective subjects as the father had to the
various members of his household, as, in the same way, its
members owed obedience to the father. In sixteenth-century
England the importance of the family as a social unit was reflected, too, in the organization of the House of Commons,
where family connexion provided such coherence as existed in
the pattern of voting. Certainly family connexion was all-
important in the system of office-holding, as it was in the world
of trade. The family was the universal frame of reference.
Harmony and concord within it was the safeguard of its stability, and its break-up in *King Lear* provided the elements of
catastrophic tragedy both for the father and for the king. The
Wars of the Roses, Edward Hall reminded the readers of his
*Chronicle*, should always be kept in mind as an example of the
dangers of discord 'so that all men, more clearer than the sun,
may apparently perceive that as by discord great things decay
and fall to ruin, so the same by concord be revived and erected'.[1]

[1] Edward Hall, *The Union of the Two Noble and Illustrate Families of Lancastre
and Yorke* (1548), Sig. A i *verso*.

Varying the metaphor, Malynes criticized usury because it 'overthroweth the harmony of the strings of the good government of a commonwealth, by too much enriching some and by oppressing and impoverishing some others, bringing the instrument out of tune'.[1]

Church, State and family, then, were patriarchal groups where unity based on obedience and acceptance of authority was the essential prerequisite. Certainly the modern notion of actively and positively training children for early independence from the family would have been quite alien to sixteenth and seventeenth-century England, where sons and daughters continued, even after adolescence, to be subject to parental discipline, and even after marriage it was not unusual for the young married couple to remain in the father's house. Nor was the educational rôle of the family confined to a narrowly-conceived moral training based on the Fifth Commandment. In the family was reared the future citizen. As William Gouge put it:–

> This is to be noted for satisfaction of certain weak consciences, who think that if they have no public calling they have no calling at all . . . a conscionable performance of household duties in regard to the end and fruit thereof may be accounted a public work. . . . A family is a little church and a little commonwealth whereby trial may be made of such as are fit for any place of authority or of subjection in church or commonwealth. Or rather it is a school wherein the first principles and grounds of government and subjection are learned.

In other words, the family was to be regarded as 'a seminary for all other societies'.[2]

The family, then, was an educational institution of prime importance, a fact well-recognized by both Church and State. In contributing to the education of his children the father's duty was to catechize them and introduce them to the Scriptures, 'for God's graces may as well be exercised in the family as in the cloister', whilst at the same time so disciplining them in the virtues of obedience to himself that their duties of obedience to the State and the Church also became apparent to them. 'Thou

---

[1] Gerard de Malynes, *St. George for England* (1601), Sig. A 6; cf. Jean Bodin, *Six Books of the Commonwealth* (1606), Book I, Chaps. ii–v.

[2] William Gouge, *Works*, I, 10–11 and 610; William Perkins, *Christian Oeconomie Englished by Thomas Pickering* (1609), Dedicatory Epistle.

art both a king and bishop too over thy house and family, a king by government to keep in awe and a bishop by instruction to teach.' The same idea is found in Vives's *Office and Duetie of a Husband* (1550): 'every man is a king in his own house and therefore as it beseemeth a king to excell the common people in judgment and in example of life and in the execution and performance of the thing that he commandeth so he that doth marry must cast off all childishness'.[1]

To help and guide him in such responsibilities the father could rely on the numerous pocket-size manuals that came off the printing presses in increasing numbers during the sixteenth century. One of the earliest was *A Werke for Householders* (1530) by Richard Whitford, whom we have already met as the translator of Thomas à Kempis's *Imitation of Christ*. Chaplain to the fourth Lord Mountjoy and later to Bishop Fox, Whitford was very much a member of what might be termed 'the More circle'. In his *Werke for Householders* he reminds the father of his duty to teach his children the Pater Noster, the Ave and the Creed 'as soon as they can speak . . . and not only your children, but also see you and prove that all your servants what age soever they be can say the same'.[2] To these prayers he adds a selection of prayers for family use, with short commentaries on each of them.

Very soon the short selection of prayers added to the manual by way of illustration developed into separate collections of prayers for family and other occasions, such as *The Patheway to Prayer* (1542), *The Flower of Godly Prayer* (1551) and *The Pomander of Prayer* (1558). Works such as these ran into many editions as well as providing the base for 'entirely new' collections under different titles. Alongside them, and in similar profusion, was the 'Brief and Necessary Instructions' type of manual, of which Edward Dering's *Briefe and Necessary Instruction very needeful to be known of all Householders whereby they may the better teach and instruct their families in such points of Christian religion as is most meete* (1572) is typical. In it he deplores the fact that

---

[1] Perkins, *A Reformed Catholick* (1598), in *Works*, I, 586; John Stockwood, *Sermon at St. Paul's Cross* (1578), p. 69; Vives, *Office and Duetie of a Husband* (1550), Sig. Q iii *verso*.
[2] Op. cit., Sig. B ii *verso*.

we have printed as many bawdy songs (I am lothe to use such a loathsome word save that it is not fit enough for so vile endeavours), to this purpose we have gotten our songs and sonnets, our Palaces of Pleasure, our unchaste fables and tragedies and such like sorceries more than any man can reckon . . . and have not been ashamed to entitle these books *The Court of Venus*, *The Castle of Love* and many such other as shameless as these.[1]

It is to oppose such a trend, he says, that he presents his own text, which is really a catechism on the whole duty of man. It ran into ten editions by 1605, and was followed in 1576 by his *Godly and Private Prayers for Householders to meditate upon and to say to their families*. In 1582 the two works were printed together as a *Short Catechisme for Householders with prayers to the same adjoining*, of which fourteen editions were produced by 1631.

Edmund Tilney in his *Briefe and Pleasant Discourse of the Duties of Marriage, or the Flower of Friendship* (1568) had a separate chapter which exhorts the husband, 'To be careful in the education of his children . . . for much better they were unborn than untaught', whilst Josias Nichols's *Order of Household Instruction* (1596) recommends that two hours per week be spent 'to instruct your children and servants according to the order of this book', starting with 'some short stories or sentences out of the holy scriptures' followed by the Catechism, and supplemented by Biblical extracts with 'interpretations' probided by the author.[2] Edward Hake's *Touchestone for This Time Present . . . whereunto is annexed a perfect rule to be observed of all parents and scholemasters in the training up of their children and scholars in learning* (1576) made some concession to the reader by casting it in rhymed couplets, but the book is more important in that it foreshadows Richard Mulcaster's more famous emphasis on the need for close co-operation between parent and teacher. It is, too, one of the few texts of its kind which deplores the typically harsh relationship between parent and child which Calvin had adumbrated as necessary and divinely-ordained. Mulcaster was, of course, the first systematic advocate of a closer relationship between parent and teacher and of the need for both to share the moral education of the child.

---

[1] Op. cit., Sig. A iii.
[2] Tilney, op. cit., Sig. C vii *verso*; Nichols, op. cit., Sig. B 7 *verso*.

The parent, he claimed, must 'bear in mind that he is bound more to his country than to his children, as his child must renounce him in countermatch with his country'. The master for his part is to be

> in nature of a counsellor to join with the parent if he will be advised. Therefore to have this thing perfectly accomplished I wish the parents and masters to be friendly acquainted and domestically familiar, and though some parents need no counsel as some masters can give but little, yet the wise parent will hear and can judge and the skilful master can judge and should be heard . . . parents and masters should be familiarly linked in a unity and continual conference for their common care, and that the one should have a good affiance of judgement in the thing and of good will toward himself reposed in the other.

In the same way parents and teachers should co-operate in matters of punishment, 'for the rod may no more be spared in schools than the sword in the prince's hand. By the rod I mean correction and awe. . . . For the private, whatsoever parents say, my lady birchely will be a guest at home or else parents shall not have their wills. . . . The same faults must be faults at home which be faults at school.'[1]

In direct instruction the parent would be concerned only with the elementary part of his child's education,

> as the Elementary professeth itself in the course of learning and in trade of school to be the first and best seasoner of the untrained mind, so ought the parents also for their own part both before and during all the elementary time to provide so at home as there be no ill liquorice inconsiderately poured into the green cask which may so corrupt it as it will either quite refuse the good elementary humour, or unwillingly receive it and not to such a good as it useth for to work where the cask if not corrupt. . . . Those parents therefore which will look for the best liquor in schools must not in any way use corrupt humour at home.[2]

To exhort was one thing, of course; to achieve the requisite end was another, for as John Stockwood pointed out

> among all the diseases that these our days and times are grievously sick withal, there is none where with they are either more generally

---

[1] *Positions*, pp. 142ff, 155–6, 273–6.
[2] *Elementarie*, pp. 25–26.

or more dangerously infected than with this, that the most part of schoolmasters like as father and householders think it no part of their duty to meddle with instructing their scholars and pupils in the word of the Lord and principles of the Christian religion, whereas without the fear of the Lord there is no wisdom neither is it possible for youth to go well-informed in virtue and good manners, things as necessary as learning.

The important thing is to start young, Stockwood declared, for 'the soft ware will receive any print', and here the parents must lead the way. Reluctantly he admitted that 'this thing doth the Papists of our time full well understand and therefore have picked schoolmasters privately to nousel up their children in their houses in the Pope's religion that they may taste and smell thereof when their parents be dead and rotten'. But after a long diatribe against Popish schoolmasters and parents Stockwood ends by exhorting his hearers and readers to emulate such zeal and efficiency.[1]

In Renaissance England the classic case of a family engaged in its educational function was that of Sir Thomas More's household. As Erasmus pointed out, 'You would say that in that place was Plato's Academy. But I do the house injury in likening it to Plato's Academy. I should rather call it a school or university of Christian religion. For there is none therein who does not study the branches of a liberal education. Their special care is piety and virtue.'[2] This reminds us, too, that the changed attitudes to married life and its corollaries, the rôle of the wife and the status of women, were as much a result of pre-Reformation influences, of humanism in fact, as of the Reformation itself. It is true that Luther and Calvin emancipated marriage from the negative overtones of criticism arising out of the superior monastic ideal of celibacy, with its emphasis on women as a temptress and its implication that marriage was a less-demanding and spiritually less-rewarding type of existence. But, as we have seen, Alberti and others a hundred years before had also rejected the monastic view, emphasizing in its place the traditional consecration of marriage by the church and the

[1] Stockwood, op. cit., pp. 88ff.
[2] Erasmus to John Faber, n.d., cited by F. Watson, ed., *Vives on the Education of Women* (1912), p. 175; cf. More to Gonell, 22 May ?1518, in Rogers, op. cit., No. 63, pp. 120–3 and More to his Children, c. 1517, in Bradner and Lynch, op. cit., pp. 108–10 and 230–1.

recognition of the child-rearing function of the parents. What the reformers did achieve, however, was an improvement in the status of women, and more particularly in the mutually-sustaining companionship inherent in the married state. It was a mutual relationship, however, which still operated within a patriarchal system in which the father, to whom unquestioning obedience was expected, was held in awe and esteem, and who himself fulfilled the rôles of sovereign, breadwinner and pastor of the family. On the other hand, if it was the father's duty to educate his children, it was also his responsibility to educate his wife. 'He doeth not his duty that doth not instruct and teach his wife—if she cannot read these things nor yet by instruction learn them, her husband must so familiarly and plainly teach her that she may remember them and use them when need shall require.' As William Gouge put it, a wife was 'an help as for bringing forth so for bringing up children; and as for erecting so for well-governing the family', and the prime need would, of course, arise when the wife shared with her husband in the moral and religious upbringing of their children.[1]

Evidently a prerequisite of this was the education of women to fit them for the rôle both of companion to their husband and educator of their children, and this meant something more than a mere offering of book-learning. It implied a view which attributed to a woman qualities of character and personality, initiative and self-reliance, and a sense of personal dignity, which hitherto had been denied her. A woman should be an object of interest and expectation in real life and not simply, as in the chivalric tradition, in some cloud-cuckoo land of unreality, impossible to achieve. The old medieval paradox, inherent in a view of woman which saw her as Eve the wife of Adam on the one hand and Mary the mother of Christ on the other, was a long time in being resolved. Richard Hyrde, for example, who translated Vives's *De Institutione Feminae Christianae* (1524) found it necessary, in his preface to Margaret Roper's translation of Erasmus' *Treatise Upon the Pater Noster* (1524), to counter the current argument of those who

> put great doubt whether it should be expedient and requisite or not a woman to have learning in books of Latin and Greek . . .

[1] Vives, *Office and Duetie* . . . (1550), Sigs. P vi and viii; Gouge, *Domesticall Duties* (1626), in *Works* (1627), I, 122–3.

alleging for their opinion that the frail kind of women, being inclined of their own courage unto vice and mutable at every novelty, if they should have skill in many things that be written into the Latin and Greek tongue compiled and made with great craft and eloquence, where the matter is haply sometime more sweet unto the ear than wholesome for the mind, it would of likelihood both influence their stomachs a great deal more to that vice that they say they be too much given unto of their own nature already, and instruct them also with more subtlety and conveyance to set forward and accomplish their froward intent and purpose.[1]

In the same way even those who advocated the education of women found it difficult to persuade themselves that women needed very much in the way of education. The medieval attitude of Philip de Novain (d. 1270) that 'women have a great advantage in one thing, they can easily preserve their honour, if they wish to be held virtuous by one thing only . . . for a woman if she be a worthy woman of her body all her faults are covered, and she can go with a high head where so ever she will, and therefore it is in no way needful to teach as many things to girls as to boys', is still to be found in a humanist such as Vives, who declared that 'though the precepts for men be innumerable, women yet may be informed with few words. For men must be occupied both at home and abroad both in their own matters and for the common weal. Therefore, it cannot be declared in few books . . . as for women she hath no charge to see to but her honesty and chastity, wherefore when she is informed of that she is sufficiently appointed.' Despite the attention he paid to the education of girls in his *Positions* Mulcaster, too, maintained that 'the bringing up of young maidens in any kind of learning is but an accessory by the way'. Even so he recognized the positive benefits of such education, for

is not a young gentlewoman, think you, thoroughly furnished which can read plainly and distinctly, write fair and swiftly, sing clear and sweetly, play well and finely, understand and speak learned languages and those tongues also which time most embraceth, with some logical help to chop and some rhetoric to brave

[1] Watson, op. cit., pp. 14 and 163.

. . . (and) if she be an honest woman and good housewife were she not worth the wishing and worthy the shriving?[1]

Of more importance, perhaps, outside court circles than within, there was a further virtue considered to be essential to a 'woman well-regarded', that of silence.

For there is nothing that doth so command, advance, set forth, adorn, deck, trim and garnish a maid as silence. And this noble virtue may the virgin learn of that most holy pure and glorious Virgin Mary which when she either heard or saw any worthy or notable thing blabbed it not out straightways to her gossips as the manner of woman is at this present day, but being silent she kept all those sayings secret and pondered them in her heart.[2]

The Mary Legends had continued to maintain their remarkable popularity well into the sixteenth century, and this particular aspect was taken over wholesale by the Puritans in their attitude to women. Indeed Becon's whole section 'Of the Duty of maids and young unmarried women' gives a clear idea of current views, with a good deal of the traditional still remaining alongside the humanist plea for the education of women. Sir Thomas More, it is true, claimed equality for his daughters, when he wrote to William Gonell, his children's tutor,

If they are worthy of being ranked with the human race, if they are distinguished by reason from beasts, that learning by which the reason is cultivated is equally suitable to both. Both of them, if the seed of good principles be sown in them, equally produce the germs of virtue. But if the female soil be in its nature stubborn and more productive of weeds than fruits, it ought in my opinion, to be more diligently cultivated with learning and good instruction to correct by industry the defects of nature.[3]

But in this he was quite exceptional and untypical of his age.

Nevertheless, the attitude to women and their rôle in the home and in society changed a good deal during the Renaissance. Throughout the medieval period, in the absence of their husbands

---

[1] *De Quartre Tens d'Aage d'Ome*, cited by Eileen Power, 'The Position of Women', in G. G. Crump and E. F. Jacob, eds., *The Legacy of the Middle Ages* (Oxford, 1926), p. 404; Watson, op. cit., p. 34, and Mulcaster, op. cit., p. 181.

[2] Thomas Becon, *A New Catechisme* (1564), in *Works* (Parker Society, 1844), p. 369.

[3] Rogers, op. cit., No. 63, p. 122.

at war, on pilgrimage or in trade, women had often taken on the burden of responsibility of running their lords' estates, a burden which was made the heavier in an age of slow communications. The picture of Agnes Paston, writing letters, keeping and checking accounts, supervising the estates of her husband, fending off litigious neighbours and seeing to the education of her children, though a very full one was by no means untypical. Even at a lower level we find women tenants in the manorial court rolls of the period, and in towns borough law accepted the woman trader. By the fifteenth century women were breaking out of their restricted sphere of interest, and not only in the household and practical arts. In Italy particularly the rapid increase of prosperity had meant that womenfolk of the well-to-do, free from the constraining influence of the nursery and the kitchen, could pay more attention to their intellectual and emotional life. As a result the courts of Italy were graced by womenfolk like Elizabeth Gonzaga at Urbino, Vittoria Colonna at Rome, Isabella D'Este at Mantua and her sister Beatrice Sforza at Milan. All were proficient Latinists, accomplished singers and lute players, patrons of the artists and poets of Renaissance Italy and capable of sharing in and contributing to the lively intellectual life of the humanist courts of the period. In France, Marguerite d'Angoulême, the sister of Francis I, Jeane de Lestouac, the sister of Montaigne, and Louise Labé of Lyons, the poetess and leader of a salon, had similar claims to fame.[1]

England had few women who could compare with these, though there is plenty of evidence both of educated women and of their education. Margaret Beaufort, Countess of Richmond and Derby and mother of Henry VII, was the founder with John Fisher of Christ's College and St. John's College, Cambridge, and she was also the patron of Caxton and Wynkyn do Worde. Catherine of Aragon may be regarded as one who patronized and encouraged the education of women rather than as having claims of her own. Lady Jane Grey, Mary Tudor, and Elizabeth, on the other hand, were all accomplished linguists. Ascham, who was tutor to both Lady Jane and Elizabeth, found the former reading Plato's *Phaedo* when he visited her at

---

[1] Cf. E. K. Varty, 'The Life and Legend of Louise Labé', *Nottingham Medieval Studies*, III (1959), pp. 78–100.

Broadgate.[1] She numbered Latin, Greek, French and Italian among her languages and even had a smattering of Hebrew and Arabic. William Fox the martyrologist, another of her tutors, thought her superior to Edward VI in her learning and ability. Elizabeth, of course, enjoyed an enormous and deserved reputation, and in a letter to Sturm, Ascham likened her to a central star among a court of young ladies, all of whom he considered more learned than the daughters of Sir Thomas More had been.

> French and Italian she speaks like English; Latin with fluency, propriety and judgment; she also spoke Greek with me, frequently, willingly and moderately well; nothing can be more elegant than her handwriting whether in Greek or Roman characters. In music she is very skilful but does not greatly delight . . . she read with me the whole of Cicero and a greater part of Livy; from these two authors indeed her knowledge of the Latin language has been almost exclusively derived.[2]

Even when the eulogy in Ascham's testimony of Elizabeth's ability as a pupil has been sifted out there can be no doubt but that Elizabeth was a very well-educated woman.

Among the educated women at her Court the daughters of Sir Anthony Cooke, himself a tutor to Edward VI, stood out. Mildred Cooke became the second wife of William Cecil and was the mother of Robert; Anne the second wife of Sir Nicholas Bacon and the mother of Francis; Elizabeth married Sir Thomas Hoby, the translator of Castiglione's *Courtier*, and Katherine married Henry Killigrew, diplomat, painter and patron of the arts. All four were well-educated women before they married their well-educated husbands, and the same may be said of Mary Sidney, Countess of Pembroke and Lucy Harrington of Bedford.

But the court was not the only centre of women's education, though obviously it was the most sought-after. If such a position could not be achieved or aspired to the daughters of the sixteenth and seventeenth-century gentry would be sent to the houses of other families, where, under the supervision of the lady of the household and the instruction of a private tutor, they would receive an education which would fit them for their vocation—

---

[1] *Scholemaster*, p. 33; cf. Ryan, *Ascham*, pp. 102ff.
[2] Ascham to Sturm, 4 April 1550, in J. A. Giles, ed., *Whole Works* . . ., I, 191; cf. *Scholemaster*, pp. 62–63 and 105.

marriage and mistress of their own households. Lady Neville, for example, wife of Sir Anthony Neville, had in addition to her three daughters, the daughter of Sir Thomas Fenton and three other gentlewomen, Anne and Katherine Jopeliffe and Ursula Ayton, in her household. Lady Jane Grey herself had been in the household of Catherine Parr from the age of nine. Margaret Dakins, later Lady Hoby, wife of Sir Thomas Posthumus Hoby, was reared in the household of the Countess of Huntingdon. Alternatively, the daughters of the house received their education at home at the hands of a private tutor who would provide the elements of English and Latin, besides the 'accomplishments' of music and dancing. Usually a young man newly down from Oxford or Cambridge was aimed at, but just as frequently in the houses of the lesser gentry it would be an aunt or other relation who undertook the task, as was the case with Grace Sherrington, daughter of Sir Henry Sherrington of Lacock Abbey, Wiltshire. In her journal Grace gives us a vivid picture of what must have gone on in innumerable houses up and down the country:–

> When she did see me idly disposed she would set me to cypher with the pen and to cast up and prove great sums and accounts and sometimes set me to write a supposed letter to this or that body, concerning such and such things, and other times let me read in Dr. Turner's *Herball* and Bartholomew Vigoe, and other times set me to sing psalms, and other times set me to some curious work, for whe was an excellent workwoman in all kinds of needlework.
> . . . Every day as my leisure would give me leave . . . I did read a chapter of the Book of Moses, another in one of the Prophets, one chapter in the Gospels, another in the Epistles to the end of Revelation and the whole psalms appointed for the day, also every day spent some time in playing on my lute and setting songs of five parts thereunto and practicing my voice and singing psalms and prayers . . . also every day I spent some time in the *Herball* and books of physic. . . . Also every day I spent some time in (needle) work of my own invention, without sample or pattern before me for carpet of cushion work and to draw flowers and fruit to their leaf. . . .[1]

[1] Rachell Weighall, 'An Elizabethan Gentlewoman', *Quarterly Review*, CCXV (1911), pp. 119–38. The references are to William Turner, *Newe Herball* (1551) and *The Most Excellent Workes of Chirurgereye . . . by Master J. Vigon . . . translated into English* (by Bartholomew Treheron) (1543).

In much the same way were the children of Sir Robert and Lady Sidney of Penshurst kept busy, as Roland Whyte, Sir Robert's agent in London reported to his master, the Governor of Flushing: 'Mistresses Mary and Kate do much profit in their book, Master William (aged 5) dances a gaillard in his doublet and hose.' Mary, Sir Robert's eldest daughter, he later wrote, 'is very forward in her learning, writing and other exercises she is put to, dancing and the virginals'. On another occasion he reported that all the children 'are kept at their books, they dance, they sing, they play the lute, and are carefully kept unto yet'.[1] Music increasingly played an important part in the home life of the middle and upper classes, and an expertise in the madrigals, rounds and catches to say nothing of the religious music of that 'golden age' of Elizabethan composers, which included Christopher Tye, Thomas Tallis, William Byrd, Thomas Morley, Thomas Weelkes and a host of others, was considered an indispensable part of one's education. The point is brought home by Thomas Morley in his *Plaine and Easie Introduction to Practicall Musicke* (1597), when he has Philomathes report, 'But supper being ended and music books according to the custom being brought to the table the mistress of the house presented me a part earnestly requesting me to sing. But when after many excuses I protested unfeignedly that I could not every one began to wonder and some whispered to others demanding how I was brought up'.[2] The printing press once again facilitated matters and produced Nicolas Yonge's *Musicae Transalpina*, the first collection of madrigals, in 1588, Thomas Watson's *First Set of Italian Madrigals Englished* in 1590 and Thomas Ravenscroft's *Pammelia* and *Deuteromelia* in 1609. These were collections of rounds and catches, the latter including the famous 'Three Blind Mice'. Thomas Pilkington's *First Boke of Songs or Ayres* (1605) is obviously devised for home use, for a song arranged for four voices is set out by the printer on a double page with the four parts so printed that the singers could sit or stand round the single copy and read their part simultaneously. For instruction in the lute recourse could be had to John Alford's *Briefe and Easye Instruction to Learne*

---

[1] Cited by L. C. John, 'Roland Whyte, Elizabethan Letterwriter', *Studies in the Renaissance*, VIII (1961), pp. 230 and 234.

[2] Op. cit., Sig. B 2.

*the Tableture to conduct and dispose thy hand unto the Lute* (1568) or Thomas Robinson's *The Schoole of Musicke, wherein is taught the perfect method of true fingering of the lute, pandora, orpharion and viol da gamba with most infallible generall rules both easie and delightful, also in method how to be your own instructor for prick song* (1603) or his *New Citharen Lessons* (1609).[1]

Dorothy Osborne's letters to William Temple perhaps best of all are indicative of the changes wrought in the sixteenth century in ideas about women's education, and though Lucy Apsley, later the wife of Colonel Hutchinson, seems to lack Dorothy's vivacity she was nevertheless obviously well-tutored and well-educated. Even so, not every one looked upon the education of women in a favourable light. Thomas Salter insisted that 'for such as compare the small profit of learning with the great hurt and damage that cometh to them, by the same shall soon perceive how for more convenient the distaff and spindle, needle and thimble were for them with a good and honest reputation that the skill of well using a pen or writing a lofty verse with dissowne and dishonour if in the same there be more erudition than virtue'. And the same point was made by Thomas Powell in Dorothy Osborne's day :—

> Instead of song and music let them learn cookery and laundry; and instead of reading Sir Philip Sidney's *Arcadia* let them read the ground of good housewifery. I like not a female poetess at any hand. Let great personages glory their skill in music, the posture of their bodies, their knowledges of languages, the greatness and freedom in their sports and their arts, in arreigning of man's affections at their flattering faces. This is not the way to breed a private gentleman's daughter.[2]

Nor was all sweetness and light even when a girl's parents did believe it important to educate her. Elizabeth Paston suffered a good deal at the hands of her mother, the redoubtable Agnes,

---

[1] Cf. G. Reese, *Music in the Renaissance* (1954), pp. 815ff; W. L. Woodfill, *Musicians in English Society from Elizabeth to Charles I* (Princeton, 1953), pp. 201ff; and E. Lowinsky, 'Music and Culture in the Renaissance', *J.H.I.*, XV (1954), pp. 509–53.

[2] Cf. G. C. Moore Smith, ed., *The Letters of Dorothy Osborne to William Temple* (Oxford, 1928), and C. H. Firth, ed., *Memoirs of the Life of Colonel Hutchinson by his wife* (1895); Salter, *The Mirror of Modestie Mete for all Mothers . . . to deck their young daughters and maidens by* (1579), Sig. C ii; Powell, *Tom of all Trades, or the Plaine Pathway to Preferment* (1631), Sig. G 3.

and, as her sister reported, 'hath since Easter the most part been beaten once in the week or twice, or sometimes twice in a day and her head broken in two or three places', whilst Lady Jane Grey reported to Ascham

> when I am in presence either of father or mother whether I speak, keep silence, sit, stand or go, eat, drink or be merry or sad, be sewing, playing, dancing or doing anything else I must do it as it were in such weight measure or number, even so perfectly as God made the world, or else I am so sharply taunted, so cruelly threatened, yea presently sometimes with punches, nipps, and bobbes and other ways I will not name for the honour I bear them, so without measure misordered that I think myself in hell till time come to go to Mr. Elmer, who teacheth me so gently so pleasantly with such fair allurement to learning that I think all the time nothing whilst I am with him and when I am called from him I fall a-weeping.[1]

Private tutors such as Mr. Elmer were, in fact, an indispensable part of the educational scene among the upper classes of Renaissance England, both for boys and for girls. Typical of such men was Henry Dowes, tutor to Gregory Cromwell, son of the Earl of Essex, and his two brothers Cheney and Charles, whose course not only included the usual 'writing, playing at weapons, casting of accounts, and pastimes of instruments' but also 'the daily hearing him to read somewhat in English tongue, and advertising him to the natural and true kind of pronunciation thereof expanding also and declaring the etymology and native significance of such words as we have borrowed of the nations or Frenchmen not even so commonly used in our quotidienne speech'.[2] Thomas Blundeville, whom we shall meet later as a translator, was tutor in the houses of Sir Nicholas Bacon and Justice Windham. Besides tutoring Lady Jane Grey, William Fox also taught Lady Jane Howard, daughter of the Earl of Surrey, whilst Lady Anne Clifford, later Countess of Dorset, had Samuel Daniel, the poet, as one of her tutors.

The general run of private tutors, however, often left much to be desired and Ascham bitterly complained

> that commonly more care is had, yea and that among very wise men, to find out rather a cunning man for their horse than a

[1] *The Paston Letters*, 29 June 1454; *Scholemaster*, p. 34.
[2] H. Ellis, *Original Letters*, 1st Series, I, 341–3.

213

cunning man for their children . . . for the one they will gladly give a stipend of 200 crowns a year and loth to offer the other two hundred shillings. God that sitteth in Heaven laugheth their choice to scorn, and rewardeth their liberality as it should be he suffereth them to have a tame and well-ordered horse but wild and unfortunate children and therefore in the end they find more pleasure in their horse than comfort in their children.[1]

Even tutors newly come down from Oxford and Cambridge had their imperfections and Sir Robert Sidney, for example, insisted on a Frenchman as tutor for Sir William, his eldest, because 'our Oxford men have seen nothing but the schools and need for most things themselves to be taught'. He later wrote from Flushing that he had obtained a tutor 'who speaketh both High Dutch and Low Dutch, French and some English besides Latin and Greek', and who would later make a good travelling companion for him.[2] James Cleland was obviously of the same opinion, for he insisted, in his *Institution of a Young Nobleman* (1607) that the tutor should have

> his head no less fraughted with mother wit (as we call it) than school learnings. For a dram of the first is for our purpose, worth a pound of the latter. To have such a tutor who shall be as wise as learned you must seek him abroad, and not in the schools . . . (one) conversant with the world not locked up in a study . . . who delighteth in honest company and not one who is astonished to frequent other men as the owl is to behold the light.[3]

Thomas Starkey, too, disapproved of private tutors for the children of the upper classes and suggested that 'certain places (be) appointed for the bringing up together of (the children) of the nobility to which I would the nobles should be compelled to set forward their children and heirs that in a number together they might the better profit'.[4] Ascham as we have seen preferred that the nobility improve the education of their children by paying more for their tutors and Lyly made the same point in his *Euphues*. Mulcaster, on the other hand, disapproved of private tutors altogether and especially opposed private educa-

[1] *Scholemaster*, p. 20.
[2] H.M.C., *de Lisle and Dudley MSS.*, II, 227, 269–70, 277, 434; cf. L. C. John, 'Ben Jonson's "To Sir William Sidney on his Birthday" ', *M.L.R.*, LII (1957), pp. 168–76.
[3] Op. cit., p. 26.
[4] Starkey, *Dialogue*, p. 169.

tion for those who were destined to serve the commonwealth in a public capacity:–

> Whatsoever inconveniences do grow in common schools (as where the dealers be men how can these be but maims?) yet the private is much worse, and hatcheth more odd ills. . . . By cloistering from the common it will seem to keep a countenance far above the common, even from the first cradle, whereby it becomes the puffer up of pride in the recluse, and the direction to disdain by dreaming still of betterment, the enemy to unity between the unequal, the over-swaining of oneself not compared with others, the disjointing of agreement, where the higher condemneth his inferior with scorn and the lower doth stomach his superior with spite.[1]

Yet tutors were there to stay and besides instructing their charges at home often accompanied the eldest son of the family on what was to become the most important part of his education, travel abroad. Hitherto the young nobleman had made acquaintance with foreign fields through war and pilgrimage. Now such opportunities were restricted, and in any case for the education-conscious of the sixteenth century not sufficiently controlled or susceptible enough of direct supervision. The traditional clerical student on the other hand, an inveterate wanderer, was considered to be too academic, too scholarly to serve as a model for the education of the nobleman's son, and so the compromise year or two abroad with a tutor became the practice. It fitted in, too, with the current theoretical discussions about the nature of wisdom which, as we have seen, emphasized the need for practical experience of people, of countries and of courts. As Leonardo da Vinci put it, 'wisdom is the daughter of experience'. So popular did such a trend become that by the eighteenth century particular routes had become fashionable and the local inhabitants *en route* had organized their economy to minister to the visitor. The Grand Tour had become part of the life of Europe.

But whereas the chief purpose of the Grand Tour was cultural, this was not the case in its nascent years in the sixteenth and seventeenth centuries. Then the aim was strictly 'useful' and 'practical': to gain practical experience of other countries, of foreign people, of their languages and particularly of the terrain

---

[1] *Positions*, p. 186.

and resources of these countries, all of which would be useful
in a future diplomatic or political career. At least this was the
aim enjoined upon prospective travellers and their tutors by the
many books and printed 'Letters of Advice' that were being
written from the second half of the sixteenth century onwards.
Just as Machiavelli had recommended his Prince 'to inure his
body to labour and travel, and learn to know the nature and
situation of divers places, marking the heights of mountains,
the opening of valleys to admit entrance, how the plains lie, by
this means also to know the course of the rivers, their depths,
and passages, the nature of the marsh grounds and divers other
things',[1] so also the young nobleman's travels abroad were to
be regarded as in the nature of a reconnaissance with certain
well-conceived and practical ends. Thus, Jerome Turler whose
*De Perigrinatione* (1574) was anonymously translated into
English in the following year, instructed his pupil to note 'how
many miles France or Spain is in length or breadth, what fortifications it hath, at what side is it easy or hard to be assaulted,
how many great rivers it hath that can be waded', and so on.
Nor were merely topographical or tactical matters to be noted.
In a typically Renaissance way the psychology of the different
peoples visited was to be observed:—

> What is the chief force or virtue of the Spaniards? and what of the
> Frenchmen? What is the greatest vice in both nations? Wherein
> doth the one or the other most regard themselves or takes greatest
> delight? In what thing the nobility of France doth differ from the
> nobility of Spain? . . . and what manner the subjects in both
> countries show their obedience to their prince or oppose them-
> selves against him?

Notice should be taken of 'public works, whether profane or
Holy', i.e. market places, schools, theatres, hospitals, or cathedral churches, monasteries, abbeys, etc., not for their architectural
or historical interest but as an index of the country's prosperity and stability. Finally and most important of all, the traveller
should 'mark how in every kind of government the Empire is
either continued or increased or lost, and in what new laws,
magistrates, officers they use to furnish them'. All this varied
information should be noted down in the daily journal and copied

---

[1] *The Prince*, Chap. 14.

into a 'relation', which must either be sent back or presented on return, for such information 'maketh men meet and fit to give counsel and to govern the Commonwealth'.[1]

John Stradling who produced his *Direction for Travellers taken out of Justus Lipsius for the behoof of the right honourable lord the young Earl of Bedford being now ready to travell* (1592) took a slightly wider view: 'If therefore you will be a profitable traveller and come home a better man than you went out . . . you must seek to be enriched with three things . . . they are wisdom of policy, knowledge or learning, manners or behaviour.' As a preliminary to travel Stradling recommended the young Earl to 'read the several histories of those nations that you are to travel . . . (in which) you shall find the nature, manners, and behaviour of the people; the cities, the ways, and the commodities of the country set down'. In addition, on arrival there 'talk with the learned of the land where you go . . . question and discourse of fashions, laws, nobility and kind of warfare of the people. . . . Be friendly to all, familiar to a few and speak but seldom. In countenance be as courteous as you can, and as your state will bear', but above all

> have diligent care . . . least you fall into the natural fault of those nations where you travel. For even as every man so every nation hath her proper vice, as for example the Frenchman is light and inconstant in speech and behaviour, the Italian hypocritical, luxurious and (which is the work of all ills) jealous. The Spaniard is imperious, proud, disdainful, pretending more than ever he intendeth to do. The German and the Netherlander ambitious, gluttonous, drunkards, always malcontent.[2]

One of the most reasoned and comprehensive of such texts was Thomas Palmer's *Essay of the Means How to Make Our Travels into Foreign Countries the More Profitable* (1606) which he produced 'for the youngest sort of such noble gentlemen as intend so recommendable a course'. Too many, he complained, embark on their travels too young. The best age would be after their twenty-fifth birthday, by which time the prior knowledge

---

[1] *The Traveiler* (1575), pp. 46–47, 55–58, 61; cf. Edward Moorcroft's description of his travels to William Cecil, 1 January 1567, *Cal. S.P. (Foreign), 1566–8,* No. 879, pp. 161–2.

[2] Op. cit. (1592), Sigs. B–B 3 *verso,* C2–C3 *verso.*

so essential for the full enjoyment of the tour could be adequately obtained. Languages, practice in weapon handling, skill in music, dancing and drawing, as well as a knowledge of 'the natural and mathematical arts', i.e. astronomy and astrology, cosmography, geography and hydrography, geometry and arithmetic, military architecture, an introduction to all of these is important, 'for the better men are grounded in these the more profit shall they make of their travels'. Once abroad the pupil's aim is 'to get knowledge for the bettering of himself and his country', which knowledge may be confined 'under six general heads . . . the tongue, the nature of the people, the country, the customs, the government, of the state, and the secrets of the same which are to be sought out wheresoever these shall come . . . (for) these things are the utensils and materials of statesmen concerning foreign matters'.[1]

One of the few occasions on which the *beauty* of foreign countries is mentioned is in a letter of advice which the Earl of Essex wrote for Roger Manners, Earl of Rutland, concerning his future visit to the Continent.[2] Look at the beauty of foreign countries, get to know the manners of the people, learn their languages, and these 'may serve for amusement . . . and delight'. Yet 'the last thing I am to speak of is but the first you are to seek. It is *knowledge* . . . without it there can be no liberality'. By 'study, conference and observation . . . the three helps to knowledge' his lordship might equip himself for his future responsibilities, for 'the true end of knowledge is clearness and strength of judgement and not ostentation or ability to discourse, which I do rather put your lordship in mind of because the most part of noblemen and gentlemen of our time have no other use or end of their learning but their table talk'.[3] Generally the aim could not have been better expressed than by Sir Thomas Bodley who recounts in his autobiography, 'I waxed desirous to travel beyond the seas for attaining to the knowledge of some special modern tongues and for the increase of my experience in the managing of affairs, being then wholly addicted

---

[1] Op. cit., pp. 18, 38–39, 52–54.

[2] June 1596, printed in William Davison, *Profitable Instructions describing what special observations are to be taken by travellers in all nations states and countries* (1633).

[3] Op. cit., Sigs. E 1 *verso*, E 6 *verso*. Davison also prints a similar letter from Philip Sidney to his brother, Robert.

to employ myself and all my cares into the public of the state'.[1]

Sometimes the young nobleman abroad stayed in the house of the resident ambassador, as Sir Philip Sidney did in Francis Walsingham's house when the latter was ambassador in Paris in 1572. But it was often an onerous duty for the ambassador, as Sir Amias Paulet reminded Walsingham five years later:–

> This bearer Mr. Throckmorton hath prayed me to give him leave to repair into England being hereunto required by his mother, as he sayeth, who hath promised to get him licence to travel into Italy, because having now gotten the French tongue in good perfection he cannot make any other profit by his abode in France. To be plain with you I think myself very happy that I am honestly delivered of him. He is a very young man and hath his imperfections, which riper years and good counsel may remove from him. He may not go into Italy without the company of some honest and wise man and so I have told him, and in many other things have dealt plainly with him.

Even when a young man did not live in the ambassador's house it was the latter's duty to know about the affairs and doings of any of his countrymen who visited his area, and Sir Amias was able to report to Sir George Peak, for example, that he was

> not unacquainted with your son's doing in Paris and cannot commend him enough to you, as well for his diligence in study as for his honest and quiet behaviour. . . . Paris is a place that will try the disposition of young men, so as for this experience which I have had of your son and of your servant Poole I may be so bold to say this much unto you that the one is able to govern himself and the other sufficient in honesty and discretion to govern any man's son that I know in the west parts of England.[2]

Obviously Sir George's son was in good hands and making the most of his education abroad.

The young Arthur Throckmorton's stay in Paris seems not to have impressed his elders, though to be fair we have only Paulet's word for this period of his life. Certainly when he travelled through the Netherlands, Germany and Italy in 1580–2 the evidence of his diary suggests that he made better use of his

---

[1] *The Life of Sir Thomas Bodley written by himself* (Oxford, 1647), p. 4.

[2] O. Ogle, ed., *Copybook of Sir Amias Poulet's Letters during his Embassy in France* (1577) (Roxeburgh Club, 1866), pp. 16–17, 89–90.

time, learning the languages, buying large numbers of books, studying astronomy and chemistry, taking lessons in singing and the lute, and noting in his diary every detail of his journeyings.[1]

As we have have seen, Thomas Palmer recommended twenty-five as the best age for such a journey, but William Cecil, Lord Roos, great-nephew of Robert Cecil went to Paris in 1615 aged fifteen; William Lord Cranborne went with his tutor Matthew Lister when he was eighteen, and Henry, Lord Clifford when he was nineteen. Sir John Harington went to Florence in 1608 with his tutor 'Mr. Tovey' when he was sixteen. Edward Herbert, on the other hand, was just twenty-five when he went to Paris 'taking with me for my companion Mr. Aurelian Townshend, a gentleman that spoke the language of French, Italian and Spanish in great perfection and a man to wait in my chamber who spoke French, two lacqueys and three horses'.[2] Sir Philip Sidney, who received a licence from the Queen in 1572 'to go out of England into parts beyond the seas . . . for his attaining the knowledge of foreign languages', was seventeen when he left, his travels taking in Paris (during the massacre of St. Bartholomew), Frankfurt, Heidelberg, Strasbourg and Vienna. From Vienna he made an excursion into Hungary and, on returning to Vienna, went into Italy where he stayed at Venice and Padua, with short visits to Florence and Genoa. He then returned to Vienna where the English Resident was the much-travelled Edward Wotton. Finally he retraced his steps through Germany to Antwerp and a sea passage home, having been away for nearly three years.[3]

Sir Thomas Puckering and William, Lord Clifford, on the other hand, 'made a stay' in Paris where they both attended the famous academy of M. de Pluvinel. Puckering's tutor, Thomas Lorkin, provides details of their studies at the academy in a letter to Adam Newton, tutor to Prince Henry:–

> Our days therefore are thus divided. In the forenoon Mr. Puckering spends two hours on horseback, from seven to nine one morning from nine to eleven another. Two other hours he spends in French one in reading the other in rendering to his teacher some part of a

[1] A. L. Rowse, *Raleigh and the Throckmortons* (1962), pp. 80ff.
[2] S. Lee, ed., *Autobiography of Edward, Lord Herbert of Cherbury* (1886), pp. 89–90.
[3] Buxton, op. cit., pp. 33ff.

Latin author by word of mouth. A fifth hour is employed in learning to handle his weapon, which entertain him till twelve of the clock when the bell warns him to dinner, when the company continues together till two o'clock, either passing the time in discourse or some honest recreation pertaining to arms. Then they are warned by the bell to dancing which holds them till three, when he retires himself to his chamber and there employs with me two other hours in reading over some Latin author, which done he translates some little part into French, leaving his faults to be corrected the morrow following by his teacher. After supper we take a brief survey of all.

Clifford's tutor, William Becher, provided similar details in his letters to the boy's father. Besides the room reserved in the Academy for his lordship, Becher also rented a house next door at £80 per annum; 'the gates of the academy being kept very strictly his lordship will be more at liberty in his own house, and it were to no purpose to distaste him with unnecessary severity'. In addition to the riding, fencing, dancing and lute playing, Clifford seems also to have attempted some mathematics and philosophy, though with what 'severity' is not recorded.[1]

'Exercises' obviously played a great part in such an education, though Sir Robert Dallington warned his readers: 'there is danger but of one in France, and that is tennis play, this is dangerous (if used with too much violence) for the body and (if followed with too much diligence) for the purse'. Dancing, too, was to be part of the course only if 'he means to follow the court, otherwise I hold it needless and in some ridiculous'.[2]

The cost of such an education would vary, of course, with the rank of the pupil. As Dallington observed,

Money, the sinews of war and the soul of travel as at home and so abroad, is the man. They say you should have two bags, the one of crowns, and the other of patience. . . . If he travel without a servant, four score pounds sterling is a competent proportion, except he learn to ride; if he maintain both these charges he can be allowed no less than one hundred and fifty pounds and to allow above two hundred pounds were superfluous and to his hurt. And this rateably according to the number he keepeth. The ordinary

[1] Lorking to Newton, 6 November 1610, in H. Ellis, *Original Letters*, 2nd Series, III (1827), pp. 221–2. J. W. Stoye, *English Travellers Abroad 1604–70* (1952), pp. 47–94.

[2] Dallington, *Method of Travel* . . . (?1605), Sig. B 4 *verso*.

rate of his expense is this: ten gold crowns a month his own diet, eight for his man at the most, two crowns a month his fencing, as much his dancing no less his reading and fifteen crowns monthly his riding. . . . If he carry money over with him (as by our law he cannot carry much) let it be in double pistolets or French crowns by weight; by these he is sure to sustain loss in no place and in Italy to gain above twelve pence in the pound.[1]

Becher reckoned that the cost of the rented house, the Academy and tuition amounted to £150 per annum. Household expenses including liveries and horses, a further £350, leaving £300 for clothes and other expenses. On another occasion he calculated the annual expenses to be £1,150. This was in 1610. James Cleland, on the other hand, thought £200 per annum sufficient for the pupil, his tutor and two servants, allowing ten French crowns for his pupils diet, eight for the tutor's, six for the man's and four for the page's, 'and the other four crowns which remain of your hundred French francs monthly for keeping you in use of your exercises, which I suppose you have learned here at home, except you continue in learning to ride, which will cost you fifteen crowns monthly. As for the other hundred pounds English, it will be little enough for your clothes, books, travelling and sundry extraordinary charges.' In 1618 Lord Percy, son of the 'wizard Earl' of Northumberland, set out on his foreign tour with his tutor, Mr. Dowse, the latter being given £100 for the journey, with a further £200 being drawn later to be at Lord Percy's disposal whilst in France. James Howell, writing in 1642, reckoned that £300 per annum would be required, with £50 apiece extra for the servants: 'I include therein all sorts of exercises, his riding, dancing, fencing, the racket, coach-hire with other casual charges together with his apparell.' Howell also refers to 'the divers academies in Paris, college-like', where he claims, 'for 150 pistoles a year which come to about £110 sterling per annum of our money one may be very well accommodated with lodging and diet for himself and a man to be taught to ride and fence, to manage arms, to dance, vault and ply the mathematics'.[2]

---

[1] Ibid., Sigs. C–C2.
[2] Cleland, op. cit., p. 254; G. R. Batho, 'The Education of a Stuart Nobleman', *B.J.E.S.*, V (1957), pp. 141–2. Howell, *Instructions for Forreine Travell* (1642), pp. 49 and 51.

Even if one were not a Clifford, it was obviously an expensive business, but this was the least of the complaints that followed hard upon the increasing popularity of foreign travel as part of a young gentleman's education. Turler noted in 1574 'There is an ancient complaint made by many that our countrymen usually bring three things with them out of Italy, a naughty conscience, an empty purse and a weak stomach.'[1] The major criticism was on grounds of religion, both France and Italy, to say nothing of Spain, offering all kinds of dangers to 'unsuspecting' Protestant youths—or so their elders claimed. It was Italy which came in for the major share of the blame, however. Roger Ascham visited Italy for a short period in 1550 and on that occasion his long letter to Edward Raven, fellow of St. John's showed no sign of the hostility which produced his famous diatribe in the *Schole-master* in 1570, when he claimed that 'Some Circe shall make him of a plaine Englishman a right Italian, and at length to hell or to some hellish place he is likely to go.'[2] After the Papal Bull of Excommunication and the Ridolfi Plot on behalf of Mary Queen of Scots, Catholicism in England was identified with treason and the dangers of travel to Italy were accentuated. 'Let him beware of Rome,' Palmer was still writing in 1606, 'the forge of every policy that setteth princes at odds, or that continueth them in debates, little or much, the tempter of subjects to evil dissensions and the setter of all wickedness and heathenish impieties and practices that are unmeet subjects for these worthy travellers to spend their time about.'[3] Sir Dudley Carleton reported to Salisbury 'that one Hole (i.e. Francis Hole) a fellow of Exeter College, Oxford and tutor to two of Sir Robert Dormer's sons . . . spared not to tell me that he had been with his young gentlemen to see Cardinal Bellarmin and were courteously received by him. The ingenuity of which confession shows that it was done without malice to satisfy curiosity.' But the danger was there, as James I himself noted:—

> Many of the gentry and others of our kingdom under pretence of travel for their experience do pass the Alps, not contenting themselves to remain in Lombardy or Tuscany to gain the language there do daily flock to Rome out of vanity and curiosity to see the

[1] Turler, *The Traveiler*, p. 66.
[2] Op. cit., p. 72.
[3] Palmer, *Essay . . .*, p. 44.

antiquities of that city, where falling into the company of priests and jesuits, . . . return again unto their countries both averse to religion and ill-affected to our state and government.

To stifle such activities the king therefore forbade all those going through Venice to go farther than Florence.[1]

The dangers of proselytizing were not the only ones, however. There were moral temptations of equal force. For Thomas Nashe, who had never visited the country, incidentally, but who nevertheless joined in the chorus of dispraise, Italy was 'the academy of manslaughter, the sporting place of murder, the apothecary shop for all nations'.[2] There were young men seduced and enemies dispatched with all kinds of subtle poisons. There, too, the vainglories of fashion, in dress, in behaviour and in speech served only 'to make of a plain Englishman a right Italian' who brought home, as Harrison complained in 1578,

> nothing but mere atheism, infidelity, vicious conversation and ambitions and proud behaviour, whereby it cometh to pass that they return far worse men than they went out . . . they have learned in Italy to go up and down also in England with page at their heels finely apparelled whose face and countenance should be such as showeth the master not to be blind in his choice. But least I should offend too much I pass over to say any more of these and their demeanour, which also is too open and manifest to the world and yet not called into question.[3]

'God hath given us a world of our own, wherein there is nothing wanting to earthly contentment. Whither go ye then, worthy, countrymen, and what seek ye?' wrote Joseph Hall in his *Quo Vadis? A Just Censure of Travell as it is Commonly Undertaken by the Gentlemen of our Nation* (1617). Much the same argument had been used by Mulcaster in his *Positions*, whilst Ascham, recommending Castiglione's *Courtier*, claimed that the book 'advisedly read and diligently followed but one year at

---

[1] S. P. Venice 7/183, 12 April 1611, cited by Stoye, op. cit., p. 121. James I to Wotton, 7 December 1616, in L. P. Smith, ed., *Life and Letters of Sir Henry Wotton* (1907), I, 70 n. 3.

[2] *Pierce Pennilesse* (1592), in R. B. McKerrow, ed., *Works*, I, 186.

[3] Harrison, *Description of England*, in F. J. Furnivall, ed. (New Shakespeare Society, Series VI, Part I, 1877), pp. 129–30. Similar descriptions and criticisms are to be found in Stubbs's *Anatomie of Abuses* (1583), Gabriel Harvey's *Letter Book* (Camden Society, N.S., XXXIII, 1884), pp. 97–98, and Dallington, *Method of Travell* (?1605), Sig. B 1 *verso*.

home in England would do young gentlemen more good, I
wisse, than three years travel abroad spent in Italy'. Yet, as Sir
Henry Wotton wrote to Robert Cecil in 1605, the situation in
Italy had been changing for the better since the death of Pope
Sixtus V; and the Englishman's picture of the Italian was
changing, too, during the second half of the century.[1] The
scheming, Machiavellian poisoner and proselytizer of Ascham's
day had turned into the foppish 'Italianate' Englishmen who
would 'bring home a few smattering terms, flattering garbs,
apish cringes, foppish fancies, foolish guises and disguises without furthering of their knowledge of God, the world or themselves'. At his worst he was Barabas in Marlowe's *Jew of
Malta*, but for the most part the stereotype was Jacques in *As
You Like it*, walking with a foreign gait, bowing in the foreign
manner, picking up foreign books in preference to English ones
and often given to melancholy. Like Portia's English suitor,
Falconbridge, who 'bought his doublet in Italy, his round hose
in France, his bonnet in Germany, and his behaviour everywhere,' he was parodied unmercifully and nowhere more fiercely
than in William Rankins's *The English Ape, the Italian Imitation,
the Foote Steppes of France* (1588).[2]

For a century or more England had looked to Italy for inspiration. Now apparently she was 'dropping the pilot', though continuing to enjoy the benefit and influence of what the pilot had
to offer. For she continued to accept the *dicta* of courtesy books
as well as educational aims which had their origin in Italy, and
more particularly, in the literary sphere, to accept Italian models
as worthy of imitation and emulation, while at the same time
pouring her scorn on 'things Italian', or rather on what youthful
visitors brought back from a brief acquaintance with the seamier
side of Italian life. Undoubtedly a good many young men and
their tutors returned none the worse for the experience of
foreign travel and study, though a good many too, deserved the
adverse criticism of their elders. Until the upper classes began in
in increasing numbers to send their sons to what came to be

---

[1] Hall, op. cit., pp. 87–88; *Positions*, pp. 208ff; *Scholemaster*, p. 61; L. P.
Smith, ed., op. cit., I, 330ff.

[2] *Samuel Purchas His Pilgrimes* (1628), To the Reader. *Merchant of Venice*,
I, ii, 28; cf. G. B. Parks, 'The First Italianate Englishmen', *Studies in the Renaissance*, VIII (1961), pp. 197–216; Z. S. Fink, 'Jacques and the Melancholy Traveller', *Philological Quarterly*, XIV (1935), pp. 235–52.

distinguished as 'the greater public schools', the family, the private tutor and the nascent Grand Tour provided an educational aggregation which was at times an alternative and at others a supplement to the traditional grammar school, university and Inns of Court. 'Courtly academies' like M. de Pluvinel's failed to take root in England despite the advocacy of Sir Humphrey Gilbert. Nicholas Bacon and William Cecil both put forward schemes for the 'courtly' education of the nation's nobility, and especially of the Queen's wards, but nothing came of them.[1] With the greater experience of the Continental academies—and the increasing criticism of their products—fresh attempts were made in the seventeenth century. The nearest approach was the household of Prince Henry at Nonsuch Palace, which Cleland described as 'that true Pantheon of Great Britain . . . where young nobles may learn the first elements to be Privy Councillor, a general of an army, to rule in peace, to command in war'.[2] Sir Francis Kynaston set up his Museum Minervae in 1635 in his house in Covent Garden, and Balthazar Gerbier his own academy in Bethnal Green in 1648, as 'a means whereby to free them of such charges as they are at when they send their children to foreign academies'.[3] But neither succeeded, and the future education of the upper classes rested with the public schools and the universities.

---

[1] The schemes of Bacon and Cecil are printed in J. Conway Davies, 'Elizabethan Plans and Proposals for Education', *Durham Research Review*, No. 5 (1954), pp. 1–9.

[2] Cleland, op. cit., p. 35. For Prince Henry's household at Nonsuch cf. T. Birch, *Life of Henry, Prince of Wales* (1760), *passim*.

[3] In a broadsheet *To All Fathers of Noble Families and Lovers of Vertue* (1648).

# VIII

## Modern Languages and Literature

In his travels abroad the prime aim of the young gentleman was to acquire foreign languages which would be of service to him in his public capacity later on. Later, skill in languages came to be as much a social accomplishment as a vocational necessity and to meet both needs there arose the new class of modern language tutor whose teaching and whose texts played an important part in the cultural life of Renaissance England, more especially in the second half of the sixteenth century and after.

The teaching of French in England was, not surprisingly, older than the Renaissance, for French had been the language of the court and the upper classes since the Conquest. It was also, though not exclusively, the language of administration and law at both national and local levels.[1] To cater for the needs of both spheres manuscript texts were being produced from the end of the thirteenth century, some of them as straightforward grammatical treatises, others taking the form of dialogues which taught the various modes of address and salutation and provided phrases and sentences relating to everyday matters of buying and selling, travelling, staying at inns, changing horses and so on. A third kind consisted simply of collections of letters and other administrative forms, whilst Walter de Bibbesworth's interlined metrical French vocabulary, written at the end of

[1] Cf. H. Suggett, 'The Use of French in England in the Later Middle Ages', *T.R.H.S.*, 4th Series, XXVIII (1946), pp. 61–83.

the thirteenth century for Denise, the daughter of William Munchesney, followed Aelfric's method of providing a collection of everyday household words. The more formal *Tractatus Orthographiae* of Thomas Coyfurelly and the anonymous *Orthographia Gallica* also date from this period and provided the basis for the courses (and texts) which flourished in Oxford in the fourteenth and fifteenth centuries.[1] These courses were not part of the statutory teaching of the university, though the teachers were, in fact, controlled by university statutes. Men such as Thomas Sampson and William Kingsmill (1415–30) used these texts and produced their own, providing a basic syntax, accidence and pronunciation, and, assuming that French would be used in correspondence and administration, a collection of model letters and instruments, petitions, charters, land settlements, wills and the like. Some of the letters in fact have provided us with a good deal of lively information about the student life of the period.[2] Many of the texts remained anonymous, however, as did the fifteenth-century *manière de langage qui tensegnera bien a droit parler et escrire doulz Franceoys selon l'usage et l'accostume de France*. Written in dialogue form, it describes a day in the life of a French gentleman, who discusses household matters with his servants, rides to Orleans singing on the way *une très amoureuse chançon*, does some shopping and dines at the inn with a *très bon fillette*, to whom he sings another amorous song. This is followed by a group of conversations between the gentleman and various people of the town and concludes with other dialogues concerning everyday happenings.[3]

---

[1] Cf. Annie Owen, *Le Traité de Walter de Bibbesworth sur la Langue Française* (Paris, 1929). For the origin of Coyfurelly's work and its relationship to the *Orthographia Gallica*, cf. M. K. Pope, 'The *Tractatus Orthographiae* of T.H., Parisii Studentis', *M.L.R.*, V (1910), pp. 185–93.

[2] Cf. C. H. Haskins, *Studies in Medieval Culture* (Oxford, 1929).

[3] Cf. D. O. Arnold, 'Thomas Sampson and the *Orthographia Gallica*', *Medium Aevum*, VI (1937), pp. 193–210; M. D. Legge, 'William of Kingsmill, a Fifteenth Century Teacher of French in Oxford', in *Studies in French Language and Medieval Literature presented to M. K. Pope* (1939), pp. 241–6. A collection of such texts (All Souls MSS. CLXXXII, 15th Century) is described in C. T. Martin, ed., *Registrum Epistolarum Fratris Johannis Peckham Arch. Cantuar.* (Rolls Series, 1882), I, xlivff. A manière of 1396 and several dialogues (1415) are described by P. Meyer in *Revue Critique d'Histoire et de Literature*, V, Pt. II (1870), pp. 373–408, and *Romania*, XV (1886), pp. 262ff, and XXXII (1903), pp. 43ff. The *Orthographia Gallica* is printed in *The Eyre of Kent*, II (Selden Society, XXVII, 1912), pp. xliii–li.

Such works found their way into the offices of the royal chancery and into monasteries, were copied, recopied and pirated, and so have survived to give us a picture of non-classical type of education which flourished and satisfied a genuine need in the later Middle Ages. They also provided a pattern for future printed texts, for though French ceased to be the language of conversation at court, an ability to speak French on occasions came to be regarded as a social accomplishment as well as an essential qualification for diplomacy. To satisfy the need for instruction arising out of this, the first printed grammars of the French language were produced, together with conversation manuals which not only used a courtly type of language but also themselves developed into readers rather than dialogues, treating of rather more elevated topics than 'the everyday type of content characteristic of the traditional *manière*.[1] One of the earliest of such printed texts was Alexander Barclay's *Here Begynneth the Introductory to Write and Pronounce French* (1521), but more typical perhaps was *L'Esclaircissement de la Langue Francoyse* (1530) of John Palsgrave, one of the many foreign language tutors who served the royal family and upper classes of the early sixteenth century. Palsgrave was for thirty years tutor to court and nobility and included among his pupils Henry VIII and Mary Tudor, whom he accompanied on a visit to France, as well as Henry's son, the Duke of Richmond. Palsgrave was very conscious of his position for when he printed his text he carefully had it restricted to 750 copies, 'lest his profit by teaching the French tongue might be diminished by the sale of the same to such persons as besides him were disposed to study the French tongue'. His great rival was Giles du Wes, whose *Introduction For to Lerne to Rede to Pronounce and to Speak French Trewly* was written about the same time as *L'Esclaircissement*. Other tutors of whom we have records included Pierre Vallence, whose *Introductions in Frensche* were written for his pupil the Earl of Lincoln, Nicholas Bourbon, tutor to Robert Dudley later Earl of Leicester, Jean Bellemain, tutor to Edward VI and Elizabeth, and Nicholas Denisot, tutor to the three daughters of the Protector Somerset, Anne, Margaret and Jane. All were well-educated men who did a good deal to introduce the French Renaissance to England and who were concerned in

[1] For Caxton's *manières* see Chap. ix.

their texts and their teaching to go beyond the mere learning of catch phrases in the *manière* style and to lay good grammatical foundations on which to build a facility in writing and speaking the language. Those who were not members of the court and had no access to the court circle of tutors, could resort to the teachers of modern languages who set up private schools, such as Peter du Ploich who taught 'at the sign of the Rose in Trinity Lane' in Oxford, and who doubtless used his own *Treatise in English and French Right Necessary and Profitable for al Young Children* (1553, 1578).

The teaching of French received a great stimulus with the influx of French Huguenot refugees in the second half of the century. Anness Dyer, for example, a native of Tournai, came to England about 1568 and was still practising the 'trade' of French teacher at Tenter Alley, Southwark in 1618. The most famous of all such refugees was Claude de Sainliens (Claude Holyband), whose father had arrived in England in 1564.[1] Holyband was a born teacher. Not only was he convinced of the social importance of his work, but he had the ability to make the teaching and learning of the French language interesting and even amusing. As index of his ability is the success which met his two main teaching texts, *The French Schoolemaister* and *The French Littleton*. The former was first published in 1573 and by 1636 had run into nine other editions, whilst the latter, which appeared in 1576, a rather easier version of his first book which he 'caused to be printed in this small volume that it might be carried by any man about him,' had its tenth edition in 1630.[2] Like the earlier *manières* Holyband's chief aim was to enable his pupils to *speak* French, as the full title of the earlier work shows, *The French Schoolmaister wherein is most plainlie shewed the true and most perfect way of pronouncing the French tongue without any help of maister or teacher set forthe for the furtherance of all those which noo studie privately at their own study or houses*. The text starts with the pronunciation of letters and syllables and then goes on to a brief set of grammatical rules, after which the bulk of the text is devoted to parallel French-English dialogues, 'For

[1] Cf. W. B. Austin, 'Claudius Holyband: an Elizabethan Schoolmaster', *N. and Q.*, CLXXVII (1939), pp. 237–40, 255–8.

[2] A. W. Pollard, *Transactions of the Bibliographical Society*, XII (1913–15), pp. 253–72, shows that 1566, the date on the title page of *The French Littleton*, is a misprint for 1576.

Travellers', 'Arrival at the Inn', 'Of Scholars and Schools', 'Merchants Buying and Selling', etc., which are followed by a collection of proverbs, the Lord's Prayer, the Creed, the Ten Commandments and a group of graces before meals. The predominant tone of the text is one of liveliness and informality, as the following extract shows:—

> Ho! Frances, rise and get you to school, you shall be beaten, for it is past seven; make yourself ready quickly.
> Say your prayers, then you shall have breakfast.
> Margaret, give me my hose, dispatch I pray you.
> Take first a clean shirt for yours is foul.
> Make haste, then, for I do tarry too long.
> It is moist yet; tarry a little that I may dry it by the fire.
> Where have you laid my girdle, and my ink holder; where is my jerkin of Spanish leather? of Bouffe? Where be my socks of linen, of woollen, of cloth? Where is my cap, my hat, my coat, my cloak, my cape, my gown, my gloves, my mittens, my pumps, my moyles, my slippers. . . .[1]

Again in *The French Littleton* in a dialogue between master and pupil:—

> What is the clock?
> It is eleven.
> Is it so late?
> Yea master it is time that I go for I should be chiden if I should tarry any longer.
> Who shall chide you?
> My mistress.
> Kneel down all. Say the prayers and go to dinner. Take heed you play not by the way. Take off your cap when you pass before your betters. Come again betimes after noon.[2]

To supplement these at a rather more academic level Holyband produced his *De Pronunciatione Linguae Gallicae* (1580) in Latin and French, a detailed exposition of grammar, phonetics and teaching method, with the usual series of dialogues annexed. In the same year, too, he published a *Treasurie of the French Tongue*, a French-English dictionary which he enlarged in 1593 as *A Dictionarie French and English*, and a *Treatise for Declining Verbes* which was reprinted in 1599, 1604, 1613 and 1633. Holyband had started his teaching career as tutor to Robert Sackville,

[1] Op. cit., p. 62.
[2] Op. cit., Sig. C v *verso*.

son of Lord Buckhurst, but round about 1575 he set up his own school in St. Paul's churchyard 'by the sign of Lucrece' (the shop of his fellow-refugee Thomas Purfoot, the printer). By 1580 when he produced his *De Pronunciatione* he was 'at the sign of the Golden Ball in Paul's churchyard', though during this period he continued to teach private pupils, including among them Anne Harrington, sister-in-law of Sir James, and her daughter Lucy, later Countess of Bedford.[1]

For over thirty years his influence was a very real one, not only in popularizing the teaching of French, but also in shaping the pattern of modern language teaching. Similar works were produced, for example, by Jacques Bellot whose *Jardins de Vertue . . . plusiers belles fleurs et riches sentences avec le sens d'icelle recueilles de plusieurs auteurs* (1581) in French and English was followed by *The Frenche Method wherein is contained a perfite order of Grammar for the French tongue* (1588). In similar vein, though explicitly for women, another French tutor, Peter Erondell, produced his *French Garden for English Ladies and Gentlewomen to walk in, or a sommer daye's labour being an instruction for the attayning unto the knowledge of the French tongue wherein for to practice thereof are framed thirteene dialogues in French and English concerning divers matters from the rising in the morning till bedtime* (1605), which he followed with a revised and enlarged version of Holyband's *French Schoolemaister* in the following year. Erondell prefaced his thirteen dialogues with a brief resumé of grammar and 'Some rules of pronunciation as the gate through which we must (and without which we cannot) enter into our French Garden.' He expressly wished to avoid burdening his pupils with too much grammatical detail, which he felt to be 'rather a trouble and discouragement to the student than any furtherance'. Pronunciation on the other hand was the key to success and here the instructions are precise and thoroughly practical. For example, 'when you meet gn melt the g with the n, as ognon, mignon; pronounce i thus, onion, minion, but g before e and i is to be pronounced as gibbet, generation, gentle and gilofer in English, but not so hard,' and

---

[1] Cf. K. Lambley, *The Teaching and Cultivation of the French Language in England During Tudor and Stuart Times* (Manchester, 1920); Lucy E. Farrar, *Un Dévancier de Cotgrave, la vie et les oeuvres de Claude de Sainliens alias Claudius Holyband* (Paris, 1908); and M. St. Clair Byrne, ed., *The French Littleton of Claudius Holyband: the Edition of 1609* (Cambridge, 1953).

this is followed up in the dialogue section, where the pronunciation of the more difficult words is given in English spelling in
the margin. The dialogues themselves centre on a Lady Rime-
laine and the 'divers matters' which occupy her 'from the rising
in the morning till bed time'. They are of no great originality,
and obviously owe a great deal to Holyband. On the other hand
Erondell recognized his market and produced a text which
would efficiently meet its requirements.[1]

Giles de la Mothe's *The French Alphabeth teaching in a very
short time a most easie way to pronounce French naturally, to reade
it perfectly, so to write it truely and to speake it accordingly* (1592)
is rather more interesting because it indicates in more detail his
teaching method. The first three or four days are to be spent
mastering the letters and syllables, and then the pupil can make
a start on reading short sentences, spelling each word four or
five times to reinforce pronunciation. Once some proficiency has
been gained in reading, or rather pronouncing, words the pupil
should start on translation, using the method of double translation. 'Later, get you acquainted . . . with some Frenchman to
the end you may practice with him by daily conference together
in speech and talk . . . (and) if there be a French church get
you a French Bible or a New Testament and everyday go to hear
the lectures and sermons. The one will confirm and strengthen
your pronunciation and the other to understand when one do
speak.' Finally de la Mothe recommends that the pupil should
acquire a dictionary and 'the hardest book you can find' and then
translate it. If in difficulty he should repair to the writer 'in
Fleet Street beneath the Conduit at the Sign of St. John the
Evangelist where his book is to be sold or else in Paul's Churchyard at the Figure of the Helmet and there you shall find him
willing to show you any favour and courtesy he may'.[2] This is
presumably the method he used when tutoring the son of Sir
Henry Wallop, whilst the practice of using a French church for
other than religious devotions was evidently widespread enough
to rouse the ire of Roger Ascham, who bitterly criticized the
practice in his *Scholemaster*. De la Mothe does not indicate what

---

[1] *French Garden*, Sig. B 7 *verso*.
[2] Op. cit. (1595 edition), Sigs. A 5 *verso*. ff. Cf. J. F. Royster, 'The First
Edition of de la Mothe's *French Alphabet* and of Hollybrand's [*sic*] *French Scholemaster*', *P.Q.*, VII (1928), pp. 1–5.

kind of Frenchman his pupils should become acquainted with, but the variety of dialects spoken by the many refugee teachers created a problem of which Holyband was well aware, and to this end he included in his texts the main distinctions to be made between them and the pure French which he aimed to teach his pupils, who when joined by pupils of other tutors (he claims) 'spy the faults as soon as I . . . and which is more they will discern whether the master which taught them first was a Burgonian, a Norman or a Houyet'.[1] As for the dictionary, his pupils would have Lucas Harrison's *Dictionarie of French and English* (1571) or Holyband's *Dictionarie* (1593), at their disposal though these were later replaced by Randle Cotgrave's more detailed *French-English Dictionarie with brief instructions for such as desire to learne the French Tongue* (1611).

Tuition in French, as in other modern languages, was of course quite private and outside the range of the grammar school curriculum, and even in the eighteenth and nineteenth centuries remained an 'extra', to be taken with a visiting tutor 'out of school hours' and at an extra fee. In Scotland, on the other hand, at the beginning of the seventeenth century, the larger burghs were beginning to license and pay certain Frenchmen to act as masters in the town. In 1616, for example, 'Johanne de Beuwgrand, Frenshman' was 'admittis to be scholmaister for instructing of the youth in the French language and to tak ane schole to that effect during the guid tounis will allauerlie, and ordanis the thesaurer of the same to pay him yeirlie twentie pundis money'; and four years later 'Haifing consideration how necessor it is that thair be ane Frenche scholemaister within this burgh for trayning up of the youth of this burgh in the Frenche language and that the stipend in tymes past grantit to Jeane Beaugrand scholemr. is so meane that the same is not able to intertean him, thairfair they haif grantit to him . . . jc li . . . and this induring the guid tounes will and his service.[2]

French was undoubtedly the most popular of the modern languages taught in England, though it was rivalled by Italian, the study of which was new with the Renaissance, so that the

[1] *French Littleton*, Sig. iii *verso*.

[2] M. Wood, ed., *Extracts from the Records of the Burgh of Edinburgh, 1604–26* (Edinburgh, 1931), pp. 143 and 210. I owe these references to Mr. W. A. McNeill of Glasgow.

first text to be produced was William Thomas's *Principal Rules of the Italian Grammer with a dictionarie for the better understanding of Boccaccio, Petrarcha and Dante* (1550). The subtitle indicates clearly for whom and for what purpose the book was intended, and for this reason too, perhaps, Thomas modelled his exposition not on the traditional French *manière*, but on the Latin grammars of the Whitinton-Lily era, starting with the letters, then going on to the parts of speech. The attached dictionary was also something more than the usual collection of everyday words, containing as it did over 8,000 words. Thomas had spent a good deal of his life in Italy, had published his *Historie of Italie* in 1549 and produced his *Rules* for John Tamworth, who being in Italy asked Thomas to 'draw him out in English some of the principal rules,' later passing these to Sir Walter Mildmay who 'caused them to be put in print'.[1]

Henry Grantham's *Italian Grammar* (1575), a translation from the Latin of Scipio Lentulo and produced for Grantham's pupils, Mary and Francis Berkeley, was similarly arranged, but once again it was Holyband, and more particularly his great rival John Florio who dominated the popular pattern of Italian teaching. Holyband, who in his early days advertised himself as 'professor in the Latin, French and English tongues', produced his *Italian Schoolemaster* in 1597, his last work. Earlier he had published his *Campo di Fior or else the Floure Fielde of Foure Languages* (1583), with Italian and Latin on one page and French and English on the other, a phrase book of the 'God save you sir! Put off thy hat child! what drink ye?' type, and owing a good deal to Vives's *Exercitatio Latinae Linguae*. He annexed to the *Italian Schoolemaster* 'the petie and wittie historie of Arnault and Luecenda' which he had originally put out in 1575, a reprint of Maraffi's Italian translation of the medieval romance with Holyband's own English version alongside. With this he included a brief Italian grammar and the inevitable group of 'dialogues'. The 1597 version, expanded and revised, was in fact an exemplar of the pattern of the foreign language manual, which included grammar, pronunciation and readings under the same cover, and which John Florio perfected in his texts.

[1] Cf. E. R. Adair, 'William Thomas, a Forgotten Clerk in the Privy Council', in R. W. Seton-Watson, ed., *Tudor Studies Presented to A. F. Pollard* (1924), pp. 133–60.

Florio's father, Michaelangelo, had arrived in England as a religious refugee in the reign of Edward VI, become preacher at the Church of St. Thomas of Acon which the Italian colony in London had founded in 1550, and acted as Italian tutor to Henry Herbert, Earl of Pembroke and Lady Jane Grey, for both of whom he produced manuscript rules for the learning of Italian. John was born in London about 1553, though he was educated on the Continent, returning to England about 1572. Thereafter he spent most of his life teaching Italian to the court and the nobility and producing his own language texts. His pupils included Queen Anne and her children, Prince Henry and Princess Elizabeth, as well as Sir Edward Dyer, Fulke Greville and Stephen Gosson the poet.[1] Florio published his *First Fruites which yieldeth familiar speech, merie proverbes, wittie sentences, and golden sayings, also a perfect introduction to the Italian and English tongues* in 1578, and its sequel *Second Fruites to be garnered of twelve trees of divers but delightsome tastes to the tongues of Italians and Englishmen* in 1591, annexing to the latter his *Garden of Recreation yielding six thousand Italian proverbs.*[2] Both works stressed as their prime aim the ready speaking of Italian, or at the very least the ability to make appropriate quotations in Italian during conversation. Rising in the morning, games and play, compliments and pleasant manners are the sorts of topics included. But they go farther than what might be called the Holyband method in that the language used is infinitely more refined and courtly. In addition they included 'discourses' on the rather more elevated topics of 'Peace and War', 'Envy and Pride', 'Of Beauty, Nobility and Poverty', 'Of Wrath with certain fair sayings of Ariosto and other poets', 'Upon Fortune' and 'Learning and Philosophy'. In addition, of course, Florio was careful to include the 'necessary rules of Englishmen to learn to read, speak and write true Italian', which were comprehensive and well-arranged and paid rather more attention to accidence and syntax than Holyband had done. Altogether Florio's texts were more polished and urbane and the speakers

---

[1] Cf. F. A. Yates, *John Florio, the life of an Italian in Shakespeare's England* (Cambridge, 1934), *passim*.

[2] Cf. R. C. Simonini, *Italian Scholarship in Renaissance England* (Chapel Hill, 1952) and the same author's edition of the *Garden of Recreation* (Gainesville, Florida, 1953).

in his dialogues were usually gentlemen, who concerned themselves with news of the court and courtiers. The acquisition of modern languages was now primarily a matter of social accomplishment.

Further material for such a market was provided by Geoffrey Fenton's *Golden Epistles* (1575) which included French and Italian letters, and Charles Merbury's *Briefe Discourse of Royal Monarchie . . . whereunto is added a collection of Italian proverbs in benefit of such as are studious of that language* (1581). Indeed Florio's *Worlde of Wordes* (1598), an Italian dictionary of 46,000 words which he enlarged in 1611 as *Queen Anne's New World of Wordes* (74,000 words), was as much an encyclopaedia of general knowledge as a dictionary, and provided those who referred to it with a rich storehouse of information, phrase and fable with which to impress their friends and vistors. When he died Florio left behind him the manuscripts of 'a new and perfect dictionary', 'ten dialogues in Italian and English' and an 'unbound volume of divers written collections and rhapsodies', and it seems likely that his self-styled successor Giovanni Torriano used the first in his *Vocabolaria Italiano-Inglese* (1659) and annexed the second to his *Italian Tutor or a most compleat Italian Grammar*. In 1640, too, Torriano published his short *New and Easie Directions for attaining the Tuscan Italian Tongue*, whilst in 1659 he revised and enlarged Florio's *New World of Words*.

It is rather surprising that texts for the learning of Spanish did not appear until quite late in Elizabeth's reign, for despite a generation of political and religious enmity, trade and diplomacy between the two countries had hardly been interrupted. The first text to appear was John Thorius's *Spanish Grammar* (1590), by which, Thorius claimed with an optimism characteristic of all manual writers, 'they that have some knowledge in the French tongue may the easier attain to the Spanish and likewise they that have the Spanish with more facility learn the French, and they that are acquainted with neither of them learn either or both'. It was based on Antonio Corro's *Reglas Grammaticales para apprender la lengua Espannola y Francesca*, published in Oxford in 1586 without acknowledgement to the author, and followed the typical layout of academic grammars, with few examples, no dialogues, and little emphasis on pronunciation. It was in any case largely superseded by the more popular *Spanish Schoolemaister, containing seven dialogues accord-ing to every day of the week and what is necessary everyday to be done, wherein is also most plainly showed the true and perfect pro-nunciation of the Spanish tongue towards the furtherance of all those which are desirous to learne the same tongue* (1591). William Stepney, its author, who mentions a grammar and a dictionary as already available, was probably referring to Thorius's texts and to Richard Percyvall's *Bibliotheca Hispanica, containing a grammar with a dictionarie in Spanish, English and Latin* which contained over 100,000 words. Percyvall's dictionary and gram-mar were both augmented and published separately in 1599 by John Minsheu, who added a set of 'pleasant and delightful dia-logues' on the usual themes, together with 'speeches, phrases and proverbs out of divers authors'. But Minsheu's chief interest was in lexicography and in 1617 he published his *Guide Unto Tongues*, a lexicon of eleven languages. John Sanford, Chaplain to Magdalen College, Oxford, who published his *Entrance to the Spanish Tongue* in 1611, not surprisingly pre-sented it in a formal academic manner and the book was obvi-ously directed to those of his students who were anxious to start studying the language. In addition there were available Lewis Owen's *Key to the Spanish Tongue* (1605) and an English version by I.W. of Cesar Oudin's *Grammar Spanish-English* (1622) which included a group of dialogues of the Florio type.

The upper classes of Tudor England were obviously well-served both in tutors and in texts for the learning of foreign languages. In many ways that part of the grammar school train-ing which made use of the Erasmus type of colloquy would serve the student of modern languages in good stead, for un-doubtedly the *Colloquia* greatly influenced the method of instruc-tion adopted by the language tutors. To a greater or lesser degree, depending on the writer, the formal side of grammar found its way into their texts but it is clear from the majority that a facility in conversing rather than an academic knowledge of the language and its structure was the chief aim. John Sanford, who produced formal grammars for French (1605) Italian (1605) and Spanish (1611), and Gabriel du Gres, whose *Breve et Accuratum Grammaticae Gallicae Compendium* (1636) and *Dialogui Gallico-Anglico-Latini* (1639) appeared whilst he was teaching privately in Cambridge and Oxford, were obviously writing for undergraduates, whereas Holyband and Florio were writing for the court. A third kind of reader, the merchant, will be dealt with later.

The number of accomplished modern linguists must not, of course, be exaggerated. But undoubtedly there were many who would have a smattering which would serve for most occasions, just as an acquaintance with the classics had become an expected and accepted part of a gentleman's equipment. And as the majority would rely on the Holyband-Florio type of texts for their modern languages, so too for the most part the upper classes relied on the spate of translations of classical texts which came pouring from the presses during the sixteenth and seventeenth centuries.[1] Their very profusion is an indication of a persistent demand and it is plain that the 'gentleman's library' was becoming a cultural institution in the second half of the sixteenth century. Once again the prime purpose of such books was practical and useful, part of a self-educative process. Even the poets of the period set themselves aims which were primarily didactic and only secondarily to delight. William Barker's preface to his translation of Xenophon's *Cryopaedia* (?1560) admirably sums up the motivation underlying what was undoubtedly the extensive reading of the upper classes: 'those authors (should) chiefly be read which have not only by fineness of wit and diligence of study attained to an excellency but also have had the experience of manners, of men, and diversity of places, and have with wisdom and eloquence joined the two together', a far cry from Pace's horn-blowing gentleman who scorned letters as being appropriate only to the 'sons of rustics', and a triumphant vindication of the humanist thesis that 'practical wisdom is born from its parents judgment and experience. . . . Experience is either personal knowledge gained by our own action, or the knowledge acquired by what we have seen read and heard of in others.'[2]

So great was the output that between 1475 and 1640, it has been estimated, one out of every eight books printed was a translation, and by 1600 'with the exception of Greek lyric poetry and drama the whole of the classical heritage was within

---

[1] Cf. H. R. Palmer, *English Editions and Translations of Greek and Latin Classics Printed Before 1640* (1911) and H. B. Lathrop, *Translations from the Classics into English from Caxton to Chapman 1477–1620* (Madison, 1933).

[2] F. Watson, ed., *Vives's De Tradendis*, p. 228.

the grasp of a travelled man though he possessed little Latin and less Greek'.[1] As Bolgar has pointed out, the question of Shakespeare's classical education is unimportant for he had an ample supply of translations at his disposal. Even the glosses by E.K. on the classical allusions in Spenser's *Shepheard's Calendar* (1579), it has been shown, had their origin not in his knowledge of the classical texts themselves nor indeed in the translations, but in the great dictionaries of the day, of Cooper, Calepine, and Stephanus, which were themselves gold mines of classical knowledge.[2]

The output of the translators reflects two aspects of education in Renaissance England. Their work was an expression, first of all, of the claim for the common man to understand the content and ideas of literature providing the language barrier was removed and the text presented in the vernacular; and, secondly, of its corollary that learned men should play their part in the task of popularization and dissemination of knowledge. The Renaissance period was optimistic in the sense that it not only recognized this claim but firmly believed that education, widely spread, would produce a better society. The more limited task was one of educating a benevolent governing class, whose education would be put at the disposal of the Commonwealth. John Knox was ahead of his time, however, when he included the poor in his famous insistence in 1561 that 'if they be found apt to letters and learning they may not neither the sons of the rich nor of the poor be permitted to reject learning. They must be charged to continue their study so that the commonwealth may have some comfort of them.'[3] The sons of the poor did become governors, of course, but only after they had moved up the social scale. The vast majority of governors were already there. But what the translators made quite clear in their prefaces and dedications was the practical aim of their labours, which was 'the relief of man's estate' and only secondarily the personal pleasure of the reader.

A second aspect of the translator's work had to do with the

---

[1] Bolgar, op. cit., p. 328; E. L. Klotz, 'A Subject Analysis of English Imprints for every tenth year from 1480 to 1640', *H.L.Q.*, I (1938), p. 4.

[2] D. T. Starnes, 'E. K.'s Classical Allusions Reconsidered', *S.P.*, XXXIX (1942), pp. 143–59.

[3] Knox, *First Book of Discipline*, in D. Laing, ed., *Works* (six vols., Edinburgh, 1846–64), II, 211.

development of English, as a language appropriate for serious writing and therefore as a medium of instruction. This was a part, in fact, of the *questione della lingua*, which as we have seen was being debated in Italy in the fifteenth century. England had no great defence of the vernacular to match Bembo's *Prose della Volgar Lingua* (1525) or du Bellay's *Deffence et Illustration de la Langue Françoyse* (1549), but the argument went on just the same, and the development of the art of translation in the century and a half from Caxton to Chapman and Holland was the product of such arguments. Gradually the vernacular, which had long been acceptable for the imaginative prose romance, became recognized as worthy not only for translations but also for original works. Even the religious controversies of the period were carried on in the vernacular as well as in Latin, and Calvin's own translation into French of his *Institutiones* (1541) was a shrewd recognition of the link between oral instruction and vernacular reading. The initial opposition to English as a written language and the later arguments about borrowing words and concocting 'inkhorn' terms, in which academics like Cheke and Wilson and Ascham took part, served to stimulate thought about structure and orthography, without which the language of Elizabethan and Jacobean literature could hardly have developed as it did. Nor could the word-for-word translations of Caxton's day have developed into the autonomous prose, 'the translation that is creation',[1] of North's Plutarch or Chapman's Homer. Caxton would hardly have dared to claim, indeed was not equipped to claim, that 'the office of the translator consisteth not only in the faithful expressing of his author's meaning, but also in a certain resembling and shadowing out of the form of his style and the manner of his speaking'.[2]

For their instruction and edification, then, those who 'hath not the ancient tongues' had at their disposal a vast range of literature, covering morals and religion, government, politics and law, manners and courtesy, poetry, history and biography, most of which had its origins in classical literature, though some of it came via French and Italian texts and some few from original works in English. Of all the classical authors which Renaissance England found most congenial Plutarch perhaps stands

---

[1] H. A. Mason, *Humanism and Poetry in the Early Tudor Period* (1959), p. 265.
[2] North, op. cit. To the Reader.

out, eclipsing even Cicero.[1] Most Englishmen with any educa-
tion at all gained their first acquaintance with his works through
the *Adagia* and *Apophthegmata* of Erasmus and the various
English translations of those two works, but the essay *De
Tranquillitate Animi* from the *Moralia* was translated by Wyatt
(*c.* 1528) and later by Blundeville (1561) and Clapham (1589).
In the same way the *De Educatione Puerorum* was translated by
Elyot in 1530, by Blundeville in 1561 and by Grant in 1571.
Then in 1579 Sir Thomas North published his translation of the
*Lives* from the French of Jacques Amyot, and Philemon Holland
translated the *Morals* in their entirety in 1603.

Holland has been called the 'translator-general in his age',
but in his own way Arthur Golding anticipated the wide-ranging
nature of Holland's contribution half a century earlier. In 1564,
for example, he translated Justinus's *Historia* and in the following year published his version of Caesar's *Commentaries* and
Ovid's *Metamorphoses*. In 1578 he produced his *Worke of the
Excellent Philosopher Lucius Annaeus Senecae concerning Benefyt-
ing that is to say the dooing, receyving and requyting of good turnes*
which 'showeth what a benefit is, why, how, and when, to what
end and on whom it is to be bestowed; what reward is to be
looked for in the doing of it and what fruit it yieldeth again.
Likewise how and when we should requite it or remain still
debtors for it, and by what means a man may be either beneficial
or thankful even without cost or pain.'[2] Not surprisingly in an
age when 'benefits', 'gifts', patronage or bribery (attitudes to
such practices have changed and with such changes the words we
use to describe them) played an important part in easing the
machinery of government and administration, Golding thought
it 'expedient' for his book 'to come in a courtier's hands'.

Golding's translation of Caesar, which was given a second
edition in 1590, was one of many books of the period which
aimed at providing instruction in the art or science of war. Peter
Whitehorne's *Arte of Warre* (1560, 1573, 1581), for example, a
translation of Machiavelli's *L'Arte della Guerra*, and Thomas
Styward's *Pathewaie to Martiall Discipline* (1581, 1852, 1585)
as well as Ascham's *Toxophilus* (1545, 1571, 1589) were all very
popular in the period, as their repeated editions show. Even

[1] Cf. M. H. Shackford, *Plutarch in Renaissance England* (1929).
[2] Op. cit., Epistle Dedicatorie.

more explicitly a military text was Sir Clement Edmunde's *Observations upon the Five First Bookes of Caesar's Commentaries setting forth the Practice of the Art Military at the time of the Roman Empire.* This was no mere piece of antiquarianism, but a series of 'observations' on selected portions of the *Commentaries.* The 1604 edition included in addition 'the manner of our modern training or tactic practice', with a wealth of information on the organizing and drilling of foot soldiers, and once again we get the characteristic reminder that 'Reading and discourse are make a soldier perfect in the art military how great soever his knowledge may be which long experience and much practice in arms hath gained.'[1]

None of Golding's works, however, can be compared with the massive work of George Chapman who started publishing his translation of the *Iliad* in 1598 and of the *Odyssey* in 1613, or the enormous output of Philemon Holland whose translations of Livy's *History* (1600) and Pliny's *Natural History* (1601) were followed by Plutarch's *Morals* (1603), Suetonius's *History of Twelve Caesars* (1606) and Xenophon's *Cryopaedia* (1621), to say nothing of the various versions he produced of Boethuis, Caesar, Justin and Aristotle. It was through translations such as these that the classical heritage, which the Italian humanists had resuscitated, was gradually assimilated into the general culture of the educated classes of Renaissance England. Without them the widespread acquaintance with classical literature could hardly have been possible.

The busy and the impatient could even by-pass the translations and rely on the sixteenth-century equivalents of the medieval *florilegia* of which Caxton's *Dictes and Sayings of the Philosophers*, printed twice in 1477, again in 1480 and 1489, and later by Wynkyn de Worde in 1528, was an early progenitor. It was followed in 1539 by Richard Taverner's *Garden of Wysedome* and Sir Thomas Elyot's *Banket of Sapience.* Each was several times reprinted and augmented and obviously satisfied a growing demand, but perhaps the most popular of such texts in the second half of the century was William Baldwin's *Treatise of Morall Philosophie Contayning the Sayings of the Wise.* First published in 1547 it was reprinted in 1550, enlarged (without permission) by Palfreyman in 1555 and 1557 and reissued by

[1] Op. cit., p. 1.

Tottel, 'twice augmented by T. Palfreyman and now once again enlarged by the first author', in 1564. Altogether twenty-three different editions were printed between 1547 and 1651.[1] Here was an obvious stand-by for the public speaker and conversationalist, but in addition it, too, made its contribution to the spread and acceptance of humanist ideas about those subjects most dear to the men and women of the sixteenth and seventeenth centuries, religion and politics, morals and manners, in other words 'the good life'. The authors represented in the *Treatise* included Aristippus, Aristotle, Chilon, Hermes, Isocrates, Pythagoras, Plato, Plutarch and Socrates, and from their works and the works of a host of lesser writers Baldwin collected material for the four headings of his book: Lives and Witty Answers of the Philosophers, Precepts and Counsels, Proverbes and Adages, Parables and Semblables (i.e. Similes).

Books such as Abraham Kendall's *Floures of Epigrammes* (1577) and Haly Heron's *Kayes of Counsaile* (1579), Crewe's *Nosegay of Morall Philosophie* (1580) and Gascoigne's *A Hundred Sundry Flowers gathered partely (by translation) in the fyne outlandish gardins of Euripides, Ovid, Petracke, Ariosto and others, and partly by invention, out of our more fruitfull orchardes in England* (1575), John Bodenham's *Wit's Commonwealth* (1597) and Francis Mere's *Palladis Tamia: Wits Treasurie* (1598), continued to serve a similar demand. Gradually, however, the anthologists were casting their net wider, beyond the classics, to include 'the moderns' both in prose and in poetry. In addition what had originally been, in effect, printed commonplace books gradually transformed themselves either into books of essays, acting as pace-makers for Bacon's *Essays* (1597), or into anthologies of contemporary poetry. R. Allott's *England's Parnassus* (1600) and Anthony Munday's *Belvedere or the Garden of the Muses* (1600), for example, were both simply dictionaries of quotations, 'the choycest floures of our modern poets'. Nicholas Ling's *England's Helicon* (1600), however, was a true anthology of complete poems on the same lines as *Tottel's Miscellany* (1557), consisting mostly of Sidney's poems

[1] Cf. E. L. Feasey, 'William Baldwin', *M.L.R.*, XX (1925), pp. 407–18; D. T. Starnes, 'Sir Thomas Elyot and the "Sayings of the Philosophers" ', *Texas University Studies in English*, XIII (1933), pp. 5–35; and C. F. Buhler, 'A Survival from the Middle Ages: William Baldwin's Use of the "Dictes and Sayings" ', *Speculum*, XXIII (1948), pp. 76–80.

but including also those of Drayton, Lodge, Spenser, and Shakespeare.[1] William Vaughan's *Golden Grove* (1600), on the other hand, 'a worke very necessary for such as would know how to govern themselves their houses and their country', continued in the Baldwin tradition. Comprehending them all were encyclopaedic texts like Peter de la Primaudaye's *French Academie* first published in 1577 and many times reprinted, a mammoth compilation of Renaissance knowledge and piety, with chapters including 'Of Science, of Study of Letters and of Histories', 'Of Nature and Education', 'Of Riches', 'Of Idleness, Sloth and Gaming', 'Of Education and Instruction of Children', 'Of the Education of a Prince', 'Of a Council and Councillors of State'. In the same way, Italian poetry and literature was introduced into England largely through collections such as William Painter's *Palace of Pleasure* (1566), Geoffrey Fenton's *Certain Tragical Discourses* (1567), William Pettie's *Palace of Pleasure* (1576) and many others, which did much to satisfy the 'Italianate' streak in Elizabethan society, despite Ascham's complaint that 'more Papists be made by your merry books of Italy than your earnest books from Louvain'.[2]

The inclusion of poetry in such miscellanies in no way impaired their didactic nature. Arthur Golding, for example, in the metrical Preface to his translation of Ovid in 1565, was careful to point out

Their purpose was to profit men and also to delight

. . .

And therefore who so doth attempt the Poet's work to read
Must bring with him a staid head and judgment to proceed
For as there be most wholesome hests and precepts to be found
So are there rocks and shallow shelves to run the ship aground.[3]

Until the seventeenth century poetry was still regarded as a branch of rhetoric, and the poet's 'delighting' of his readers was at best the sugar coating to the didactic pill. Philip Sidney's *Apologie for Poetry* (1583), Thomas Lodge's *Defence of Poetry* (1579), George Puttenham's *Arte of English Poesie* (1569), all make the same point:—

[1] Other examples are listed in C. Crawford, ed., *Allott's England's Parnassus* (Oxford, 1918), pp. xviiff.

[2] *Scholemaster*, p. 80.

[3] *The Fyrst Fower Bookes of P. Ovidius Nasos Worke intituled Metamorphosis* (1565), Sig. B iii *verso*.

Our chief purpose herein (i.e. in writing poetry) is for the learning of ladies and young gentlemen, or idle courtiers, desirous to become skilful in their own mother tongue, and for their private recreation to make now and then duties of pleasure, thinking for our own part none other science so fit for them as that which teacheth *beau semblant* the chief profession as well of courting as of poesie.

The poet, like the translator and the manual writer, aimed to edify his reader and for this reason deplored with William Webbe 'the uncountable rabble of rhyming Ballet-makers and compilers of senseless sonnets who be most busy to stuff every stall full of gross devices and unlearned pamphlets'.[1]

Of all the branches of knowledge prized by the man of affairs, history perhaps had the largest claim, because it seemed to him to be most immediately useful. A sense of history was, of course, one of the characteristic features of humanism, not only in the way Renaissance man showed his sense of the past, his awareness of his place in time, his conscious seeking after origins in the classical world and imitation of all that was best there, but also in his conscious awareness of posterity. 'Desirous to enhance lady Fame and suppress that deadly beast Oblivion',[2] he so ordered his life that it would be found worthy of remembrance, even facilitating the recollection by, for example, collecting, rewriting and arranging his letters for the benefit of posterity and his own reputation. But in addition to this, Renaissance historians as well as those who read the histories stressed the notion that the study of history was morally and politically profitable.

By the fifteenth century the medieval chronicle with its annalistic method no longer appealed to the rhetoricians versed in Cicero and Quintilian, who regarded stories of the past as part of the man of affairs' stock-in-trade. Cicero's *De Oratore* provided the humanist historian with the justification for such a view, 'as History, which bears witness to the passing of the ages, sheds light upon reality, gives life to recollection and guidance

---

[1] Puttenham, op. cit., in G. C. Smith, *Elizabethan Critical Essays*, two vols. (Oxford, 1904), II, 164–6; Webbe, *Discourse of English Poetrie* (1586), in ibid. I, 246.

[2] Edward Hall, *The Union of the Two Noble and Illustrate Families of Lancastre Yorke* (1548), Dedication to Prince Edward.

to human existence'.[1] Bruni repeated this in his *Florentine History* as well as in his *De Studiis et Litteris*, 'for the careful study of the past enlarges our foresight in contemporary affairs and affords to citizens and to monarchs lessons of incitement or warning in the ordering of public policy. From history also we draw our store of examples of moral precepts'.[2] We find it for the first time in English in Caxton's *Proheme* to his 1482 edition of Higden's *Polychronicon*. The student of history, he reminds his readers,

> may by reading of histories containing diverse customs, conditions, laws and acts of sundry nations come unto the knowledge and understanding of the same wisdom and policy . . . sitting in his chamber or study (he) may read, know and understand the public and noble acts of all the world as of one city . . . and by the same to know what is requisite and profitable for his life and eschew such errors and inconveniences by whom other men have been hurt . . . therefore the counsels of ancient and whitehaired men in whom old age hath engendered wisdom (hath) been greatly praised of younger men, and yet histories so much more excell them as the diurnity or length of time includeth more examples of things and laudable acts than the age of one man may suffice to see.[3]

The reading and understanding of histories are, furthermore, 'most profitable to young men' making them 'semblable and equal to men of greater age . . . but also histories are able and make right private men worthy to have the governance of Empires and noble realms . . . (history) sheweth honesty and maketh vices detestable . . . advanceth noble men and despiseth wicked men and fools.'[4]

Those who produced the educational treatises of Renaissance England repeated what the Italian humanists had had to say about history and its part in the education of a gentleman destined for the public service. Elyot, for example, stressed that wisdom was based on experience and that history could provide that vicarious experience of public and private affairs, in both

---

[1] Op. cit., II, ix, 36.
[2] In Woodward, *Vittorino*, p. 128.
[3] W. J. B. Crotch, ed., *The Prologues and Epilogues of William Caxton* (E.E.T.S., Orig. Series, CLXXVI, 1928), pp. 64–66.
[4] *Governour*, II, 384.

positive and negative ways, teaching the reader to follow the example of virtue and to eschew evil policies. The anonymous writer of *The Institucion of a Gentleman* (1553), discussing the dangers of idleness, recommends the characteristic physical 'exercises' of the period, but goes on 'yet the mind of man may be occupied much to the increase of his knowledge and understanding, wherein there can be nothing more meet for gentlemen than the reading of histories . . . most profitable and very necessary to be read of all those which bear office and authority in the commonwealth'. By reading history, 'they may learn the right institution of their lives . . . (and) moreover it maketh private men worthy to become rulers over others, provoketh captains in wars to seek immortal glory through their worthy deeds . . . it feareth evil-disposed men and maketh them oftentime refrain from doing of mischief by reason of the shame that cometh thereof, registered in histories of their dishonour'.[1] In a letter (1596) to the Earl of Rutland, the Earl of Essex enjoined him: 'above all the books be conversant in histories for they will best instruct you in matters moral, politic and military by which and in which you must settle your judgment'.[2] Walsingham, too, advised his nephew to read as much history as he could:—

> for that knowledge of histories is very profitable study for a gentleman, read you the lives of Plutarch and join thereto all his philosophy . . . read also Titus Livius and all the Roman histories . . . as also all books of state both old and new as Plato *De Republica*, Aristotle *Politica*, Xenophon and the orations, and as in these, the reading of histories, as you have principally to mark how matters have passed in government in those days, so have you to apply them to these our times and states, and see how they may be made serviceable to our age or why to be rejected, the reason whereof well-considered shall cause you in process of time to frame better courses both of action and counsel as well in your private life, as in public government.[3]

In his preface to *The Historie of Leonard Aretine* (*i.e. Bruni*) *concerning the Warres between the Imperialles and the Gothes for the possession of Italy* (1563), Arthur Golding claimed that it was

---

[1] Op. cit. (1568 edition), Sig. G ii *verso*.

[2] Davison, op. cit., Sig. E 6 *verso*.

[3] Cited by Conyers Read, *Mr. Secretary Walsingham and the Policy of Queen Elizabeth* (Oxford, 1925), I, 18.

a token that a man loveth his country not to be ignorant in the original and proceedings thereof or whatsoever else hath fortuned unto it in times past. Furthermore the knowledge of histories doth greatly delight the mind because all we men do of nature covet to know things and also it bringeth great profit for as much as it containeth the examples of like affairs, and what end they come, and giveth experience in many things, through the which old men are accounted wiser than young because they have seen more things in their lives time, and by experience not only of their own but also of other men's perils, are made more ware and are therefore able to give better judgement and are wont to be led by better counsel. For when they read of the rulers and Empires of the greatest kings and puissantest nations and experience how soon they come to decay they understand by and by what a folly it is to boast and be proved for those things, which no man is able to assure himself that they will continue with him until night. Thus doth a history make us both more wise and more modest in our doings.[1]

Undoubtedly the most widely read history book was Plutarch's *Lives* and particularly so after North's translation (1579). In it the reader would be told:—

> history is a very treasury of man's life . . . the surest, safest and durable monument that man can leave of their doings in this world to consecrate their names to immortality . . . a certain rule and instruction which by examples past teacheth us to judge the things present and to foresee things to come, so as we may know what to like of and what to follow, what to dislike and what to eschew . . . an historie is the schoolmistress of Princes, at whose hand they may without pain in way of pastime and with singular pleasure learn the most part of things that belong to their office.

For all of these reasons (North claimed)

> there is no profane study better than Plutarch. All other learning is private, fitter for the universities that the cities, fuller of contemplation than experience, more commendable in the students themselves than profitable to others. Whereas stories are fit for every place, reach to all persons, serve for all times, teach the living revive the dead, so for excelling all other books as it is better to see learning in noblemen's lives than to read it in philosopher's writings. . . . If Englishmen will read these what service is

---

[1] Op. cit. Preface to the Reader.

there in war, what honour in peace which they will be ready to do for their worthy Queen.[1]

The study of history, then, not only taught by example in a way that applied to both the public and private life of the reader, the political and the moral, but was meant also to encourage patriotism.[2] Rulers were notable patrons of the historians, though what they patronized was apologetics rather than objective history. The Tudors, for example, never denied the direct ancestry from King Arthur which sixteenth-century historians claimed for them, and Polydore Vergil came under severe attack from the chroniclers of the period for his scathing disbelief in Arthur as an historical personage. Here is raised the dilemma which faced Renaissance historians, who generally recognized the need to avoid 'bad history' yet at the same time were reluctant to deny the providential nature of history and insisted on the didactic nature of the historian's task. If the humanist historian was careful to establish the facts he nevertheless reserved the right to select those facts which would persuade the reader of the virtues of certain princes and of the rightness of their policies, and to express this in an appropriately rhetorical style which would ensure the achievement of such an aim. Bacon's *History of Henry the Seventh*, for example, was expressly written in the hope that the young Prince Charles would find it instructive and useful in practical statecraft, dealing with questions such as: How should a king deal with men who oppose him? How command the allegiance of his subjects? How persuade when he chooses not to command? It was essentially a realistic introduction to the psychology of government far removed from, say, Fortescue's idealized picture provided for Prince Henry, son of Henry VI. In the same way, when Richard Knolles translated Bodin's *Sixe Books of a Commonwealth* (1606) he put forward as the chief point in its favour the fact that Bodin was 'a man much employed in public affairs of both his Prince and country', who had produced not 'a certain imaginary form of perfect commonwealth' (as had Plato and More) but one 'with the good and the evil, the perfections and the imperfections, incident unto the

---

[1] Op. cit. Dedication to the Queen and Preface to the Reader; cf. M. H. Shackford, *Plutarch in Renaissance England* (1929).

[2] Cf. F. S. Fussner, *The Historical Revolution: English Historical Writing and Thought 1580–1640* (1962), *passim*.

same, and many other matters and questions most necessary to be known for the maintenance and preservation of them.' Certainly, if 'those which have consumed all their time in histories, do know nothing in the end but the descents, genealogies, and pedigrees of noblemen, and when such a king or Emperor reigned or such like stuff', their study of history must be regarded as a waste of time.[1]

The study of history, then, was considered a basic part of a gentleman's education. It did not, however, become a formal part of the university curriculum until the early seventeenth century, when the Camden Chair was set up in 1621 'to maintain within the university one Reader who shall be called the Reader of Histories . . . (and who) should read a civil history and therein make such observations as might be most useful and profitable to the younger students of the university to direct and instruct them in knowledge and use of history, antiquity and times past'. Its first incumbent was Degory Wheare, fellow of Exeter, who read lectures on Lucius Florus in accordance with Camden's wishes, but it was not until 1688 that the Chair got its first real scholar, Henry Dodwell, and he was very soon deprived for refusing to take the oath to William and Mary. Thereafter, for the next eighty years, the Camden Chair lapsed into intellectual bankruptcy. A history lectureship was also set up at Cambridge by Fulke Greville, Lord Brooke, at the end of 1628 and since no Cambridge scholar was deemed suitable for the place of a Dutchman, Isaac Dorislaus, was appointed. His choice of Tacitus' sombre annals of despotism as the subject matter for his lectures was, however, considered to be an indirect criticism of the monarchy and he was prohibited from lecturing. The prohibition was later withdrawn but he lectured no more, and even though Brooke left an endowment for a Chair in his will (1628) no one seems to have given the lectures.[2]

But though the teaching of history as a university subject did not flourish, undoubtedly 'histories' were read by those

---

[1] Op. cit. To the Reader; T. Blundeville, *The True Order and Method of Wryting and Reading Histories* (1574), Sig. H. iv *verso*.

[2] Cf. H. S. Jones, 'The Foundation and History of the Camden Chair', *Oxoniensia*, VIII–IX (1943–4), 169–92; W. H. Allison, 'The First Endowed Professorship of History and its first incumbent', *Am.H.R.*, XXVII (1921–2), pp. 222–7; and Mullinger, III, 83–89, whose Appendix C prints the statutes for Brooke's lectureship.

undergraduates who read at all, and certainly the educated gentleman considered it an essential part of his reading, whether he had been to university or not. The printing press and the translator were his two allies. Without them the kind of man who enlivened the debates of the Elizabethan parliaments and who provided the essential patronage for the poets and dramatists of the period could hardly have existed.

# IX

<hr>

# Merchants, Navigators and Landowners

<hr>

So far we have been concerned either with the education of the professions, the clerics, the teachers, the lawyers, or with the education of men at the top of the social hierarchy, men like Sir Philip Sidney, courtier, diplomat, scholar, poet, patron and traveller, and of 'the many gentlemen excellently learned among us (who) . . . effected to row and steer their course in his wake'.[1] We have briefly mentioned, too, another type of 'man of affairs', the merchant, whose education was to be quite different. Of growing importance in Renaissance England the merchants were not only becoming very rich but also politically and socially ambitious. Their social ambitions led them to invest their profits in land, the ownership of which was essential if they were to achieve their ambition of rising in the social scale. But such investment led them also into the intricacies of estate management in an age when land values were soaring and when traditional methods of management were no longer satisfactory. Their horizons were widening, and as a consequence, too, their skills and expertise. We turn now, then, to study the ways in which they prepared themselves both for their 'craft and mysterie' and for their new rôle as landowners and estate managers.

The traditional path which led to membership of a craft or trade guild was that of the apprentice, a path which, with the growth of urban population and the rise of new trades, became

[1] Nowell Smith, ed., *Sir Fulke Greville's Life of Sir Philip Sidney* (Oxford, 1907), pp. 34–35.

increasingly subject to the oversight of the guilds and Livery Companies, in whose halls were found 'a combination of the activities of a ducal estate office with those of a charity organization society and a department for technical education'.[1] In addition, of course, by controlling apprenticeship regulations the guilds could ensure not only a supply of those skilled in their trade or craft, but also, and particularly in the late fifteenth and sixteenth centuries, a virtual monopoly against competition, whether skilled or not. Such regulations could and did control quantity as well as quality.

The system worked through a definite contract of service, in the form of an identure between master and apprentice (or, rather, those acting for him) for a stated term of years. By the time of the Renaissance this had long been the case, the number of years varying considerably. The fishmongers, for example, stipulated in 1312 that 'no apprentice should be received for a less term than seven years according to the ancient usage'. The goldsmiths, on the other hand, more usually stipulated ten years, whilst the stationers varied the term from seven to sixteen years. The Statute of Apprentices (1563), in laying down a period of seven years, merely made general an accepted custom of long-standing. By his indenture the apprentice was bound to live in his master's house, to serve him diligently, obey 'reasonable' commands, keep his master's secrets, protect him from injury, abstain from dice, cards and haunting of taverns, contract no matrimony, commit no fornication, nor absent himself without permission. In return the master undertook to provide the boy (or girl, for girls were regularly admitted as apprentices) with bed, board and lodging and to instruct him in the 'trade, craft or mystery'. During the fifteenth century, too, instruction in the three R's was being expected of the master. In the Goldsmith's Company, for instance, fines were levied for failure to have apprentices taught to read and write, and for refusing to take apprentices who could not read and write, and in 1498 an apprentice agreed to serve an extra year providing his master would keep him one year at a writing school.[2]

---

[1] G. Unwin, *Gilds and Companies of London* (3rd edition, 1938), p. 192.

[2] O. J. Dunlop, *English Apprenticeship and Child Labour* (1912), pp. 150ff; R. F. Seybolt, *Apprenticeship and Apprenticeship Education in Colonial New England* (New York, 1917), p. 15; W. S. Prideaux, *Memorials of the Goldsmiths Company* (1896–7), I, 27, 28, 36.

This form of education, domestic in every sense, for the master stood *in loco parentis* to the apprentice, was subject also to the oversight of the guild, and had wider ramifications than the merely technical instruction of the apprentice. The master's social and moral responsibilities for his charge were continually emphasized. On the other hand, the guild's oversight applied as well to the craftsmanship of the master himself, whose standard of workmanship was subject to investigation by 'searchers', the H.M.I.'s of the guild system. By the beginning of the sixteenth century, however, the power of guild supervision was increasingly being used for negative ends to maintain a restrictive monopoly, and the educative function consequently declined in significance. The guilds continued to associate themselves with traditional grammar school education through the endowment of chantry priests and grammar schools, or by acting as trustees for schools founded by their members, but this had little to do with the professional preparation of apprentices.

The decline of the apprenticeship system as an educational institution was, however, countered by the production of manuals especially designed for the instruction of the merchant. For their origins we have once again to go back to Italy where manuscript manuals teaching arithmetic, book-keeping and accounts, as well as compendia of useful information about weights and measures in various countries, the drawing up of instruments of credit and exchange, and conditions on the various trade routes, were produced. The manuals themselves had the backing of the municipal vernacular schools in Italy, where in the Florence of 1338 the chronicler Giovanni Villani found that those attending the grammar schools of the town were outnumbered two to one by those attending the city's six schools teaching writing and commercial arithmetic. Pirenne has noted such schools in Flanders in the twelfth century, though it was not until the fourteenth century that private teachers, mostly scriveners, began to teach commercial subjects to the sons of Hanseatic merchants, and even then we find a Jacob Fugger and a Lucas Rem considering it more worthwhile to go to school in Venice for their commercial education.[1]

---

[1] R. Pernoud, *Les Villes Marchandes au XIV et XV Siècles* (Paris, 1948), p. 225. Cf. H. Pirenne, 'L'Instruction des Marchands du Moyen Age', *Annales*, I (1929), pp. 13–28; A Fanfani, 'Le Préparation Intellectuelle et Professionelle a l'Activité

The arithmetic texts had as their prototype Leonardo Fibonacci's *Liber Abaci* (1202) whose fifteen chapters ranged from numeration in Greek, Roman and Arabic figures through the four basic arithmetical processes to problems of buying and selling, the division of profits among partners, and exchange operations, with four final chapters on progression and proportion, cubes and squares. A similar pattern was followed by Paolo Dagomari of Prato in his *Tractate d'Abacco* (1339) and by the more famous text of Lucas Pacioli, whose section on what might be termed business arithmetic in his *Summa de Arithmetica, Geometria Proportioni et Proportionalita* (1494) was republished separately in 1504 as *La Scuola Perfetta Dei Mercanti*, and provided the model for most of the printed texts of the sixteenth and seventeenth centuries.[1] In addition to the arithmetical processes, he included instruction in the keeping of the inventory, journal, memorial and ledger books and introduced the reader to the method of double-entry book-keeping, which by the fifteenth century had become the accepted method in Italy. Pacioli himself, it should be said, made frequent use of Piero Borgi's *La Nobel Opera De Arithmetica* (1484), which had been expressly 'prepared for merchants' and was reprinted no fewer than sixteen times by 1557.

Alongside these computational texts were the compendious manuals for merchants of which *La Practica della Mercatura* of Francesco Balducci Pegolotti is perhaps the most famous.[2] Pegolotti worked for the banking house of Bardi, at a time when Florence was in the heyday of her prosperity as an industrial and commercial centre. The firm had connexions all over Europe and Asia Minor and Pegolotti travelled widely in its service. Treating of 'things needful to be known to merchants of divers

[1] *La Scuola Perfetta . . .*, reprinted in facsimile with English translation in J. B. Geijsbeck, *Ancient Double Entry Book-keeping* (Denver, 1914). Cf. R. E. Taylor, *No Royal Road: Lucca Pacioli and his times* (Chapel Hill, 1942).

[2] A. Evans, ed., *La Pratica della Mercatura of Francesco Balducci Pegolotti* (Cambridge, Mass., 1936).

Economique en Italie du XIV au XVI Siècle', *Le Moyen Age* LVII (1951), pp. 327–46; A. Sapori, 'La Cultura del Mercante Medievale Italiano', *Rivista di Storia Economica*, II (1937), reprinted in translation in F. C. Lane and J. C. Riesmersma, *Enterprise and Secular Change: Readings in Economic History* (1953), pp. 53–65.

IX. (i) Renaissance Song Book: from Thomas Pilkington, *First Booke of Songes and Ayres* (1605).

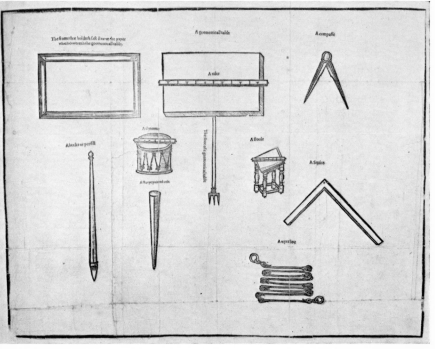

IX. (ii) Sixteenth-century Surveyor's Instruments: from Cyprian Lucar, *Lucar's Solace* (1590).

X. The Ambassadors by Hans Holbein the Younger, 1533.
(National Gallery, London.)

parts of the world and for those to know who deal in merchandise and exchange', his text obviously took many years to compile, but appears to have been completed about 1340. Other texts which have survived include *La Practica della Mercatura* (1442) of Giovanni di Antonio da Uzzano and Giorgio Chiarini's *Libro che tracta di mercatantie et usanze de paesi* (1458), a book of customs, exchanges, monetary systems, weights and measures, letters and bills of exchange, information relating to tolls, the products and commercial prospects of a particular area, together with its fiscal system, everything in fact needful for a travelling merchant. Written about the same time as Pegolotti's text and most effectively supplementing it was an anonymous Venetian *Tarifa zoe noticia dy pexi e mexure di luogi e tere che s'adovra marcadontia per il mondo* ('Tariffs and knowledge of weights and measures of the regions and countries who address themselves to commerce across the world'). With the advent of the sedentary merchant who had less first-hand knowledge of the areas with which he traded, such texts became all the more valuable to him, as they did to his factors, who not only bought on his behalf, but also had to seek out buyers, negotiate the hazards of exchange, and when all was done work out their own 'provision', their $2\frac{1}{2}$ per cent. commission. Glossaries and phrase books, topographical dictionaries and legal formularies, with moralizings about usury and the just price, monopolies and ingrossers—'very useful admonitions and good advice to the merchant', as Pacoli put it—thrown in for good measure, these manuals were obviously much more than mere ready reckoners, though in time their financial sections tended to become predominant.

The popularity of such books and the complexity of their contents, as well as the recent research which shows an increasing sophistication of commercial practice and techniques from the twelfth century onwards, effectively deny the Sombartian thesis that the medieval merchant was very largely illiterate and primitive in his commercial techniques. The buying and preparing of goods in the country of their origin, their transportation, their sale abroad, and the management of credit and payments were all activities of a continuous character requiring the presence of several persons in different places, and such transactions required an education well above the general level. The manuscript texts provided an essential framework of knowledge which passed virtually unchanged into the printed texts on which the merchants of sixteenth-century England relied. They even took over the Italian terms of business: debit (debito), credit (credito), inventory (inventorio), journal (giornal), cash (cassa). Written in the vernacular they also provide further evidence of the growing laicization of education, which now looked beyond the clerics to those who would become men of affairs in the secular world of business.[1]

Though the first of such texts to be produced in England was dated 1543, English merchants' connexions with Italy evidently acquainted them with the Italian methods of book-keeping and merchandising well before that date. In 1476, for example, James Harrison was apprenticed to Christopher Ambrose, a Florentine by birth, who traded from Southampton and took English apprentices into his household where he undertook to introduce them to the mysteries of his trade. Again in the last decade of the century Marco Strozzi, who had lived for a while in Southampton, took the son of a London draper to Pisa, 'there to be at school'. Details of the boy's schooling have survived in the Chancery Court proceedings, since the boy's mother, after her husband's death, refused to reimburse Strozzi for the money he had spent on the boy's schooling and up-keep in Pisa.[2]

The successful merchant, his factors and his apprentices owed much to the school of experience but they also needed direct instruction in book-keeping and accounting. They would want to know something about the new cosmography and its applications to navigation, and in their travels abroad and in their dealings with foreign merchants they would need also some command of foreign languages. For all these requirements they would look in vain to the grammar schools and universities. The vernacular schools of Italy and Flanders, organized by the municipality, found little favour in England where those seeking instruction in these 'arts' relied instead on the private teacher and the

---

[1] M. M. Postan, 'Economic and Political Relations in England and France 1400–75', in *Studies in English Trade in the Fifteenth Century* (1933), p. 146. Cf. R. D. Face, 'Techniques of Business in the Trade between the Fairs of Champagne and the South of Europe in the Twelfth and Thirteenth Centuries', *Ec.H.R.*, 2nd Series, X (1957–8), pp. 426–38.

[2] H. W. Gidden, ed., *Book of Remembrance of Southampton, 1270–1600* (1951), pp. 202–3.

manual of instruction. Only exceptionally does one find schools such as Jesus College, Rotherham and the grammar school at Acaster providing, in addition to the grammar and song masters, a third 'knowing and skilled in the art of writing and reckoning and able to teach to write and all such things as belong to the scrivener's craft'.[1]

During the sixteenth century, however, a widening field of commerce arising from the discovery of a greater world and from the development of techniques of industrial production, made the need for a sound technical education the more acute for an ambitious merchant. In default of any response from the traditional seats of learning, private schoolmasters, producing their own texts, once again met the need.

The first of such texts to appear in England (though not now extant) was the *Profitable Treatyce called the Instrument or Boke to Learne to knowe the good order of the keeping of the famous reconyng, called in Latyn Dare et Habere and in English Creditor and Debitor* (1543). It was written by Hugh Oldcastle, who, we are told by John Mellis, another such teacher, had his school in Mark Lane in the parish of St. Olave. Mellis, himself, who produced a revised edition of Oldcastle as *A Briefe Instruction and Maner how to Keepe Bookes of Accomptes after the Order of the Debitor and Creditor* (1588), kept a school 'at Mayes Gates, nie Battle Bridge', in the parish of the same name across the river in Southwark, and, as he indicates in the *Shorte and Plaine Treatise of Arithmeticke in Whole Numbers* which he 'adjoined' to the *Briefe Instruction*, he had been teaching these subjects 'nigh on thirty years'. He undertook the work, he explained,

> forasmuch as it behoveth every good discreet merchant to have knowledge and cunning in reading and writing, also to be prompt and ready in his accounts and reckoning, and most especially that he hath the cunning and feat of arithmetic, with pen and counter. And also more that he hath a perfect order in holding and keeping of accounts and parcels of all his reckonings in his books thereto appertaining.'[2]

The two texts, bound up together, certainly provided the learner with most of what he would want to know, whether with respect

[1] Leach, *Edvcational Charters* (1911), p. 425.
[2] *Shorte and Plaine Treatise . . .*, fol. 53 *verso*. *Briefe Instruction*, Sig. A 2, To the Reader.

to setting out his various books of account, the inventory, memorial, journal or ledger books, or with the arithmetic on which the conduct of the counting-house was based. The *Treatise* set out the various basic arithmetical processes, and went on to cover the Rules of Loss and Gain, of Company or Partnership, of Barter and Exchange, of 'alligation' and 'false positions', with a worked example to illustrate each.

The rule of alligation, for example, is illustrated thus:—

> A mercer has six several pieces of satin of diverse prices and colours of £10 10s. the piece, of £12 6s, £14 2s, £15 12s, £17 9s, and £8 6s, and a chapman is come and will have all these several pieces but not at the prices aforesaid, but so rated that he will give but one ordinary price for them all, one with another. The question is what ordinary price the mercer ought to give his chapman to please him and to save himself harmless without one penny damage.

The method and answer are concisely put: 'First add up the six several pieces and find them £78 6s. Then divide that by six, the number of pieces, which gives £13 0s 10d, the common price he ought to make of them to the contentation both of the buyer and the seller'. In the same way the rule of false position, i.e. 'supposed' position, has for its example

> Delivered to a merchant a certain sum of money for a term of five years to have the loan of it at £10 per hundred for a year. At the end of five years I received both for principal and gain £420. The question is . . . what sum of money was delivered to the merchant at first. Answer, . . . take £300 supposed to be the principal first delivered, the interest whereof for five years amounteth to £150 which joined with the £300 maketh £450, which is £30 more than was delivered. But then to find the just sum, say by the Rule of Three direct. If £450 came of £300 whereof cometh £420: multiply and divide and find £250 which is the first sum of money delivered at the first.[1]

Shortly after Oldcastle's pioneer work had been published there appeared *A Notable and Very Excellente Woorke how to keepe a boke of accomptes* (1547). This was an English translation of a text by Jan Ympyn Christoffels, originally published in Flemish in 1543 and translated into French in the same year.[2]

[1] *Shorte and Plaine Treatise . . .*, fols. 46 *verso* and 50.

[2] R. de Roover, *Yan Tympyn: essai historique et technique sue le premier traité flamand de comptabilité* (1543) (1928).

It was followed by *The Maner and Fourme how to keepe a perfect reconyning after the order of the most worthy and notable accompte of Debitour and Creditour* (1553) of James Peele, citizen and salter of London. He dedicated his work to the Company of Merchant Adventurers, and cast it in the well-tried form of a dialogue, or rather of two dialogues, one between merchant and schoolmaster and the other between master and scholar. He revised and enlarged it in 1569 as *The Pathway to Perfectness in the Accomptes of Debitor and Creditor*, and included in his new edition advice to farmers on how to keep their accounts. To all merchants he repeats the age-old maxim of account:—

. . . receive before you write, and write before you pay,
So shall no part of your accompt in any wise decay.

The same kind of precise procedure is recommended in the matter of letter-writing, when Peele suggests the keeping of a duplicate letter book, 'the readier to answer all causes that may chance in variance between you, your factors, servants or any other'.[1]

All of these texts gave instruction in the Italian method of double-entry book-keeping. John Weddington's *Brieffe Instruction and maner how to keepe marchants Bokes of Accomptes after the Order of Debitor and Creditor as well for proper accomptes, partable factor and other very nedeful to be knowen and used of all men in the feattis of marchandize* (1567), however, suggested that instead of using three books of account—the Waste Book or Memorial, the Journal, and the Great Book or Ledger, the permanent record of all business transacted—the Journal posting might be dispensed with by splitting up the book of original entry, the Memorial, into separate books or parts, each devoted to a particular category of transaction, each serving as a posting medium direct to the Ledger. Weddington's text has a further distinction in that it is the first English text to have Arabic numerals throughout in the money columns, in the entry narratives as well as in the totals. Once again a practising merchant (Weddington imported linen into Antwerp and was subsequently agent in that part for Sir Thomas Gresham) was providing a ready introduction into the merchant's 'mysterie'.[2]

[1] Op. cit., Sig. B vi *verso*.
[2] Cf. B. S. Yamey, 'John Weddington's *A Briefe Instruction . . .*, *1567*', *Accounting Research*, IX (1958), pp. 124–33.

Like Weddington, Richard Dafforne, the author of *The Merchant's Mirrour or Directions for the Perfect Ordering and Keeping of Accounts* (1645), had spent a good deal of his life as a merchant, this time in Amsterdam. In 1630 he returned to London, where he set up school 'at Abchurch Lane towards Lombard Street' as a 'practitioner and teacher of this famous and rewarding art of accountantship; as also of arithmetic with great facility, in English or Dutch (and) likewise rectifieth books of accounts abroad and at home in any method or state whatsoever.' During this period of teaching he also published *The Apprentices Time Entertainer Accomptantly or a Methodical Means to Obtain the Exquisite Art of Accomptantship* (1640) to which he 'adjoined' with a separate title-page *The Young Accomptants Compasse or Briefe Directions how the inexperienced accomptant that betakes himself into the service of the Honble. Coy. of Merchants of London Trading to the East Indies or elsewhere is to begin to prosecute and compleatly finish his office*. Weddington's manual survives in a unique copy at Blair College, Aberdeen. Oldcastle's we know only through Mellis's revised edition. The present rarity of copies of these early manuals may be simply explained by their contemporary usefulness and popularity. They were concerned, not with definitions, classes and properties of numbers, but with the practical applications of arithmetical processes, with the Rules of Two, Three and Five, with the dividing of a calculated profit or loss in proportion to the parties whose capital was involved, with simple and compound interest, and with the calculation of rates of exchange, in an age when coinage was chronically unstandardized. More often than not they provided, too, some instruction in elementary book-keeping. As such they would be used, either by the pupil at school or by the apprentice, the factor and the merchant himself in the counting-house, until they dropped to pieces.

It was no coincidence that among the paraphernalia which Holbein included on the shelves of the two-tiered bench on which his two 'Ambassadors' leaned, was a copy of Peter Apian's *Eyn Newe Undd Wolgegrundte Underwesing Aller Kauffmanns Rechnung* (1527) (a New and Well-grounded Instruction in all Merchants' Arithmetic), and it is much more likely that the small book which Holbein painted into his portrait of the merchant Georg Gisz standing in his counting-house is a similar kind of manual, rather than the volume of Latin poetry which Dr. Winchester suggests in her *Tudor Family Portrait*.[1]

Accounting operations such as we have mentioned obviously required something more then the elementary instruction provided in Clement and Coote for the grammar school 'petties', who in any case would be concerned much more with the elements of reading and writing as a preparation for their grammatical studies. Once again, however, for those who required it there were texts available. The earliest in English, *An Introduction for to Lerne to Recken with the Penne or Counters*, appeared in 1537 from the press of John Herford at St. Albans, and was based on two earlier works, one a Dutch text *Die Manière om te Leeren Cyffren* (1508) and an independent, though similarly-titled, French work *La vraye manière pour apprendre a Chiffres* (*c.* 1530–7). The author of the English text was, however, no slavish imitator. Though he included in the first part of his six-part text the rules of 'this feat of algorisme', he omits the traditional sections on the rules of duplation (doubling) and mediation (halving) on the grounds that 'whereas in other copies is set duplation, triplation, and quadruplation, all that is superfluous, for so much as it is contained under the kind of multiplication'. The practical nature of the arithmetic he dispenses is well shown in this example :—

> Four merchants lay money together for winning for a certain time of whom the first hath laid 10 francs for two years, the second 20 francs for three years, the third 100 francs for one year and the fourth hath laid 40 francs for four years, and they have gained 452 francs. I demand how much each one ought to have of winning after the money he hath laid and after the time he hath holden his money in gain for company.[2]

The book was an immediate success. It was reprinted in London by Nicholas Bowman in 1539, and at least six times before the

---

[1] Winchester, op. cit., p. 209; cf. my 'Holbein's "Ambassadors" and Sixteenth Century Education', *J.H.I.*, XXI (1960), pp. 99–109, and P. Ganz, *The Paintings of Hans Holbein* (1950), Cat. No. 74, Plates 113–16; see also Plates 85 and 98.

[2] Op. cit. Sig. D *verso* and Sig. G viii. Cf. P. Baekstalle, 'Notes on the First Arithmetics Printed in English', *Isis*, LI (1961), pp. 315–21; A. W. Richeson, 'The First Arithmetic Printed in English', ibid., XXXVII (1947), pp. 47–56; R. Steele, ed., *The Earliest Arithmetics in English* (E.E.T.S., Extra Series, CXVIII, 1922), and L. L. Jackson, *The Educational Significance of Sixteenth-Century Arithmetic* (Columbia, 1906).

end of the century. Such examples were the common feature of sixteenth-century arithmetics, practical, useful and related to the everyday experience of the counting-house, though the academic arithmetics continued to be produced. Gemma Frisius, for instance, practical cosmographer though he was, could still produce an example such as this from his *Arithmeticae Practicae Methodus Facilis* (1540, and fifty-five editions thereafter):—

> A man having a certain number of aurei bought for each aureus as many pounds of pepper as equalled half the whole number of aureis Then upon selling the pepper he recieved for each 25 pounds as many aurei as he had at the beginning. Finally he had 20 times as many aurei as he had at first. The number of aurei and the quantity of pepper are required.[1]

Of more practical use was the classic arithmetic of the sixteenth-century Robert Recorde's *The Grounde of Artes* (1543), which was later revised and enlarged by John Dee in 1561, and more significantly by teachers of accounts like John Mellis (1582, and at least nine other editions by 1610) and Robert Hartwell (1618, and at least nine other editions by 1654). By the time Hartwell's 1623 edition appeared the text was one of 613 pages, though still printed in pocket size. Both Mellis and Hartwell concentrated on showing how to get the answer to an example as quickly as possible, adding at the same time a number of reference tables, including exchange values, aliquot parts of the pound and the shilling and the calculation of interest. Rivalling Recorde's text was Humphrey Baker's *Wellspring of Sciences which teacheth the perfect work and practice of arithmetic*, originally published in 1546 and reprinted and revised at least twelve times by 1687. Dedicated to the Company of Merchant Venturers, Baker's text is marked by the copiousness of the examples illustrating each of the processes involved, and must have been the standard textbook in his school 'on the north side of the Royal Exchange next adjoining the sign of the Ship', where besides merchant's arithmetic and book-keeping he taught geometry and mensuration, cosmography and navigation. Dionis Gray's *Storehouse of Brevitie in Woorkes of Arithmetike* (1577), dedicated to the Goldsmiths' Company, provided the same kind of instruction, though Gray went so far as to provide

---

[1] Cited by Jackson, op. cit., p. 176.

rules for the elementary processes in verse. For addition he wrote:—

> To the figures in first place set
> First see ye do resort
> And of the sum which they do make
> Set digit under line
> And for each ten in article found
> One shall ye thence transport
> Unto the next and second place
> By memory right fine.[1]

In the same way Thomas Hughes's *The Art of Vulgar Arithmetic* (1600) taught the aliquot parts of money:—

> A farthing first finds forty eight
> And half penny hopes for twenty four
> Three farthings seeks out sixteen straight
> A penny puts a dozen lower.

For the grammar school pupils who wished to go farther than petty arithmetic, Brinsley recommended Recorde and the private school: 'If you do require more for any you must seek Recorde's Arithmetic or the like and set them to the cyphering school.' For his own part Recorde regretted England's backwardness in producing counting-house clerks, attributing this to the reluctance of learned men to produce texts 'for the aid of the unlearned', and Francis Bacon made the same point in his *Advancement of Learning* where he wrote, 'the wisdom touching negotiation or business hath not been hitherto collected into writing, to the great derogation of learning and the professors of learning'.[2] By Bacon's day, as we have seen, some attempt at least had been made to meet the demand of such texts and such instruction, though in nothing like the degree in which the Dutch tackled the problem. Indeed by the mid-seventeenth century English writers were attributing to this fact the success of the Dutch as a mercantile power and called for increased attention to commercial education in this country.[3]

---

[1] *Storehouse* . . ., Sig. B iii and *verso*.

[2] Brinsley, op. cit., p. 26; Bacon, *Works*, III, 447.

[3] G. P. Gooch, *English Democratic Ideas in the Seventeenth Century* (2nd edition, 1927), p. 25; Thomas Mun, *Discourse of Trade* (1621) and *England's Treasure by Forraign Trade* . . . published by his son in 1664, but written several years earlier, both printed in J. R. McCulloch, ed., *Early English Tracts in Commerce*

Such demands emphasized the wide range of a merchant's experience and serve to lead us, now, from the purely financial aspects of commerce to the other skills and information considered necessary in this field. Doubtless some few merchants with a knowledge of Italian could make use of the compendious texts of Pegolotti and company, but it was not until 1589 that an English text was available, one which aimed at providing a *vade mecum* for the aspiring merchant. The arithmetics and book-keeping texts occasionally included in their pages pieces of information and tables which would be of use, but none set out to do more than this until John Browne, merchant of Bristol, wrote his *Marchants Avizo*.[1] A handbook of seventy pages designed expressly for factors and apprentices by a merchant with long experience in the Portuguese trade, it gives information about foreign currencies and the keeping of accounts, and includes specimens of various business documents, such as model letters, insurance policies, and bills of exchange. On the topic of business letter-writing Browne's book was, in fact, recommended by Angel Day, the author of the standard letter-writing handbook of the day, *The English Secretorie* (1586).

An important part of Browne's text is the section headed 'certain godly sentences necessary for youth to meditate upon', for it gives a clear picture of mercantile morality, or at best a standard towards which sixteenth-century merchants might be expected to work. In it he laid down an elaborate code governing the conduct of those apprentices and young factors who, released from the discipline of their master's house, might be exposed to the temptations of life in a foreign country. Mixing moral maxims with practical business advice Browne exhorts his reader:—

> Take heed of using a false balance or measure . . . covet not over familiarity amongst men it maketh thee spend much loss of time.

[1] Cf. P. McGrath, ed., *The Marchants Avizo by J(ohn) B(rowne), Marchant 1589* (Cambridge, Mass., 1957).

---

(2nd edition, Cambridge, 1954), pp. 44–45 and 122–4. For similar French manuals cf. N. Z. Davis, 'Sixteenth-Century French Arithmetics on the Business Life', *J.H.I.*, XXI (1960), pp. 18–48. For Dutch texts cf. P. G. A. de Waal, *De Leer Van Het Boekhouden in de Nederlanden in de Zestiende Eeuw* (1927) and O. ten Have, *De Leer van Het Boekhouden in de Nederlanden Tidjens de Zventiende en Achtiende Eeuw* (1933), for which references I am indebted to Professor Yamey.

Be not hasty in giving credit to every man, but take heed to a man that is full of words, that hath red eyes, that goeth much to law, and that is suspected to live unchaste. . . . When thou promiseth anything be not stuck to perform it, for he that giveth quickly giveth double. . . . Fear God. . . . know thy Prince . . . love thy parents . . . give reverence to thy betters . . . be courteous and lowly to all men . . . be not wise in thine own conceit.[1]

Profit was still the aim of course, but despite the decline in the influence of the Canon Law, the old prohibitions—against seeking wealth for its own sake and beyond what was requisite for a livelihood in one's station, exploiting a customer's difficulties to extract an extravagant price, excessive interest charging, engrossing to 'corner the market'—remained a part of the mercantile scene, and evidently men like Browne, who had served his apprenticeship in his home town and had risen to be its mayor, still honoured the master's rôle *in loco parentis* in respect of his apprentices.

As for handwriting itself, an art 'very necessary' for the merchant and counting-house clerk alike, it was increasingly being taught by teachers such as Peter Bales, who kept school at 'the upper end of Old Bailie, near the Sign of the Dolphin', where doubtless he made use of his own *Writing Schoolmaster* (1590). Previously undertaken by the priest or parish clerk the teaching of writing was becoming a reluctantly-accepted part of grammar school work, as we have seen. But there was a great deal of difference between the standard achieved in the grammar school and that required for the writing up of ledgers, the penning of letters and the drafting of legal documents in the counting-house world of commerce. Indeed, as Brinsley admitted, 'you shall find very few good writers in grammar schools unless either they have been taught by scriveners or by themselves are marvellously apt hereunto'.[2] At Giggleswick Grammar School in 1592 it was arranged for the master to absent himself for three weeks in the year 'to be appointed when he thinketh it most convenient, for his scholars to be exercised in writing under a scrivener for their better exercise in that faculty'. Occasionally some masters of the small grammar schools seized on the opportunity to claim an extra fee for writing

[1] Op. cit., pp. 55ff.
[2] Brinsley, op. cit., p. 28.

lessons. Generally, however, writing came low in the hierarchy of studies, and the governors of Blackburn Grammar School were obviously apprehensive that the status of the school might be impaired if too much of this kind of instruction was allowed to take place, when they prescribed in 1592 'that no scrivener shall teach writing school terms without urgent cause oftener than one in the year for the space of a month'.[1] The writing school which Dame Ramsey provided for within Christ's Hospital was quite exceptional, and more often than not, if someone wished to improve his handwriting or achieve the skills necessary to cope with counting-house business, then recourse would be had to the growing number of writing masters who were setting up their schools towards the end of the sixteenth century, and who enjoyed their heyday in the eighteenth century. And this was true not simply of those going into commerce. Arthur Wilson, for example, related in his autobiography how, his father falling into financial difficulties and unable to send him up to university, he was found a clerkship in the Exchequer (c. 1611). 'But I could not write the court and chancery hands (he relates), so my father left me for half a year with Mr. John Davies in Fleet Street (the most famous writer of his time) to learn those hands'.[2] Davies' *Writing Schoolmaster* ( ?1631) was a typical example of the sort of handbook which came off the presses in this period. The earliest in English was Jean de Beauchesne's *Book Containing Divers Sorts of Hands* (1570). Based on a long tradition of Continental writings masters, it was published by Thomas Vautrollier, the famous scholar-printer, who later produced *A Newe Booke of Copies containing Divers Sorts of Sundry Hands* (1574). Each has a woodcut showing 'How you ought to hold your penne' and a set of 'Rules made by E.B. for children to write by'. Frances Clement's *Petie Schole* (1587), also published by Vautrollier, and Edmund Coote's *English Schoolmaster* (1596) include plates of copy, as well as instructions about choosing and cutting and holding one's quill. Even the making of ink was dealt with. But neither compared in either level or detail with Beauchesne or with Peter Bales's *Writing Schoolmaster* (1590), Richard Gething's

---

[1] Cf. H. C. Schultz, 'The Teaching of Handwriting in Tudor and Stuart Times', *H.L.Q.*, VI (1943), p. 399.
[2] F. Peck, *Desiderata Curiosa* (1732), I, Book XII, p. 7.

*Coppie Book* (1616) or Martin Billingsley's *The Pen's Excellencie* (1618). It was to these texts and teachers that those in search of proficiency with the pen would go for further tuition, and to John Browne's *Marchants Avizo* for model business letters, rather than to collections of letters such as Abraham Fleming's *Panoplie of Epistles as a looking glasse for the unlearned contayning a perfect platform of inditing letters of all sorts* (1576) or William Fulwood's *Enemie of Idleness: teaching the manner and stile how to endite, compose and write all sorts of epistles* (1568). Owing more to the Latin formularies of Erasmus and Macropaedius, Fulwood and Fleming had little that would be of professional help to the merchant, who looked rather to the continuation of the tradition of *ars dictaminis*, developed by the Bolognese notaries and fostered by the professional writing masters.[1]

The ability to speak a foreign language was, in the same way, an important part of a merchant's equipment, and professional expertise and texts to help him in this sphere were readily available. One of Caxton's first printed books was a *manière de langage*, printed in 1463. No more than a phrase book, the text had limited aims, but of its value to the young apprentice or factor travelling abroad in the early stages of his career there can be no doubt. Drawn up in parallel columns of French and English it included salutations, a widely-based vocabulary, a list of crafts and trades, instructions about the exchange value of foreign coinage, weights and measures, a list of fairs, and phrases likely to be used by those travelling and making use of inns. As Caxton put it in his introduction, 'Who this book will learn may well enterprise or take in hand merchandises from one land to another, and to know many wares which to him shall be good to be bought or sold, for rich to become. Learn this book diligently, great profit lieth therein truly'.[2]

---

[1] Cf. K. G. Hornbeak, *The Complete Letter Writer in English, 1568–1800* (Northampton, 1934); J. Robertson, *The Art of Letter Writing: an essay on the handbooks published in England during the sixteenth and seventeenth centuries* (Liverpool, 1942); A. Heal, *The English Writing Masters and their Copy Books* (Cambridge, 1931); F. Plaat, ed., *Wolfgang Fugger's Handwriting Manual entitled A Practical and Well-grounded Formulary for Divers Hands, 1553* (1960).

[2] H. Bradley ed., *Dialogues in French and English by William Caxton* (E.E.T.S., Extra Series, LXXIX, 1900), pp. 3–4. For a full discussion of *manières* cf. Lambley, op. cit., pp. 42ff.

A similar *Good Book for to Learne to Speake Frenshe* was printed by both Pynson (*c.* 1492) and Wynkyn de Worde (*c.* 1498) and included the traditional salutations, together with phrases to do with buying and selling, inquiring the way and conversation at the inn, as well as two model business letters, one from an apprentice to his master reporting on business undertaken in Paris and the consequent shortage of money, and the other from one merchant to another describing the arrival of laden ships in London and Southampton and suggesting that they should stock up their shops. Books for the use of English merchants were also being published abroad during the sixteenth century; one example was Gabriel Meurier's *French Grammar* (1557), published in Antwerp and dedicated to the English merchants of that city. A similar text, also published in Antwerp, was the *Familiare Communicators no leasse proppre then verrie proffytable to the Inglish nation desirius of redinge the ffrench language* (1563).

In addition to the *manières* and grammars there were new polyglot dictionaries for the use of merchants and travellers, such as the one printed in Venice in 1540 which covered English, Latin, French, Spanish, Italian and German and was later re-printed several times in France. With the growth in popularity of language teaching in Elizabethan England more texts which took into account the needs of the merchant came on the market. William Stepney's *Spanish Schoolemaster* (1591), for example, included sections especially for the merchant, as did Giovanni Torriano's *Italian Tutor* (1640). The latter was dedicated to the Company of Turkey Merchants, 'of all the famous companies of this city none affecting the Italian tongue so much as yours', and was written 'that the hopeful youth which is daily trained up under your care whether your sons or your servants might reap most benefit thereby'.

But all of these manuals catered for what might be called the private sector of educational provision. John Dury advocated the teaching of French, Italian and Spanish in common schools specially provided for those destined for commerce and quite separate from the classical school (as was later recommended by the Taunton Commission in the 1860s). It was not, however, until the Dissenting Academies of the late seventeenth century and the Scottish burgh academies of the mid-eighteenth century were founded that modern languages began to enjoy a regular place in the secondary school curriculum. In the meantime private language schools flourished, resting on the assured tradition of teaching established by Holyband and Florio and catering for the practical needs of the aspiring merchant as well as the more genteel requirements of the gentleman's sons and daughters.

The merchants of Renaissance England would, then, need to know something not only of the goods they were dealing in, but of the countries in which they traded and of the languages of these countries. Of equal importance to them would be some knowledge of the science or art of navigation. Many of them sailed in their own ships, but even those who did not would want, from their counting-house, to be able to calculate the estimated time of arrival of their ships, which route would be best, whether the ship was well-equipped in navigational aids, whether the shipmasters were competent in the business of navigation and so on. In a highly competitive age it became necessary for the merchant to be aware of the crucial importance of compass variation, and of the accuracy of his tables of the sun's declination. Even if not expert himself, he would need to be knowledgeable about these matters, and certainly those who sailed for him would need to be expert if the maximum profit were to be wrung from each venture.

This was an area of educational enterprise which expanded enormously in our period, when a new world of land and sea and sky was being discovered. The universities, as we have seen, had little in the way of systematic teaching to offer in this field. Once again, however, the printer and private teacher came into their own, producing maps and books about maps, cosmographical surveys and books on the newly-discovered lands, navigational manuals for seamen, and technical works on the science of navigation and the instruments necessary for precision sailing. The merchant found himself at the centre of all of this, though, of course, he himself must be set in the wider context of the rise of new scientific ideas and mathematical techniques, which were at one and the same time the producer and product of those great voyages of discovery which spanned the two hundred years of our period.[1]

The earliest of the navigational aids were the *peripli* of the

[1] Cf. M. Boas, *The Scientific Renaissance, 1450–1630* (1962), *passim*.

Ancient World and the *portolani* of the medieval Mediterranean, sets of coastal sailing directions which indicated the navigational hazards of rocks, reefs and shoals for the coasts and harbours of the Mediterranean and provided the requisite courses from headland to headland. A second kind of aid was the sea chart itself, on which the navigator could keep a record of his course and distance run when out of sight of land. This did not, of course, develop until the Portuguese voyages took mariners and merchants farther afield, but it was the association on the sea chart of the wind-roses of the *portolani* with the magnetized needle pointing north which resulted in the modern compass rose.

For the mariner of the fifteenth and sixteenth centuries several problems posed themselves, problems which for a long time seemed incapable of solution. How, for example, could he reconcile the straight line course he plotted on his plain-chart with the sphericity of the ocean on which he sailed? How could a compass be produced which remained accurate wherever his voyages took him, or instruments which were sufficiently accurate to enable him to take precise observations of the altitude of the sun and other heavenly bodies? What method could be devised for solving the age-old difficulty of longitude? The solution and practical application of each of these problems were of more than academic interest when the accuracy of the shipmaster's sailing affected the profits of the merchant for whom he sailed.

With the growth of trade the two constituents of the *portolani*, the chart and the sailing directions, gradually became more detailed and began to evolve a life of their own. Both, of course, must be distinguished from the world maps which the academic geographers and cosmographers produced. The former were essentially practical aids for practical seamen, and both the chart and the directions (the *roteiros*, *routiers* or rutters of the sixteenth century) underwent considerable changes in their degree of sophistication and accuracy. The earliest English rutter laid more emphasis on tidal information, soundings and shoal banks than on distances between ports. For most of the sixteenth century Englishmen made use of Robert Copland's *Rutter of the Sea* (1528), a translation of Pierre Garcie's *Grant Routier et Pilotage* (1502), with woodcut illustrations of the coastline's

XI. Title-page of Robert Recorde's Arithmetic Book
*Grounde of Artes* (1543).

XII. Title-page of Anthony Ashley's translation of Lucas Wagenaer's
*Mariner's Mirrour* (1590).

silhouette and produced, as Copland wrote in his Prologue, 'to the erudition and safeguard of our merchants and others haunting the sea'. Six other editions of Copland's text were produced by 1587, but in 1588 it was replaced, once and for all, by Anthony Ashley's *Mirrour of the Sea*, a translation from the Dutch of Lucas Janszoon Wagenaer. Wagenaer came from Enkhuizen, one of the most famous of the Zuider Zee ports, at the time when Amsterdam dominated Dutch trading enterprises. In 1584 and 1585 he produced an entirely new set of charts, the first batch covering the west coast of Europe from the Zuider Zee to Cadiz, the second covering the North Sea and the Baltic. Published by the great Plantin, they were the culmination of almost a century of Dutch *entrepôt* trade during which the Dutch seamen had come to know these waters like the back of their hand. So important were they that in 1588 Lord Howard of Effingham, the Lord High Admiral of England, persuaded the Privy Council to commission an English edition in which the text associated with the charts was translated by Anthony Ashley. The text itself set new standards in accuracy, and included a short treatise on cosmography and navigation, various tables for the sun's declination, for finding the time of the new moon and the age of the moon, a list of important stars, sections on how to calculate latitude, how to use the cross-staff, and how to trace a copy of a chart, together with courses and distances for the west coast of Europe, the latitudes of the ports and harbours, tide tables, soundings for banks and shoals round the shipping lanes, and so on. It was well named *The Marriners Mirrour wherein may playnly be seen the courses, heights, distances, depths, soundings, flouds, ebbs, rising of lands, rocks, sands and shealds with the marks for entrings into harbourroughs, havens and ports of the greater part of Europe. . . .*[1]

Similar works continued to appear, most of them translations from the Dutch, such as Robert Norman's *Safeguard of Saylers or Grand Rutter* (1590), which included sailing directions for the British Isles, France, Spain, Flanders and Denmark, and was revised by Edward Wright in 1605 and John Tapp in 1612.

[1] Cf. G. R. Crone, 'The Mariners Mirrour, 1588', *Geographical Journal*, CXIX (1953), pp. 455–8, and D. Gernez, 'Lucas Janszoon Wagenaer: a chapter in the history of guide books for seamen', *Mariners Mirror*, XXIII (1937), pp. 190–7 and 332–50.

But for twenty or thirty years *The Mariners Mirrour* had no rival, the very word 'Waggoner' becoming part and parcel of the professional terminology. In 1617, however, an English translation of Willem Janszoon Blau's more up-to-date *Licht der Zeevaert* (1608) was produced under the title of *The Light of Navigation* covering 'all the coasts and havens of the West, North and East Seas'. It was reprinted in 1620 and 1622 and remained the standard work throughout the seventeenth century.

All of these rutters and the charts associated with them, covering relatively small areas of the globe, assumed that the mariner was sailing on a non-spherical sea, and the charts were called, therefore, plain- or plane-charts. In other words it was assumed that the straight-line course which the master laid on his chart corresponded to his actual passage through the water. Mariners were, of course, well aware that this in fact was not the case, and either shrugged off the inaccuracy as something that was part of nature or looked forward to the day when a chart could be produced on which a straight line course would correspond to their actual course. Such a chart was produced in 1569 by Gerard Mercator whose world projection, taking into account the converging of the meridians towards the pole, was a systematic distortion in which the parallels and meridians showed as right angles. But Mercator was a geographer or cosmographer not a navigator, and it was not until the 1590s that his method and its crucial importance to the ocean navigator, as opposed to the coastal pilot, became known in any widespread sense. The application of Mercator's method was first worked out by Edward Wright, but he was slow to publish the results of his work and it was not until 1599 that his *Certain Errors in Navigation* appeared. In the meantime he had communicated his ideas to the Dutchman, Hondius, who produced a chart incorporating Mercator's and Wright's ideas in 1594. In 1597 William Barlowe's *Navigator's Supply* added to the volume of criticism directed towards the plain-chart and lauded the virtues of the Mercator-type chart, which he described as 'resembling the ordinary Sea Cards save that the degree of the meridians in it do proportionately increase from the Equator toward each pole upon good reason and firm demonstration, thereby showing the true position of any place in respect of any other which the usual cards in a far distance cannot do, being yet the very principal point that the navigator desireth'.[1] A chart based on the new method appeared in the 1599–1600 edition of Hakluyt's *Principal Navigations*, and so effective was this popularization by Hondius and Wright that by 1630 most of the charts produced at Dieppe, the greatest chart factory in Europe, were based on the Mercator projection. It was Wright who first used the balloon metaphor to explain Mercator's methods and who provided too, a table of 'meridional parts' which would enable seamen to read off for every degree of latitude the proportional change in scale which would take place at each parallel. Even without the tables a seaman could at least rest assured that he would be sailing in the right direction if he followed the course laid out on his chart. Using the table he could more accurately estimate his distance run and thereby make a more accurate estimate of his land-fall and his time of arrival in port.

The sphericity of the ocean, then, had important repercussions for the navigators as voyages both of discovery and of commerce increased in length. A further difficulty concerned the accuracy of the ship's compass. Columbus had already noted the disturbed and disturbing behaviour of his compasses as he sailed farther west, unaware that the variation of the instruments, that is the difference between true north and magnetic north, changed with different parts of his chart. In the coastal waters of Europe the 'north-easting' or 'north-westing' of the mariner's compass was apparent but known by experience to be small, and was in any case often corrected when the compass-maker was setting his needle in relation to the compass rose. Any changes thereafter would be blamed by seamen on faulty instrument-making or neglectful intrument-makers. The earliest *map* to indicate compass variation was in Peter Apian's *Cosmographiae Introductio* (1529), but it was not until towards the end of the century that it came to be regularly indicated on printed *charts*. One of the earliest known examples of its indication on a chart is on the MS. chart drawn by Martin Frobisher in 1576, on which he recorded his own observations of the phenomenon. William Borough, too, had been collecting similar information, and it was this kind of information which the instrument-maker, Robert Norman, drew on to supplement his own experience of 'eighteen to twenty years at sea', when

[1] Barlow, op. cit., Sig. K 4 *verso*.

he published his *Newe Attractive* (1581), dedicated to Borough and including the latter's own *Discourse of the Variation of the Cumpas*.[1] It was in the *Newe Attractive*, too, that Norman presented the world his observations and experiments on another phenomenon, the dipping of a compass needle away from the horizontal as a result of the earth's magnetism, which hitherto had been regarded as yet another manifestation of the unreliability of compass-makers. Norman's book, described by Thomas Blundeville as 'of an easy price meet for every poor man's purse', was a true popularizer, in which the practical seaman and instrument-maker presented the most up-to-date of material in a way that would be intelligible 'to the unlearned'.

Even so, neither Borough nor Norman was aware of the fact that the variation of a compass at a particular place changed with the years. Confirmation of the secular variation of a compass could, in any case, only be achieved by comparing systematic observations of the phenomenon over a period of years, and it was largely through men like Borough and Norman and the masters of ships who heeded their advice to record compass variation, that it was eventually possible for Henry Gellibrand, Gresham Professor of Geometry, to clear the matter up in his *Discourse Mathematicall on the Variation of the Magneticall Needle* (1635). By comparing his own recordings of variation at Deptford with those of Borough and Norman in 1580 and of his predecessor, Edmund Gunter, in 1622, he was able to show that the variation was gradually decreasing.

By the end of the sixteenth century more and more books like that of Norman were creating among navigators an informed climate of opinion which increasingly rejected the old rule of thumb methods. Mariners were, and still are, the most conservative of men, and there were many at this time who continued to deride 'the Star-Shooters'. On the other hand the repeated calling for translations, reprints and revised editions of general navigational texts such as Richard Eden's translation of Cortes's *The arte of Navigation* (1571) and Taisnier's *Very Profitable and Necessary Book Concerning Navigation* (1574), or John Hampton's translation of Medina's *Arte of Navigation* (1571), and Edward Wright's *Haven-Finding Art* (1599) from the Dutch

[1] William Borough's chart is reprodued in Hakluyt, *Principal Navigations* (Hakluyt Society, Extra Series, III, 1903), p. 224.

of Simon Stevin, as well as original works such as William Bourne's *Regiment of the Sea* (1573), John Davis's *Seamen's Secrets* (1594), John Tapp's *Seamen's Calendar* (1607), John Smith's *Sea Grammar* (1627) and *Accidence of the Sea* (1636), make it clear that English seamen were learning both from the experience of other nations and from the investigations of their own countrymen. When Sebastian Cabot was Chief Pilot of England a navigator's knowledge and expertise were his most closely guarded secret. Under successors like Richard Chancellor and Stephen Borough every effort was made to spread what knowledge was accumulating. As William Borough put it,

> Therefore I wish all seamen and travellers that desire to be cunning in their profession first to seek knowledge in arithmetic and geometry, which are the grounds of all sciences and certain arts, of the which there is written in our English tongue sufficient for an industrious and willing mind to attain to great perfection, whereby he may not only judge of instructions, rules and precepts given by others, but also be able to correct them and devise new of himself, and this not only in navigation but in all mechanical sciences.[1]

Just as navigational techniques were disseminated so, too, information about the newly-discovered parts of the globe was passed on in books like Eden's *Treatyse of the Newe Indies* (1553) and *Decades of the Newe Worlde* (1554), and Frampton's *Briefe Description of Portes, Creekes, Bayes and Havens of the Weast India* (1578) and *Account of the Empire of China* (1579). The most important contributor to this field was, of course, Richard Hakluyt, whose *Diverse Voyages* (1582) and *Principal Navigations* (1589) were later supplemented by Samuel Purchas in his *Hakluyt Posthumus or Purchas his Pilgrims* (1625, etc.). All of these writers were popularizers in the way that Robert Recorde had been when he produced his *Castle of Knowledge* (1556), which aimed at doing for astronomy and cosmography what his *Grounde of Artes* (1542) had done for arithmetic and his *Pathway to Knowledge* (1551) for geometry.[2] Robert

---

[1] *Discourse*, Preface to the Travellers, Seamen and Mariners of England.

[2] For Recorde's contribution cf. F. R. Johnson and S. V. Larkey, 'Robert Recorde's Mathematical Teaching and the Anti-Aristotelian Movement', *Huntington Library Bulletin*, No. 7 (1935), pp. 59–87, and L. D. Patterson, 'Robert Recorde's Cosmography, 1556', *Isis*, XLII (1951), pp. 208–18.

Norman and Edward Wright did the same for navigation. William Bourne's aim was a common one:–

> my meaning is to instruct the simplest sort of seaman. . . . For this is general amongst seamen and also gunners, how simple and without the skill soever they may be, if that they have once taken charge to be master of a ship he [*sic*] thinketh great scorn to learn at any man's hand. . . . But I do hope that in these days that the knowledge of the masters of ships is very well mended, for I have known within these twenty years that they that were ancient masters of ships have derided and mocked them that have occupied their cards and plats, and also the observations of the altitude of the Pole (Star) saying that they care not for their sheep-skins, for he could keep a better account upon a board, and when they that did take the latitude they would call them star-shooters and sun-shooters and would ask if they had stricken it.[1]

In the same way John Davis declared in his *Seamen's Secrets* (1595) that 'To manifest the necessary conclusions of navigations in brief and short terms is my only intent and therefore I admit the causes and terms and definitions of artificial words as superfluous to my purpose, neither have I laid down the cunning conclusions apt for scholars to practice upon the shore but only those things that are needfully required in a sufficient seaman'.[2] Significantly, too, Davis chose the time-honoured pedagogical device of the dialogue in which to cast his book, as had Thomas Hood in his *Use of Two Mathmeticall Instruments* (1592) and *Use of Both Globes* (1592) and John Wolfe in his *Treatyse Very Necessary for all Seafayringmen in which by way of a conference betweene two pilotes are very necessary things discussed besides the most desired arte of shooting East and West and the observacion of the Sun* (1598), a translation from the Dutch of Mathijs Syverts of Enkhuizen.

Wolfe's was one of many texts published in the second half of the sixteenth century and later which gave instruction in the making and use of navigational instruments, texts which were often produced by those who were themselves instrument-makers. Most navigational texts had something to say about the astrolabe, the cross-staff, the backstaff, the nocturnal, the quandrant and so on. Some, on the other hand, were specialized

---

[1] *A Regiment for the Sea* (1577), To the Reader.
[2] Op. cit., Dedicatory Epistle to Lord Charles Howard of Effingham.

texts devoted solely to the instruments. William Barlowe's *Navigators Supply* (1597) for example, which drew on the work of Borough and Norman, was concerned with the supply of instruments, and recommended that 'If any one desire more simple instruction concerning the use of these instruments he may repair unto John Godwin, dwelling in Bucklersbury, teacher of the ground of these arts', going on to make the point that 'two months learning of a skilful teacher and three years practice in a few good voyages . . . shall get more perfection . . . than he could otherwise with twenty years experience according to the ordinary ignorant practice'.[1]

Barlow was here touching on a matter which is to be found in a good many aspects of the Renaissance, the relationship between the scholar and the practical craftsman, one part of which was the oft-repeated plea for scholars to make their contribution by popularizing the results of their work and especially its practical applications. 'Except there be a uniting of knowledge with practice there can be nothing excellent.' Barlow's comment is echoed in dozens of other texts. The sixteenth century saw, in fact, the beginnings of a breakdown of the traditional disdain, Platonic in origin, for instruction in the fields of technical enterprise. Vives and Rabelais had each in their writings urged the importance of technical instruction and the value of learning from artisans and technicians, as had Leonardo da Vinci in the field of the fine arts. Henry the Navigator had tried to achieve this kind of co-operation among those who congregated at Sagres, but much more effective was the work done at the *Casa da Contratacion* in Seville. Doubtless Sir Humphrey Gilbert had such work in mind when he laid down, in his scheme for a 'Queen Elizabeth's Academy' (1570), that whilst the first of his two mathematicians should concentrate on the applications of his art to military affairs, the second

> shall read one day cosmography and astronomy and the other day tend the practices thereof only to the art of navigation, with the knowledge of necessary stars, making use of instruments appertaining to the same: and also shall have in his school a ship and a galley made in model, throughly rigged and finished, to teach unto his auditory as well the knowledge and use by name of every part thereof, as also the perfect art of shipwright and diversity of all

[1] Op. cit., Sig. K 2.

sorts of moulds appertaining to the same, and shall yearly be allowed £66. 13. 4d.

In addition there was to be 'one who shall teach to draw maps, sea-charts etc., and to take by view of eye the plat of anything, and shall read the grounds and rules of proportion and increasing perspective and measuration belonging to the same, and shall be yearly allowed £40'.[1]

The need for expert guidance had been recognized as early as 1540 in the 'Act for the Maintenance of the Navy of England', and French specialists had been imported by Henry VIII in the 1540s to survey the ports and train pilots. A plea for some systematic instruction had been made in 1562 when Stephen Borough, who had sailed with Richard Chancellor in search of the North-East Passage and was Chief Pilot of the Muscovy Company, petitioned the Privy Council in a *Discourse on the Need for Instruction in Navigation and in the appointment of a Chief Pilot of England*. In 1558 Borough had visited the *Casa da Contractacion*, which since its foundation by Charles V in 1503 and its early days under Pilot-Major Amerigo Vespucci had acted as a clearing house for all that was new in the arts of navigation and cartography, as well as being the place where all aspiring pilots and navigators acquired the obligatory certificate which alone entitled them to take charge of a ship. Its activities had already been described by Richard Eden in his translation of Peter Martyr's *Decades of the Newe Worlde* (1554). Returning from his 1558 visit Borough had brought back with him a copy of Martin Cortes's *Arte de Navegar* (1551) and persuaded the Muscovy Company to have it translated for the benefit of English seamen. The result was Richard Eden's *Arte of Navigation* (1561), which included sections on making charts and instruments as well as instruction in the art of navigation. But Borough recognized, too, the value of the systematic instruction which went on at Seville and in his petition asked that the Crown appoint 'a learned and skilful man in the art of navigation to teach and instruct', at the same time seeking for himself the post of Chief Pilot of the Realm, who would have power to examine and appoint all masters and pilots of ships of forty tons

---

[1] Op. cit., p. 5; cf. E. G. R. Taylor and M. W. Richey *The Geometrical Seaman: a book of early nautical instruments* (1962).

burthen and upwards. A draft Commission was in fact drawn up for the Queen but was never put into operation, probably owing to the opposition of the members of the Trinity House of Deptford whose original charter of 1514 had empowered them to examine and select the masters of the king's ships, to control the pilotage of the Thames and to provide an adequate 'store of skilfull Pilotes'.[1]

After Borough's death the task was taken up by Richard Hakluyt, who wrote to Walsingham in 1584 from Paris, where he had found a mathematical lectureship set up by Peter Ramus in operation. He stressed the great value that two navigational lecturers would have—one in London for practical seamen and the other in Oxford where a scholar might further the mathematical side of a navigation—suggesting that each be paid a stipend of £50 per annum.[2] He repeated his suggestion in the preface to his *Diverse Voyages* (1582) and again in the Dedication to his *Principal Navigations*, in which he 'greatly wished there were a lecture of navigation read in this city (of London) for the banishing of our former gross ignorance in marine causes and for the increase and generally multiplying of the sea-knowledge of this age'. Like Borough he quoted the system at Seville, and did indeed manage to persuade Sir Francis Drake to put up £20 a year towards the appointing of a fit person; but the candidate having insisted on a stipend of twice that sum, the scheme once again fell through.[3]

In 1588, however, such a lectureship was in fact founded and put into operation when Sir Thomas Smith, later to be the first Governor of the East India Company, together with other merchants of the City of London, contributed funds for 'a mathematicall lecture'. The initial stimulus at the time of the founding of the lectureship was the threat of invasion, and the first lecturer, Thomas Hood, was instructed to show the application of mathematics to military affairs for the especial benefit of the 'Captains of the Trained Bands'. With the lessening of tension, however, Hood's lectures turned to more profitable

[1] D. W. Waters, *The Art of Navigation in England in Elizabethan and Early Stuart Times* (1958), pp. 103ff and Appendices 6A and 6B.

[2] S.P. 12/170, No. 1, printed in Waters, op. cit., pp. 544–5.

[3] E. G. R. Taylor, ed., *The Original Writings and Correspondence of the Two Richard Hakluyts* (Hakluyt Society, 1938), I, 24–25, 54–55, 179–80, 209, and II, 429–32, 473, 510.

applications, i.e. to navigation, 'the chiefest pillar of your gain', as Hood described it in his inaugural lecture.[1] The practical bent of Hood's lectures, which covered 'geometry, astronomy, geography, hydrography and the art of navigation', was well brought out in his remarks about geometry:–

> Then if geometry reach so high that it can justly measure the cope of heaven, no doubt in earth it performeth most excellent things. Let geography witness in universal maps, let topography witness in several cards, let hydrography witness in the mariner's plat, you yourselves may witness in martial affairs, let the gunner witness in planting his shot, the surveyor in measuring land, witness all those which labour in mines and those which practice conveying of water. . . .

His lectures obviously in large degree fulfilled the aims which Gilbert had set out for his academy and their popularity when printed points to their meeting a real need. His inaugural address was promptly published by Edward Allde, a prominent printer of navigational texts.[2] In 1590 appeared *The Use of the Celestial Globe in Piano* and *The Use of Two Mathematicall Instruments, the Crosse-Staffe . . . and the Jacobs' Staffe*, which were followed in 1592 by *The Use of Both Globes, Celestiall and Terrestriall* and *The Marriners Guide*, the latter designed as an addition to accompany the 1592 and subsequent editions of Hood's revision of Bourne's *Regiment of the Sea*. In addition Hood produced a translation of Peter Ramus's *Elements of Geometry* (1590) and of Christian Urstitius's *Elements of Arithmetic* (1596).

Originally the sum raised was intended for two years' lectures, but before the time expired the Privy Council ordered the continuation of the lectures for another two years, and 'for so much longer as the Lord Mayor of the City will give the same allowance or more than is at this present is granted'. The exact date of the demise of the lectures is not known; it was certainly not after 1594, by which time 'the Lord Mayor and the City' were probably thinking in terms of putting into practice the

[1] Printed in F. R. Johnson, 'Thomas Hood's Inaugural Address as Mathematical Lecturer of the City of London, 1588', *J.H.I.*, III (1942), pp. 94–106; cf. F. R. Johnson, *Astronomical Thought in Renaissance England* (Baltimore, 1937), pp. 196–205.

[2] On whom cf. R. B. McKerrow, 'Edward Allde, a typical trade printer', *The Library*, 4th Series, X (1929), pp. 121–62.

scheme devised by Sir Thomas Gresham. Hood in any case continued to publish his works and to teach privately, as the advertisement in his *Use of Both Globes* tells us, including among his pupils both navigators and 'land measurers'.

Hood's lectures were not, of course, unique. The famous Dr. John Dee had for many years acted as adviser in matters navigational to the Muscovy Company, instructing their navigators and particularly stressing the relevance of mathematics in the practical problems of navigation. Indeed, almost every great navigator of the day consulted him at his house in Mortlake, where his library of over 4,000 scientific books and his collection of instruments were put at their disposal. Thomas Hariot provided similar instruction for Raleigh and his captains prior to the Guiana voyage in 1595. Edward Wright lectured on navigation to the East India Company until his death in 1616, whilst instrument-makers like John Goodwin and John Tapp, who taught 'near the Bulwark Gate in Tower Hill', and 'mathematical professors' like Robert Hartwell, who, besides producing new editions of Recorde's *Grounde of Artes* and Blundeville's *Exercises*, taught 'the arts and sciences mathematical' at his house 'near the Golden Lyon in Fetter Street', were part of an important group of private teachers. Such teachers were mostly to be found in London, but others evidently taught in the other great ports of England. Francis Jones, for example, was paid £4 in 1618–19 by the Society of Merchant Venturers at Bristol, being 'one year's fee allowed him for instructing poor sailors in the art of navigation'.[1]

As we have seen, in the mid-1590s the Lord Mayor and City of London were reluctant to provide further funds for the Hood lectureship because of the likelihood of their being able to put into operation the provisions of the will of Sir Thomas Gresham. Sir Thomas had laid down that, subject to a reservation to his wife for life, the revenues from the land and the buildings comprising the Royal Exchange and his house in Bishopsgate were to be used to provide stipends of £50 per year for seven professors of Law, Rhetoric, Divinity, Music, Physics, Geometry and Astronomy. He died in 1579, but his wife lived on

[1] P. McGrath, 'Merchant Shipping in the Seventeenth Century', *Mariners Mirror*, XLI (1955), p. 27. For a full list of teachers cf. E. G. R. Taylor, *Mathematical Practitioners of Tudor and Stuart England* (Cambridge, 1954), Pt. ii.

until the end of 1596, so that it was not until Michaelmas 1598 that the seven Gresham professors were duly installed. Once appointed, however, the professors of Geometry and Astronomy provided, on a permanent basis, the sort of applied mathematical instruction which Thomas Hood had offered ten years earlier.[1] Their leading light was Henry Briggs, first Gresham Professor of Geometry, who, with the Professors of Astronomy, Edmund Gunter (appointed 1619) and Henry Gellibrand (appointed 1626), notably contributed to the practical applications of mathematics which were taking place during these early years of the seventeenth century. To Briggs must go the credit for the amazingly rapid dissemination of Napier's logarithms. The latter's *Mirifici Logarithmorum Canonis Descriptio* appeared in 1616. It was at Brigg's suggestion that Edward Wright undertook the translation into English, *A Description of the Admirable Table of Logarithms*, and it was Briggs himself, Wright having died in 1615, who completed the work and saw it through the press in 1616. It was Briggs, too, who, having twice travelled to Edinburgh to visit and consult Napier, saw, with Napier, the inconvenience of the base to which the latter's logarithms were calculated, and undertook, with Napier's encouragement, the calculation of logarithms to the base 10, our common logarithms. Briggs, produced his first set of tables, covering the numbers 1 to 1,000 in 1617. In 1620 Edmund Gunter published tables of logarithmic sines using the decimal base, and four years later, having since been appointed to the Savilian Chair of Geometry at Oxford, Briggs published his *Arithmetica Logarithmica* (1624), in which he provided tables for the numbers 1–20,000 and 90,000–100,000. Finally in 1628, the Dutchman Adrian Vlacq completed the series, with tables for 20,000–90,000, and for the next 250 years the Briggs-Vlacq tables served as the basis for mathematical calculation.[2]

It was characteristic of the period that the practical usefulness of Napier's invention was immediately seen and publicized. In

[1] Cf. F. R. Johnson, 'Gresham College, The Precursor of the Royal Society', *J.H.I.*, I (1940), pp. 413–38; D. McKie, 'The Origins and Foundation of the Royal Society of London', in Sir Harold Hartley, ed., *The Royal Society: its origins and founders* (1960), pp. 1–37; R. H. Syfret, 'The Origins of the Royal Society', *Notes and Records of the Royal Society*, V (1948), pp. 95–137.

[2] C. G. Knott, ed., *The Napier Tercentenary Memorial Volume* (1915), pp. 1–32 and 111–37.

a prefatory verse to Wright's translation Richard Lever pointed out

> Their use is great in all true measuring
> Of lands and plots, buildings and fortification.
> So in astronomy and dialling,
> Geography and navigation,
> In these, and like, young students soon may gain.
> The skilful, too, may save cost, time and pain.

Aaron Rathborne called for pocket-sized tables in his *Surveyor* (1616). Briggs and Gunter lectured in the new technique at Gresham College. John Speidell taught 'the use of logarithms' at his school in Queen Street, off Drury Lane, and published a modified set of tables, *New Logarithms*, in 1619 and again in 1622. John Pell, of Trinity College, Cambridge, on the other hand, could apparently get no help in the university in 1628, when he was trying to master logarithms on his own, and had therefore to write to Briggs himself at Oxford.[1] The same story of the practical application of mathematical techniques may be told of the development of decimal fractions. These were first clearly advocated in the *De Thiende* (1585) of Simon Stevin, who produced his treatise for the benefit of those 'astonomers, land-meaters, measurers of tapesty, gaudgers, stereometers in general, money masters, and all merchants' who required the 'easy performance of all reckonings computations and accounts without broken numbers'. His work was the indispensable prelude to the development of logarithms, though his symbolism was clumsy and was soon replaced by other methods.[2] Robert Norton's English translation, *Disme or the Art of Tenths* appeared in 1608, and was followed by *The Art of Tenths or Decimal Arithmaticke* (1619) of Henry Lyte, who claimed he had been teaching the subject for the past ten years, during which time he had been distributing manuscript copies of the text, 'some for accounts, some for measuring and dividing land into acres, some for measuring cloth, glass, board, timber, etc.'

The last half of the sixteenth century saw in England a

---

[1] Cf. Briggs to Pell, 25 October 1628, in J. O. Halliwell, *Collection of Letters Illustrative of the Progress of Science in England* (1841), p. 57, cited by Curtis, op. cit., p. 245.

[2] For the early history and development of decimal symbolism, cf. D. E. Smith, *History of Mathematics* (Boston, 1925), II, 23ff.

growing insistence on a methodology based on the habitual observation and recording of data, and on experimentation, the results of which could be quantified. Such a development was undoubtedly stimulated by the fruitful cross-fertilization between scholar and practitioner, and by the books which both sides produced. Rarely in the universities of England do we find this conscious attention to scientific method. But, if the institutionalized dissemination of the new science was lacking, certainly there was no lack of less formal channels along which these ideas could flow. The 'familial groups' which centred round John Dee at his house in Mortlake and round the Wizard Earl of Northumberland at Syon House and in the Tower of London, actively concerned themselves with scientific experiments and observations, and in so doing sought the help of instrument-makers and other non-academic 'scientists'.[1] Gunter and Gellibrand each spent a good deal of time in the naval yard at Deptford, working with John Wells, the Keeper of the Naval Stores and author of *Sciographia or the Art of Shadows* (1635), in which the construction of various dials and the astronomical method of finding the meridian are described. It was in Wells's garden, too, that Gellibrand made the observations of compass variation which enabled him to confirm the existence of secular variation in 1634. Perhaps the classic case of this marriage between theory and practice, however, is to found in the work of William Gilbert, who freely acknowledged, in *De Magnete* (1600), his indebtedness to the instrument-maker and mariner, Robert Norman, for his knowledge of magnetic dip. Gilbert devotes a quarter of his space to navigation and the instruments necessary for navigation, and when he quotes other writers it is the work of contemporary cosmographers to which he refers and not the Aristotelian and Ptolemaic texts which formed the basis of university studies. His insistence on the need for experimentation and his search for knowledge 'not in books but in things themselves' have been called the first systematic exposition of modern experimental science. Yet in a very real sense Gilbert's work reflected a growing attitude to which

[1] C. F. Smith, *John Dee, 1527–1608* (1909), pp. 236ff and *passim*; Batho, *B.J.E.S.*, V (1957), pp. 137–9; J. W. Shirley, 'The Scientific Experiments of Sir Walter Raleigh, the Wizard Earl and the Three Magi in the Tower', *Ambix*, IV (1949), pp. 52–66.

mathematical practitioners and Gresham professors alike contributed, and it is significant that the origins of that 'Invisible College' which was later to become the Royal Society are to be found in informal meetings amongst the Gresham professors of geometry and astronomy and their friends, long before they began to meet in Dr. Wilkins's chambers at Wadham College, Oxford.[1]

At the root of all this work was a belief not only that human knowledge might be extended indefinitely, but also that the end-product of such extension was the perfectibility of man himself. It was a belief, without which, to go no farther, the English followers of Comenius could hardly have developed their own educational ideas. Nor could they have written books such as George Snell's *Right Teaching of Useful Knowledge* (1648), for example, which claimed 'to fit scholars for some honest profession such as any man needeth (that is not a teacher) in all knowledges, in one school, in a shorter time, in a more plain way and for much less expenses than ever hath been devised. . . .' Francis Bacon modestly (for once) places himself in this context when, in suggesting his House of Salomon as a 'clearing house' for the dissemination of the new science, he remarked, 'I shall content myself to wake better spirits, like a bell-ringer which is first up to call others to church.'

With the help of the printing press, 'science' was now making its presence felt in a field of human endeavour where rule of thumb had reigned for so long, and what was becoming true of commerce and navigation was becoming true, too, of that most conservative of industries, agriculture. During the sixteenth century, landowners, whether those of ancient lineage or the newly-rich merchants, lawyers, civil servants, Crown officials and thrifty yeomen whose estates were recently acquired and who alike were encroaching on the traditional preserve of the aristocracy, were finding it increasingly necessary to become efficient if they wished to survive the effects of inflation.

[1] Cf. E. Zilsel, 'The Origins of William Gilbert's Scientific Ideas', *J.H.I.*, II (1949), pp. 1–32, and 'The Genesis of the Concept of Scientific Progress', ibid., VI (1945), pp. 325–49; A. C. Keller, 'Zilsel, the Artisans and the Idea of Progress in the Renaissance', ibid., XI (1950), pp. 235–40; R. P. Stearns, 'The Scientific Spirit in England in the Early Modern Times', *Isis*, XXXIV (1943), pp. 293–300; R. P. Adams, 'The Social Responsibilities of Science in *Utopia, New Atlantis* and after', *J.H.I.*, X (1949), pp. 374–98.

The debates about gentility, to which we have already referred, always included the question of whether a gentleman should encumber himself with the day-to-day details of farming. Landowning was one thing, but actively concerning oneself with or indeed equipping oneself to take care of the details was quite another. Most of the texts frowned on any day-to-day concern on the part of the gentleman, but this might be expected in works whose origins were to be found in Italian models, catering for the gentleman of urban court life, for whom the countryside was merely a place where occasional draughts of fresh air might clear the head for further activity at court. Though the anonymous *Institucion of a Gentleman* (1555) did make the point that the landowner should know something about his estates, if only to safeguard himself against his servants' indolence or dishonesty, Lawrence Humphrey's *The Nobles or of Nobilyte* (1563) was most unusual in insisting on the benefits of good husbandry and well-surveyed estates.[1]

But in England the gentry were the landed gentry, and as Henry Percy, Ninth Earl of Northumberland, explained to his son, ignorance of estate management could prove fatal. He attributed his own difficulties on succeeding to his patrimony to

> want of knowledge in mine own estate, an ignorance fostered in me by my father's concealing of what was fit for me to have been made acquainted withal, either to cause obedience in keeping me under or to hinder some prodigal expense in small trifles. Hand in hand with these followed many inconveniences that my time hath tasted of, and the ground, as I said before, by not being taught the secrets of my estate before I had use thereof.

His advice, therefore, was plain and to the point: 'understand your estate generally better than any of your officers, for ordinarily I have marked that all men that consume their estates are for the most part ignorant of what they have, what the worth of it is, what the particular commodities thereof may be . . .' Sir Walter Raleigh was of the same opinion. His 'rules to be observed for the preserving of a man's estate' were 'that thou know what thou hast, what everything is worth that thou hast and to see that thou art not wasted by thy servants and officers'.

---

[1] *Institucion* . . ., Sig. C iii *verso*, *Nobles* . . ., Sig. I vii ff.

Furthermore, 'if thou trust any servant with thy purse, be sure thou take his account ere thou sleep'.[1]

In the end the plain facts of the case could not be ignored. Gentility apart, if a landowner wished to safeguard his estates and his revenues in a fiercely competitive and litigious age, then he would need to equip himself with the details of estate management, whether in its legal or its agricultural aspects. He could do this by consolidating widely scattered properties and by ridding himself of long leases when they fell due. Fixed freehold and copyhold tenures could be dealt with in the same way. There were legal devices in plenty for this, and, as we have seen, the lawyers were not slow in producing the necessary instruments. But ultimately it came down to husbandry, as the 'good husbandry' clauses in the new leases testified, when they insisted on adequate manuring or prohibited the disturbance of courses, when they laid down precise standards of fencing and ditching or regulated timber conservation. Gone were the days when the classical texts on agriculture, those of Pliny and Virgil, Cato, Varro and Columella, could be deemed to be of practical use to the English landowner or tenant. In Dr. Overbury's *Characters* it is the 'mere scholar' who 'gives directions for husbandry from Virgil's *Georgics* and for cattle from his *Bucolics*'.[2] Now both landowner and tenant had to seek practical advice.

Demands for institutionalized agricultural education did not come until the middle of the seventeenth century. Gerbier's Academy included in its curriculum the study of soils, fruit production and general husbandry. John Dury aimed at setting up a 'Colledge of Husbandry' in 1651, and repeated his call in his *Legacy of Husbandry* (1655). William Sprigge even went so far as to suggest, in his *Model Plea for an English Commonwealth against Monarchy* (1659), that agriculture should be included in his reformed curriculum for the universities. John Bellers's *Proposals for Raising a College of Industry of all Useful Trades and Husbandry* (1695) were actually approved and accepted by the Society of Friends, starting a trend in Quaker

[1] G. B. Harrison, ed., *Advice to his Son by Henry Percy, Ninth Earl of Northumberland* (1609) (1930), pp. 30 and 76. Raleigh, *Instructions to his Son and Posterity* in Adys and Birch, eds., *Works* (1829), VIII, 565–6.

[2] E. F. Rimbaud, ed., *Miscellaneous Works . . . of Sir Thomas Overbury* (1890), p. 88.

education which remained a characteristic feature for over two hundred years.[1] But what was lacking in institutional education was quite adequately made good by the printed book, which gradually replaced the manuscript treatises of the medieval period. These were the treatises of estate management and estate accounting which enabled the stewards of monastic and manorial lands to obtain the maximum revenue from their respective estates, and which paralleled the legal manuscript treatises to which we have already referred.[2] Like their predecessors, the printed books were supremely practical in their approach, and an indication of the sort of text which was to become increasingly available for those who needed it is provided by Anthony Fitzherbert's *Boke of Surveying* (1523), whose general aim is exemplified by the heading of its fortieth chapter, 'How to make a township that is worth XX marks a year worth XX pounds a year'. Fitzherbert energetically championed methods of enclosure as allowing of better methods of husbandry and thus increasing the value of the land. In the same year he produced his *Boke of Husbandry* in which he set down the most up-to-date methods of arable farming, giving details of tools and equipment, advice on capital outlay, methods of manuring, draining, ploughing, rick-building, and so on.

These two books, out of date as they were soon to become, nevertheless not only epitomize the changes in agriculture of the period, but also the way in which the new outlook was disseminated. By 1600 Thomas Wilson could report that the gentlemen of England 'are now for the most part grown to become good husbandmen and know as well how to improve their lands to the uttermost as the farmer and the countryman, so that they take their farms into their hands as the leases expire, and either till them themselves or else let out to those who will give most'.[3] Such a change was facilitated by, and indeed could

---

[1] For other mid-seventeenth-century schemes cf. G. H. Turnbull, *Hartlib. Dury and Comenius* (Liverpool, 1947), pp. 57–65.

[2] Cf. H. G. Richardson, 'Business Training in Medieval Oxford', *Am.H.R.*, XLVI (1941), pp. 259–80 and 'An Oxford Teacher of the Fifteenth Century', *B.J.R.L.*, XXIII (1939), pp. 436–57; D. Oschinsky, 'Medieval Treatises on Estate Accounting', *Ec.H.R.*, XVII (1947), pp. 52–61, and 'Medieval Treatises on Estate Management', ibid., 2nd Series, VII (1956), pp. 296–309.

[3] F. J. Fisher, ed., *The State of England Anno Dom. 1600 by Thomas Wilson* (Camden Miscellany, XVI, 1936), p. 18.

hardly have taken place so quickly and on such a wide scale without, the manuals which came off the presses in increasing numbers. It is significant, too, that whereas Peter Crescenzi's *Ruralia Commodia*, a well-known medieval text, was printed in Augsburg in 1471 as a handsome (and expensive) folio volume, Fitzherbert's book was produced in 1523 by Pynson as a small quarto and in 1526 by Berthelet in duodecimo. Crescenzi would probably have found a place on the sixteenth-century gentleman's library shelves. Fitzherbert on the other hand would have been in constant use, carried about in the pocket.

All aspects of farming were catered for an in a variety of ways. Thomas Tusser's *Hundred Good Pointes of Husbandrie* (1557), which ran through many editions and was enlarged in 1573 into *Five Hundred Good Pointes of Husbandry*, was written in doggerel verse and cast in the form of a farmer's calendar, a method which continued to be popular on into the nineteenth century.[1] More orthodox and detailed texts, which eventually replaced Fitzherbert and Tusser, included Barnaby Googe's *Four Bookes of Husbandrie* (1577), revised and enlarged in 1614 as *The Whole Art and Trade of Husbandry*, Gervase Markham's *The Country Farme* (1616), *The English Husbandman* (1613–15) and a revised edition of Googe's work in 1631, Gabriel Plattes's *Treatise of Husbandry* (1638), many times 'revised and enlarged', and Walter Blith's *English Improver* (1649) and *English Improver Improved* (1652). In addition to such general texts, which covered every aspect of arable and pastoral husbandry, there were dozens of manuals dealing with particular aspects of farming. Leonard Mascall, for example, a prolific writer on matters agricultural, produced *A Booke of the Arte and Maner how to Graft and plant all sortes of trees* (?1569), *The Husbandrie, Ordering and Government of Poultrie* (1581) and *The First Booke of Cattel* (1596). Sir Hugh Plat was responsible for *Sundrie New and Artificial Remedies against Famine* (1596), *The Jewel House of Art and Nature contayning Sundrie experiments in the Art of Husbandry* (1594) and *The Newe and Admirable Arte of Setting Corne* (1600). In addition to his general texts that most prolific of agricultural writers (and plagiarizers) Gervase Markham produced books on horsemanship and farriery, on

---

[1] Cf. G. E. Fussell, 'Farmers' Calendars from Tusser to Arthur Young,' *Economic History*, II (1933), pp. 521–35.

veterinary remedies, on water meadows and even on the kitchen garden. In the era of the 'great rebuilding' it is not surprising that there were plenty of texts on gardens and orchards, of which the earliest was Thomas Hill's *A Most Briefe and Pleasant Treatise teaching how to dress sowe and sette a garden* (1563). It reached an eighth edition by 1608, by which time it included treatises on 'the governing of bees', 'yearly conjectures mete for the husbandman to know' and 'the art of grafting and planting of trees', and with these additions appeared in a fourteenth and last edition in 1656.

But tending one's land according to the best agricultural practice was not all. In an age of inflation and of litigation one needed to know the exact extent of one's holding. No longer was it sufficient simply to set down acreages *per estimationem*. Too much was at stake, and, indeed, a report drawn up by Sir Robert Johnson in 1602 showed that the poverty of the Crown was much increased by the 'want of authentic surveys' of Crown lands.[1] This was a criticism of the Crown as a landowner, for the wherewithal was immediately to hand in the new professional class of surveyor, whose expertise and whose texts were yet another example of the geometrical revolution at work. In this case the application of triangulation to varying topographical features enabled a skilled surveyor, using a new range of instruments to supplement the traditional rod and cord, to survey 300–500 acres a day with a great degree of accuracy. As in the case of navigation, the instrumentation of such an exercise was elaborate and remarkable. The plain table and the theodolite were by the end of the century standard equipment, thanks to the advocacy of men like Leonard and Thomas Digges, as well as of professional surveyors like Edward Worsop, Ralph Agas, Aaron Rathborne and John Norden.

Although the earlier texts such as Fitzherbert's *Boke of Surveying* (1523), Richard Benese's *Maner of Measurying All Maner of Lande* (1540), and Valentine Leigh's *Treatise of Measuring all kind of lands* (1562) were a vast improvement on the medieval texts, they still relied on the perch rod and compass dial, and in any case were concerned more with how to set down the results of a survey than with the methods of producing

---

[1] *Cal.S.P.Dom.*, *1601–3*, pp. 176–7, printed in C. Hill and E. Dell, *The Good Old Cause* (1949), p. 155.

an accurate 'plot'. By the mid-century, however, geometrical methods were beginning to make headway. Gemma Frisius had laid down the principles of topographical survey by triangulation in 1533, when he appended a treatise of his own on that subject to his second revised edition of Apian's *Cosmographia*.[1] Apian's work was widely read and Frisius's method was, therefore, quickly disseminated. Its usefulness was first made plain in an English text in 1556, with the publication of Leonard Digges's *Booke named Tectonicon briefly showing the exact measuring and speedie reckoning all maner of land, square timber, etc.*, which was reprinted four times by the end of the century. The practical value of such works is exemplified in the new surveying texts which followed, written by professional surveyors. Ralph Agas, for instance, in his *Preparative for Plotting Lands* (1596), explains that at the beginning of his career he used the plain table 'sometimes directed by needles, sometimes by the former station as is now used, sometimes in the middle of the Close, sometimes by the bounders'.[2] Later, however, he abandoned it for the 'Theodelitus' or 'Topographical Instrument' of Leonard Digges, details of which had been published in *Pantometria* by Digges's son Thomas in 1571, and from which the modern theodolite with its telescopic sights is derived. In the same way Edward Worsop, in his *Discoverie of Sundrie Errours Committed by Landmeaters Ignorant of Arithmetick and Geometrie* (1582), pays tribute to the value of the scholarly texts of men like Digges and Recorde and Dee, without whose groundwork the surveyor could not expect to master the new methods. Indeed, those who had been reluctant to accept and master the new methods, whether landowner or surveyor, came in for a good deal of criticism. As Worsop put it, 'when the blind leadeth the blind they fall both into the ditch'. His whole text is studded with signs of that growing professionalism which marked much of the late sixteenth and early seventeenth centuries. Worsop might, in fact, be claimed as the first advocate of an Institute of Chartered Surveyors. He wrote :–

[1] Cf. E. G. R. Taylor, 'The Earliest Account of Triangulation', *Scottish Geographical Magazine*, XLIII (1927), pp. 341–5, 'The Plane Table in the Sixteenth Century', ibid., XLV (1929), pp. 205–11, and 'William Bourne, a chapter in Tudor Geography', *Geographical Journal*, LXXII (1928), pp. 329–41.

[2] Op. cit., p. 4.

Such sufficient skill as a surveyor should have before he ought to execute that office cannot be attained but by a longer study and a greater practice than is commonly thought to be had thereto. It is also one of the chargeablest studies that one can enter into. There are few that will take the pains to give perfect instructions to young beginners and to set them in the right course of study and practice, which is a great cause of much vain expenses. The mathematical part seemeth so dry and hard at the first entrance that some (as wearied) give over before they have passed half-way. Also measurers ignorant of geometry can make quicker dispatches than the learned and skilful can, which so pleaseth the ignorant because it diminishes the present charge, that they little regard him that make true measure, which in truth is penny wisdom and pound foolishness. . . . If the learned and skilful did use conferences and devise ways how these inconveniences might be redressed, true knowledge advanced and ignorance depressed, as the learned in other professions do, great utility would ensue. . . . If surveyors were in such order, as by good reason they should . . . then as the learned in other professions are known from the unlearned so might they. Not any student of the law can be admitted to the Bar except by the Benchers he be thought sufficient.

None can be admitted in the universities to any degrees of learning but by the allowance of the ancient graduates of the same profession. If the skilful in the parts mathematical, legal and judicial would friendly and singly join together to reform and instruct each other and to reduce survey to a perfect order, without doubt many which now understand but parts and pieces right, but more things erroneously or lamely, would in short space prove sufficient men. Also excellent good ways for the best instruction of young students thereof would soon be had.[1]

Such instruction was already available. It came from the private teachers, the 'mathematical practitioners', whom we have seen teaching navigation, as well as from the manuals written either by the teachers themselves, or by the professional surveyors. John Norden, topographer, cartographer and surveyor, who carried on the work of the great map-maker, Christopher Saxton, produced his *Surveyor's Dialogue* in 1607. William Folkingham's *Feudigraphia, the synopsis or epitome of surveying methodized* appeared in 1610 and Aaron Rathbone's *The Surveyor* in 1616. Rathborne, perhaps above all others,

---

[1] Op. cit., Dedicatorie Epistle and Sigs. I i, K i *verso* ff.

epitomizes the new professional attitude. He was probably a pupil of John Godwyn, whom William Barlow had recommended in *The Navigators Supply* (1597). His own *Surveyor* constantly refers to the teachers of his day, men such as Thomas Bretnor, who taught in Cow Lane, near the Smithfield, and John Speidell, who shared Rathborne's interest in logarithms, and who was one of the 'professors' appointed to teach in Kynaston's Museum Minervae (1634). By the mid-century the profession was well-established, and in its turn Rathborne's text was superseded by *The Complete Surveyor* (1653) of William Leybourne, whose many works (his last was published in 1704) contributed to the education of the generation which carried out the surveys for the parliamentary enclosures of the eighteenth century. The landowning gentry, too, valued the accuracy of the new methods, and saw the point of Peacham's advice to become at least acquainted with such matters:—

> in brief, the use you shall have of Geometry will be in surveying your lands; affording your opinion in building anew or translation; working your mills as well for grinding corn as for throwing forth water from your lower grounds and bringing water far off for sundry uses; seeing the measure of timber, stones and the like (wherein gentlemen are many times egregiously abused and cheated by such as they trust); to contrive much with small charge and in less room.[1]

Whether amateur or professional, then, in commerce and agriculture (as in law), the man of affairs in Renaissance England found himself more and more concerned with the technical details of his enterprise. In order to cope with this new situation he found it increasingly necessary to turn to the private teacher and the printed manual, those non-traditional means of education which throughout the latter part of our period were becoming a crucial part of the total educational provision in England. And it was against a background such as this that 'the new philosophy' of the seventeenth century, the science of Descartes and Newton, developed; a background which owed much to Robert Recorde, John Dee, the Gresham professors and their like. Without it Descartes could not have written,

> It is possible to attain knowledge which is useful in life, and

[1] Op. cit., p. 77.

instead of that speculative philosophy which is taught in the schools, we may find a practical philosophy by means of which, knowing the force and the action of fire, water, air, the stars, the heavens and all other bodies that environ us, as distinctly as we know the different crafts of our artisans, we can in the same way employ them in all those uses to which they are adapted, and thus render ourselves the masters and possessors of nature.[1]

[1] *Discourse on Method* (1637), Pt. vi.

# Conclusion

H o w e v e r much we might deplore certain aspects of education in Renaissance England—the disputes between the 'Greeks' and the 'Trojans', the cobwebs of Ciceronianism, the inhibiting effects of religious polemic on standards of scholarship—the period was nevertheless one in which there was a passionate regard for education, one in which it was realized that education could serve the welfare of the community just as much as the political and religious interests of a sovereign. As an object of study 'knowledge for its own sake' would not have occurred to a Renaissance humanist, and Vives's enjoinder that 'having acquired our knowledge we must turn it to usefulness and employ it for the common good'[1] remained an important theme throughout our period. The notion underlies much of the social literature of the sixteenth century, and continued as a major plank in the platform of Comenius's Pansophism in which 'the relief of man's estate, . . . the general good and comfort of mankind' was the dominant aim. William Petty, indeed, looked forward to the millennium

> when one man or horse shall do the work of three and everything (be) improved to strange advantage. There would not then be so many fustian and unworthy preachers in Divinity, so many pettifoggers in the Law, so many Quack-Salvers in Physick, so many Grammaticasters in country schools, and so many lazy serving men in gentlemen's houses, when every man might learn to live otherwise, in more plenty and more honour.[2]

Such writers often placed a faith in education which strained its capacity to achieve what was hoped for, and their optimism could verge on the naïveté which can be detected in Erasmus and Bacon just as much as in lesser writers such as John Kytchin,

[1] Watson, *Vives on Education*, p. 283.
[2] W. Petty, *Advice on W.P. to Mr. Samuel Hartlib for the Advancement of Some Particular Parts of Learning* (1648), p. 23.

who promised the readers of his *Court Baron* (1580) that 'for sweatless labour (they might) receive satisfaction in exchange', or George Snell, who claimed to achieve success 'in one school, in a shorter time, in a more plain way and for much less expense than ever before hath been used'.[1] Yet society needs such optimism, however naïve or even ludicrous some of its exponents may appear to be. Certainly it had its place in Renaissance England, injecting a confidence into men's minds about what scholarship could achieve or technology effect on their behalf.

The attempts to 'methodize' knowledge and to communicate it to a lay public, and the startling success with which the printing press was put to work as the prime agent of this process, were proof of the concern to bring knowledge under control for the benefit of the common weal. Education had become 'modern', in the sense that knowledge, and especially the knowledge associated with the various professions, callings and trades, was no longer secret, something to be guarded and passed on only to those chosen few who were members of the 'mysterie'. The vernacular manual literature which we have examined is the supreme exemplification of the modern notion that knowledge should be shared, and that such sharing, far from jeopardizing the interests of the few, would benefit them as well as the community at large. As a result, an increasing proportion of the population was actively encouraged and enabled to satisfy its political, religious, cultural and technical needs. It was not simply that small boys and undergraduates no longer needed to rely on oral work and the painful copying of texts. Reading became an out-of-school activity, for instruction and edification as well as for pleasure. Though this was far from being an age of mass education the gap between the educated clerk and the illiterate layman was considerably reduced, and the change was very largely the result of the new adult education, or adult self-education, through the 'teach yourself' manuals.

This secularization of education had its effects on virtually every level of society. Most important of all, however, the new ideas about education and its rôle provided for and produced a ruling class whose members were not necessarily confined to

---

[1] Kytchin, op. cit., Epistle Dedicatory; Snell, *The Right Teaching of Useful Knowledge* (1649), Title page.

those of ancient lineage, and whose education was based on a book-learning which alone, it was considered, could fructify 'practical experience'. If anything about the gentry 'rose' it was their standard of education, and this was as true of their literary and cultural interests as it was of that part of their education which fitted them for public life.

The new books which were being read and studied in the home and the private school did not, however, merely provide a new content for education, whether it was English literature, history and geography, or the scientific, technical and commercial subjects. They reinforced the growing feeling that such subjects should be included in the curriculum of the traditional institutions of education. During the Commonwealth period the idea made some headway, but thereafter 'traditional learning', however badly taught, continued to predominate and remained until comparatively recent times a major influence in secondary and university education. It is for this reason, presumably, that the other, non-classical, type of education has been neglected by historians in the past. In course of time, however, the two kinds of provision, classical and technical-commercial, interacted to modify each other. The former widened its curriculum to admit new subjects, though their status in that curriculum remained that of the poor relation. The latter, recognizing the dangers of a too-narrowly vocational approach, attempted to 'liberalize' its studies. Yet, even now, we cannot claim a complete fusion of aim. The problem of what constitutes a liberal education remains for the mid-twentieth century to solve.

# Index

*Anthologia Graeca*, 63
Antonino, St., 31
Anwykyll, John, 106, 108
Aphthonius, 110f, 112f
Apian, Peter, 262, 275, 292
*Apologie for Poetry*, 245
*Apology*, 145
*Apophthegmata*, 110, 242
*Apprentices Time Entertainer*, 262
apprenticeship, 254f
Aquinas, St. Thomas, 14
architect, 33
Aretino, Pietro, 47
Argyropulos, John, 53
Aristippus, of Catania, 53
Aristotle, 10, 13, 21, 23, 26, 30, 44, 50, 57, 65, 71, 73, 141, 145ff, 151, 248
arithmetic, study of, 3, 32, 84, 100, 156, 255, 259ff, 282
*Arithmetica Memorativa*, 151
*Arithmeticae Practicae Methodus Facilis*, 264
Arnold, Thomas, 130
*Ars Magna*, 150
*Arte de Navegar*, 280
*Arte della Guerra*, 242
*Arte of English Poesie*, 245
*Arte of Logicke*, 164
*Arte of Navigation*, 276, 280
*Art of Tenths or Decimal Arithmaticke*, 285
*Arte of Rhetorique*, 112
*Art of Vulgar Arithmetic*, 265
*Arte of Warre*, 242
*Arte or Crafte of Rhetoryke*, 111
*Artes of Logicke and Rethorike*, 112
*Abcedarium Anglico-Latinum*, 115
Abelard, Peter, 8f, 57
Academies, 226, 289
Academies, Courtly, 82, 220ff
Academies, Dissenting, 270
*Accidence*, 107
*Accidence of the Sea*, 227
*Account of the Empire of China*, 277

'Achademy, Queen Elizabeth's', 82 156, 279f
*Acolastus*, 109
*Adagia*, 242
Adam of Buckfield, 14
Adelard of Bath, 8, 14
*Ad Herennium*, 110f
adiaphora, 60
*Advancement of Learning*, 154, 265
*Advice to a Son*, 84
Aelfric, 11, 228
Aeneas Sylvius Piccolomini, (Pius II), 49, 51, 105
*Aesop's Fables*, 103, 110, 146
Agas, Ralph, 292f
agriculture, study of, 288ff
Alberti, Leon Battista, 22, 31ff, 36, 51, 57, 69, 81, 85, 204
Albertus Magnus, 14, 59
Alexander of Hales, 14
Alford, John, 211
Allde, Edward, 282
Alleyn, Thomas, 93
Allott, R, 122, 244
*Alvearie*, 115, 123
*Amendment of Orthographie*, 103, 122
Amyot, Jacques, 242
Andrewes, Lancelot, 118
*Annotationes in Dialectica Johan Setoni*, 125
Ascham, Roger, 79, 84ff, 105, 109f, 122, 120, 124, 137, 142, 161, 208f, 213, 223f, 233, 241f
Ashley, Anthony, 273
Ashton, Thomas, 117
astronomy, study of, 3, 82, 84, 156, 279ff
*As You Like It*, 225
Augustine, St. of Hippo, 5f, 23
*aulae*, 13
Aulus Gellius, 51, 56
Averroes, 65

Bacon, Anne, 209

301

Bacon, Francis, xi, 128, 154, 182, 209, 244, 250, 265, 287, 297
Bacon, Nicholas, 98, 155, 172, 209, 213, 226
Bacon, Roger, 52
Bainbridge, Christopher, 55
Baker, George, 166
Baker, Humphrey, 264
Baldwin, William, 243
Bales, Peter, 267f
Ball, Thomas, 148
*Banket of Sapience*, 243
Barclay, Alexander, 79, 229
Baret, John, 115, 123
Barlowe, William, 274, 279, 295
Barnes, Robert, 60
barristers, 170ff
Basil, St., 23
Beauchesne, Jean de, 268
Beaufort, Lady Margaret, 132, 141f, 208
Beaumont, Robert, 139
Bec, 7
Beccari, Antonio, 45
Becher, William, 221f
Becon, Thomas, 207
Bede, the Venerable, 6
Bekynton, Thomas, 43, 47
Bellemain, Jean, 229
Bellers, John, 289
Bellot, Jacques, 232
*Belvedere, or the Garden of Muses*, 244
Bembo, Cardinal, 241
Benchers, 179ff
Benese, Richard, 292
Bereford, C. J., 170
Bernard, of Chartres, 8, 37
Bernard, Richard, 164f
Bernard, St., 7, 17
Berthelet, Thomas, 191, 291
Bess of Hardwick, 97
Bibbesworth, Walter de, 227
*Bibliotheca Eliotae: Eliot's Librarie*, 116
*Bibliotheca Hispanica*, 238
Bildestone, Nicholas, 43
Billingsley, Henry, 151
Billingsley, Martin, 269
Bilney, William, 60
Blau, Willam Janszoon, 274
Blith, Walter, 291
Blount, William, Lord Mountjoy, 68
Blund, John, 14
Blundell, Peter, 93

Blundeville, Thomas, 164, 213, 242, 276, 283
Boccaccio, 30, 42, 50
Bodenham, John, 244
Bodin, Jean, 250
Bodley, Sir Thomas, 118, 218
Boethius, 6, 57
*Boke of Noblesse*, 76
*Boke of St. Albans*, 75
*Boke of Surveying*, 290, 292
*Boke of the Justice of the Peas*, 191
*Boke of the Ordre of Chyvalry*, 76
Bole, Richard, 43, 52
Bologna, 10, 12, 41, 46, 52
bolting, 173f
Bonaventura, St., 57
*Book Containing Divers Sorts of Hands*, 268
*Book of Entries*, 189
*Book of Hawking, Hunting and Blazing of Arms*, 75
*Booke named Tectonicon*, 293
*Booke of the Art how to Graft*, 291
book-keeping, teaching of, 255, 259ff
books, manuscript, 15, 294, 227ff, 255ff
Boorde, Andrew, 120
Borgi, Piero, 256
Borough, Stephen, 277, 280
Borough, William, 275ff
Bourbon, Nicholas, 229
Bourne, William, 277f, 282
*Bref Grammar for English*, 122
Brethren of the Common Life, 59
*Breve et Accuratum Grammaticae Gallicae Compendium*, 238
*Brevia Placita*, 187
*Brief and Ease Instruction to Learne the Tableture . . .*, 212
*Briefe & Necessary Instruction . . .*, 201
*Briefe & Pleasant Treatise . . . to sette a garden*, 292
*Briefe Description of Portes, Creekes, Bayes etc.*, 277
*Briefe Discourse of Royal Monarchie*, 237
Briggs, Henry, 284f
Brinkwell, John, 56
Brindsley, John, 105, 109, 112f, 117ff, 123ff, 153, 265
Brooke, Chair of History, 251
Brooke, Sir Robert, 188
Browne, Anthony, 93
Browne, John, 266, 269
Browne, Thomas, 128

Brunelleschi, Phillippo, 37
Bruni, Leonardo, 22, 27, 28ff, 36, 40, 43ff, 49f, 52f, 57, 69, 85, 168, 247f
Bullokar, John, 123
Bullokar, William, 103, 122
Buonaccorso, 37, 49, 77
Bucer, Martin, 146, 158
Buck, Sir George, 169, 172
Buckley, William, 151
*Bucolics*, 289
Butler, Charles, 112, 152
Buxtorf, Johannes, 118
Byngham, William, 132, 134
Byrhtferth, 11

Cabot, Sebastian, 277
Caesar, Julius, 242
Celephine, Friar, 240
Calvin, John, 101, 124, 202, 204, 241
Cambridge;
    Christ's College, 132, 148, 208
    Clare Hall, 160
    Emmanuel College, 93, 146, 160
    God's House, 132
    Gonville and Caius College, 97, 135, 166
    King's College, 131, 139, 151
    Magdelene College, 148
    Pembroke College, 60
    Queen's College, 136, 148
    St. Catherine's College, 133
    St John's College, 60, 97, 125, 133, 134, 146, 208, 223
    St Nicholas Hall, 133
    Sidney Sussex College, 160
    Trinity College, 131, 133f, 144f, 147, 285
    Trinity Hall, 46, 133, 166
Cambridge, University of, 13, 46, 60, 62f, 73, 94, 97, 133f, 136, 140, 142, 146, 151, 155, 157, 159, 214, 285
Camden, William, 97, 118
Camden, Chair of History, 251
Campaldino, battle of, 30
*Campo di Fior*, 235
Capella, Martianus, 6
Capellanus, Andreas, 18
Capello, Francesco, 80
Cardan, Giralamo, 150
Carleton, Sir Dudley, 223
Carter, Peter, 125
Cary, Robert, 155, 172
Cartwright, Thomas, 134

*Casa da Contratacion*, 279
*Casa Giocosa*, 36, 124
Cassiodorus, 6
*Castell of Health*, 120
Castiglione, Baldassare, 82f, 209, 224
Castiglione, Zano, 43f
Catechism, 94, 98ff, 105, 119, 200, 202
Catherine of Aragon, 208
Cato, 103, 110, 289
Cauis, John, 133, 136, 144, 166
Cavendish, Sir William, 97
Cawdrey, Robert, 123
Caxton, William, 76f, 120, 208, 241, 243, 247, 269
Cecil, Robert, 209, 220, 225
Cecil, Sir William, 83, 109, 140, 146, 151, 156, 209, 226
Cecil, William, Lord Roos, 220
*Certain Tragical Discourses*, 245
Chaderton, Laurence, 152
Chalcondyles, Demetrius, 54
Chancellor, Richard, 277, 280
Chancery, Inns of, 172f, 185
Chancery Lane, 170, 173
Chandler, Thomas, 54
*chansons de geste*, 18f
chantries, 89ff
chantry priests, 61
Chapman, George, 241, 243
Chalres V, 70
Chartres, cathedral school of, 7f, 10
Chaucer, William, 13, 42, 77
Cheke, John, 109, 142, 150, 159, 241
Chiarini, Giorgio, 257
Chilworth, John, 50
Chomeley, Sir Roger, 93
chivalry, 16ff, 75, 82, 96
Christoffels, Jan Ympyn, 260
Chrysoloras, Manuel, 45, 53
Cicero, 5, 25, 27, 29, 34, 49ff, 56f, 65, 81, 110, 121, 128, 146, 148, 209, 242, 246
Ciceronianism, 128, 153, 297
citizenship, 26ff, 33
Citeau, 7
*Civile Converzatione*, 84
Clapham, John, 242
Claymond, John, 56
Cleland, James, 84, 193, 214, 222, 226
Clement, Francis, 104, 262, 268
Clement, John, 56
Clement, Vincent, 43, 47
Clenardus, 117

Clifford, Lord William, 220, 223
Clifford's Inn, 193
Coke, Sir Edward, 183, 187ff
Colet, John, 41, 52, 55, 57ff, 63, 68, 98, 107f, 110, 117, 159
*Colloquies*, 110, 146, 238
Colonna, Vittoria, 208
Comenius, Jan Amos, xi, 104, 123, 130, 297
*commensales*, 132f
*Commentaries*, 242
*Compendium Grammatice*, 16, 106
*Compleat Gentleman*, 84
*Consolacion for our Grammar Schools*, 105, 123
*Controversia de Nobilitate*, 49, 77
Cooke, Anthony, 209
Cooke, Elizabeth, 209
Cooke, Katherine, 209
Cooke, Mildred, 209
Cooper, Thomas, 116, 240
Coote, Edmund, 104, 263, 268
Copland, Robert, 272
*Coppie Book*, 269
Corderius, Marthurin, 110
*Cornucopiae*, 144f
Corro, Antonio, 237
*Cortegiano, Il*, 82f, 209, 224
Cortes, Martin, 276, 280
*Cosmographicae Introductio*, 275, 292
cosmography, study of, 156, 275, 292f
Cotgrave, Randle, 234
Countre, Thomas, 91
*Country Farme*, 291
*Country Justice*, 192
*Court de Baron*, 194, 298
Courtenay, Peter, 50
courtesy, books of, 19, 82ff, 225
*Courtier, The*, 82f, 209, 224
*Courtier's Academy*, 84
courtly love, 18
Coverdale, William, 60
Cox, Leonard, 92, 111
Coyfurelly, Thomas, 228
Cranborne, Lord William, 220
Cranebrook, Henry, 43
Cranmer, Thomas, 70, 73, 137
Crescenzi, Petro, 291
Cromwell, Thomas, 61, 70f, 73f, 97
Curtis, Mark H., 145f, 148, 150f, 167
cyphering, 100
*Cyropaedia*, 239, 243

da Bisticci, Vespasiano, 44
Dafforne, Richard, 262
Dagomari, Paolo, 256
Dallington, Sir Robert, 221
Dalton, Michael, 192
d'Andeli, Henri, 10
d'Angoulême, Marguerite, 208
Dante, Alighieri, 24, 27, 30, 42
Dati, Gregorio, 28f, 58
Davies, John, 268
Davis, John, 277f
Day, Angel, 266
*De Amicitia*, 49f
*De Avaritia*, 57
*De Bono Solitudinis*, 24
*Decades of the Newe Worlde*, 277, 380
*De Casibus Virorum Illustrium*, 51
Decembrio, Pier Candido, 44f
*Declamacion of Noblesse*, 77
*De Conscribendis Epistolis*, 114
*De Consolacione*, 57
*De Constructione*, 107
*De Contemptu Mundi*, 21
*De Copia*, 110f, 128
*De Dignitate et Excellentia Hominis*, 37
*De Disciplina Scholarum*, 57
Dee, John, 97, 151, 264, 283, 286, 293, 295
*De Educatione Puerorum*, 242
*De Elegantiis*, 146
*Defence of Poetry*, 245
*Deffence et Illustration de la Langue Françoyse*, 241
*De Finibus*, 51
*De Fructu*, 55
*De Grammaticis*, 49
*De Humani Corporis Fabrica*, 166
*De Ingenius Moribus*, 28, 34
*De Institutione Feminae Christianae*, 205
de la Mothe, Giles, 233
*De Laudibus Calvitii*, 50
*De Laudibus Legum Angliae*, 172
de la Vigne, Pierre, 42
de Lestouac, Jeanne, 208
*De Liberis Recte Institutendis*, 72
Della Casa, 83
*Della Famiglia*, 31ff, 81
*Della Pittura*, 33
*Della vita Civile*, 33, 78
del Monte, Piero, 43
*De Magnete*, 286
de Moleyns, Adam, 43
Demosthenes, 57, 117f, 128, 146

Denisot, Nicholas, 229
De Nobilitate, 37, 57
Denton, Thomas, 155, 172, 176
De Officiis, 34, 121
De Oratore, 34, 51, 246
De Oratoribus, 49
De Perigrinatione, 216
De Physica, 148
de Pluvinel, Antoine, 220, 226
De Pronunciatione Linguae Gallicae, 231
De Ratione Studii, 109
De Re Aedificatoria, 33, 51
De Regimine Principe, 81
De Rerum Natura, 49
Dering, Edward, 201
De Saeculo et Religione, 26
Description of England, 144
Descartes, René, 295
Description of the Admirable Table of Logarithms, 284
Desiderius, Bishop of Vienne, 6
De Sonorio, 51
De Sphaero, 54
De Studiis et Litteris, 34, 247
de Taramo, Simon, 43
De Thiende, 285
De Tradendis Disciplinis, 109, 117, 124
De Tranquillate Animi, 242
De Tyranno, 27, 52
Deuteromelia, 211
De Vita Activa et Contemplativa, 57
De Vita Solitaria, 23
d'Ewes, Sir Simonds, 186
dialectic, study of, 3f, 10
Dialecticae Institutiones, 112
Dialogue between Pole and Lupset, 61, 71f, 154
Dialogui Gallico-Anglico-Latini, 238
Dialogorum Sacrorum, 110
Dictes and Sayings of the Philosophers, 243
Dictionarie French and English, 231
Dictionarie of French and English, 234
Dictionariolum Puerorum, 115
Dictionarium Linguae Latinae et Anglicae, 116
dictionaries, 114ff, 102, 122f, 231, 234
Digges, Leonard, 292f
Digges, Thomas, 292f
dignity of man, 24ff, 35ff, 49
Diogenes, 32
Dionysius of Halicarnassus, 117
Direction for Traveilers, 217

discipline, school, 124f
Discorsi, 84
Discourse Mathematical on the Variation of the Magneticall Needle, 276
Discourse of English Poetrie, 246
Discourse of the Duties of Marriage, 202
Discourse of the Variation of the Cumpas, 276
Discourse on Need for Instruction in Navigation, 280
Discoverie of Sundrie Errurs Committed by Landmeaters, 293
Disme, or the Art of Tenths, 285
Disputationes Camaldulenses, 51
Distichs, 103, 110
Dissenting Academies, 270
Diverse Voyages, 277, 281
Dives Pragmaticus, 103
Divine Comedy, 11, 25
divinity, study of, 58, 62
Doctor and Student, 190
Doctrinale, 10, 16
Doddington, Bartholomew, 159
Doddridge, John, 190
Dodwell, Henry, 251
Dogget, John, 50, 52
Dominican Order, 13f
Donatus, Aelius, 5, 10, 16, 98, 106f
Dorislaus, Isaac, 251
Dormer, Sir Robert, 223
Dorp, Martin, 64
Double Reader, 175
Dowes, Henry, 213
Downes, Andrew, 159
Drury, John, 121
du Bellay, Joachim, 241
Dudley, Edmund, 80
Dugard, William, 99
Dugdale, Sir William, 172, 177
du Gres, Gabriel, 238
Duns Scotus, 57, 65, 141
Dunstan of Glastonbury, 11
du Ploich, Peter, 230
Duport, James, 148, 153
Dury, John, 270, 289
du Wes, Gil, 229
Dyer, Sir James, 188f


Eadmer, 11
East India Company, 281, 283
Eden, Richard, 276ff
Edinburgh Review, 168

Edmunde, Sir Clement, 243
*Education of Children in Learning*, 104f, 112
Edward III, 174, 176
Edward, VI, 89f, 93, 108, 209, 236
Egerton, Sir Thomas, 112
Egidius, Romanus, 22
*Eirenarcha*, 192
*Elegantiae Lingua Latina*, 50
*Elementarie*, 100, 102
*Elements of Arithmetic*, 282
*Elements of Geometry*, 282
Elizabeth, Queen, 93, 96, 108, 140, 146, 158, 208f
Elyot, Sir Thomas, xi, 70, 78, 82ff, 85, 115, 117, 120, 124, 128, 135, 138, 155, 175f, 186, 195, 242f, 247
Emmanuel of Constantinople, 53
*Enemie of Idlenesse*, 269
*England's Helicon*, 244
*England's Parnassus*, 122, 244
*English Ape, the Italian Imitation*, 225
*English Expositor*, 123
*English Husbandman*, 29
*English Improver*, 291
*English Improver Improved*, 291
English language, 102, 116, 119ff, 122, 240f
*English Lawyer*, 190
*English Schoolmaster*, 104, 268
*English Schools at the Reformation*, 89ff
*English Secretarie*, 266
*Entrance to the Spanish Tongue*, 238
*Epistolae ad Atticum*, 27, 50f, 110
*Epistolae ad Familiares*, 27, 45, 51, 110
*Epitome*, 111
Erasmus, Desiderius, 41, 51, 57, 59f, 61, 63ff, 68, 70f, 79ff, 84, 107ff, 116, 123f, 128, 146, 159, 168, 204, 238, 241, 269, 297
Erondell, Peter, 232
*Esclaircissement de la Langue Françoyse*, 229
*Essay . . . how to make our Travels . . . the more profitable*, 217
Essex, Earl of, 218, 248
Ethelward, 11
*Ethics, Nichomachean*, 45, 50, 52f
Eton Grammar, 108
Euclid, 151
*Euphues*, 84, 214
Everard de Bethune, 11, 16
*Every Man Out of His Humour*, 195

'exercises', 82
*Exercitatio Lingua Latinae*, 235

Facio, Batholomew, 37
*Facetiae*, 43
*Faithful Shepheard*, 164f
*Familiare Communicators . . . of reading the ffrench language*, 270
family, 31ff, 199ff
Fenner, Dudley, 112
Fenton, Geoffrey, 237, 245
Ferrara, 47, 49
*Feudigraphia*, 294
Fibonacci, Leonardo, 256
Ficino, Marsilio, 38, 52, 57, 61
*First Boke of Songs and Ayres*, 211
*First Booke of Cattel*, 291
*First Fruites*, 236
*First Set of Italian Madrigals Englished*, 211
Fisher, John, 60, 63, 133f, 146, 208
Fisher, Robert, 51
Fishacre, Robert, 14
Fitzherbert, Sir Anthony, 188f, 191f, 290ff
*Five Hundred Good Pointes of Husbandrie*, 291
Fleet Street, 173, 268
Fleming, Abraham, 115, 269
Fleming, Richard, 48
Flemmyng, Robert, 48ff, 52
Fletcher, R. J., 173
Florence, 22, 24ff, 27, 54, 255f
*Florentine History*, 247
*florilegia*, 11, 243
Florio, John, 235ff, 239, 271
*Floures for Latin Speaking*, 110, 212
*Floures of Elegant Phrases*, 110
*Floures of Epigrammes*, 244
Flower, William, 108
*Flower of Godly Prayer*, 201
Folkingham, William, 294
Fortescue, Sir John, 145, 172, 176
*Foundacion of Rhetorike*, 111
*Four Bookes of Husbandrie*, 291
Fox, Richard, 51, 55ff, 63, 124, 133, 145f, 159, 168, 201
Fox, William, 209, 213
Frampton, John, 277
Franciscan Order, 13
Fraunce, Abraham, 126
Free, John, 43, 48, 50
*French Academie*, 245

*French Alphabeth* . . ., 233
*Frenche Methode* . . ., 232
*French-English Dictionarie* . . ., 234
*French Garden for English Ladies*, 232
*French Grammar*, 270
*French Littleton*, 230f
*French Schoolemaister*, 230f
French, study of, 155ff, 172, 220, 227ff, 269ff
Friends, Society of, 289
Frisius, Gemma, 264, 292
Frobisher, Martin, 275
Frulovisi, Tito Livio, 45
Fulbecke, William, 189
*Fulgens and Lucres*, 77
Fuller, Thomas, 136
Fulwood, William, 269

*Galateo*, 83
Galen, 54, 166f
Garcie, Pierre, 272
*Garden of Eloquence*, 112
*Garden of Recreation*, 236
*Garden of Wisdome*, 110, 243
*Gawain and the Green Knight*, 20
Gellibrand, Henry, 276, 286
Gellius, v. Aulus Gellius
Gentili, Alberico, 166
gentility, concept of, 81ff, 288
*Gentleness and Nobility*, 78
geography, study of, 32, 85, 148, 277
geometry, study of, 3, 156, 282ff
George of Trebizond, 51
*Georgics*, 289
Gerald of Wales, 12, 42
Gerbier, Balthazar, 226, 289
German, study of, 157
Gething, Richard, 268
*Godly and Private Prayers for House-holders*, 202
Godwyn, John, 279, 283, 295
*Golden Epistles*, 237
*Golden Grove*, 122, 245
Golding, Arthur, 123, 242, 245, 248
Goldsmith's Company, 254, 264
Gonell, William, 73, 207
Gonzaga, Elizabeth, 208
*Good Book for to Learne to Speke Frenshe*, 270
*Goodly Prymer in Englishe*, 101
Googe, Barnaby, 29
Gouge, William, 152, 160, 200, 205
*Governour, The*, xi, 82, 117

*Graecismus*, 10, 16
grammar schools, 14ff, 89ff
*Grammar Spanish-English*, 238
grammar, study of, 3, 10, 15, 35, 98, 105ff, 143
*Granarium*, 43, 52
Grand Tour, 215ff
Grant, Edward, 118, 242
Grantham, Walter, 235
Gratian, 10
*Grant Routier et Pilotage*, 272
*Graunde Abridgement*, 188
Gray, Dionis, 264
Gray's Inn, 138f, 170ff
Greek, study of, 51ff, 56, 63ff, 73, 99, 116ff, 127, 142, 145, 148, 155f, 159f
Gregory, the Great, 6
Gresham College, 155, 167, 276, 295
Gresham, Sir Thomas, 261, 283
Greville, Fulke, 97, 251
Grey, Lady Jane, 208, 210, 213, 236
Grey, William, 43, 48ff, 52f, 70
Grimald, Nicholas, 121
Grindal, Edmund, 163
Grocyn, William, 41, 51f, 54f, 63
Grosseteste, Robert, 14, 52
*Grounde of Artes*, 151, 264, 277, 283
Guarino Veronese, 34, 43, 45, 48ff, 105f, 127
Guazzo, Stephen, 84
*Guide unto Tongues*, 238
guilds, 90, 92, 253
Gunter, Edmund, 276, 284, 286
Gunthorpe, John, 48, 50, 52
Gunthorpe, Thomas, 91
Gianotti, 29
Gilbert, Sir Humphrey, 82, 155ff, 226, 279, 282
Gilbert, William, 286f
Gill, Alexander, 122f, 125
Giotto, 37
Guicciardini, Francesco, 29

Haddon, Walter, 144
Hakluyt, Richard, 275, 277, 280
Hall, Edward, 199, 202
Hall, Joseph, 224
Hastings, Henry, Earl of Huntingdon, 162
Hariot, Thomas, 283
Harrington, Sir James, 232
Harrington, Sir John, 220
Harrington, Lucy, 209

Harrison, Lucas, 234
Harrison, William, 144, 224
Harsnett, Samuel, 97, 126
Hart, John, 103
Hartwell, Robert, 264, 283
Harvey, Gabriel, 152
Harvey, William, 167
Hatton, Christopher, 138
*Haven Finding Art*, 276
Hebrew, study of, 116, 118f, 142, 145,
    148, 156, 158ff
Hegendorf, Christopher, 114
Heliodorus, 117
Hemminge, Nicholas, 164
Henry IV, 47, 176
Henry VIII, 67, 73, 89, 108, 124, 131,
    133, 141, 145, 155, 160, 166, 172,
    181, 188, 229
Herodotus, 57
Heron, Haley, 244
Hesiod, 117, 146
Hexter, John, 135, 139, 141, 150
Higden, Ranulph, 247
Higgins, John, 110, 115
Hill, Thomas, 292
Hippocrates, 166
*Historiae Florentini Populi*, 29
*Historie of Italy*, 235
*History of Henry the Seventh*, 250
*History of Twelve Caesars*, 243
history, study of, 29f, 35, 42, 81, 84,
    168, 217, 246ff
Hoby, Sir Thomas, 83, 209
Holbein, Hans, the Younger, 262
Holborn, 170, 177
Holdsworth, Richard, 143, 145ff, 150,
    153
Holdsworth, W. S., 176
Hole, Francis, 223
Holes, Andrew, 43f, 47, 50, 53
Holgate, Robert, 91, 94
Holland, Philemon, 97, 241f
Holles, Gervase, 185
Holles, Sir John, 185f
Holte, John, 106, 128
Holyband, Claude, (Claude de Sain-
    liens), 230ff, 236, 238f, 271
Homer, 146, 241
*Homilies*, 61
Hood, Thomas, 278, 281ff
Hooker, Richard, 61, 158
Hoole, Charles, 105, 112, 117f, 153
Horace, 5, 110, 146

Horman, William, 109
Horn Book, 101
Horsfall, John, 164
*hospitia*, 13
House of Commons, 85, 137ff, 147, 195,
    199
Howell, James, 222
Hughes, Thomas, 265
Huloet, Richard, 115
Humphrey, Duke of Gloucester, 43ff,
    48f, 52
Humphrey, Lawrence, 84, 288
*Hundred Good Pointes of Husbandrie*, 291
*Hundred Sundry Flowers*, 244
*Husbandrie, Ordering and Government of
    Poultry*, 291
Hutchinson, Lucy, 212
Hyrde, Richard, 205

*Idiotismes*, 146
*Iliad*, 243
*Image of Governance*, 78
*Imitation of Christ*, 59, 201
Inner Temple, 138, 170ff
Innocent III, 21
Inns of Court, xi, 82, 85, 137f, 145, 166,
    169ff
*In Praise of the New Chivalry*, 17
*Institucion of a Gentleman*, 84, 191, 248,
    288
*Institutes*, 189
*Instititutio Oratoria*, 34, 45
*Institution of a Christian Prince*, 84
*Institution of a Young Noble Man*, 84,
    193, 214
*Institutiones Rhetoricae*, 111
*Introductio ad Sapientiam*, 124
*Introduction to Lerne to Recken with the
    Penne or Counters*, 263
*Introduction to Lerne to Rede to Pro-
    nounce and to Speak French Trewly*, 229
*Introductions in Frenshe*, 229
*Introductory to Write and Pronounce
    French*, 229
*Invective against the Florentines*, 27
*Invective Against the Great and Detest-
    able Vice Treason*, 74
"Invisible College", 287
Ireland, John, 127
*Isagogicon*, 45, 50, 52
Isidore, of Seville, 6
Isocrates, 4, 57, 117f
*Italian Grammar*, 235

*Italian Schoolemaster*, 235
Italian, study of, 157, 234ff, 270
*Italian Tutor*, 237, 270
Italiate Englishmen, 225ff

James, I, 223
*Jardins de Vertue*, 232
Jennyngs, Stephen, 92
Jerome, St., 5, 23, 58
*Jewel House of Art and Nature*, 291
Jewel, John, 142, 145, 158, 162
*Jew of Malta*, 225
John of Garland, 11, 16, 114
John of Salisbury, 10, 42
Jones, Francis, 283
Jones, William, 84
Jonson, Ben, 122, 195
Jordan, W. K., 96, 129
Jowett, Benjamin, 168
Judd, Sir Andrew, 92, 93, 95
Judges' Orders, 180, 182, 184
*Jurisdictions . . . of Courts Leet, Baron etc.*, 194
Justinus, 242f
Juvenal, 57, 146

*Kayes of Counsaille*, 244
Keckermann, Bartholomew, 148, 164
Kempe, William, 104ff, 112
Kempis, Thomas à, 201
Kendall, Abraham, 244
Keper, John, 84
*Key to the Spanish Tongue*, 238
Killigrew, Henry, 209
*King Lear*, 199
Kingsmill, Thomas, 158
Kingsmill, William, 228
Knolles, Richard, 250
Knollys, Sir Francis, 138
Knox, John, 130, 244
Kynaston, Sir Francis, 226
Kytchin, John, 194, 297

Labé, Louise, 208
*Lac Puerorum*, 106
Lambard, William, 192
*Lamentation Against Rebellion*, 74
Landino, Christoforo, 51, 57
Langton, Thomas, 55
Latimer, Hugh, 59f, 61f, 73, 85, 137, 161
Latimer, William, 51, 70

Latin, teaching of, 51f, 65, 99ff, 127, 155f, 172, 211, 220
Laud, William, 151, 163
*Laudatio Florentinae Urbis*, 28
*Laudatio Johannis Strozzae Equitis Florentini*, 29
Law, Canon, study of, 3, 41f, 46, 56, 131, 166, 169
Law, Civil, study of, 3, 41, 46, 71, 131, 142, 155, 157, 166, 169, 190f
Law, Common, study of, 157, 169ff, 191
Law French, 174, 176, 190f
Law Latin, 176
*Laws of Ecclesiastical Polity*, 158
Lay Feofees, 163
Leach, A. F., 89ff
Lee, John, 50
*Legacy of Husbandry*, 289
Leigh, Valentine, 292
Leland, John, 48, 97
Leonico, Tomeo, 54f, 70, 73
Letter-writing, teaching of, 42, 114, 266ff
Lever, Ralph, 62, 153
Levins, Peter, 116
lexicography, 116, 238
*Liber Abaci*, 256
*Liber Epistolaris*, 42
libraries, 44, 48ff, 55, 57
*Libre del Ordre de Cavayleria*, 19
*Libro che tracta di mercatantie*, 257
*Licht der Zeevaert*, 274
*Light of Navigation*, 274
Lily, George, 55
Lily, William, 63, 107f, 117f, 121, 127, 235
Linacre, Thomas, 41, 51f, 54f, 63, 68, 70, 167
Lincoln's Inn, 170ff
Ling, Nicholas, 244
*Lingua Latina Exercitatio*, 110, 124
Lipsius, Justus, 148
*litterae bonae*, 64f
Littleton, Thomas, 189f, 193
Livy, 115, 146, 209, 243
Lively, Edward, 160
Lodge, Thomas, 245
Lodi, 34
logic, study of, 4, 9, 141, 143, 145f, 148
*Logonomia Anglica*, 122f
Lombard, Peter, 9
Lombardo, della Seta, 24
Lorich, Richard, 112

Lorkin, Thomas, 220
Loschi, Antonio, 27
Louvain, University of, 123, 151
Lucan, 146
Lucian, 63
Lucretius, 49
Ludham, John, 164
*Ludus Literarius*, 105
Lull, Ramon, 19
Lupset, Thomas, 57, 97
Luther, Martin, 204
Lyceum, 4
Lyly, John, 84, 153, 214
Lyte, Henry, 285

Machiavelli, Niccolo, 216, 225, 242
Machyn, Henry, 185
McIlmaine, R., 165
Macropaedius, 114, 269
*Magnum Abbreviamentum*, 188
Malory, Thomas, 75
Malynes, Gerard, 200
*Maner of Measurying All Maner of Lande*, 292
Manetti, Gianotto, 37, 47
*manières*, 228ff, 235, 269f
*Manipulus Vocabulorum*, 116
Manners, Roger, 218
*Manual of Prayers or the Primer in Englysh and Laten*, 101
*Manuale Scholarium*, 11
Manutius, Aldus, 54, 57, 128
Mapletoft, John, 167
*Marchant's Avizo*, 266, 269
Markham, Gervase, 291
Marlow, Christopher, 225
*Marriners Guide*, 282
Martyr, Peter, 158, 280
Marwood, Roger, 93
Mary, Queen, 95, 156, 161, 208, 229
Mascall, Leonard, 291
mathematics, study of, 82, 84, 222, 279ff
Matten, Richard, 153
Mead, Joseph, 148, 153
Medici, family of, 25, 30, 38, 47
medicine, study of, 3, 54, 56, 142, 157, 166f
Medwall, Henry, 77
Melanchthon, Philip, 111f
Mellis, John, 259, 262, 264
Merbury, Charles, 237
Mercator, Gerard, 274

Mercer's Company, 69, 92
Merchant Adventurer's Company, 261, 264, 283
*Merchant's Mirrour*, 262
Merchant's Taylor's Company, 92
Mere, Francis, 122, 244
*Metamorphoses*, 242
meteorology, study of, 32
*Methode . . . to Reade English*, 103
Meurier, Gabriel, 270
Michill, Richard, 125, 127
Middle Temple, 170ff, 186
Mildmay, Sir Walter, 93, 235
Milton, John, 122, 127
Minsheu, John, 238
*Mirifici Logarithmorum Canonis Descriptio*, 284
*Miscellanea*, 56
*Mirror of Modestie Mete for all Mothers*, 212
*Mirrour of the Sea*, 273
*Model Plea for an English Commonwealth*, 289
modern languages, study of, 82, 155ff, 227ff, 234ff, 269ff
*Modus tenendis curiam baronis*, 194
moots, 174, 177ff
monasteries, 6, 9, 13
*Moralia*, 242f
More, Margaret, 109, 205
More, Sir Thomas, xi, 41, 52, 54, 63ff, 80, 106, 109, 124, 128, 204, 207, 209, 250
Morley, Thomas, 211
*Morte D'Arthur*, 75
Moryson, Richard, 73f
Morwent, Robert, 56
Mosellanus, Petrus, 110f
Mulcaster, Richard, 100, 102, 104f, 118, 120, 122, 124f, 202, 206, 214, 224
Munday, Anthony, 244
Muscovy Company, 283
Museum Minervae, 226
music, study of, 3, 32, 156, 283
*Musicae Transalpinae*, 211
*Myrrour or Glasse of Maners*, 121

Napier, John, 284
Nash, Thomas, 127, 224
*Natura Brevium*, 189
*Natural History*, 243
navigation, study of, 157, 271ff, 284ff

*Navigator's Supply*, 274, 279, 295
Nicholas of Cusa, 61
Nicholas the Greek, 52
Nichols, Josias, 202
Niger, Thomas, 80
Nizolius, Marius, 128
Neale, Sir John, 135, 137ff, 147f, 150, 167, 185, 195
Nenna, Giovani Battista, 84
*Nennio or a treatise of Nobilitie*, 84
neo-Platonists, 36f, 39
*New Atlantis*, xi
Newbury, Thomas, 103
*New Citharen Lessons*, 212
*New Discovery of Old Art of Teaching School*, 105
*Newe and Admirable Arte of Setting Corne*, 291
*Newe Attractive*, 276
*Newe Boke of Presidents*, 193
*Newe Book of Copies*, 268
*Newe Herball*, 210
*New Logarithms*, 285
Newton, Adam, 220
Newton, Isaac, 295
Neville, Anthony, 210
Neville, George, 53
*Nobel Opera de Arithmetica*, 256
nobility, concept of, 37f, 74ff, 59ff, 288
*Nobles or of Nobilyte*, 84, 288
*Noctes Atticae*, 56
Nonsuch Palace, 226
*Nosegay of Morall Philosophie*, 244
Norden, John, 292, 294
Norgate, Robert, 148
Norman, Robert, 273, 275ff, 286
North, Sir Thomas, 241f, 249
Northumberland, Earl of, 286, 288
Norton, Robert, 285
Norton, Thomas, 101
Novain, Philip de, 206
*Novum Testamentum*, 60, 69
Nowell, Alexander, 92f, 101, 118, 131

*Observations . . . on Caesar's Commentaries*, 243
Oderic Vitalis, 11
Odo of Cluny, 6
*Odyssey*, 243
*Office et authoryte de Justyces de Peas*, 191
*Office and Duetie of a Husband*, 201
*Old Abridgement*, 187

Oldcastle, Hugh, 259, 262
Oldham, Hugh, 99
*On the Education of Children*, 34
*Orationes*, 50f
*Oration on the Dignity of Man*, 38
*Order of Household Instruction*, 202
*Organon*, 148
*Origines Judicales*, 172
Orleans, cathedral school of, 7, 10
*Orthographia Gallica*, 228
*Orthographie*, 103
*Ortus Vocabularium*, 114
Osborne, Dorothy, 212
Oswald, 11
Oudin, Cesar, 238
Overbury, Thomas, 289
Ovid, 11, 18, 57, 110, 146, 242, 245
Owen, Lewis, 238
Oxford, university of, 12f, 46, 49, 52ff, 58, 60, 63f, 69, 134, 136, 140, 142, 151, 155, 157, 228, 284
    All Soul's College, 133, 141, 151, 166
    Balliol College, 48, 50, 139
    Brasenose College, 131, 145, 153
    Cardinal College, 70, 73, 146
    Christ Church College, 13
    Corpus Christi Collge, 51, 55ff, 124, 133, 145f, 148, 158
    Exeter Hall, 54
    Exeter College, 223
    Lincoln College, 48, 50
    Magdalen College, 56, 106, 125, 133, 138, 141, 238
    Merton College, 13f, 151
    New College, 54, 131, 141
    Queen's College, 141, 145
    St. John's College, 131, 145
    St. Mary's Hall, 138
    Trinity College, 159
    University College, 13
    Wadham College, 283

*Pabularium*, 43
Pace, Richard, 55, 63, 70, 80, 239
Pacioli, Lucas, 256f
Padua, 27f, 46, 48ff, 54f, 70, 166
Painter, William, 245
Palaeologos, Demetrius, 53
*Palace of Pleasure*, 245
*Palearium*, 43
*Palladis Tamia*, 122, 244
Palmer, Thomas, 217, 220, 223

Palmieri, Matteo, 22, 33, 47, 78
Palsgrave, John, 109, 229
*Pammelia*, 211
*Panoplie of Epistles*, 269
*Pantometria*, 293
Paracelsus, Philippus, 166
*Paraphrases*, 61
Paris, Cathedral School of, 7, 10
Paris, University of, 9, 10, 12, 52, 151
Parker, Matthew, 60, 93, 142, 146, 158
Parr, Catherine, 210
*Parve Latinitates*, 121
Paston, family of, 193, 208, 212
Paulet, Sir Amias, 219
*Pathewaie to Martiall Discipline*, 242
*Patheway to Prayer*, 201
*Pathway to Knowledge*, 277
*Pathway to Perfectness in Accomptes*, 261
Peacham, Henry, 84, 112, 295
Peak, Sir George, 219
Peckenham, Humphrey, 91
Peele, James, 26
Pegolotti, Francesco Balducco, 256f, 266
Pell, John, 285
*Pen's Excellencie*, 269
Percyvall, Richard, 238
Perkins, John, 190
Perotti, Nicholas, 48, 106, 114
Peter Lombard, 60
Peterson, Robert, 84
*Petie Schole*, 104, 268
Petrarch, 22f, 27, 30, 35, 40, 42, 44, 57
Pettie, William, 84, 245
"petties", 98ff
Petty, William, 297
Petworth, Richard, 43
*Phaedo*, 53, 208
*Phaedrus*, 45, 52
Phayer, Thomas, 193
*Philanthropy in England*, 129
philology, 40, 42, 45
Physicians, Royal College of, 167
physical education, 18
Pico della Mirandola, 38, 61, 66, 69
Piccolomini, Aeneas Sylvius, (Pius II), 49, 51, 105
Pilgrimage of Grace, 73
Pilkington, James, 93, 99
Pilkington, Thomas, 211
Pius II (Aeneas Sylvius Piccolomini), 49, 51, 105
*Plaine and Easie Introduction to Practical Musicke*, 211

Plat, Sir Hugh, 29
Platina, 48, 57
Plato, x, 3f, 23, 30, 44f, 52, 57, 118, 204, 208, 248, 250
Platte, Gabriel, 29
Plautus, 146
Pliny, 51, 243, 289
Plowden, Edmund, 186, 188f
Plutarch, 34, 43f, 51f, 65, 84, 241, 243, 249
Poggio Bracciolini, 27, 34, 38, 43, 49, 57
Pole, Reginald, 51 n.3, 70, 73, 159
Politian, (Angelo Poliziano), 54, 56
*Politics*, 45, 52, 248
*Polychronicon*, 247
*Pomander of Prayer*, 201
Pope, Sir Thomas, 159
Porter, H. C., 146
*portolani*, 272
*Positions*, 100, 105, 206, 225
poverty, virtue of, 30, 32
Powell, Thomas, 212
Puckering, Sir Thomas, 220
*Purchas, His Pilgrimes*, 277
Pirchas, Samuel, 277
Purfoot, Thomas, 232
Puttenham, George, 245
*Practica della Mercatura*, 256
*Practis of Preaching*, 164
*Praise of Folly*, 64, 81
*Preacher or Method of Preaching*, 164
preaching, 163ff
*Preparative for Plotting Lands*, 293
Preston, John, 148
priesthood, education of, 49, 61f, 71, 96, 155, 157ff
Primaudaye, Peter de la, 245
prince, education of, 74f, 81ff, 216
*Principal Navigations*, 275, 277, 281
*Principal Rules of the Italian Grammar*, 235
Priscian, 10, 106
Proclus, 54
*Progymnasmata*, 63, 111f
*Profitable Booke Treating of the Lawes of England*, 190
*Promptorium Parvulorum*, 114
*Proposals for Raising a College of Industry*, 289
*Prose della Volgar Lingua*, 241
*Proverbs or Adagies*, 110
*Prymer in Englyshe and Latyn*, 101

Pynson, Richard, 106, 189, 270, 291
*Queen Anne's New World of Wordes*, 237
Quintilian, 5, 34, 43, 51, 56f, 81, 110, 128, 246
*Quodlibeta*, 141
*Quadrivuim*, 3
*Quo Vadis? A Just Censure of Travell*, 224

Rabanus Maurus, 6, 9
Rabelais, François, 127, 279
Rainolde, Richard, 111f
Raleigh, Sir Walter, 83, 288
*Ramae Rhetoricae*, 112
Ramus, Peter, 112, 146, 148, 151, 153, 165, 281f
Rankins, William, 225
Rastell, John, 188
Rastell, William, 189, 191
Rathborne, Aaron, 285, 292, 294
Raven, Edward, 223
Ravenscroft, Thomas, 211
reading, teaching of, 98, 102, 104, 254
Readings, 174f, 180ff
Recorde, Robert, 151, 264f, 277, 283, 293
Rede, Sir Robert, 141
Redman, Robert, 188
Regent Masters, 132, 134, 141, 143f
*Regiment of the Sea*, 277, 282
Regius professorships, 133, 141f, 153ff, 166, 168
*Reglas Grammaticales*, 237
*Remedy Against Sedition*, 74
*Reports*, 188
*Republic*, 4, 45, 248
Rheims, university of, 151
Rich, Richard, 93, 96
Richard of Bury, 42
rhetoric, study of, 3, 10, 110ff, 128, 141, 143, 146, 148, 153, 164
*Rhetorica*, 51
*Rhetorica Ecclesiasticae*, 164
*Rhetoricae Libri Duo*, 153
riding, teaching of, 156f, 220f
*Right Teaching of Useful Knowledge*, 287
Robert of Chester, 14
Robinson, Thomas, 212
Roger of Hereford, 14
Rolle, Henry, 188
Rolle, Richard, 59
*Roman de la Rose*, 11, 20
Rome, 4, 48, 51, 55
Romei, Annibale, 84

Rood, Theodorick, 53
Roper, Margaret, 205
Royal College of Physicians, 54
Royal Grammar, 108
Royal Society, xi, 154, 168, 287
*Rudimenta Grammatices*, 107, 121
*Rule of Reason*, 112
*Ruralia Commodia*, 291
*Rutter of the Sea*, 272
rutters, 272f

Sadoleto Jacopo, 72
*Safeguard of Saylers*, 273
St. Germain, Christopher, 190f
St. Paul, 58, 60
St. Paul's Cross, sermons at, 162, 165
Salamanca, university of, 52
Sallust, Gaius, 56
Salomon, House of, 287
Salter, Thomas, 212
Salutati, Coluccio, 22, 26f, 29, 44, 69
Sampson, Thomas, 228
Sanford, John, 238
Savilian Chair of Geometry, 284
Saxton, Christopher, 294
*Scholemaster*, 84, 105, 109, 223, 233
*Schoole of Musicke*, 212
Schoolmasters, discipline, 124, 246ff
Schoolmasters, oath, 95
Schoolmasters, salary, 124f
Schools;
    Acaster, 259
    Ashbourne, 93f
    Ashby, 162
    Ashby-de-la-Zouch, 105
    Bangor, 117
    Beccles, 121
    Blackburn, 117, 119, 268
    Brentwood, 93
    Bridgnorth, 92
    Bury St. Edmunds, 96, 99, 104
    Canterbury, 98
    Chelmsford, 97
    Chigwell, 126
    Chipping Norton, 92
    Christ's Hospital, 99, 268
    Colchester, 97, 99, 116
    Cromer, 92
    Cuckfield, 129
    East Retford, 91, 94, 117, 119
    Eton, 97f, 109f, 117f, 124, 129, 131, 159
    Felsted, 93, 96, 116

Schools—*continued*
Giggleswick, 267
Harrow, 117f
Hawkeshead, 120
Heighington, 99
Heptonstall, 125
Hertford, 124
Highgate, 93
Horsham, 92
Houghton-le-Spring, 99
Hull, 15
Ilminster, 91
Ipswich, 70, 91, 97, 108
Jesus College, Rotherham, 259
Kirkby Stephen, 95, 99
Launceston, 90
Leeds, 91
Leicester, 162
Little Waltham, 91
Liverpool, 90
Louth, 92
Ludlow, 92
Magdalen College, 106, 111, 110, 127
Manchester, 99, 107, 125
Merchant Taylors', 98, 104, 118, 125, 131
Middleton, 93, 131
Newent, 90
Norwich, 117, 124
Oundle, 119
Peterborough, 99
Plymouth, 104
Reading, 91f, 107, 111
Repton, 97
Rivington, 93, 99, 114, 117, 119, 124
Rochdale, 93
Rolleston, 99
Rugby, 93
Ruthin, 99
Saffron Walden, 92, 129
St. Albans, 15, 91, 98, 116
St. Bees, 117
St. Paul's, 55, 92, 97f, 107, 110, 117, 122, 129
St. Saviour's, 117
Sandwich, 93
Sherborne, 129
Shrewsbury, 91, 97, 117, 124
Stafford, King Edward VI, 91
Stevenage, 93
Stockport, 92
Stone, 93
Stratford, 92
Tiverton, 93
Tonbridge, 92, 165
Towcester, 91
Uttoxeter, 93
Walthamstow, 92
Week St. Mary, 90
Westminster, 92, 118, 124, 129
Whalley, 125
Winchester, 129, 131
Wolverhampton, 92
Schools, cathedral, 6f, 14f, 89
Schools, chantry, 15, 89ff
Schools, endowment of, 129f
Schools, monastic, 6f, 14f
*Schools of Medieval England*, 89
*Sciographia or the Art of Shadows*, 286
Scotland, 234, 270
*Scriptores Astronomici Veteres*, 54
*Scuola Perfetta dei Mercanti*, 256
*Sea Grammar*, 277
*Seaman's Calendar*, 277
*Seaman's Secrets*, 277f
*Seconde Fruites*, 236
*Secretum*, 23, 36, 57
Sellyng, William, 51, 54
*Sentences*, 60
Serbopoulos, Johannes, 53
Serjeants-at-Law, 173ff
Servius, 106
sermons, see preaching
Seton, John, 147, 153
Severus, 78
Sforza, Beatrice, 208
Shakespeare, William, 113, 119, 239, 245
Shirwood, John, 51, 53, 57
*Shepheard's Calendar*, 240
Sherborne, Robert, 98
Sheriff, Lawrence, 92
Sherrington, Grace, 210
Sherry, Richard, 111
*Shorte & Plaine Treatise of Arithmeticke*, 259
*Shorte Catechism for Householders*, 202
*Shorte Dictionarie for Yonge Beginners*, 115
*Shorte Introduction of Grammar*, 108
*Shorte Introduction on Guiding to Print, Write and Reade Inglish Speech*, 122
Sidney, Mary, Countess of Pembroke, 209

Sidney, Philip, 83, 97, 128, 153, 219f, 244f, 253
Sidney, Robert, 153, 211, 214
Simon, Joan, 90
*Sir Amadis*, 20
*Sir Eglamon*, 20
*Sixe Books of a Commonwealth*, 250
Sixtus V, 225
Smith, John, 142, 277
Smith, Thomas, 281
Snell, George, 287, 298
*Spanish Grammar*, 237
*Spanish Schoolemaister*, 238, 270
Spanish, study of, 157, 237, 270
*Speculum*, 57
Speidell, John, 285
Spenser, Edmund, 83, 122, 240
Spicer, William, 129
Sprigge, William, 289
Stafford, George, 60
Stafford, Thomas, 60
Stanbridge, John, 106f, 109, 114
Stapleton, Thomas, 66
Star Chamber, Court of, 166, 185, 190
Starkey, Thomas, 60, 71ff, 154f, 191, 214
Statham, Nicholas, 188
*Statham's Abridgement*, 188
Stationers' Company, 119
Statute of Apprentices, 254
Statute of Uses, 182, 192
Stephen of Blois, 17
Stepney, William, 238, 270
Stevin, Simon, 277, 285
Stockwood, John, 165, 203f
*Storehouse of Brevitie in Woorkes of Arithmetike*, 204
Stowe, John, 172
Stradling, John, 217
Sturm, Johannes, 84, 110, 209
Styward, Thomas, 242
Suetonius, 49, 51, 146, 243
Sulpitius, 106
*Summa de Arithmetica . . .*, 256
*Summa Moralis*, 31
*Summer's Last Will and Testament*, 127
*Sundrie New and Artificial Remedies against Famine*, 291
Surigone, Stephano, 54
surveying, teaching of, 285, 290ff
*Surveyor*, 294
*Surveyour's Dialogue*, 294
Susenbrotus, 111f

Sydenham, Thomas, 166
*Symbolaeographia*, 193
Synesius, 50

*Table Alphabeticall*, 123
*Tabulae*, 111
Tacitus, 49
Taisnier, Johannes, 276
Talaeus, Audomarus, 112, 151, 153, 165
Tallis, Thomas, 211
Tamworth, John, 235
Tapp, John, 273, 277, 283
Taverner, Richard, 110, 243
*Tectonicon*, 293
Terence, 57, 109, 115, 146
Temple, William, 152, 212
*Tenures*, 189, 193
Theobald of Etampes, 12
Theocritus, 146
*Theologia Platonica*, 38
theology, study of, 3, 5, 9, 57f, 65, 133, 145, 148, 157, 164
Thierry of Chartres, 8
Thomas à Kempis, 59
Thomas of Capua, 42
Thomas, Thomas, 116
Thomas, William, 235
Theodore, of Gaza, 117
*Third Universitie of England*, 172
Thorius, John, 237
Thorne, S. E., 171, 187
Thring, Edward, 127
Throckmorton, Arthur, 219
Thucydides, 57
Tilney, Edmund, 202
Tiptoft, John, 48ff, 53, 70, 77
*Tom of All Trades, or the Plaine Pathway to Preferment*, 212
*Topography of Ireland*, 12
Torriano, Giovanni, 237, 270
Tottell, Richard, 188, 243
*Touchstone for this time present*, 202
Townshend, Aurelian, 220
*Toxophilus*, 120, 202
*Tractate d'Abacco*, 256
*Tractatus Orthographiae*, 228
translations, 83, 85, 101, 164, 205, 211, 213, 235, 240, 242, 245, 250, 260, 272, 276ff, 285
travel, 46, 215ff
Traversari, Ambrogio, 47
*Treasurie of the French Tongue*, 231

*Treatise for Declining Verbes*, 231
*Treatise in English and French*, 230
*Treatise of Husbandry*, 291
*Treatise of Measuring All Kinds of Lands*, 292
*Treatise of Morall Philosophie*, 243
*Treatise of Schemes and Tropes*, 111
*Treatise of the Figures of Grammar and Rhetorike*, 111
*Treatise Upon the Paternoster*, 205
*Treatyse of the Newe Indies*, 277
Trebizond, v. George of
*Trivium*, 3
Tunstall, Cuthbert, 60, 68
Turler, Jerome, 216, 223
Turner William, 210
Tusser, Thomas, 291
tutors, private, 97, 135, 209f, 213ff, 220, 223, 229, 238, 270
tutors, university, 145ff, 150f
*Tyrannicida*, 63

Udall, Nicholas, 92, 110, 121
Urbino, Dukes of, 34, 82
Urstitius, Christian, 282
*Use of Both Globes, Celestiall and Terrestriall*, 282
*Use of the Celestial Globe*, 282
*Use of Two Mathematicall Instruments*, 278, 282
usher, 100, 105f, 124f, 155f
*Utopia*, xi, 66, 68f, 80
Uzzano, Giovanni da, 257

vacations, learning, 171, 174, 180
Valerius Maximus, 51, 56
Valla, Lorenzo, 50, 56, 58, 106, 146
Vallance, Pierre, 229
*valor naturalis*, 31
*valor usualis*, 31
Varro, 5, 289
Vaucluse, 24
Vaughan, William, 122, 245
Vautrollier, Thomas, 268
Venice, 55
Vergerio, Pier Paolo, 27f, 34f
Vergil, Polydore, 45, 250
Veron, John, 115
Vesalius, Andreas, 166
Vespasiano, Battista, 47
Vespucci, Amerigo, 280
Vienne, Council of, 52
Vigerius, 146

Vigoe, Bartheolomew, 210
Vincent of Beauvais, 57
Villadei, Alexander, 10, 16, 106
Villani, Giovanni, 25, 255
Virgil, 5, 6, 11, 50, 289
Visconti, family of, 25, 28
*vita activa*, 22ff, 29f
*vita contemplativa*, 22ff
*Vita Henrici Quinti*, 45
*Vitae Pontificum*, 57
Vittelli, Cornelio, 54
Vittorino da Feltre, 34, 36, 45, 124
Vitrivius, 57
Vives, Juan Luis, 57, 108, 110f, 117, 123f, 201, 205, 235, 279, 297
Vlacq, Adrian, 284
*Vocabolaria Italiano-Inglese*, 237
*Vocabula*, 114
vocabularies, 227f
Volz, Paul, 61
*Vulgaria Terentii*, 109
'vulgars', making of, 109f
Vulgate, 60, 64

Wagenaer, Lucas Janszoon, 273
Wakefield, Thomas, 160
Walcher, Prior of Malvern, 14
Wallis, John, 151
Walsingham, Sir Francis, 138, 219, 281
Ward, John, 166
Ward, Seth, 160
Watson, Thomas, 211
Waynflete, William, 53, 133
Wells, John, 286
Webbe, William, 246
Weddington, John, 261f
*Wellspring of Sciences*, 264
*Werke for Householders*, 201
Wesley, John, 124, 146
West, William, 193
Wheare, Degory, 251
Whethamstede, John, 43, 45f, 52
White, Sir Thomas, 131, 145
Whitehorne, Peter, 242
Whitelocke, Sir James, 118
Whitaker, William, 101
Whitford, Richard, 201
Whitgift, John, 61, 134, 142, 146, 153, 161f
Whitington, Robert, 107, 109, 121, 235
*Whole Art and Trade of Husbandry*, 29
William of Champeaux, 8

William of Salisbury, 11
William of Worcester, 53
Wilson, Thomas, 112, 241
Winter, Thomas, 71
wisdom, idea of, xi, 21, 34, 40, 75
Withals, John, 115
*Wit's Commonwealth*, 244
Wolfe, John, 278
women, education of, 205ff
Worde, Wynkyn de, 106, 208, 243, 270
*Worlde of Words*, 237
Worrall, Thomas, 153
Worsop, Edward, 292
Wolsey, Thomas, 55ff, 70, 73, 91, 97, 108
Wotton, Edward, 57, 220

Wotton, Sir Henry, 225
Wright, Edward, 273ff, 278, 283f
*Writing Schoolmaster*, 267f
writing, teaching of, 98ff, 156, 254f
Wulfstan, 11
Wyatt, Thomas, 242
Wykeham, William of, 131, 134
Wylford, Edmund, 141

Xenophon, 44, 52, 57, 118, 239, 243

Year Books, 187ff
Yonge, Nicholas, 211
*Young Accomptant's Compasse*, 262
Young, Bartholomew, 84

Zwingli, Ulrich, 124